"We need this book now more than eve[...] now than at any point in human history. With *Visual Delight in Architecture*, Heschong redirects our gaze and reimagines what it means to create truly humane indoor environments. Every person desires a view to the outdoors to satiate their appetite for light. This is a fundamental human need and its provision should be a basic human right..."

Kevin Van Den Wymelenberg, PhD,
Director, Institute for Health in the Built Environment;
Professor of Architecture, University of Oregon

"Architects, and anyone, interested in creating a more humanitarian world need to read this book, *immediately*! As the preeminent architect who demonstrated how daylit buildings can improve learning, working, and selling, Lisa Heschong brings us up to date with added attention to views. Skillfully synthesizing research, literature, and design imperatives, Heschong summarizes why both daylight and views are needed in our buildings to better serve all building occupants, our society, and the future of the planet."

Margo Jones, FAIA, NCARB, LEED-AP,
Founding Partner, Jones Whitsett Architects, Massachusetts

"There is so much more to *Visual Delight in Architecture* than seeing – from rhythm to health to cognition to community to beauty to survival – Lisa Heschong brings another brilliant treatise to life, for all of us who design and inhabit architecture."

Vivian Loftness, FAIA, *Paul Mellon Chairholder and University Professor in Architecture, Carnegie Mellon University*

"Now, three generations after my architect father Richard Neutra started to write pleas for researched responsible design, architect and researcher Lisa Heschong is showing us how far we have come and how far we have to go in understanding the deep biological impact of what reaches us through our eyes."

Dr. Raymond Neutra, *Epidemiologist, Past President of the International Society for Environmental Epidemiology, Chair of the Richard Neutra Foundation, Past (Associate and Assistant) Professor of Public Health, UCLA and Harvard University*

Visual Delight in Architecture

Visual Delight in Architecture examines the many ways that our lives are enriched by the presence of natural daylight and window views within our buildings. It makes a compelling case that daily exposure to the rhythms of daylight is essential to our health and well-being, tied to the very genetic foundations of our physiology and cognitive function. It describes all the subtlety, beauty, and pleasures of well-daylit spaces and attractive window views, and explains how these are woven into the fabric of both our everyday sensory experience and enduring cultural perspectives.

All types of environmental designers, along with anyone interested in human health and well-being, will find new insights offered by *Visual Delight in Architecture*. The book is both accessible and provocative, full of personal stories and persuasive research, helping designers to gain a deeper understanding of the scientific basis of their designs, scientists to better grasp the real-world implications of their work, and everyone to more fully appreciate the role of windows in their lives.

Lisa Heschong is an architect and founding principal of the Heschong Mahone Group (HMG), a building sciences consulting firm, where she led ground-breaking research showing a relationship between daylight and student test scores, retail sales, and office worker performance. Heschong is the author of the classic *Thermal Delight in Architecture*, along with many technical publications about daylighting and energy efficiency in buildings. A graduate of UC Berkeley and MIT, she is a Fellow of the Illuminating Engineering Society (IES), and received the ARCC 2012 Haecker Award for Architectural Research. Heschong lives in Santa Cruz, California, with her husband, two horses, and a sailboat, where she never tires of watching the changing colors of the surrounding ocean and sky.

Visual Delight in Architecture

Daylight, Vision, and View

Lisa Heschong

Illustrations by Garth von Ahnen

Routledge
Taylor & Francis Group

LONDON AND NEW YORK

First published 2021
by Routledge
2 Park Square, Milton Park, Abingdon, Oxon OX14 4RN

and by Routledge
605 Third Avenue, New York, NY 10158

Routledge is an imprint of the Taylor & Francis Group, an informa business

British Library Cataloguing-in-Publication Data
A catalogue record for this book is available from the British Library

Library of Congress Cataloging-in-Publication Data
Names: Heschong, Lisa, author.
Title: Visual delight in architecture: daylight, vision and view / Lisa Heschong.
Description: Abingdon, Oxon; New York: Routledge, [2021] |
Includes bibliographical references and index.
Identifiers: LCCN 2020046164 (print) | LCCN 2020046165 (ebook) |
ISBN 9780367563226 (hardback) | ISBN 9780367563233 (paperback) |
ISBN 9781003097594 (ebook)
Subjects: LCSH: Daylighting. | Architecture–Human factors. |
Architecture–Health aspects.
Classification: LCC NA2794 .H47 2021 (print) |
LCC NA2794 (ebook) | DDC 729/.28–dc23
LC record available at https://lccn.loc.gov/2020046164
LC ebook record available at https://lccn.loc.gov/2020046165

ISBN: 978-0-367-56322-6 (hbk)
ISBN: 978-0-367-56323-3 (pbk)
ISBN: 978-1-003-09759-4 (ebk)

Typeset in Times New Roman
by Newgen Publishing UK

In loving memory of my artful brother Eric, and in hope that my dear grandchildren may all read this someday.

Contents

PART 4: MEANING

Author's Preface

The cover photo of this book has an interesting backstory. I had been searching far and wide for an image which would exemplify many of the ideas in this book. It was far more challenging than I expected. Although I know of many wonderful daylit buildings, with beautiful views, it turns out that not many architects take photos from the inside of their buildings, looking out. Not many architects take photos of their buildings completely daylit, with all the electric lights turned off; nor after they are fully inhabited, with people comfortably settled into daily routines.

I soon realized I would need to arrange for the photograph myself. However, as I was finishing the book's manuscript, the COVID-19 pandemic descended and access to buildings everywhere was restricted. Travel became impossible. I thought perhaps I might find the right window up on the nearby campus of the University of California, Santa Cruz. Years earlier, I had taught a course there on green buildings. The introductory assignment for this senior seminar was very open-ended: *"Describe your favorite place on campus, and what about it makes it a special place for you."* I was only mildly surprised when 28 out of the 30 responses prominently featured a favorite view somewhere on campus—a dorm balcony, a rooftop garden, a roadside bench, even a perch at the top of a tree. The UC Santa Cruz campus sits high above Monterey Bay and is famous for its spectacular views of meadows stretching out to the Pacific Ocean far beyond. However, most of the campus buildings are set back deep within the dense redwood forest that covers the Santa Cruz Mountains.

I remembered that a number of my students described their favorite indoor place as a seat near the big windows of the Science and Engineering Library. They described the calm focus they found sitting at the foot of the big trees, looking up into fragments of a soft sky. Intrigued, I went to investigate further and learned the building had been designed by a venerable California architecture firm, Esherick Homsey Dodge and Davis, and had received many design awards at the time of its opening in 1991. Nestled into a sloping site, the three-story library follows a zig-zag plan, which deftly preserved the integrity of the surrounding forest. The building's many corners have tall, floor-to-ceiling windows extending slightly beyond the concrete walls on both sides, such that on each floor those corners are suffused with daylight filtering through the towering trees. A grid of red metal window frames contrasts with the evergreen foliage outside. It was these corner windows that the students described.

Later I learned that Chuck Davis, the design architect, had laid out the building specifically to preserve views into the native forest. Creating a comfortable place to enjoy close-up views of the trees was the driving idea behind every design decision he made, from site plan to structural system to interior design. He had previous experience building in the redwoods, whereupon he had discovered both the opportunity for magical views of the trees, and the feasibility of building so close to them. Davis explained to me: *"Back during the design phase, the campus arborist insisted that trees around the building would be damaged by construction and die, and so we needed to cut many more of them down. I was sure we could build very close to them, and I was eventually proved right."*

Ultimately, only 11 trees were sacrificed for the library's construction. Some of the original redwoods remain within four feet of the foundation of the building.[1]

As I learned from my own students, those efforts paid off in a level of affection that students have for the place, seeking out their favorite spots for study or reflection. But only very recently, when I returned to take the cover photo, did I learn those windows also had a specific monetary value. After decades of service, it was time for a major renovation to the building. The library needed to transition from the paper-based libraries of the twentieth century into the digital library services of the twenty-first. A growing student population needed more places to study, with access to charging stations and rapid internet services. They no longer needed access to rows of stacks filled with paper journals that were easier to access online. Worried about the magnitude of the needed improvements, University Librarian Elizabeth Cowell looked to find donors willing to augment the university's meager available construction funds.

She took one potential donor, who had been an undergraduate there when the library first opened, on a tour of the library to explain the proposed renovations. *"Don't ever change that corner!"* he exclaimed, then explained: *"That chair, by that corner window—that was my spot! I went there every day to study, staring out into those trees, rain or shine."* Then, via their family foundation, Alec Webster and his wife promised first five, then seven million dollars in support of the library's renovations. At that point in time, this was the largest private donation in the history of the campus. Once completed, the new digital furnishing plan radically transformed the library, opening up views across the floors, while maintaining big comfortable reading chairs nestled up next to the windows.[2]

Wanting to understand more of his motivation, I interviewed Webster, who explained he felt strongly about investing in the preservation of buildings and adapting them for new uses. *"Just tearing down buildings to modernize them is crazy! This building was an incredible place to be. It was totally peaceful. Its windows just draw you in."* Elaborating further, he explained: *"Good windows attract people. They bring them into the library and tie the campus community together. We need more places like that. They give us a sense of shared history."* Clearly, Chuck Davis's original efforts to preserve the view of the forest had a significant financial payoff for the library decades later and have helped ensure the library's continuing function for decades to come.

It is actually extremely difficult to capture, via a mere photograph, the experience of looking out at a view from inside of a building. This story about the cover photograph shows that there is a lot more going on than just the patterns of light and color one sees on a printed page. After reading this book, maybe you can find some especially wonderful windows in a building near you, and then go uncover their backstory: how they came to be and how they have helped sustain the building's meaning for its many inhabitants over the years. If so, please be sure to appreciate the architect and everyone else involved in the construction and management of the building who brought those windows into your world.

Introduction

Set wide the window. Let me drink the day.

Edith Wharton

This book examines the many ways that our lives are enriched by the presence of natural daylight illumination and window views within our buildings. It makes the case that appropriately timed exposure to daylight is essential to the very genetic foundations of our physiology and cognitive function. It explores the many delights and pleasures of being in a daylit environment, why we are so attracted to interesting views of the outdoors, and how they shape our cultural perspectives. It reviews the history of daylight and views in various types of settings, from homes to schools, workplaces, and hospitals, and also considers the many types of threats, from urban design to technological innovations, that reduce our opportunities to enjoy daily access to daylight and views.

We modern humans spend over 90% of our lives inside of buildings. I ask that you give that little piece of information some deep thought. What does it mean for our overall health and well-being that we live out the majority of our lives, from infancy through old age, indoors?

This has not always been the case. In prehistoric times, humans spent the vast majority of their days outdoors—certainly while gathering food, hunting, fishing, and farming, but also while preparing food, eating, playing, and even sleeping. Even just 100 years ago, many human activities were normally performed outdoors. But now in modern societies, our time outdoors has been steadily shrinking. This is true across all professions and age groups. One large study in the United States found that on average, children spent just nine minutes more per day (!) outdoors than the average adult.

Since we now spend most of our lives inside of buildings, it matters a great deal how those buildings are designed. The indoor environment is now our (un)natural habitat! The forms, details, and functions of buildings profoundly impact our physical health and mental well-being, they set the stage for how we perceive the environment around us, they influence our social relationships, and they both form and inform our culture.

Humans are highly visual creatures. Whereas dogs understand their world largely through their sense of smell, and creatures with exceptionally large ears or long whiskers may rely more on sound or touch, we humans use our sense of sight as our primary mode for understanding the world. In many ways, due to the very evolutionary perfection of our eyes, our interaction with the visual environment is often so seamless, so very easy, that it does not demand much thought or reflection. But the design of our buildings importantly determines the visual environment in which we spend our lives. This book is an effort to begin to take that visual world apart into component pieces, different cultural perspectives and design applications, and thus help to build a more comprehensive theory of the indoor visual environment.

Visual Delight is what results when the design of our visual environment is working so well, so perfectly in tune to all of our needs, that it is a source of continuing pleasure and joy.

Is Daylight Essential, or an Optional Amenity?

I first realized that I needed to write this book when I was working with a team of colleagues on a proposal that one of our national 'green' building codes should require at least 50% of all workspaces to have access to a view of the outdoors. We called it our 'view proposal.'

My team had already succeeded in persuading this same code group to adopt minimum requirements for daylight illumination, which they considered to be a reasonable expression of best practices. I knew from my experience that, a decade or two earlier, general building industry attitudes had been strongly arrayed against daylight illumination. As a design architect, I had struggled to get daylighting design included in the schools and office buildings I was working on. However, in 1999, I completed a major research study which showed that elementary school children in classrooms with more daylight progressed faster on their math and reading curriculum. The study's findings quickly made national and international headlines, and soon 'natural daylight' became a preferred feature for high-performance school design. In the years since, many other researchers' findings have supported the positive effects of daylight, and other codes and standards groups had already moved to adopt minimum daylighting requirements. Thus, after decades of effort by many people to persuade the building industry to embrace daylight illumination, a sea-change in attitudes had indeed happened.

However, the national code committee's reaction to our view proposal was very different. After many long discussions, it was soundly voted down by over 70% of the committee! The most succinct statement of the opposition that I received was that "*a view requirement is not appropriate for a green building code because it has no health or environmental impacts: views are an amenity.*" An amenity is a real estate term for something for which you must pay extra. Fresh air used to be considered an amenity, back in the days when industrial air pollution was pervasive in our cities. Now it is recognized as fundamental to human health. I realized we had a long way to go to persuade these code officials, the building industry, and the public at large, that access to views mattered, at least as much as daylight illumination and maybe more so. It can take a long time to change widespread attitudes and assumptions.

The Cusp of a Design Revolution

I wrote a little book called *Thermal Delight in Architecture* in 1979. It was written at the height of the 'energy crisis' of the 1970s, when I felt that there was a need to look beyond the established architectural assumptions of the day in order to find new design ideas for a more energy efficient architecture, one which could respect basic human physiological needs, while also providing sensual pleasure, emotional engagement, and deeper cultural meanings. That little book has continued to find resonance with new readers over the decades, as they also explore new ways of thinking about this most basic of building function: how to keep the occupants happy, healthy, and comfortable, while using the desire for thermal comfort as an inspiration for humane and meaningful design.

We may be at a similar cusp today, with recent revolutions in lighting and technology enabling radically new approaches to our visual environment. Our buildings are getting ever bigger, our cities ever denser, as the world's human population continues to inexorably expand. Given the times we live in, high-tech solutions, such as daylight and view replicators, are often aggressively marketed instead of the much simpler and proven approaches to the design of our buildings and cities, such as windows and skylights. At the very same time we are learning ever more about how fundamental genetic mechanisms tie all aspects of our physiology to planetary rhythms of light and dark, and the essential contribution that daylight makes to our overall well-being. Which solutions will be most appreciated by following generations?

Back when I wrote *Thermal Delight*, I assumed that the visual functions of architectural design were so basic, obvious, and well developed that they did not need further elaboration. Little did I know at the time that I would spend most of my professional career documenting the benefits of using daylight to illuminate buildings, first to reduce energy use and then to make a more humane environment.

A Personal Story

It was while working on a series of daylighting case studies that I initially noted the remarkable change in mood and attitude among people working in nicely daylit spaces. My client at the time, a large utility company, Southern California Edison, had been promoting the use of skylights in large open spaces, referred to as 'big box' buildings—such as industrial buildings, warehouses, large retail stores, or school gymnasia—for over a decade. When I arrived on the scene, they already had quite a bit of experience with good daylighting designs for this building type, and many examples of businesses who were happy with their decision to adopt skylights as a standard element of design. My primary mission was to document how cost-effective skylights could be at reducing energy use, given the lighting technology at the time. However, along the way, I encountered far more nuanced stories about what motivated building owners to adopt daylighting.

I was sent north of Los Angeles to two new manufacturing plants that used skylights, Remo Inc. and Standard Abrasives. Their new buildings had been built after the 1994 Northridge earthquake destroyed their original facilities. The owners of these two companies were actually friends—Standard Abrasives supplied materials that Remo used in their drumheads—and so they had talked to each other about the design of their new buildings. The owner of Remo had been at work at 4:30 in the morning when the magnitude 6.7 earthquake struck. When I interviewed him, he described the sheer terror of finding himself in a heavily damaged, swaying building, in total blackness after the power went out. He decided then and there he would never again work in a building without windows and skylights, so that he could always have some light, even if it was only the light of the moon or starlight, to find his way out.

His new building featured lots of skylights, enough so that he could turn off ¾ of all the electric lights on most days.[1] In the sunny weather around Los Angeles, he could turn off his metal halide factory lights within an hour after sunrise and keep them off all day until an hour before sunset. Southern California Edison considered this a great success story for reducing peak daytime electricity loads. The owner liked the money he was saving from the skylights, but even more, he told me, it was the loyalty of his employees that was the real payback. After the earthquake, he had to temporarily close down his operations for a few months, while he built this new building 30 miles away, near Santa Clarita. He worried if he could get people to come work at the new location, given the difficulties of commuting in Los Angeles. In the end, he said, all 100+ of his original employees moved to the new location. He credits the skylights. Once they saw the beautiful new building, they signed up and stayed on.

He then urged me to go visit the building that his buddy at Standard Abrasives had built after seeing his skylights. This manufacturing building was smaller, about 1/4 the size of the first. The owner of Standard Abrasives had decided to relocate his factory to a less congested location, where he easily could live nearby, just over the county border in Simi Valley. His new factory was on a slight rise above the valley, and he decided that in addition to being skylit, it should also take advantage of some of the beautiful views across the valley. So, following the lead of his friend from Remo, he commissioned a new warehouse-style building, with plenty of skylights, but also with huge openings in the walls that allowed floor to ceiling windows, each about 15 feet wide and 30 feet high.

I interviewed the workers at Standard Abrasives about the quality of the lighting in their workplaces. They reported they barely noticed when the overhead electric lighting (a mixture of florescent and metal halide) switched off when there was sufficient daylight from the skylights—it certainly did not bother them. Sure, they liked the lighting system overall: it was high quality and it made their jobs easier. But they *loved the views!* Young Latina women, who could barely speak English, couldn't stop talking about the window views, and how good it made them feel at work. They loved the trees, the sky, the daylight, the changing colors. I had been interviewing lots of workers in different buildings, but this level of response was different. I had also never been in a factory building with views before. I was very impressed: it felt like a happy place. I went to interview the owner. I still remember him as one of the happiest people I have ever interviewed. He was happy to answer all my questions. He loved the new building and the energy savings from the skylights. He loved his job. He loved his company. He was proud of his workers. I came away from that experience curious about the specific power of views in the workplace. That experience was the beginning of the journey that led to much of my later research, and ultimately, the writing this book.

The Structure of this Book

I have since had many formative adventures learning about people's relationship with daylight and views in their workplaces, studying both old designs and new technologies. Many of those experiences shaped my overall perspective and have found their way as stories into this book. Almost everyone seems to have a formative story about windows—from their early childhood, their school days, or a critical time in their adult lives. When I ask people to remember an important moment in their education, and then describe the physical setting, it almost always prominently features a window as part of the indelible memory.

This book draws not only on my experience, but also asks you to draw on yours. Unlike most books about architecture, there are no photographs and/ or plans to explain individual buildings. Instead, I encourage you to go online to seek out more information about the buildings I describe, and try to form your own evaluation of their visual quality. Even better, I hope you will start to look at your own home, workplace, or favorite coffee shop with new eyes, considering the contribution that daylight and views make to your preferences in those places.

In addition to the many stories and personal experiences, this book also draws heavily on recent research findings from a wide range of fields. Looking for inspiration and insight, this book casts a very wide net, from neuroscience to public health, from urban design to interior design, from economics to education, from history to technology. Uniting all of these perspectives is my point of view as an architect, asking the question: how can we use this information to design better buildings in which we all work and live?

The book is divided into four parts: *Prediction, Perception, Motivation,* and *Meaning*, each with a handful of chapters. At the end, a brief Conclusion summarizes the many arguments made throughout. (You are welcome to read the Conclusion first, if you are really pressed for time!) Words and acronyms which may be unfamiliar to the average reader or have an unusual usage in this book are designated on first usage with blue font, and defined in the Glossary at back of the book.

Part 1: Prediction, addresses the fundamental physiological mechanisms of our circadian, visual, and cognitive systems and their relationships to daylight and view. Timing is key, as each system strives to stay in synchrony with each other, with planetary rhythms, and anticipate any likely changes. The communication between our eyes and brains is much more of a two-way street than previously thought, such that each is helping to prepare the other for the next moment in time.

Part 2: Perception, explores human sensory experience. It launches with an exploration of how we learn to see, and how visual perception changes with age. It then continues to explore many visual aspects particular to daylight, from color to glare, and the dynamics of daylight, along with various daylighting design strategies. It differentiates between daylight illumination and window views, and considers what content and qualities of window views that are most meaningful for building occupants.

Part 3: Motivation, considers human social interactions and architectural constructs. It probes how daylighting and views have been deployed in almost every type of building, beginning with schools and ending with healthcare. It recounts some of the research that details how people perform differently in daylit buildings, and how views change the economics and perceived value of places. In between, there are stories from manufacturers, retailers, realtors, writers, office workers, judges and jurors which consider issues of privacy and privilege, security and social connection, focus and expansiveness.

Part 4: Meaning, explores how daylight, view, and the visual environment interact with cultural understandings. It steps back to look at iconic views and daylight designs that epitomize cultural attitudes and philosophies. It explores how concepts of nature have varied over time and across cultures, and how newer concepts of biophilia and technophilia are being translated into building design. In some places and moments, as with the fractal nature of gothic cathedrals or the view of Earth from the International Space Station, the very presence of daylight or a view can create a transcendent experience, connecting us more deeply with both our inner and outer universes.

Observations from Vitruvius

If all of the topics mentioned above seem a tad overwhelming, let me suggest a perspective from a very old friend from ancient Rome to encourage you to embrace new areas of learning. Vitruvius was an architect living in the time of Julius Caesar. He wrote the sole surviving contemporary treatise on the architecture of the Roman empire, *The Ten Books on Architecture*, which were rediscovered in the early fifteenth-century Italy and soon became the design basis for much of Renaissance architecture. Vitruvius opens his first book with a wonderful disquisition about all the types of knowledge that an architect must master: "*The architect should be equipped with knowledge of many branches of study and varied kinds of learning, for it is by his (or her) judgment that all work done by the other arts is put to test. This knowledge is the child of practice and theory ... It follows, therefore, that architects who have aimed at acquiring manual skill without scholarship have never been able to reach a position of authority to correspond to their pains, while those who relied only upon theories and scholarship were obviously hunting the shadow, not the substance.*" As well as: "*Let him (or her) be educated, skillful with a pencil, instructed in geometry, know much history, have followed the philosophers with attention, understand music, have some knowledge of medicine, know some opinions of the jurists, be acquainted with astronomy and the theory of the heavens ... perhaps to the inexperienced it may seem a marvel that human nature can comprehend such a great number of studies and keep them in memory. Still, the observation that all studies have a common bond of union and intercourse with one another, may lead to the belief that this can easily be realized."*

In other words, the architect must be a proud generalist, and draw knowledge and inspiration from many fields, in which others will always be far more expert. And yet, in the process of creating the buildings and cities where we live, all other arts and knowledge are *"put to the test"* in order to usefully inform the design of a physical environment that is supportive of human life. I hope that all of you reading this book, whether simply as a daily building occupant—or in a more professional role as a building designer, student, government official, or scientist—will find ways to collaborate in the process and help inform the next generation of buildings and cities.

I have come to believe that some of the greatest gifts that architects can give to the occupants of their buildings are beautifully daylit spaces, with ample views out to the surrounding world, spaces where the rhythms of the planet can be fully experienced. The creation of such buildings, and the cities that enable their success, is an enduring contribution to the well-being of humanity.

I hope that this book will convince you that the visual delight provided by daylight and views should be a daily experience for *everybody*. If that can be achieved, then our world will be generally healthier, more prosperous, and sustainable, and full of places that make people feel joyful and blessed, both now and into the future. I further hope that, having read this book, you can find a way to help bring more visual delight into the daily lives of other people.

Part 1: Prediction

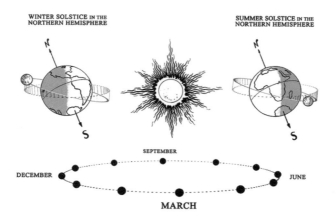

1. Planetary Rhythms

All life forms on our planet must find ways to adapt to environmental changes in order to stay healthy, grow, and reproduce. Those that are most successful also correctly *anticipate* major environmental changes—those that might impact their ability to metabolize, grow, and reproduce—so that they can prepare and quickly adapt to the new condition. Humans are no exception. Thus, the more successfully we can predict the future, the more successfully we can thrive.

The most fundamental environmental change experienced on our planet is the daily cycle of light and dark. Predicting that day will follow night might sound ridiculously obvious and simplistic, since we have all lived with regular cycles of day and night since birth. However, the extreme environmental contrast between day and night—brighter, warmer days fueled with intense solar radiation, followed by darker, colder nights—and the continual variation of that rhythm, have profound implications for every life form on the surface of the Earth.

We all know that as Earth orbits around the sun, it also spins on its axis every 24 hours. Yet not every planet does this: the 24-hour time period is unique to our planet. Early in the evolution of life, single-celled organisms developed an internal genetic clock, called a circadian rhythm, to help predict the timing of day versus night. These internal clocks have been found in the genetic mechanisms of every life form so far studied on the surface of the planet,[1] including the most primitive cyanobacteria, and have been preserved through millions of years of evolution in the DNA of every cell in the human body.

There are, in addition, two other very important planetary rhythms which further complicate things: yearly seasons and lunar cycles. Because the Earth tilts on its axis as it orbits the sun (at 23.5°), the intensity of solar radiation and the length of day versus night varies with the seasons. On the side of the planet tilting towards the sun it is summertime, with longer days and shorter nights, while on the other half tilting away it is winter, with shorter days and longer nights. Twice a year the tilt perfectly aligns with the plane of the Earth's orbit, on the days called the equinox. On just those two days, once for the spring equinox and once for the fall equinox, everywhere on the surface of the planet, day and night are of exactly equal length, 12 hours each. In between those two special days, the days grow progressively longer until midsummer, known as the summer solstice, and progressively shorter until midwinter, known as the winter solstice. At the extreme conditions, at the North and South Poles, there are many days where the sun shines continuously for 24 hours during the summer and never rises above the horizon during the winter. Adapting to the continuously changing lengths of day versus night is a key function of our circadian system.

The second complicating factor, lunar cycles, are created by the moon's orbit around the Earth about once a month (every 29.53 days). The moon's gravity pulls the oceans towards the moon, creating a complex pattern of daily and monthly tide cycles: a lunar rhythm which profoundly influences marine organisms. In addition, sunlight reflects off of the moon, following a monthly pattern of waxing and waning between a very bright 'full' moon and a completely dark 'new' moon. This change in the brightness of moonlight at night is also extremely important to nocturnal organisms, as they either hope to hide from predators in the darkness or seek out food and mates in the moonlight.

The interaction of these three planetary rhythms—the Earth's daily rotation, its tilted yearly orbit around the sun, and the moon's monthly orbit around Earth—creates enormous rhythmic complexity. All life forms, including humans, have found ways to respond to this rhythmic complexity, using a variety of sensors and mechanisms that collect information and provide continuous feedback about changes and trends, enabling better prediction of future conditions.[2]

Calendars

Humans have been trying to understand the interactions of these rhythms since ancient times. In every known culture across the planet, people have been preoccupied with measuring, recording, and predicting the passage of time. Neanderthals may have counted days and months with scratches on bones and stones. Stonehenge and other Neolithic structures were created as solar and celestial observatories in order to predict the seasonal timing of sunrise and moonrise. The earliest written records of a calendar are from Sumer and Egypt. The priestly classes were charged with correctly keeping the calendars to predict the best planting and harvest times and determining the days for yearly rituals. However, every few years these early calendars inevitably drifted a few days out of sync with true solar time, necessitating an official declaration to make a formal correction.

The Romans also struggled with creating a civil calendar, based roughly on lunar months, which would stay properly aligned with the solar year. They did this by adding a few extra days during the winter, when needed: February was their preferred 'flexi-month' to bring the coming calendar year into better alignment. The Julian calendar instituted by Julius Caesar in 46 BCE added one extra day to February every four years to account for the extra six hours that were not included in a 365-day calendar. But the Julian calendar was slightly too long and still required occasional adjustments by decree. By the sixteenth century it had drifted by ten days. A revised calendaring system, named the *Gregorian calendar* for Pope Gregory XIII, was instituted by the Catholic Church in 1582, and gradually adopted by governments around the world, to the point where it is now the most widely used civil calendar internationally.

We humans are now fluent in thinking of the passage of time via the days, months, and years of our calendars. With various types of clocks, we found ways to subdivide our days into hours, minutes, and seconds. With ever more sensitive instruments, we have found ways to use the natural vibration rate of electrons pulsating around an atom to enable measurement of increasingly smaller units of time, such as nano-seconds—one billionth of a second. This precision enables our global communication, via signals from satellites which keep our computers, cells phones, and GIS mapping systems all in tight synchrony. However, this continuing progress in technological competence may have made tracking time so easy, so obvious, as to have blinded us to the essential relationship of all life forms to planetary rhythms, and our fundamental dependence on that timing for our own health and well-being.

Subtle variations in daylight are some of those planetary cues that help every cell in your body know what time it is. If your bedroom has a clear window in it, the light receptors in your eyes will sense the arrival of dawn even before you open your eyes. The slow fading of daylight at sunset, from the last amber rays of the sun to the darkening night sky, also primes your body to get ready for restorative sleep. Thus, exposure to natural patterns of daylight illumination, especially via windows in our buildings, wherein we spend the majority of our days, and indeed, the majority of our lives, provides a profound biological link to planetary rhythms.

Adequate exposure to daylight illumination for all humans was something that could easily be taken for granted in earlier times, when people spent more of their lifetimes outdoors. However, in today's more technological world, people can easily spend days, or even months, entirely indoors. Thus, the design of our habitations, workplaces and cities to provide sufficient access to daylight for everyone is a critical challenge for our time. Done well and artfully, it will not only help to maintain the health and well-being of our growing population, but also provide the visual delight that sustains us emotionally.

Life's Daily Breath: Chlorophyll and Oxygen

Before we delve into the implications for urban and architectural design, it is instructive to consider the deep evolutionary roots of our circadian patterns. From the oceans we can more easily understand the fundamental ways that the sun's radiant energy during the day, and lack of it at night, drives oxygen cycles, food cycles, circadian biology, and vision. It was about midway through our planet's existence, i.e. about two to three billion years ago, that photosynthesis evolved, creating a new way to transform the radiant energy of the sun into chemical energy that could be stored as sugar. A new molecule mastered the process of using the energy in visible light to transform a handful of water molecules and dissolved carbon dioxide (along with two by-products, some extra oxygen and water) into one molecule of sugar. This is the chemical process of chlorophyll-A, which forms the essential basis of most plant life, and of oxygen production on Earth.

In order to utilize chlorophyll successfully, early organisms had to find just the right balance of solar radiation within the ocean's waters. The chlorophyll molecule absorbs light energy at the two ends of the visible spectrum, in the long red and short blue wavelengths, while reflecting most of the green wavelengths in the middle. This is why organisms with chlorophyll appear greenish. Ultraviolet radiation (UV), on the other hand, inhibits the production of chlorophyll. UV is so energy-intensive that it can break down organic molecular bonds within a cell and destroy DNA. Thus, in order to survive and to find just the right energy balance to produce their sugars, these simple photosynthetic organisms, collectively called phytoplankton, need to float deep enough in the water to avoid most UV radiation, while still receiving enough blue and red light to manufacturer their sugars. Finding just the right balance of light to support photosynthesis in ocean waters is a highly dynamic process, because the ratio changes with the daily and seasonal angle of the sun, along with the changing clarity or murkiness of the water.

At night, in order to continue fueling their metabolism, phytoplankton reverse the process and consume some of the sugar stores and extra oxygen they made during the day. Thus, during the day when they have sufficient light to make chlorophyll, they are producing oxygen and releasing it into nearby waters, while at night they are reabsorbing some of the oxygen. The chlorophyll production is therefore also driving the daily oxygen (and carbon dioxide) balance in the upper layers of the ocean, increasing oxygen levels during bright days and decreasing it during the dark nights. Like a daily breath, they are exhaling oxygen during the day and inhaling it at night.

Zooplankton and Bioluminescence

Zooplankton are another type of plankton, but which cannot make their own food supply via chlorophyll. Instead they survive by eating those who do, and thus they are classified as animals. Zooplankton tend to reverse the movements of the phytoplankton, sinking deep into the ocean's waters during the day, feeding off the nutritious 'snow' of dead micro-organisms drifting down towards the bottom, while avoiding UV radiation and any surface-dwelling predators. Then at night, they engage in a great vertical migration, moving upwards to feed on the phytoplankton living closer to the surface. This daily vertical migration has been called the largest migration in the world, based on sheer biomass and the range of organisms involved.

This vertical migration is driven primarily by light, or rather the lack there of. The zooplankton are seeking darkness. Research suggests that much of this vertical migration is driven by circadian rhythms embedded in the genetics of each creature, and controlled by melatonin, the same hormone that in humans signals the presence of darkness. However, there is also evidence that these tiny creatures have photoreceptors that are prompting them to moderate their migrations, because it has been observed that the height of their migrations is less in the presence of moonlight and greater when the moon is darkened by cloud cover and or a lunar eclipse.[3] Such photoreceptors in microscopic organisms driving their behaviors might be considered the evolutionary beginning of vision.

Zooplankton have another very surprising feature: they can make their own light. Most have a capability for bioluminescence, i.e. they can glow like a firefly. Indeed, Dr. Steven Haddock, a bioluminescence researcher at the Monterey Bay Aquarium Research Institute in California, has developed evidence that upwards of three-quarters of all marine organisms have the ability to make their own light via bioluminescence![4] If these creatures are seeking darkness, why would they need to glow?

Some deep-sea organisms are known to use bioluminescence as a lure, to attract prey with a little glow imitating the movements of their favorite fish, or like fireflies, as a sexual attractant to find mates. While there are many possible evolutionary theories for the survival value of bioluminescence, one of the most intriguing is to create a cloak of invisibility. The color of almost all bioluminescent molecules is blue-green, the same color as the ocean above. By self-glowing blue-green, the creatures no longer cast a shadow or create a silhouette, especially when viewed from below against the brighter waters above. Rather, by glowing themselves, they can blend into the sparkles, reflections, and diffuse blue-green glow of sunlight or moonlight. Thus, they are most likely making their own light not to see, but to be un-seen.

It is striking how these extremely simple organisms organize their lives around the cycles of light and dark. Zooplankton exhibit photosensitivity that drives their activity, and which likely informed both the evolution of both daily hormonal cycles and vision in more complex animals. Continuing scientific advances have enabled ever more insight into the fundamental role of light (and darkness) in the basic genetic and biochemical mechanisms of life.

Seasonal, Lunar, and Circadian Rhythms

The daily and seasonal rhythms of life on our planet have been long obvious to the primitive peoples of the world. Hunters know when each type of animal will be most active or asleep, will migrate or wean their babies. Fisherman likewise pay careful attention to seasonal and lunar cycles of fish behavior, such as the trout feeding frenzy when the mayflies all hatch during sunset on a new moon.

You may have noticed that some flowers bloom only at a certain time of day, such as morning glories and evening primrose, their timing even evidenced in their common name. Magnificent fields of giant sunflowers not only track the sun throughout the day, but then rewind at night so that they are once again facing east in time for the morning sunrise. Flowers also time the release of their fragrance for when their pollinators are most actively foraging: daytime for those pollinated by bees and night for those pollinated by moths. Red flowers, like roses, tend to be most fragrant during daytime hours when they are most visible, while white flowers, like many jasmine species, peak their perfumes in the late twilight and early evening hours. Thus, it is not only the behavior of individual species that is controlled by a circadian clock, but entire ecosystems, engaging in an elaborate daily dance.

Thoughtful building design should also reflect these changes, taking advantage of the change in sun path over the course of the seasons, and the resulting cycles in weather and vegetation. Just like gravity, the path of the sun through the sky is fully understood, and thus completely predictable. We can easily predict how much sunlight can strike a window or enter a skylight on any given hour and day of the year. We can just as easily predict the length and location of shadows at any hour of the year. Computerized tools are now available online to produce this information for any point on the planet (see page 129).[5] Others computerized programs can account for the probability of weather patterns based on historical data. It is not the knowledge of these patterns that is missing, rather we often neglect the art of applying them with greatest benefit to building occupants. Imagine a city where our buildings and streets are designed to be as precisely attuned to our daily and seasonal patterns as a field of sunflowers tracking the sun.

2. Chronobiology and Human Health

In spite of commonplace experience with daily and seasonal rhythms, the influence of biological rhythms on human physiology, mood, and cognitive behavior was not widely recognized in the twentieth century. The study of biological rhythms remained a small, niche area of study. Few scientists conducted their experiments accounting for, or reporting on, time of day effects or the lighting conditions in their labs. Their favorite test subjects—rats, rabbits, or fruit flies—were often kept in interior labs that had no exposure to daylight, and often also under continuous night lighting. Thus, we can assume that many test animals were living under severe circadian disruption conditions. How did this impact their findings relative to human psychology, pharmacology, or pathology? We don't know, and it is disturbing to ponder.

This changed dramatically in 2017, when three Americans, Jeffrey C. Hall, Michael Rosbash, and Michael W. Young, were awarded the Nobel Prize in medicine and physiology. Recognition for their discoveries about how internal clocks and biological rhythms govern many metabolic processes greatly accelerated interest in the wide reach of circadian biology, and has elevated the new scientific discipline called chronobiology. Scientists have since discovered molecular and genetic rhythms embedded in every cell in our body. Indeed, a study sponsored by the Salk Institute found that over 80% of all protein-coding genes in primate tissues follow a daily rhythm.[1] This finding has enormous implications for medical diagnosis and treatment, and the prescription of drugs which are likely to have a greater efficacy at specific times of the day.

However, it also has similar implications for the design of cities and buildings that promote human well-being. If our fundamental physiology is tied to well-synchronized circadian rhythms, at all levels of expression, from social behavior down to the rhythmic genetic activity making and unmaking the basic protein building blocks of our metabolism, then helping people maintain robust circadian rhythms is a key public health issue.

Many rhythms which were ignored or overlooked in the twentieth century are now being rediscovered as essential to our relationship with the visual and built environment. We can now consider not only a wide variety of circadian, lunar, and seasonal rhythms expressed throughout our body, but also synchronization of other micro-rhythms, such as walking, blinking, breathing, heart beats, and even the most fundamental rhythms of the brain that set the pace of our thoughts and dreams. These many rhythms will be explored further in the upcoming chapters on the eye and the brain, but first, let's consider human circadian physiology in a bit more detail, especially by considering what can go wrong.

Circadian Disruption: Jetlag, Shiftwork, and SAD

The first recognition of problems with human circadian disruption began via 'jetlag.' Jet-powered commercial airplane travel began in the 1950s and became the norm for long distance flights in the 1960s. Before jet-travel, people were simply not traveling fast enough to get noticeably out of synchronization with local time. Pilots, airline crew, and frequent flyers began to realize that they felt rather out of sorts after traveling through three or more time zones: getting hungry and sleepy at odd times, falling asleep in business meetings, and becoming ravenously hungry in the middle of the night. As scientists began to study the jetlag phenomenon, they realized that it took a number of days, or even weeks, before a person's body adapted to the new time zone. (Current belief is that it takes at least *one day* of adjustment time for *each hour* of shifted time zone to fully adjust and get all body processes back in sync with each other.) In parallel, industrial health researchers realized that sift work was very similar in its effects of circadian disruption—it was like jet lag without going anywhere—and that shift workers' health was suffering.

In the 1980s the United States National Institutes of Health began to research a newly identified phenomenon of seasonal depression, named seasonal affective disorder or SAD. This form of depression was characterized by depressed mood in the late fall and early winter, as days grew shorter, and was associated with an increase in lethargy, carbohydrate cravings, and weight gain. (SAD could be thought of as a kind of counterpoint to 'spring fever,' when people find that they are strangely agitated and students feel a compelling need to skip classes and lie out in the sunshine on the campus quad.) It was noted that there was a higher prevalence of SAD in the more northern regions of Europe and North America, and especially in people who had moved north from countries nearer the equator. Suspecting that SAD was a chronobiological disorder, early therapists demonstrated that SAD was treatable with 'light therapy,' where patients would sit in front of a bright light box for 30 to 60 minutes every morning to jump-start their daytime mental and physical functions.

However, these early treatments did not have the benefit of a deeper understanding of the complexities of the circadian clock. Thus, many of these early studies simply reported on treatment with 'bright light,' with no concern for reporting the specifics of the light source, its intensity, or the spectral content of the light. The two variables of interest were typically just timing and duration: how long should a subject sit in front of the light box, and when?

Similarly, as biologists began to investigate circadian disruption in laboratory animals, they focused primarily on the *timing* of light–dark patterns, rather than the qualities of the light or the rate of change. Fluorescent lights were simply switched on and off, in 12/12 hour or 8/16 hour patterns. Researchers commonly reported that they administered 'bright light,' followed by 'dim light' at night, with no appreciation of how very little light might suppress melatonin production at night.

A Newly Discovered Photoreceptor: The ipRGC

A major breakthrough occurred when scientists first identified the specific cells in the eye which were responsible for initiating the signal to the mammalian circadian system. These were identified as specialized ganglion cells in the retina, which previously were thought to be merely intermediate connector nerve cells with no receptivity to light. There are about 3 million retinal ganglion cells (RGC) which send information from the eye to the brain, reporting on the activity of the rods and the cones (see Figure 2.1).

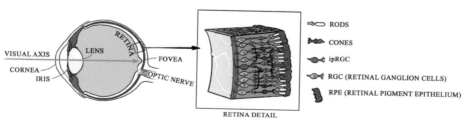

Figure 2.1: Cross section of eye and retina, with location of rods, cones, and ipRGC

In 2003, a group of scientists first reported that a tiny percentage of these RGC, less than 5%, were photosensitive themselves.[2] These ganglion cells were found to contain an ancient photoreceptor chemical, melanopsin, that is more similar to that found in the eyes of insects than in the rods and cones of mammals and birds.[3] This discovery has since caused a revolution in the understanding of light and health. These receptors are now most commonly referred to as the intrinsically photosensitive Retinal Ganglion Cells or ipRGC. Although it may be an awkward name, it is worth remembering because the ipRGC contribute an important part of the story about daylight and health.

Once identified, there was a rush to understand the function and communication pathways of the ipRGC. It was quickly learned that these cells are quite different from the other well-known photosensors in the retina, i.e. the rods and cones. The ipRGC are rather sluggish, taking seconds, instead of milliseconds, to respond to light.[4] Yet once activated, the ipRGC also sustain their signal for an exceptionally long time. They are uniquely sensitive to blue light, around 480 nanometers (nm), which not coincidentally is also the color of a blue sky and the segment of solar radiation with the greatest intensity in the visible spectrum. (see Figures 3.3 and 7.1) Thus, the ipRGC are uniquely suited to provide a stable representation of the presence of ambient daylight intensity. When the ipRGC are firing, an animal, or human, can assume "*It is now daytime*" and "*I should be going about my business doing daytime type activities.*"

Indeed, the extremely long tails of these ipRGC nerve cells, their axons, were found to go directly to the brain's primary controller of circadian rhythms, the suprachiasmatic nucleus, or the SCN for short. The SCN then communicates with many regions of the brain. One important pathway leads to the pineal gland, which produces the hormone melatonin. The pineal gland begins to manufacture melatonin with the onset of dim light in the evening, with concentrations peaking later in the middle of the night and gradually dissipating with the arrival of morning light.

This peak production of melatonin at night is true for all animals, regardless of whether they are nocturnal or diurnal. For example, for nocturnal rats and bats, high melatonin levels are associated with active behaviors, like looking for food and mates, whereas for diurnal humans and mammals, high melatonin levels are associated with sleep. Thus, melatonin is a biochemical indicator of darkness (and not, as often misrepresented, a 'sleep hormone'). It translates the physical absence of blue light photons into a chemical message that diffuses throughout the body of the animal. Thus, it provides an internal representation of the external dark-light cycle. Melatonin has been called the conductor of the circadian orchestra, providing the 24-hour pulse to which all other intra-cellular clocks in tissues throughout the body synchronize their rhythm.

With the discovery of the ipRGC and their sensitivity to blue wavelengths, researchers had a new hypothesis about the mechanism controlling human and animal circadian rhythms. Maybe it was retinal exposure to blue wavelengths, activating the ipRGC and signaling the pineal gland to cease production of melatonin, that was the primary driver of human circadian rhythms? Maybe it was unnatural timing of exposure to blue wavelengths that was resetting people's circadian clocks, causing jetlag, shiftwork syndrome, SAD, and other problems associated with disrupted sleep? Research into circadian disruption had an exciting new impetus and spread into many new fields of inquiry.

Sleep Disruption and Health Impacts

At the same time that jetlag, shiftwork syndrome, and SAD were being identified, research into sleep disruption was also gaining recognition. In the 1950s researchers first started using electronic equipment to observe and record sleep patterns, observing people sleeping via infrared cameras and electroencephalography (EEG). The EEG machines attached electrical sensors to the outside of the sleeping subject's scalp, and recorded changes in brain wave patterns. These studies helped to identify different phases of sleep, from the lightest to the deepest phases of sleep, and rapid eye movement (REM) sleep which was highly correlated with dreaming. By recognizing a structure to sleep, researchers began to identify which phases contributed to which recuperative functions of sleep, and how different types of sleep disruption could contribute to poor outcomes.

Americans and other westerners had become increasingly dependent on medications to help them sleep through the night, plus caffeine and other stimulants to stay awake at other times. Sleep researchers also began to realize that many chronic sleep problems might have a circadian root cause, and furthermore, that large populations were becoming chronically sleep deprived, including about 20% of workers engaged in shift work, the elderly with poor sleep patterns, and most especially, teenagers! In 2018 the US Centers for Disease Control reported that fully three-quarters of American high school students did not get enough sleep, staying up too late doing homework or shift work at a part-time job, and getting up too early for classes.[5]

The US Department of Defense also became increasingly concerned about poor sleep quality, not just as a public health issue, but also as a national security issue: if soldiers and sailors are sleepy at the wrong time, it could have serious consequences in any military operation. Indeed, many of the worst industrial accidents of the twentieth century happened in the middle of the night and when workers were sleep deprived, such as the Exxon Valdez oil spill and the Chernobyl nuclear meltdown. Similarly, the more recent collisions of US Navy destroyer ships USS Fitzgerald and USS John S. McCain with commercial ships happened when sailors were sleep deprived.[6] Researchers at the Monterey Naval Postgraduate School subsequently reported in 2019 that according to a recent survey, 72% of American active duty service members had sleep disturbance problems.[7]

The authors emphasized the significance of this finding, succinctly summarizing the extensive literature on the impacts of sleep disturbances: *"According to the consensus recommendation, sleeping less than 7 hours per night on a regular basis is associated with adverse health outcomes, including weight gain and obesity, diabetes, hypertension, heart disease and stroke, depression, and increased risk of death. Sleeping less than 7 hours per night is also associated with impaired immune function, increased pain, impaired performance, increased errors, and greater risk of accidents."*

The scope of the long-term health impacts of circadian disruption should be shocking: weight gain, obesity, diabetes, heart disease and stroke, depression, and increased risk of death! The authors explain that short-term impacts, such as increased errors, risk of accidents and injury, are compounded further since once injuries have occurred healing is also slowed: *"Sleep also affects the rate of healing through the secretion of growth hormone during deep sleep and the inhibition of cortisol secretion."* Not only is poor sleep associated with increased levels of disease and injury, but also with more general cognitive and physical decline: *"From a clinical viewpoint ... medical and psychiatric disorders are frequently associated with impairments in sleep quality and quantity, and ultimately can result in degraded cognitive and physical performance."*

The evidence of the pervasive public health consequences of poor sleep duration and quality are massive, and growing. The authors conclude simply: *"It is evident that for anyone seeking to optimize human performance, sleep is vital."*

Russell Foster, a professor of neurology and ophthalmology at Oxford University was one of the early researchers of neural circadian mechanisms.

He has since become a passionate advocate for improved 'sleep hygiene.' He explains in a TED Talk how 36% of a person's life is spent asleep, or 32 years out of a 90-year lifespan![8] He recommends taking a 'photon shower' every morning, by experiencing the brightening of the sky on an early morning walk outside in order to stay in tune with planetary rhythms and keep one's circadian system in fine tune. Foster describes a stark contrast between pre-industrial attitudes towards sleep, which valued slumber and dreams as an essential part of life, such as the Shakespearean quote from the play Julius Caesar which suggests: *"Enjoy the honeyed heavy dew of slumber"* versus the attitude of post-industrial societies, where sleep is considered to be a hindrance to productivity. Foster quotes Thomas Edison, the famous nineteenth-century inventor who patented the incandescent light bulb and bragged about sleeping less than five hours per day, as declaring with great hubris that: *"Sleep is a criminal waste of time, inherited from our cave days."*

On the value of sleep, Shakespeare seems to have been more prescient than Thomas Edison.

Circadian Complexity

Most of the early studies of the effect of light on human melatonin production were done at night, to see which wavelengths would most effectively activate the ipRGC and suppress the production of melatonin. It was found that very little light indeed could have a profound effect, on the order of just a few lux, especially around the peak color sensitivity of the ipRGC in the blue light wavelengths. (See Figure 3.1 for examples of common illuminance levels as measured in footcandles and lux.)

However, it has since been realized that the sensitivity of the circadian systems is, itself, circadian! In other words, the sensitivity of ipRGC to input varies by time of day, and likewise, the response of the SCN, pineal gland, and melatonin receptors throughout the brain and body also vary by time of day. Thus, while tiny changes in the amount of blue light might have a major effect on melatonin production in the middle of the night, increasing the amount of blue light in the middle of the day may have no measurable effect because melatonin suppression has already been fully achieved.

It is critical to understand that biological rhythms are not driven by simple on-off switches. Rather, the circadian systems in our bodies operate much more like an ecological system. Changes from one state to another are a complexly unfolding process, which may become unstable if interrupted. First, messenger chemicals, such as melatonin, initiate multiple receptors, which then induce a 'biochemical cascade' of further transformations. At each stage of the process, there are intricate systems of feedback loops that work to either increase or decrease signals, inhibiting or accelerating production and secretion of other biochemicals at different time scales. This clock mechanism works not just to coordinate with the external world, but also to also synchronize rhythmicity within the cellular environment.

It is also interesting to note that many fundamental elements of this system have multiple functions, most of which are still poorly understood. Consider, for example, the role of dopamine. At the start of the day, increasing light and declining levels of melatonin signal the time to begin the manufacture of dopamine, a neurotransmitter often described as the 'pleasure' chemical in the popular press, because it is associated with the reward system in the brain. Dopamine, along with its precursors and antagonists, has become a key component of drugs used in the treatment of depression, schizophrenia, ADHD, and the motor tremors of Parkinson's disease. However, outside of the brain, dopamine also has important functions in regulating blood pressure, plus the activity of the kidney, the pancreas, and the intestine, among others. Furthermore, dopamine rhythms are critical to vision: it is also manufactured in the retina, exclusively during daylight hours, where it enhances the activity of cone cells to improve the clarity of daytime vision. Dopamine is also found in most all multicellular organisms, including the simplest of flatworms and jellyfish, where it is consistently connected to forms of motor control.[9] Thus, dopamine seems to be an ancient organic molecule, which has been repurposed many times throughout evolution to fulfill many functions, but all of those likely having something to do with behaviors or metabolic activities which are most necessary or appropriate during daylight hours.

Sunlight Pros and Cons

In recognition of the complexity of the circadian system, some researchers are starting to propose that health problems resulting from circadian disruption are not solely attributable to inappropriate exposure to small amounts of blue light at night and the resulting melatonin suppression, but perhaps equally attributable to a complementary mechanism of inadequate exposure to daylight and sunlight during the day.

Indeed, Michael Smolensky, an early practitioner of chronotherapy at the University of Texas Houston Medical Center, makes the case that many diseases can be traced to either lack of vitamin D synthesis during the day or lack of melatonin synthesis at night, or more properly, an imbalance of the two. He has proposed that lack of daytime exposure to sunlight can be an equivalent circadian disrupter as exposure to blue light at night.[10] His hypothesis is that the arrival of daylight's blue light at dawn alerts the circadian system to prepare for vitamin D synthesis via exposure of the skin to sunlight's UV-B, which would normally peak around noon when the sun is highest in the sky. Likewise, he hypothesizes that the gradual departure of blue light at dusk signals the change-over to melatonin production, which peaks around 2am in the middle of the night. If so, then experiencing the gradual brightening of the sky at sunrise, and the gradual dimming of the sky at sunset would be key functional components of maintaining a robust synthesis of vitamin D during the day and melatonin at night.

Smolensky also published a summary of about 50 diseases and syndromes that are known to have a circadian component, including those that affect the skin, intestinal tract, neural system, kidney, eyes, musculoskeletal system, psychiatric and behavioral disorders, and autoimmune diseases.[11] His assertion is that patient care for these types of rhythmic disorders should first establish an individual's circadian status and then work to stabilize it. Once a patient's rhythm is understood, medical treatments can then be administered with optimum timing, ranging from simple allergy medications to chemotherapy for cancer. Stabilizing the circadian rhythm of patients would then logically become an important objective for hospital design and for other facilities that are responsible for the care of any patient with a circadian related disease or syndrome.

Some people have expressed concern that additional exposure to sunlight might result in higher rates of skin cancer. However, there may be important countervailing health benefits to sunlight exposure, as a 2016 paper in the journal *Medical Hypotheses* discussed: "*During the last decades new favorable associations between sunlight and disease have been discovered. There is growing observational and experimental evidence that regular exposure to sunlight contributes to the prevention of colon-, breast-, prostate cancer, non-Hodgkin lymphoma, multiple sclerosis, hypertension and diabetes. Initially, these beneficial effects were ascribed to vitamin D. Recently it became evident that immunomodulation, the formation of nitric oxide, melatonin, serotonin, and the effect of (sun)light on circadian clocks, are involved as well.*"[12]

This controversy will not be resolved soon, until large-scale studies can compare the pros and cons of various doses of sunlight exposure across all these risks. However, some suggestion of overarching benefits of daylight and sunlight is potentially coming from a number of large studies looking at health outcomes related to time spent outdoors,[13] or simply residential proximity to parks and other green space,[14] which are finding greater long-term public health benefits than expected.

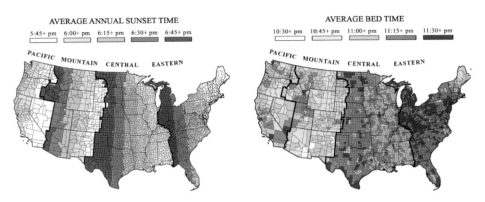

Figure 2.2: Time zones and bedtimes across continental USA

Now that the comprehensive nature of circadian biology is being better understood, other researchers are starting to consider interactive effects, at many levels. For example, a group at the US National Institutes of Health considered how different patterns of light exposure might change susceptibility to environmental exposures of toxins and pathogens.[15] Similarly, at the University of Oregon, researchers have been testing how the complex of micro-organisms that inhabit our buildings, known as the micro-biome, change with exposure to daylight. They have found that, just as humans and animals have preferred circadian patterns, so do bacteria. Initial studies have suggested that pathogens are happiest growing in darker areas, while increased daylight reduces the count of those bacteria which cause human diseases.[16] Thus, there are also many indirect pathways whereby daylight and circadian stimulus might influence our exposure or susceptibility to disease.

Some of the most compelling, and surprising, studies looking at circadian rhythms and public health considered the impact of a person's geographic position within a time zone. The first map in Figure 2.2 illustrates first the difference in true solar time relative to 'social' clock time each USA standard time zone.[17] The second map shows average annual bedtime per county, for a large population wearing the Jawbone digital tracking device. Using public health data by county, one study found significant increases in both general and specific cancer rates as a function of the county's relative position in the time zone, from east to west.[18] Other studies have similarly found poor health and economic outcomes for divergences in solar time versus social time in Europe and China, and due to daylight savings time.[19,20]

Collectively, these studies suggest that even small disruptions in our natural pattern of daylight exposure, *on the order of less than one hour per day* between social clock time and actual solar time, can have significant negative impacts on long-term health outcomes. To the extent that the design of cities and buildings can help keep our circadian rhythms in sync with the planet, we are likely to see improvements in public health.

Our Daily Exposure to Daylight

The question thus arises: *"How much time do we actually spend outdoors? How much time are we normally exposed to daylight in the course of our lives?"* The first question is a bit easier to answer than the second. If a person is outdoors, there is an almost 100% probability that they will be simultaneously exposed to daylight (unless they are always wearing very dark sunglasses). However, very little is known about typical daylight exposures inside of buildings, where we spend a majority of our time. Current thinking is that it may be the overall daily pattern of exposure to light and dark that is most important in determining circadian health, rather than any particular minimum 'dosage.'

In recent decades not only have people been experiencing a sharp decline in sleep quality at night, but also a reduction in time spent outdoors during the day. Large population studies, begun in the 1980s, have consistently shown a surprising decline in the amount of time modern people spend outdoors. Back in 1989 Wayne Ott at Stanford University analyzed extensive demographic data from 12 Western countries and concluded that modern industrialized people spend 92% of their time indoors, 6% in transit, and only 2% of their time outdoors.[21] This was certainly an alarming estimate.

Subsequently, in 2001 a large team of scientists and statisticians, led by the UC Berkeley School of Public Health, published an even more comprehensive National Human Activity Pattern Survey (NHAPS).[22] This ambitious study collected 24-hour diaries from over 9,000 Americans of all ages to provide a detailed picture of where Americans spent their days—such as homes, schools, offices, hospitals, vehicles, bars, and restaurants. This study concluded that, on average, Americans spent 7.6% of their time outdoors, 5.5% inside of vehicles during commutes, and thus the remaining 86.9% of time inside of buildings. The analysis also differentiated between children under 12 and everyone else, showing that American children spent an average of *nine minutes* more outside during that day then their elders. On an average day, 41% of adults and 39% of children never went outside at all!

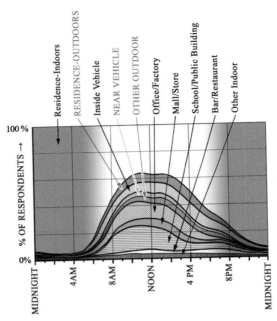

Figure 2.3: Average time indoors and outdoors, NHAPS study of 9,000 Americans

Similar studies in Canada and Europe replicated these results. It should be noted that these studies were conducted before the ubiquitous presence of laptops and smart phones in our lives. Later, a 2011 follow-up study in Britain found that children were spending one half the amount of time outdoors than their parents had 25 years earlier.[23] Another follow-up survey of American children in 2019 found that time spent outdoors was strongly biased by ethnic affiliation, such that Black and Asian children experienced more cultural barriers to spending time outdoors, and that increased time on computers and cell phones was one of the primary reasons cited that children spent less time outdoors.[24]

These numbers should be a wake-up call for how very little time we currently spend exposed to the natural elements outdoors. Instead, we are living out our lives inside of buildings. As Wayne Ott declared after his study back in 1989: *"We are basically an indoor species."*

As an indoor species, we should thus try to understand more about our indoor environment, and how it can best support our health. According to the same NHAPS study quoted earlier, as a population-wide average, Americans spend about half of their daytime hours inside their homes, approximately another 20% in schools or other public buildings, 10% in various offices or factories, and the remaining 10% in retail stores, restaurants, bars, or other types of buildings, as illustrated in Figure 2.3. So, to answer the second question, *"how much daylight are we exposed to?"* we need to consider more specifics about daylight availability in each of these different types of buildings.

Daylight Exposure Inside of Buildings

A while ago I drew a conceptual diagram, shown below in Figure 2.4, comparing our modern ambient light exposure to our ancestral pattern, long before electric lighting was invented, when humans were still living primarily outdoors under the sky and sleeping in complete darkness at night. In contrast, modern humans rarely sleep in compete darkness, with streetlights shining in their bedroom windows and little indicator lights glowing

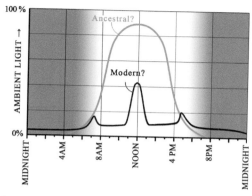

Figure 2.4: Daily exposure to ambient light (conceptual), ancestral versus modern lifestyles

incessantly throughout the house. During the day, working adults may have only brief exposure to high levels of daylight illumination when they step outside to commute to and from work or school, and perhaps take a brief walk outside at lunch time. The rest of the time is spent inside of buildings where ambient illumination levels are determined predominantly by electric lighting.

Increasingly, studies have attempted to track daily illumination exposure levels for a representative population, such that we could add real data to this conceptual diagram. In 2013 a Dutch team collected light exposure data for 42 participants on a university campus, continuously for three days each, collected over the course of a full year.[25] For the whole study group, they found that the average hourly light exposure rose from a low of 30 lux in the morning to a midday average of about 200 lux, then dropped back down to 60 lux in the evening. These are very low illumination values, representative of electrically lit buildings. Common daylight levels outdoors could easily be ten to 100 times greater.

The Dutch group found that peak exposures, >1,000 lux at the eye (such as might occur from stepping outside, or looking out of a window), occurred on average for less than five minutes per hour. Interestingly, these peak exposures varied seasonally, with almost 17 minutes of cumulative exposure during spring, compared to only two minutes in the autumn (perhaps an expression of a 'spring fever' lust for more circadian stimulus?). These researchers also found that the intensity of light exposure, whether measured to represent vision or circadian stimulus, was significantly correlated with greater feelings of 'vitality.' This was true whether they considered light-level exposures averaged over the previous hour, or shorter periods, from the previous five, ten, 15, or 30 minutes. Thus, a brief exposure to bright light was found to have a significant impact on mood for the following hour. Unfortunately, the Dutch researchers did not report the participant's location indoors versus outdoors, so we don't know if people were walking outside or looking out of a window when they had those high light exposures.

It is important to recognize that for any study of circadian stimulus, it matters a great deal what people *look* at when they are inside of buildings. For example, while my office desk may have an ambient daylight level of 100 lux, I can easily receive ten times that amount by merely looking out of the window. However, we also have little information about how much time people actually spend looking out of windows. Some researchers at EPFL recently conducted a study for other purposes, using eye-tracking devices to record when and for how long people looked out a window adjacent to their computer. They found that, given the opportunity, the participants spent a large percentage of their work time, up to 40%, looking out the window, with many frequent glances. (Also see page 123.)

The bottom line is we do not yet know what average, normal, optimal, or sub-optimal exposure to daylight might be for modern populations.[26] However, even without this knowledge, some electric lighting companies are already eagerly marketing their products as capable of meeting all of our circadian needs. Not coincidently, those same companies are also funding most of the current research efforts in this area. They clearly have hopes of developing a standard prescription, an R_x, for daily light exposure (using their products, of course!).

In the meantime, both the International Commission on Lighting (CIE)[27] and the American Medical Association (AMA)[28] have issued statements urging caution before jumping to conclusions about the correct R_x for light exposure. Currently their recommendations focus on avoiding unnecessary exposure to blue wavelengths at night, especially for a few hours before sleep, but offer no recommendations for daytime lighting. They do note, however, that the natural pattern of very bright days and very dark nights is the evolutionary norm for circadian entrainment.

An Appetite for Light

Long ago, I experienced a strange craving for daylight after a long transcontinental flight. I had been traveling from east to west and, after hours on the airplane, disembarked into morning's first light. I went into the women's restroom at Chicago's O'Hare airport, which had large diffusing windows facing the sun. I found myself riveted by the windows radiating brightly diffused sunlight. I realized I didn't want to leave. Ever! *"What is this feeling?"* I wondered, understanding that it was rather odd behavior to be transfixed by glowing windows in a public bathroom.

Was I *starved* for daylight? Or was I satisfying a deep *thirst*? Which is a better term to describe this feeling? Thirst is a very basic instinct of all animals. This is because an imbalance of fluids, too little or too much, can kill you. Our bodies seek to maintain a very precise balance between the hydrostatic pressure inside and outside of cells. While some animals, like camels, can go for days without drinking, humans need to replenish their store of liquids on a daily basis, in order to maintain proper kidney function. When you are really thirsty, drinking pure water is usually the best solution. Indeed, according to recent research, we have taste receptors that reward us for drinking pure water when we are especially thirsty, by making it taste extra delicious.

Appetite, on the other hand, is a more general desire to consume food. An appetite can be the simple result of hunger pangs, the physical churning of our stomach when it is expecting food, or an appetite can be the result of acquired tastes, more of a social construct of learned preferences. We can have healthy appetites for nutritionally balanced food, or unhealthy appetites for addictive sugars and salts. Appetites on over-drive can make you fat or lead to other unhealthy outcomes. Appetite, and hunger, also comes and goes. It is more of a circadian signal 'time to eat!' than an alarm bell for a dangerous bodily imbalance. Whereas an unsatisfied thirst can kill you within a few days or even hours, humans can go without food for a long time: completely for weeks or months, or slowly wasting away for years. As a result, we have often learned not to trust our appetite as a guide to what we really need.

So, which is a better metaphor for light: thirst, or appetite? Do we need to sip daylight throughout the day, like we sip water? Or is 'snacking' on daylight a better metaphor? Is daylight better confined to certain 'mealtimes,' where we consume it in big doses? Given that humans have survived in so many poorly lit places, in prisons and dungeons, in submarines and basements, it is clear that lack of daylight will not kill you, at least not immediately and directly. One of the evolutionary strengths of humans is our very adaptability. We can thrive on many dietary types, from tropical to arctic, from Neolithic to modern. The same is true of our patterns of exposure to light, given successful human settlements from the tropics to the arctic, from caves to modern skyscrapers.

Given this, I believe that an *appetite* for daylight provides the more appropriate metaphor, of a subtle urge that we must combine with many other daily demands, pleasures, and constraints. We are still trying to learn which appetites are most healthy, and how to weave those healthy appetites best into our daily lives and customs.

In later chapters in Part 2, Perception, we will discuss all the many pleasures of our visual sense and how we perceive the visual environment around us. These are the sensory rewards that reinforce our visual appetites and motivate us to seek more of a good thing. First, however, we'll delve deeper into the mechanisms of the eye, and then explore how vision is perceived by the brain.

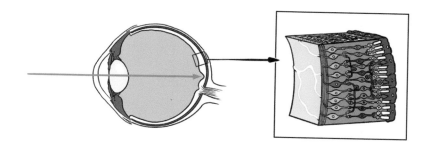

3. The Evolving and Aging Eye

The eye has been called the miracle of evolution. Early evolutionary scientists could not fathom how such an amazing instrument as the eye had evolved, and the perfection of human vision was given as proof of 'intelligent design' from a divine being, rather than via the more random and slow evolutionary processes suggested by the Darwinian theory of natural selection.

Darwin, on the other hand, was acutely aware of this critique, and even in spite of how little was understood at the time about the functions and physiology of the eye, he resolutely maintained that such amazing complexity and precision could be developed over the course of time via the naturalistic process of evolution. In his journals he wrote: *"Reason tells me, that if numerous gradations from a simple and imperfect eye to one complex and perfect can be shown to exist, each grade being useful to its possessor, as is certainly the case; if further, the eye ever varies and the variations be inherited, as is likewise certainly the case and if such variations should be useful to any animal under changing conditions of life, then the difficulty of believing that a perfect and complex eye could be formed by natural selection, though insuperable by our imagination, should not be considered as subversive of the theory."*[1]

It is not so difficult today to explain the key steps of evolving from a primitive light sensitive organism, such as zooplankton, through the very primitive 'eye spots' of a worm, the wide variety of eyes found in insects and fish, to the more advanced capabilities of birds and mammals. It is worthwhile to learn more about the visual capabilities and perception of other animals, as it helps to put the 'miracle' of human vision in context, and give us pause to consider the implications of our own particular visual strengths and weakness. The following pages provide just a few highlights. (Please refer back to Figure 2.1 for the basic anatomy of the human eye and retina.)

From an evolutionary perspective, the first function to develop was likely the day/night detection of the circadian system, along with detecting the direction of the source of light. As we learned earlier, primitive light detection systems exist in even the tiniest zooplankton, enabling them to adjust their daily migrations up and down the water column. We now understand that the primary mammalian circadian receptors, the ipRGC, are located within our retina, and influence a wide range of metabolic, cognitive and visual functions.

The next basic eye function likely to have evolved is detecting the movement of objects, indicating if the object might be alive and therefore prey or predator. The sudden arrival of a shadow is usually the cause for a fly to flee! The detection of movement, however, is greatly complicated if the sensing animal itself can also move: an animal that can move then needs the cognitive processing power to determine if a spot of light on its retina is moving due to some external changes in the environment, or due to its own internal body movements. To factor in its own body movements, an animal needs to develop self-awareness. The more types of movement an animal is capable of, the greater the mental processing power required. Thus, it is thought that the evolution of complex movement, vision, and brain power go hand-in-hand. This is a key concept to keep in mind as we explore other aspects of vision and the visual environment.

Once an animal can successfully detect movement that might indicate predator or prey, the next question to resolve is what kind of object is moving, and how fast, all of which requires greater visual acuity. Visual acuity involves the detection of edges—the boundary between the object and everything else—along with determining distances, three-dimensional shapes, and textural patterns. Visual acuity is increased with better optics, such as a lens and eyeball that can be adjusted to focus on objects at different distances, and a higher resolution of the image, via a greater density of photoreceptors and more neural connections to transmit and process the information.

Humans may win the contest for most neural connections to process visual information, but some birds have up to ten times more photoreceptors in their retinas than humans, all packed into smaller eyes. The photoreceptor density of bird eyes is as if the resolution on a digital camera was transformed from 100 pixels per inch to more than 1,000 pixels per inch. However, bird eyes manage their optical focusing strategies very differently than we do, resulting in a perpetual wide-eye stare. We humans are keenly interested in tracking what others are looking at, to better understand what they are thinking and feeling. Thus, creatures without the same eye movements as humans can seem strangely alien and soulless to us.

Color vision is perhaps the most evolutionarily advanced visual capability, allowing subtle discrimination of light intensity by wavelength. Many nocturnal animals and those that live solely in the ocean depths or underground do not have the ability to perceive colors. Their vision is provided by photoreceptors which report the intensity of light, but cannot differentiate its wavelength. This type of photoreceptor can be exquisitely sensitive in dim light, but they tend to saturate and thus cease to function under bright light, leaving the animal blinded by the light. Many nocturnal frogs and salamanders, for example, are completely unable to function under illumination much brighter than the full moon, and thus become dazed and confused under electric outdoor lighting.

Animals functioning during the daytime evolved a second visual system that supports color vision, but which requires higher levels of illumination. While most vertebrates and invertebrates have color vision, their eyes have very different optical structures and photoreceptor chemistry. Some insects, fish, and birds can perceive ultraviolet wavelengths, enabling them to see other creatures that appear completely transparent to us, or see additional colors and patterns in flowers or feathers. The visual capabilities of animals may also change over their lifetimes to accommodate new ecological niches. For example, as salmon migrate down from the clear waters of a mountain stream into the murky green waters of an estuary and then out into the blue depths of the open ocean, and then reverse the process to spawn, their eyes also remarkably change color sensitivity: some visual receptors elongate and increase their sensitivity while others retract and lose sensitivity.[2]

Current evolutionary theory holds that while dinosaurs reigned supreme during the daytime, the first mammals were small and primarily nocturnal. To help find food in the darkness of night, their sense of smell became primary over vision, such as it still is for dogs and rats. Many mammals also developed whiskers to help them feel around in the dark. Early mammalian eyes reflected this shift to nocturnal behaviors, with a higher density of rods most sensitive in the dark of night, and a loss of color vision capabilities compared to birds. Some nocturnal mammals, especially carnivores, developed a special reflective surface at the back of their retina, called the *tapetum lucidum*, which greatly enhances night vision. This is why cats' eyes can sometimes seem to glow in the dark, and why flash photography of wildlife often shows critters with strangely bright eyes.

Human Vision: Daytime versus Nighttime

We have our primate ancestors to thank for a return to daytime activity and thus the evolutionary restoration of greater human color vision capabilities than most mammals. Indeed, humans have two visual systems with distinctly different structures and functions: our daytime vision system, called photopic vision, driven primarily by our cones, and our nighttime vision system, called scotopic vision, driven primarily by our rods. Rods provide most of our peripheral vision, and all of our dim-light (nighttime) black and white vision, while cones provide our bright light (daytime) color vision and the high acuity in our central, focal vision.

Given early mammals' specialization in nighttime living, it is understandable that most of the human retina consists of rods. In the human eye there are about 15–20 times more rods than cones. This adds up to about 120 million rods versus 6–8 million cones. Our rods are up to 10,000 times more sensitive to light than cones.

When fully adapted to night vision, human rods can detect a light source which is emitting just a few dozen photons per second, such as a distant star. However, to get to that level of dark adaptation may take up to 45 minutes. This is because our night vision is dependent upon processing retinal, a form of vitamin A which circulates in our body. Under bright light conditions, when rods are less active, most of the retinal is outside of the eye, circulating through the liver so that it can be regenerated for the next use. Under natural outdoor conditions, sunset provides a natural transition time, when our eyes prepare for the coming darkness. During this transitional period, called mesopic vision, both rods and cones are active. As retinal returns to the eye, the rods become the dominant signaling pathway, and we can see deeper into the shadows. By the end of twilight (at about one lux or less of ambient light), we have lost most all color vision, and our world appears instead in shades of gray.

Figure 3.1 below provides some examples of photopic, mesopic, and scotopic illuminance ranges, in both the imperial units of footcandles, and the more widely used metric units of lux (it is handy to remember that 1 footcandle

Time	Illuminance Range	Outdoor Examples	Indoor Examples	Approximate Footcandles or Lux		Dominant Photoreceptors	
Day Time	photopic	Sunlight		10,000	107,527	cones	
	photopic	Blue Sky	Atrium	1,000	10,753	cones	
	photopic	Heavy Overcast	Skylit Bigbox	100	1,075	cones	
	photopic		Sidelit Office	30	323	cones	
	photopic	Dark Stormy Day	Sidelit Lounge	10	108	cones	
	photopic		Interior Hallway	3	31	cones	
	photopic mesopic	Early Twilight	Garage/Storage	1	11	cones	rods
Night Time	mesopic	Deep Twilight		.1	1.1	cones	rods
	scotopic mesopic	Full Moon		.01	.11	cones	rods
	scotopic	Quarter Moon		.001	.011		rods
	scotopic	Starlight		.0001	.0011		rods
	scotopic	Overcast Night		.00001	.00011		rods

Figure 3.1: Table of illuminance ranges and examples

equals roughly 10 lux, or more precisely, 10.7639 lux). Figure 3.1 shows that humans can successfully navigate in outdoor environments that span more than ten orders of magnitude of illuminance, from starlight to sunlight. At any given time our eyes can successfully function within four or five of these orders of magnitude. However, it is important to understand that our perception of brightness does not follow the linear scale of our measuring instruments, but rather follows more of a logarithmic progression. Thus, all things being equal, an increase in *measured* illuminance levels from ten to 100 lux will only be *perceived* as about twice as bright. But all things are rarely equal! And our perception of illumination is highly contextual. Thus, the gloom of a 'dark stormy day' may actually measure 1,000 times brighter in terms of lux than a joyful 'brightly moon-lit night.'

Given today's world of pervasive artificial illumination indoors and outdoors, people living in cities rarely experience a need to navigate the world using only their rods and nighttime vision. They generally are most comfortable operating under mesopic conditions at nighttime where they can still perceive some color. As we will discuss in the later chapters, visual perception is a learned mental process, and without experience, many modern humans have not fully developed their nighttime perceptual abilities. Rods are located most densely in the human eye at about 20 degrees off the center line. Thus, your visual perception of details at night under scotopic visual conditions should be noticeably better at about 20 degrees off center. Pilots and sailors are often trained to consciously scan a scene at night to take advantage of this improved off-center perception.

In addition to being vastly more sensitive to low levels of light, rods also respond more slowly than cones, and with less spatial accuracy. This is because many rods and a few cones are grouped together in a mosaic of overlapping 'receptive fields.' Some receptive fields have specialized visual perception jobs, such as detecting sharp versus fuzzy edges, spots versus lines, or different colors—information which is processed directly by the ganglion cells and others that connect them. It is only recently that visual scientists realized that much of this simpler preprocessing of visual information was happening directly in the retina, before being sent up to the brain. Receptive fields tend to be largest at the periphery of the retina, giving us less visual acuity in that area. However, because of the larger receptive fields, we are also extremely sensitive to movement or flicker in our peripheral vision.

In contrast, cones completely dominate at the very center of our focal vision. The fovea centralis is the formal name for this unusual visual structure where, within 1–2 degrees of the center of our visual field, our retina is packed with nothing but cones. (This visual area is about the width of one finger held at arm's length from your face.) Other cones are scattered lightly through the rest of the retina, connected to groups of rods via the receptive fields and providing color information throughout our peripheral view.

Most of the cones in the fovea have a one-to-one relationship with an axon that feeds its visual information directly up to the brain. Thus, the fovea provides high resolution visual acuity. The fovea centralis is not unique to humans, but many other mammals such as dogs and horses have other visual organizations, such as a horizontal 'visual streak' which provides them with their most detailed vision along a horizontal axis rather than a single spot. In all vertebrates, the millions of axons connected to the photoreceptors in the fovea and the receptive fields exit the retina via the optic nerve, creating one small area of the retina that is so packed with connective nerve tissue that it has no photoreceptors, hence is it often called 'the blind spot.'

Cones, unlike rods, do not saturate in bright light under daylight conditions, but they also use substantially more energy to perform their task. Compared to rods, cones also signal visual changes to the brain at more rapid rate, which also requires more energy. Thus, by reducing the number of cones in the retina compared to birds, mammalian eyes are conserving energy and reducing the metabolic load of vision.[3] This concentration of greatest visual acuity into one tiny area of our eyes has important consequences for the health, energy intensity and the movement of our eyeballs, but first we'll talk about the color capabilities of the cones.

As mentioned earlier, while most mammals have two types of cones, humans have three types, enabling our wider range of color perception. The common mammalian two-cone system differentiates between blues, greens and yellows, but cannot distinguish shades of oranges and reds. This type of color perception is similar to that of many so-called 'color-blind' humans, where oranges and reds are seen instead more as beiges and browns.

The human three-cone system (also shared with some other primates) not only provides differentiation between oranges and reds, but also more shades of greens and yellows, and violets at the far end of blue. The three types of human cones are colloquially called the 'blue, green, and red cones,' but they are more accurately referred to by their sensitivity to different wavelengths, i.e. 'short, medium, and long,' as illustrated in Figure 3.2.[4]

While looking at Figure 3.2, you'll note that the sensitivity curves of the medium (M-cones) and long (L-cones) cones have a very similar shape and overlap a great deal. There may be a good evolutionary mystery here. It seems likely that sometime back in primate evolution, a mutation created two new types 'yellow' cones, one slightly on the blue side of yellow to create greens and the other just to the red side of yellow to create oranges and reds. These two cones function as an additive unit (M+L) when differentiating yellows from blues, but as subtractive (M–L) when differentiating greens from reds.

Interestingly, the ratio of red to green cones in the retina varies considerably in any normal population, from 2:1 to 4:1. In addition, the red or L-cones also have a great deal of intrinsic genetic variation. For example, a study of men from around the world found 85 genetic variants in the L-cone.[5] The genes for

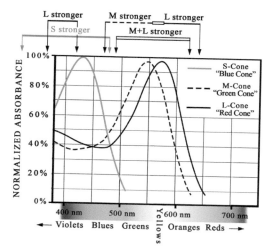

Figure 3.2: Relative spectral sensitivity of three human cones. Comparison at the top differentiates greens from reds, and violets from blues, while the second comparison differentiates blues from yellows

the red and green cones are located on the X-chromosome, but the genes for the blue S-cones are located elsewhere. This explains why common red-green color blindness is sex-linked, found much more frequently in men, who have only one X-chromosome.

Furthermore, given the wide variation in L-cone genetics, some women can have a different version of this gene on each of their two X-chromosomes. These rare women have been found to have four types of cones active in their retinas, resulting in additional perceptual abilities in the deep reds and oranges. Thus, not all humans see color the same way. There are also important differences in color perception that arise developmentally, between children, adults, and especially the elderly, as we will discuss in later in Chapter 6, Learning to See.

White Light and the Measurement of Light

When, under photopic conditions, all three types of cones are equally stimulated we perceive the light as white. Together, the sensitivity of the three cones are combined into a spectral sensitivity curve called the V-lambda curve, or the luminosity function for photopic vision. The V-lambda translates the intensity of wavelengths into human's perception of brightness; thus, this particular luminosity function is integral to our human-centric definition of 'light' and how we measure light with a variety of common metrics such as *lux, candelas, and lumens.*

However, it is important to remember that these common light metrics, both as used in this book and used widely by lighting engineers around the world, were originally derived from the subjective evaluations of white light by lots of people who were presumed to have normal vision. Thus, people who are genetically color blind, or who have different color sensitivities for other reasons, may perceive different levels brightness. Furthermore, our rods, and the iPRGC discussed earlier, have quite different color sensitivities; thus, when they are active, the perceptual brightness of light may be different than the standard photopic measurements based on cone-dominated vision. To accommodate these differences in perception under different conditions, lighting engineers have started talking about 'scotopic lux,' 'mesopic lux,' 'circadian lux,' or 'melanopic lux,' which are all measurements of light balanced to different types of retinal sensitivities. Figure 3.3 illustrates three such sensitivity curves: photopic, scotopic, and melanopic.[6] The first two have been highly standardized in the lighting industry for decades, but the third, named for the influence of melanopsin in the iPRGC, is still under development, and currently has a number of variations.

In Figure 3.3 you can see that the sensitivity of our scotopic (rod-based) nighttime vision is shifted strongly towards the shorter blue wavelengths compared to our photopic, daytime vision. This is even more true for the sensitivity of our non-visual circadian system driven by the iPRGC. Thus, an increase in blue wavelengths can change our perception of brightness at different times of the day, depending on which type of photoreceptors are most active in our retina..

All these differences in color sensitivities become important as you realize that the actual spectral content of what we perceive to be 'white light' can vary enormously. The spectral content of natural daylight varies throughout the day, sometimes dominated by blue wavelengths, other times with a greater proportion of yellow (see Figure 7.3). Yet in spite of this

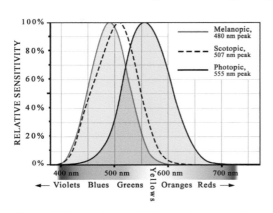

Figure 3.3: Luminous efficiency functions for the human eye: daytime vision (photopic), nighttime vision (scotopic), and circadian receptors (melanopic)

variation, our brains still perceive the light to be fundamentally 'white.' Electric light manufacturers learned long ago that they could economize on the cost and efficiency of artificial light sources by preferentially providing light stimulus at the peak of our cone sensitivity. There are lots of 'recipes' of wavelengths that will be perceived as white, although some are much better than others at fully rendering the subtlety of various colors (Figure 7.4 illustrates the spectral power distribution graphs of some of these 'recipes' for electric light sources). The type of white light produced by electric light sources has been designated informally with names such as 'cool white' and 'warm white,' or more precisely with designations of color temperature expressed in degrees Kelvin. The designation of the color temperature of a white light source is an attempt to describe the combined perceptual effects of all the colors contained in the light. Some examples are provided in Figure 3.4. However, the color temperature of a light source does not tell us the actual spectral content of the light. There are now many more precise ways to describe the color content of light sources, and thus their impact on the various photoreceptors in the retina and our resulting perception of color.[7] The study of color perception is fascinating and complex. The fundamental point here is that how we perceive light is not always perfectly aligned with how it has traditionally been measured.

Natural Light Sources	°Kelvin	Electric Light Sources
blue sky	10,000	
	9,500	
	9,000	
	8,500	
	8,000	
	7,500	computer screen
overcast daylight	7,000	
	6,500	"daylight" fluorescent
	6,000	cool white LED
	5,500	
noon sunlight	5,000	cool white fluorescent
	4,500	metal halide
	4,000	warm white LED
evening sunlight	3,500	halogen lamp
	3,000	warm white fluorescent
	2,500	40W incandescent
sunrise/sunset	2,000	
candle flame	1,500	
fire ember	1,000	low pressure sodium
	500	

Figure 3.4: Color temperature of various natural and electric light sources

Our brain has an amazing ability to continuously recalibrate what colors we perceive, such that objects are perceived to have color constancy, even as the source of the light and the resulting stimulation of the cones is changing. The implications of color constancy are explored further in later chapters. We will also discuss how color perception changes over the course of our lifetimes, from the bright-eyed vision of young children to the more restricted palate of the aged. As we learn more about the interactions among the many types of photoreceptors in our eyes and the processing of visual information in our brains, we have to recognize that the perception of the visual environment is highly subjective, and can vary substantially among individuals, as their unique physical sensitivities and cultural experiences come into play.

Movement and the Energetic Eye

The supreme density of cones and axons at the fovea is why human visual acuity is so dominated by the focal center. Nearby, the blind spot in each eye is even larger than the fovea. Our visual system compensates for both this tiny visual focus area and our blind spots by having our eyes constantly scanning and sampling the field of view. This rapid scanning allows our brains to then assemble a coherent image, even though all the information is not simultaneous!

The human eye is an extremely active sensory organ, almost constantly in motion. Indeed, the muscles surrounding the eye make some of the fastest movements in our body. (The eye is in motion not only while we are awake, but also more strangely, while we are dreaming, even while sleep paralysis suppresses movement in all other muscles.) Our eyeballs make two basic kinds of movement: smooth pursuit, whereby they continuously track a moving object such as a ball or bird in flight; and saccades (from the Old French verb *saquer*, 'to pull'), tiny jerky movements which are even faster, and mostly outside of conscious control. When looking at a scene, the motion of the eye constantly shifts between these very rapid saccades and momentary pauses, called gaze fixations. Gaze fixations typically last 1/10th to 3/10th of a second (100 to 300 milliseconds), with about three to six gaze fixations per second. The tracking of gaze fixations has become an important research tool to study attention, with applications from marketing to computer interfaces to childhood development. Figure 3.5 illustrates a variety of saccade patterns from a famous study by the Russian scientist Alfred Yarbus.[8] He recorded the eye movements of people while looking at the painting *The Unexpected Visitor*, in response to different questions, such as (D) *"What was the family doing before the visitor arrived?"* or (G) *"Estimate how long the visitor has been away."*

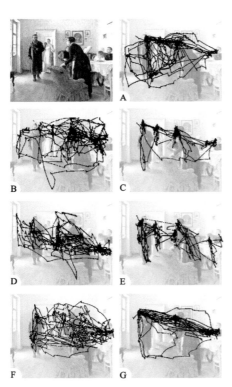

Figure 3.5: Early eye tracking study illustrating various saccade patterns

The eye's pupil is also constantly in motion, expanding and contracting the area of the iris that controls the amount of light which makes it into the back of the retina. The iris closes down to its smallest diameter in bright light, increasing the precision of our vision, just as stopping down the lens on a film camera increases the depth of field. The iris opens wider in dim light, to allow more light to stimulate the retina. However, the pupil also constricts and expands under the influence of a variety of drugs and hormones such as oxytocin, and in response to many subtle emotional and cognitive events. Because the behavior of the eye is so intimately tied to our brain, tracking tiny changes in pupil size has become an important research tool for many forms of cognitive science, as we will learn in the following discussion of the brain.

The most noticeable movement of human eyes are the eyelids, which close frequently, as a blink. The majority of blinks are unconscious, occurring once every few seconds. Our eyes blinks involuntarily in response to a perceived physical threat, and voluntarily, as in flirting. Blinks are also tied to cognitive processes and occur most frequently at the end of a thought. Film editors early on learned to look for the speaking actor's blink as the natural moment to cut to a new scene. Just as with pupillary response, hormones influence blinking rates. For example, dopamine metabolism influences blinking rate, with people suffering from Parkinson's having a reduced blinking rate, and those with schizophrenia an increased rate. Heightened levels of estrogen, such as from contraceptives, also seem to increase the blinking rate. Very young children apparently have less need to blink than adults. Newborns may blink only once or twice per minute. Blinking rates gradually increase over childhood, until late adolescence when blinking rates are similar to adult rates, averaging about once every six seconds. Strangely though, with all this blinking going on, we rarely notice discontinuities or interruptions in visual information. This is because our brains so neatly fill in for our eyes, making assumptions about what was happening while our eyes were closed.

It is not just the muscles in our eyes that are in constant motion and need a steady supply of energy to support their activity. The rods and cones in our retina are also surprisingly busy, continuously sloughing off used material, and rebuilding and re-charging themselves, in preparation for more light detection. Every day, rods and cones shed around 10% of their segmented disks. This material is then recycled through the single layer of adjacent retinal pigmented epithelial (RPE) cells that separate the rods and cones from their ample blood supply, the myriad of capillaries coursing around the back of the retina. As a result, the eye, the retina, and especially the tiny fovea at the center of the retina, have some of the highest energy demands and metabolic rates of any tissues in the body.

Keeping the eyes moving helps to pump more blood through their many muscles and delicate surrounding tissue. Movement also helps to lubricate tissues of the eyes. Thus, eye movement is essential to eye health. Most optometrists recommend that office workers should refocus their eyes on some distant view at least once every twenty minutes. Having an interesting view outside of a window turns out to be a primary motivation for us to keep our eyes in motion.

Adaptation and the Fatigued Eye

Because the photosensors in the retina are working so intensely responding to incoming light signals, they sometimes get exhausted, and need a period of recovery before they can function correctly again. At their upper limits, photosensors can become desensitized to new input, and stop signaling. This type of exhaustion is called saturation. Healthy young eyes have higher saturation limits, and recover quickly. Older eyes, and those with more restricted blood and nutrient flow, take much longer to recover.

Colors perceived during the recovery period appear to lack the color of the desensitized photoreceptors: this creates an 'after-image' effect, where the eye continues to see a bright image, but in the complementary color. For example, at night, a car's red taillight might appear to have a green trail. During the day, if you stare at a bright yellow flower long enough, it may seem to develop a blue edge. Many artists have tried to capture the dazzling dance of colors that can occur around the bright edge of objects when the eye fatigues, such as the famous impressionist Vincent Van Gogh, and more recently the Californian artist Wayne Thiebaud, with his richly colored paintings of pies and landscapes.

Scientists are only beginning to study the many interactions and feedback loops in the neural wiring of the retina, among the millions of rods, cones, iPRGC, ganglion cells, and many other types of cells. On closer examination, there are far more complexities than originally imagined in our earlier models. For example, it turns out that rods may participate much more in daytime vision than previously thought.[9] It is clear that the eye's response to light is different during the day than at night, likely a function of our circadian status and how much dopamine is coursing through our eyeballs.

There are also suggestions of seasonal sensitivity effects. One recent study, set in Antarctica,[10] attempted to resolve how the human eye responds to extended periods of night and artificial illumination. The researchers tracked a biomarker that indicates melanopsin sensitivity. They report: *"On the whole, we found that retinal sensitivity increased following the disappearance of daylight."* They found that much smaller amounts of illumination had bigger effects on melatonin suppression during the winter than during the summer, and also that their study subjects became more visually sensitive to both photopic and scotopic levels of light during the seven months of the Antarctic winter. Thus, this study suggests that there is also a long-term impact of 'light history' on perception. Just as the eye of the migrating salmon has been found to alter its sensitivities between river and ocean, so to, the human eye seems to change its sensitivities by season or after long-term exposure to new illuminance conditions.

There are other ways in which our long-term history with light impacts us, especially in our early years. The human eye is actively growing and developing from birth through adolescence. Likely there is massive 'wiring' between various receptive fields and axons communicating with the brain that is established during this period. The eye is also learning to focus on ever more distant objects and track their movement. In order to accomplish this objective, the eyeball adjusts its own growth and muscle development to achieve the best possible focus on distant objects. For most people, distant vision becomes an effortless joy. However, for an increasing number of children, their distance vision does not develop well, and objects in the distance remain blurred. We call people with this condition near-sighted.

Myopia and Dopamine

The technical name for near-sightedness is myopia. Myopia is caused by an elongated eyeball where the focal length is out of sync with the focusing power of the lens and cornea. The problem is often first identified in school, when children start to learn to read, and it can continue to develop through adolescence, at which point it stabilizes, rarely continuing to progress after age 20 or 25.

Back in the nineteenth century, when wearing glasses was unusual, especially for children, common wisdom was that children needed plenty of time playing outdoors, and plenty of bright light while reading indoors, in order to avoid developing myopia. As a child, the future US President Theodore Roosevelt was an unusually studious boy who loved reading in his wealthy father's vast library. As a teenager he discovered that he could not see as well as his friends, and eventually was outfitted with corrective lenses to correct severe myopia. He wore his trademark 'spectacles' for the rest of his life, even as he became a paragon of the robust outdoorsman.

By the early twentieth century most ophthalmologists, the doctors who study eyes, came to believe that all myopia was inherited, especially since myopic children tended to have myopic parents. However, this belief in the primacy of the genetic basis of myopia was shaken as huge populations of urban children began to develop myopia in the latter half of the twentieth century. Within one generation, Inuit and Eskimo children born in towns in Alaska and Canada developed myopia, whereas their parents who had spent their lives living out on the ice fields had perfect vision.

Childhood myopia grew to epidemic proportions in some Asian cities like Seoul and Singapore, where up to 80% of high school students were found to be myopic. Ophthalmologists (along with recruiters for the military) grew alarmed and began to study larger demographic trends. In 2000, whereas less than 2% of people over 80 years old worldwide had myopia, almost 30% of 20–30 years did. It seemed that something drastic had changed between 1920 when the 80-year-olds were born and 1970 when the 30-year-olds were born. In countries like South Korea and China, the myopia trend was clearly associated with rapid urbanization and thus spending more time inside of buildings. Looking at masses of data from around the world, researchers concluded that, if present trends continue, fully 50% of the world population will be myopic by the year 2050.[11]

The elongation of the eyeball which causes myopia is irreversible once established. The resulting poor vision can be corrected with lenses, such as eyeglasses or contact lenses, or more invasive methods, such as surgery for intraocular implants. Medicated eye drops are also now available to slow the progression of myopia, but only if used daily for many years. Myopia is also a risk factor for other types of irreversible vision loss, like forms of macular degeneration and retinal detachment later in life. Thus, prevention of myopia has major public health implications.

Returning to the older nineteenth-century theories about bright light and outdoor play, ophthalmologists recently began to investigate more seriously the relationship between the development of myopia in children and exposure to daylight. Early studies compared adults' recollection of their childhood habits, including playing sports outdoors and time indoors watching TV, and found that the more time that they spent outdoors as a child, the less myopia they had as adults.

A recent meta-study by eye doctors in Sweden and the United States who carefully documented the progression of myopia in children over time found that it consistently progressed much faster during the winter, when there are fewer hours of daylight, than during the summer months.[12] Overall, they found that: "*A person with little exposure to daylight has a fivefold risk of developing myopia*" and an additional threefold risk "*if that person also performs close-up work.*" Thus, exposure to daylight was the primary factor that explained increased levels of myopia. The authors concluded that *"dopamine, which is released in the retina in line with image brightness, inhibits eyeball length increase."*

Based on these types of findings, Australia and Singapore have since adopted recommendations that children spend a minimum of two hours outdoors per day to minimize their risk of developing myopia. However, studies have not yet isolated the precise component of daylight which has a preventive effect. While some researchers hypothesize that it may be the ultraviolet component of sunlight only available outdoors, others believe that it might be the infrared component, or the blue wavelengths which also stimulate the circadian system, or justly simply brighter white light overall.[13]

The Circadian Dance

What is clear from many avenues of research is that the eye itself is functioning differently at different times of the day, following its own intrinsic circadian cycle: sometimes preparing for functioning with full color vision in the bright daylight, sometimes preparing for extreme low light sensitivity at night, and sometimes working on repair, growth, and development while we sleep. Ranjay Chakraborty, an eye development researcher in Australia, recently summarized the role of dopamine in a paper on the circadian systems of the eye: *"Dopamine, an important neurotransmitter found in the retina, not only entrains intrinsic retinal rhythms to the light:dark cycle, but it also modulates refractive development."*[14] If so, circadian regulation of hormones and neurotransmitters within the eyeball may also be key to eye health and development.

Perhaps part of our cultural slowness in recognizing this complex circadian dance that our eyes are performing for us every day is because, for centuries, we have had a mechanistic model of the eye as an optical device or a camera, rather than thinking about the eye as the extremely intricate, wet, living arrangement of tissues that it really is. The eye is not only a sensory organ, but one that is anticipating daily changes in our environment and sending continuous updates about its status to the brain. As Chakraborty writes: *"It is now clear that many aspects of retinal physiology are under the influence of a circadian clock."* We have consistently underestimated the capabilities of the eye and over-simplified its mechanisms.

Our visual system can resolve visual details across ten orders of magnitude of illumination levels, both on the beach in full sunlight and on a moonless night, by appropriately transitioning between two completely different visual systems (photopic and scotopic); and yet, under naturally occurring daylight conditions, this adaptation across light levels is often accomplished so seamlessly that people are rarely consciously aware of the adaptation process.

Our eyes and brains, working together, do a remarkable job of creating a coherent image of the world around us, in spite of constantly changing light levels and the color content of the light, the movement of our head and eyes, rapid saccades and blinking, and our body's positioning in three-dimensional space. Active looking, which keeps our eyes constantly in motion, helps pump the blood flow which supplies the necessary nutrients to sustain the health of our eyes and delay the inevitable effects of aging.

Vision is one of the great joys of our life, and yet our eyes and brains are easily fooled by illusions. Our visual perception of the world is the result of a very complex orchestration, which includes physics, optics, genetics, biochemistry, cognitive processing, experience, and culture. In order to better understand how our brain makes sense of all this sensory input, we'll next take a brief excursion to consider some provocative recent findings in psychology, neurology, and other cognitive sciences, which may suggest ways to better understand and design our visual environment.

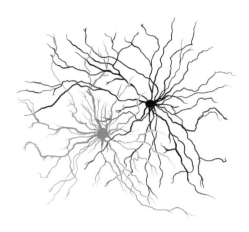

4. The Predictive Brain

Visual perception comes so easily and flawlessly to most of us that it seems effortless, when in reality the processing going on inside our brains is unimaginably complex. All sensory information arrives in the brain as pure data, based on electrical signals of the neural axons delivering the information from other parts of the body. Our visual system has 2–3 million axons delivering information to the brain from the retina, each one synthesizing the input from a 100 rods and cones on average, plus ipRGC sensors. In comparison, our hearing system has 30 times fewer nerve connections. This is just one of many forms of evidence that human brains are structured to favor visual information.

Daniel Levitin is a cognitive psychologist with a highly unusual background combining neuroimaging, computer science, and rock music production. Something of a renaissance man, he holds positions as Professor of Psychology, Behavioral Neuroscience, *and* Music at McGill University in Montreal, Canada. He also wrote a popular book, titled *This is Your Brain on Music*, wherein he makes the case for how the human brain is uniquely structured to engender our love of music. He summarizes many people's simplistic perspective on the brain thusly: *"Because we can manipulate mental images—we can zoom in on them, rotate them, in the case of music we can speed up or slow down the song in our heads—we are compelled to think that there is a home theater in the mind."*[1]

Humans are always reaching for new metaphors to describe the dazzling capabilities of their brains, often based on the most recent technological innovation that they are familiar with, whether it be the perfection of a Swiss watch in the nineteenth century, or a home theater in the twentieth. In many ways we tend to be more impressed and interested in recent technological achievements, the wizardry of computer software and hardware that have produced the latest cell phone video capability or virtual-reality gizmo, rather than amazement at what the 'wet-ware' of our brains and eyes routinely achieve.

In order to really appreciate the intimate ties between the design of our physical environment, especially as it relates to daylight and view, and our brains' sensory and processing capabilities, I would like to take you on a deeper dive into some of the ways that the brain interacts with the visual environment. I ask for patience from my readers, such as the architects and designers who may not be accustomed to some of the neurological terminology, and perhaps also from those scientists who are uncomfortable with speculation about the implications of their findings. Later in the book, many of these underlying cognitive mechanisms will reappear as themes, as we discuss the social and cultural aspects of designing buildings for daylight and views.

Environmental design is not an application that has any currency in the field of neuroscience. Certainly, no one is funding research scientists to address the kind of questions that I have as an architect. The closest type of applied research in this area might have to do with interest in the health of military personnel in extreme deployment conditions like nuclear submarines, or astronauts during long-term space travel.

As an architect, trying to understand current cognitive science is like playing the child's game of 'connect the dots,' except that the dots that outline the picture are not yet numbered and many of them are still missing. Research scientists tend to be a very conservative group, carefully trying to limit the application of their findings to what is known conclusively, providing plenty of caveats and qualifications, and avoiding speculation about the wider implications of their research. Undaunted, I have taken on that job, even though I could best be described as an interested layman in the many disciplines represented within the cognitive sciences. I have been eagerly surveying the current scientific literature in order to gain insight into two particular questions from an architectural perspective:

1   *"What are the potential cognitive benefits of looking out a window?"*
2   *"How might exposure to natural daylight, either via a window view or as part of the ambient illumination of a space, interact with those effects?"*

Expectations

Jeff Hawkins is another neuroscientist-cum-renaissance man who founded the non-profit Redwood Center for Theoretical Neuroscience, now housed at the

University of California, Berkeley. His passion has always been to understand how the brain works in order to create better models for machine learning. In 2002 he published a seminal book *On Intelligence* which lays out his theory that prediction *"is the primary function of the neocortex, and the foundation of intelligence."* He states very simply, and with conviction: *"The cortex is an organ of prediction."*[2]

A brain's predictive model allows an organism to anticipate what might happen next, and to more efficiently prepare and adjust its response, resulting in a huge evolutionary advantage for those creatures who can successfully predict the immediate future. This core cognitive function of trying to predict the future is a theme that will run through much of this book.

In order to predict the future, the brain uses the memory of past sensory information to create a predictive model of the environment. Sensory inputs that form our internal predictive models come from all our outwardly directed senses—vision, hearing, touch, taste, smell—plus our inwardly directed senses, including proprioception, interoception, and self-awareness of our own intentions. Proprioception is an essential component of mental models. It provides the sensory input of our skeletal-muscular system that tells us what our bodies are doing, where our joints are, what speed our limbs are moving, with what degree of force. It is this internal awareness that makes it impossible for us to tickle ourselves, since our brains already know where our hands are going before they arrive. Interoception, in contrast, provides information about the non-mechanical status of our body, such as core body temperature, hunger, thirst, pain, and the status of organs, like a full bladder.

A cognitive predictive model allows us to compare observations about what is currently happening to similar situations experienced in the past. It includes all outward sensory observations tightly synced in time with our interior sensory input and cognitive intent. Hawkins nicely describes common experience of a predictive model at odds with sensory experience: *"If you have ever missed a step on a flight of stairs, you know how quickly you realize something is wrong. You lower your foot and the moment it 'passes through' the anticipated stair tread you know you are in trouble. The foot doesn't feel anything, but your brain made a prediction and the prediction was not met ... you know as soon as your foot continues even a faction of an inch beyond the spot where your brain had expected it to stop."*[2]

It is the instantaneous difference between the expected model and the actual experience that grabs our attention. This difference can be either the *presence* of unexpected information, or the *absence* of expected information. It can be as subtle as a pebble in your shoe or a skipped beat in music.

When expectations are met, the brain's cognitive model is confirmed and the result is understanding, which is a rewarding and thus relaxing feeling. It also frees the brain's attentional resources for other needs. When expectations are not met, because some sensory input, sequence or timing is different than anticipated, this constitutes a novel event that attracts our attention. Depending on the importance of the difference, the novel experience might vary from mildly interesting to intensely dangerous. Either way, we are alerted to new information that should be noted and remembered so it can be considered next time. Thus, creating a successful predictive model of the environment is relaxing and emotionally rewarding, while noticing differences between the expected model and current reality is alerting, and invokes more cognitive effort to address a potential problem.

This match, or mismatch, with expectations may help explain many of our emotional reactions to window views: those which are either very familiar and predictable tend to be reassuring and relaxing. Those which are novel or unpredictable are more engaging. In later chapters we will consider the many layers of sensory, emotional, and cultural meaning that can attach to such views, whether in a vacation condo, classroom, or a high-rise office tower.

Partial Information and Inferences

The successes and subtleties of our predictive models are even more remarkable given that we rarely have complete information to inform our models. As Levitin explains: *"Much of what we see and hear contains missing information ... Sound and sights often come to us as partial information that has been obscured by other things in the environment. [From an evolutionary perspective ...] A perceptual system that can restore missing information would help us make quick decisions in threatening situations."*[3]

On the simplest level, when we see only part of a coffee mug hidden behind our computer monitor, we still perceive it as a whole mug which will properly hold the coffee without a disastrous leak. A car partially hidden behind a building is still understood as a functional car. Levitin continues, emphasizing that perception is inherently probabilistic: *"Perception is a process of inference, and involves an analysis of probabilities. Most of the time the information we receive at our sensory receptors is incomplete or ambiguous."*

We have seen in our earlier discussion of the eye how rapid saccades sample a scene to collect many bits of detailed information that are then cognitively assembled into a holistic visual perception. Blind spots are filled in. Inferences are made about missing information, especially based on recent experience. Because of this probabilistic process, our brains tend to pay more attention to information that is fuzzy, or partially obscured, in order to over-sample areas of uncertainty.[4] This is one of the reasons that mysteries are so deeply fascinating for us: they represent unresolved information. This may also be why layered views and winding paths are more interesting than flat perspectives where all objects in a scene are fully in view.

Jeff Hawkins provides a wonderful metaphor for vision that helps us to recognize what an active process vision is, such that all of our mental imagery is continuously under construction and revision, based on new visual sampling: *"Natural vision, experienced as patterns entering the brain, flows like a river. Vision is more like a song than a painting."*[5]

Proprioception and Personal Space

It is slightly amazing to contemplate how our proprioceptive-self readily extends its understanding of what constitutes 'our body' to include any tool extensions that we routinely use. Thus, for a chef, her knife can come to be perceived as part of her hand's motion, for a carpenter a frequently used hammer can become a body extension. Extremes of this phenomenon can be seen in athletes who can perceive a hockey stick as a precise extension of their arm, or a backhoe operator who can operate his machine with as much elegance and precision as a ballet dancer. In a sense, proprioception defines our concept of personal space. Personal space is our 'home base,' the three-dimensional bubble within which we can operate fluidly, that space within which we can act without encountering friction with the environment.

An example of one of the most constricted spaces we commonly experience in modern culture is the middle seat on an economy airplane ride, where there is barely room to move an elbow or knee. There is little visual relief from the seat-back directly in front of us, a few inches away. Contrast that experience with sitting in an aisle seat, where you can watch the comings and goings of the service staff, or better yet, sitting in the window seat, where a steady progression of interesting landscapes or distant sunsets are available. I confess that on occasion I have written a poem or two while traveling cross country in the window seat, as my mind expanded out into the boundless sky and landscape below; but I have never written a poem, or had much to contemplate other than my own misery, while tightly sandwiched in a middle seat.

This sense of personal space is at least partially located in the *amygdalae*, two small almond shaped structures deep in the middle of the brain. The amygdalae also play key roles in the formation of memories of emotional events, adding emotional valance to our spatial boundaries. People and monkeys with damage to one or both amygdalae display little concern about personal space.

Their boundaries of 'you-versus-me' tend to blur, with no emotional response to personal space violation. In later chapters we will explore how a sense of personal space interacts with views. Expanded personal space seems to translate into a sense of ownership, especially of views. People often describe views that they love as 'expansive' and those they dislike as 'constricting.' Their stories also often merge personal feelings of expansion with a sense of happiness, and those of contraction with stress, pressure, or unwanted constraints.

Cognitive Maps and Disorientation

We humans also have a remarkable ability to form internal representations of our place in the larger world, often called cognitive maps. Edward Tolman, a professor of psychology at UC Berkeley, first introduced the concept of a cognitive map in 1948, to explain how rats learned to navigate various mazes. Kevin Lynch, then a professor of urban planning and architecture at MIT, expanded the idea in his 1960 book, *Images of the City*, to mean the imaginary map of a place that people carry around in their heads. Lynch interviewed people in various cities, trying to understand how they formulated a mental map to help them navigate their neighborhoods. He described five types of elements that seemed to be common among the many narratives: paths, edges, districts, nodes, and landmarks. Since then the term cognitive map has come to be used much more broadly in many fields, describing any kind of mental representation of logical relationships, not just geography. In this book, I use the term as Kevin Lynch did, to mean people's understanding of the physical layout and relationships of their environment.

We have since learned that this mapping ability is also tightly connected with the formation of long-term memories. It makes sense from an evolutionary perspective that any animal, including humans, would selectively benefit from the ability to form a mental map of their territory to help them find their way back home, after traveling to find food, water, or mates. Tales of animals that have remarkable spatial navigation abilities abound, such as migratory birds and turtles who find their way across vast stretches of the planet to return each year to the same sites for foraging, breeding, or nesting. Just as remarkable is the true story of a poor Indian village boy, Saroo Bierley, who got lost on a train as a five-year old, was inadvertently transported 1,000 miles away to Calcutta where he lived on the streets as an orphan, until he was eventually adopted by a couple in Australia.[6] Twenty years later, with the help of aerial images from Google Earth, he was able to remember the unique layout and landmarks of his village—a water tower by the train station, a certain bridge near a fork in the road—in order to correctly locate his village and reunite with his family.

I recently had a similar experience when looking at Google Earth satellite images, rediscovering pathways through the empty hillsides of Los Angeles I had once explored 50 years ago on horseback, even though I had never previously seen a map or photo of those places, nor thought about the routes. Somehow my childhood brain faithfully filed away key visual details and path relationships for *50 years*. You can try a similar experiment: try looking at a satellite image of an early childhood neighborhood and testing how much spatial information you can pull out of those distant memories.

These stories all speak to our amazing human ability to understand the physical relationships of places with uncanny accuracy, and stash that information away for future use. However, not only are we remembering spatial relationships accurately, and without great effort, but our brains are also creating a miniaturized map, a scaled image, such that I could recognize my childhood paths at the minute scale of a satellite image. This ability to mentally zoom in and out of a scaled image is remarkable. It helps explain our fascination with heights and overlooks, where we can look down on a landscape from above and make sense of tiny buildings and paths that we previously experienced at full scale. It may also explain some of our fascination with fractal images, self-similar at many scales, as discussed later in Chapters 9 and 19.

An important structure of the brain that has been identified as significant for both spatial mapping and memory is the hippocampus, named long ago for its supposed resemblance to a sea horse (*hippo* = Greek for horse). The hippocampus, located deep in the center of the brain near the brain stem, is now understood as the locus of spatial orientation and navigation, and is also recognized as essential for the consolidation of short-term memories into long-term memories. For any animal that wanders about, a cognitive map would be a key component of long-term memory.

The hippocampus has been found to be enlarged in London's black-cab taxi drivers, who are famous for 'The Knowledge,' memorizing every possible path through the city, even in the old part of town where street names may change every block.[7] Similarly, other studies have shown that the hippocampus is especially compromised in Alzheimer's patients, who become easily disoriented, in both space and time. Indeed, it is interesting and probably not coincidental that the English word 'disoriented' is used to mean both losing a sense of direction in space and losing track of time.

The hippocampus is considered the home of episodic memory, pulling together the 'who, what, where, and when' of a memory trace. The co-location in the brain of these two very distinct functions—spatial orientation and long-term memory—has led to the common recommendation that you can improve your memory performance by mentally locating information in space, such as imagining walking through your house, and finding various names or dates in particular places like the hallway closet or the top of the stairs. Some people who have demonstrated amazing feats of memory, such as memorizing impossibly long strings of numbers, have used this type of spatial memory as their mnemonic technique.

It seems that exposure to daylight may also play a role in the consolidation of the long-term memories formed in the hippocampus. Recent studies by researchers at the US National Institutes of Health have found that the ipRGC, those 'intrinsically photosensitive retinal ganglion' cells in the retina, have axon projections that reach directly to hippocampus.[8] Thus, key functions of the hippocampus are likely influenced somehow by exposure to daylight. Other memory researchers worked with a type of laboratory rat which is normally active in the daytime.[9] The rats were maintained under two test conditions, 12-hour dim days followed by 12-hour dark nights, or else bright days and dark nights. After four weeks of this daily light exposure pattern, the rats were tested in a maze for memory performance. Those which were kept in the dim light conditions (50 lux) had impaired memory and performed poorly. The rats' memory impairment was reversed when they were returned to brighter daytime conditions (1,000 lux). Other physical and chemical changes in the hippocampus were also observed between the two groups, implying a decrease in hippocampus functionality for the dim light group.

At the very least, for diurnal mammals such as humans, it makes sense that their mapping center, the hippocampus, would be alerted to become active during the day when they would be most likely to be wandering about. *"Pay attention!"* it says, *"Make sure you help me remember how to get back home before nightfall!"* Furthermore, in the studies just cited, we have evidence that episodic and spatial memory formation is somehow tied to a circadian cue, such that it operates well under a strong day/night lighting patterns, but degrades when the day/night pattern is weakened. Window views can provide both the information that informs the cognitive map, helping us to locate ourselves in relationship to the outside world, and can also provide the circadian stimulus that helps set the memory. Our brains do this for us easily and automatically; it is a natural function. Having that information stored away, we feel confident and well oriented; without it there is a sense of unease, of disorientation.

Distractions

There is another mechanism whereby the physical environment, especially daylight and view, might influence memory formation and retrieval, usually referred to as 'context-dependent memory and learning.' Steven M Smith in the Department of Psychology at Texas A&M University became one of the early researchers investigating how environmental context impacts memory formation and retrieval.[10] In 1978 Smith ran a series of tests in three very different spaces in the university's psychology building: 1) a windowless classroom in the basement; 2) a very tiny compartment within the animal laboratories, but with two small windows that overlooked a courtyard; and 3) a large classroom with large windows overlooking a busy street. He was not studying the effect of windows per se, and so there were also many other environmental differences between the three rooms. The subjects were also tested at different times of the same or next day. What interested Smith was whether learning and remembering in the same or a different physical environment made a difference. He consistently found an advantage to being tested in the same environment in which students had originally learned the material. Somehow, the physical environment was helping people to remember better.

Smith's study set off a scientific scramble to try to identify which environmental features might be associated with improved memory. Test tasks varied from remembering lists of nonsense syllables to recognizing faces. However, the researchers did not seem to have any clear hypotheses about which qualities of an environmental context might be responsible for improving or hindering memory formation, other than simply 'different' or 'more complex.' They often got downright silly, such as having students taking a test while chewing gum, or in rooms scented with different fragrances. In one test, a box was put over the subject's head to simulate a new environment. Another set of researchers even tested subjects learning lists of words underwater in scuba gear. If the testing spaces included windows or daylight, they don't report it. We are left to imagine what kind of office or lab was used, most likely some typical interior room on campus. These psychology researchers definitely do not think like architects!

In 2014 Takeo Isarida, a professor of management at Shizuoka Sangyo University in Japan prepared a literature review of all recent studies examining 'environmental-context dependent memory.'[11] In general, according to Isarida, the more complex the environmental context, the better the memory storage and retrieval. But most importantly, from our perspective, researchers saw the largest effect sizes when subjects were tested a day or more later, i.e. after the subjects had had a chance to 'sleep on it.'[12] This implies that circadian stimulus may have been instrumental in helping to better 'set' the memory in relationship to its environmental context.

These studies which suggest that more a complex visual context supports better memory formation and retrieval would seem to contradict long held beliefs that window views are a source of distraction, which interrupt a student's or office worker's attention, reducing their task performance and inhibiting memory. Back when I was a student the prevailing educational theory was that windows should be minimized in a classroom to reduce all possible distractions and thereby help students focus on the teacher's lessons.

As a highly visual child, looking out of windows had been one of my great pleasures. In sixth grade I loved looking at the giant eucalyptus trees right outside my classroom windows, and anthropomorphizing them into silent sentries vigilantly watching over us. When maintenance workers showed up one day to strip off their pealing bark, I imagined that the trees were being tickled mercilessly. My giggles clearly annoyed the teacher, who promptly moved me to a seat at the front of the class with my back to the windows. Now in retrospect, I can remember the appearance of those windows far better than the appearance of that teacher, or whatever he was trying to teach us. You can conduct a similar thought experiment, remembering back to some time in school, once when you had no view, and another situation when you did have access to a view window. How do your memories differ?

In various ways, memory formation and retrieval, along with spatial awareness, cognitive maps, attention, distraction, and boredom, all seem to have some connection to our relationship with windows. The history of how scientists have studied these various mental states over the past decades is a potentially illuminating story which may shed some light (so to speak!) on our understanding of the underlying value of window views.

Memory researchers have traditionally divided the problem of studying memory into two processes: memory formation and memory retrieval. Clearly, in order to form a memory, first the information has to be perceived. For most of the twentieth century, psychologists thought that the key to better memory formation was better attention. It was assumed that people with a better ability to intentionally control and focus their attention could learn more, learn faster, and then remember and perform tasks better. If this was true, then helping people to have better attention, especially a longer 'attention span' before they succumbed to distraction, would improve learning and life skills.

5. Attention and Insight

William James, the foundational American psychologist, famously claimed in his 1890 textbook on psychology, *"Everyone knows what attention is"* implying that it was perhaps even too self-evident to discuss. However, he then proceeded to define it further, contrasting attention with its purported opposite, 'distraction.' James believed that the distracted mind was 'scatterbrained,' while attention provided clear and vivid trains of thought. Thus, for James and most of his successor psychologists, attention became the gold standard for cognitive performance.

William James also influenced the study of attention by proposing a 'spotlight' model, whereby attention had three components: a 'focus' acting as a spotlight to highlight important details; a periphery or 'fringe' area where information was less resolved; and a 'margin' or limit beyond which no more information was available. This metaphorical model of attention is clearly visual in nature and surprisingly close to what we know about how the retina actually works. In the case of vision, focus is provided by the fovea, which scans every scene like a searchlight. Information collected in the receptive fields of peripheral vision informs the movement of the saccades to direct the attention of the fovea. The margin or limit of vision can be delineated by the visual field, as constrained by the rotation of the eyeball in its sockets, obstruction by nose and eyebrows, and the range of motion of the head. Thus, I think it is fair to say, James based his psychological model of attention on his personal experience with the visual system.

However, purposefully focused attention is not an automatic function of the brain. It is a learned skill. Recognizing what information is worth paying attention to, i.e. deserving of the spotlight's focus, takes quite a while to sort out. Babies and children very gradually build up their predictive models, as they discover what sensory information will give them better predictions of future events. We have all experienced our brains ability for selective attention, via our ears, when we can hear our name even within the din of a cocktail party or pick out just a few recognizable words in a foreign language.

Just like our ears, our visual system is prepped to respond quickly to certain patterns that have been previously established as significant. If you are fluent in reading English, the words STOP or HELP! will grab your attention whether you want them to or not. If you are fluent in reading a landscape, certain details will grab your attention. For example, my husband is a sailor. As we walk by our local harbor, he will notice one new sailboat mast within a chaotic visual field of hundreds. *"Where did that new black mast come from?"* he'll ask, as I wonder what he is looking at. Meanwhile, I'm noticing an odd bird behavior. Similarly, expert eyes may quickly pick out a new model car on the highway or a new style of shoes on the basketball court that others fail to notice.

Thus, with increased expertise, we are able to develop selective visual attention, switching our focused attentional resources, like a spotlight, to just the sensory input that seems most salient at the moment, and ignoring information that does not seem relevant to our current predictive model. This is how you become inured to a view that used to excite you, and now which you rarely notice. Yet even so, as we will see, even a seemingly boring view to which we long ago ceased paying much attention may still serve an important purpose.

Working Memory

Selective attention allows us to focus on a narrow stream of sensory input. Working memory is what allows us to hold that information together in our mind while we make sense of it. Selective attention determines what goes into our working memory. Our working memory capacity determines how much information we can process in one batch. Originally referred to by cognitive scientists as 'short-term memory,' the newer concept of 'working memory' focuses more on the manipulation rather than the storage of information.

Earl Miller, a neurologist at the MIT Picower Institute for Learning and Memory, studies how attention is focused and how the brain coordinates thought and action. In a recent blog, *Working Memory 2.0*, he describes how working memory provides a central concept of how the brain supports higher level thinking: *"Working memory is the 'sketchpad of conscious thought.' It is the platform where we hold and manipulate thought and is foundational to the organization of goal-directed behavior."*[1]

Psychologists believe that people vary in their working memory capacity, and while they can be trained to expand their capacity, it also tends to be an inherent characteristic. Greater working memory improves attentional control, by making it easier to consciously choose what to pay attention to, rather than being simply reactive to the flashiest sensory input. Miller continues: *"Working memory is the fundamental function by which we break free from reflexive input-output reactions to gain control over our own thoughts."*

Thus, any environmental condition that improves working memory will also increase a person's capacity for goal-directed behavior, often referred to as executive function. You might want to keep this idea handy, in your personal working memory cache, as you read through the rest of this story about attention, vigilance, and related mental states.

Vigilance, Boredom, and Vitality

Psychologists studying attention became particularly interested in the concept of 'vigilance,' i.e. the ability to maintain sustained focused attention on a given task over time, such that any small changes would be noticed. Vigilance became extremely interesting to psychologists during the Second World War when the ability to closely monitor radar screens for tiny changes in repetitive lines and blips became a matter of life and death.[2] After the Second World War, as human–machine interactions became ever more common, interest in vigilance continued as a key performance indicator for the quality of attention.

Natural visual tasks involving sustained vigilance include, for example, lifeguarding at a lake or soldiers scanning the horizon for security threats—all visually complex environments with many activities and potential distractors. However, research psychologists interested in studying vigilance discovered that they could greatly enhance the precision of their studies by reducing tests of vigilance to computerized visual tasks conducted in the lab, where every aspect of the test could be controlled. Thus, vigilance studies were conducted under increasingly artificial conditions. The researchers' goal was to discover the threshold conditions at which their subjects lost their ability to detect weak or rare target signals, such as when a point of light randomly appeared within a grid of gray lines. Other sensory input was generally ignored by these researchers: sounds, smells, touch or other sensations were rarely tested. Studies of naturalistic vision and environmental context increasingly became a thing of the past.

Only recently did it occur to the researchers that, rather than studying *vigilance*, they might actually be studying *boredom*, since the tasks they were asking their study subjects to do were extremely monotonous and had no meaningful context or natural motivation. Psychologist John Eastwood and his colleagues at York University in Canada were perhaps the first to raise this concern. They explained the problem boredom may create for researchers: "*Research into cognitive processes, and in particular attention, relies heavily on artificially constrained and monotonous laboratory tasks. Thus, attention research is an ideal breeding ground for boredom to arise. Therefore, boredom may emerge as an important, yet largely neglected, confounding variable within cognitive neuroscience research.*"[3]

Boredom is not a trivial condition. It is more than just an absence of motivation. For many people boredom is experienced as a painful state, as evidenced in the common phrase 'bored to death.' Boredom also has an odd relationship with time, in that time seems to become excruciatingly slow, with no chance of escape. Eastwood captured this change in perception in his definition of the condition: "*Boredom is the experience of being [emotionally] disengaged and stuck in an endless dissatisfying present.*" Some people will take extreme measures to try to get relief from boredom, which can be anti-social or self-destructive, such as binge eating or alcohol abuse. Boredom is also associated with increased accidents at work; thus, it can have serious costs and public health risks.

One of the most interesting and influential studies on boredom in the past decade has been a deceptively simple observational study, conducted by some social scientists from Carnegie Mellon University in Pennsylvania. They simply asked people: "*Are you bored?*" They asked a lot of people, out in the real world, and then collected enough other information about their situation at the time to provide some interesting insights.

Published in 2016, this 'experience sampling' study collected hourly diaries from almost 4,000 US adults for ten days via cell phone prompts.[4] Large field studies like this one, where the behavior of hundreds or thousands of people going on about their normal lives are either observed or self-reported, have come to be called 'ecologically valid.' This is a term used in the social sciences to indicate that the research conditions adequately represent relevant contextual experience, as opposed to those studies of vigilance in highly artificial settings, such as monitoring a computer in a basement laboratory.

From this large dataset, the researchers analyzed the demographic and situational characteristics which best predicted boredom. The authors reported that boredom rates were always higher during the standard working hours of 9am to 5pm, when, perhaps not coincidentally, people were also most likely to be inside of buildings. Furthermore, *"respondents were 3 to 6 times more likely to express boredom while working and studying than while playing sports or exercising,"* and *"respondents were most frequently bored in schools/colleges, medical facilities, airports, and at work."* The authors also presented a graph of boredom rates by time of day: steadily rising in the morning, with a little dip at lunch time, a peak at 2pm and then slowly dropping until bedtime. To my eyes this is a classic circadian curve, similar to those seen for alertness, sleep pressure and various hormone interactions. However, the authors offered no discussion of a potential circadian or hormonal influence on boredom rates.

The opposite of boredom might be thought of as 'vitality,' a psychological characteristic defined by American clinical psychologist Richard Ryan as those times when a person has both increased physical and mental energy.[5] There is an interesting pair of studies discussed below which attempted to correlate exposure to more or less light with feelings of vitality. These two studies, conducted by the same research team a few years apart, have seemingly contradictory findings, and yet there may be an underlying lesson about daylight exposure.

In the first study, reported earlier on page 31, a Dutch research group at Eindhoven University of Technology tracked 42 people each for three days, while they went about their everyday lives.[6] Importantly, participants wore a light level sensor at eye level that recorded both white light exposure, normalized to human visual perception (lux), and blue light exposure, to better represent circadian stimulus. Data collection was distributed over a full year to represent all seasons. The researchers concluded that the intensity of hourly light exposure, whether measured to represent vision or circadian stimulus, was significantly correlated with greater feelings of vitality. Indeed, this was true whether they considered light levels averaged over the previous hour, or shorter periods, from the previous 5, 10, 15, or 30 minutes.

A second study was conducted five years later in a more controlled laboratory setting.[7] In this second study, light dosage was administered via fluorescent lamps within a large diffusing 'light box' mounted on the wall directly at eye level. The box could be controlled to provide 20 steps of illumination levels, from 20 lux to 1,000 lux at the eye, similar to the light exposure levels that had been measured in the earlier field study. In this lab study, however, the researchers found no correlation between light exposure and vitality, or any other performance or emotional outcomes.

The contradiction between the two studies could potentially be explained simply by the difference in contexts. The first study was done with 'ecologically valid' observations of people going about their everyday lives, engaged in natural behaviors, walking outside on occasion and likely looking out of windows when the urge struck them. In contrast, the second study was performed in a highly constrained laboratory setting, where there was nothing interesting to look at and no intrinsic motivation to stare at that weird light box on the wall.

How much difference might a pleasant window view make to positive feelings of vitality or negative feelings, like boredom and loneliness? Do these emotions have a circadian component, such that more or less exposure to daylight might make a difference?

One researcher who has attempted to sort this out is Won Hee Ko and her colleagues at UC Berkeley's Center for the Built Environment.[8] She constructed an experiment that tested 86 people who each worked at two computer workstations which were identical with one exception: one workstation was adjacent to a large window looking out to some nearby trees, while the other workstation, in the same room, blocked the window view with a tall continuous curtain. Ko's study combines some of the advantages of a laboratory study, in the use of a controlled physical environment, careful measurement of the test subjects' physical and cognitive states along with randomized order of testing, with the advantages of a more naturalistic field study, by using the presence or absence of a real view as the key variable.

Ko found that after her study subjects had worked next to a window for 55 minutes they experienced small, but significant, increases in positive emotions and reductions in negative emotions. Study subjects also showed small improvements in their working memory capacity and concentration when they were next to the window. Interestingly, the test subjects also perceived the thermal environment next to the window as more comfortable, even though the test room was purposely kept at a uniform temperature, and warmer than normal (28°C or 82°F). They also reported slightly fewer symptoms of dry eyes or blurred vision.

Ko's study provides yet more evidence that even short-term exposures to window views can have positive effects on people's emotional states and cognitive performance. Clearly, the 'distraction' of the window view was not impeding cognitive performance, but rather enhancing it. However, the explanatory mechanism remains elusive. Why might the simple presence of a window view have so many diverse positive effects? One possible explanatory mechanism is the many benefits of mind wandering, otherwise known as 'daydreaming,' discussed next.

Mind Wandering and the Default Mode Network

In the world of psychological theory, mind wandering had been a very minor subject of study, especially compared to attention and vigilance. Similar to William James's description of the 'scatterbrained,' it was considered the opposite of vigilance. When a person is vigilant, they are paying very close attention to the task at hand. When their mind wanders away from the task at hand, they miss key information, mistakes happen, and overall performance on the assigned tasks drops. Mind wandering, or 'distracted thinking' as it was sometimes called, was considered to be a key indicator of the type of attention problems seen in both ADHD and dementia patients. Various studies showed that increased mind wandering was associated with all kinds of social problems, including depression, alcoholism, and drug abuse. Mind wandering was also shown to be associated with unwanted 'intrusive thoughts' and negative emotions, such as might be experienced by clinical populations with obsessive compulsive behaviors or schizophrenia. Thus, the early literature took a very negative view towards mind wandering, as one of the key problems undermining sustained vigilance and focused attention, and a predictor of many negative health outcomes.

There was one psychologist, however, Jerome L. Singer, teaching at the Yale School of Medicine, who thought that there must be a positive side to mind wandering, or 'positive constructive daydreaming' as he preferred to call it. Starting in the 1960s Singer began to explore the connections between daydreaming, imagination, creativity, curiosity, and delayed gratification in children.[9] As a lonely voice in the field, he continued to hypothesize that daydreaming was a normal, positive function in both children and adults that supported planning, problem solving, storytelling, and enhanced social skills.

Beginning the 1990s, scientists started using a powerful new tool to study the inner workings of the brain. Functional magnetic resonance imaging (fMRI) uses magnets to detect changes in blood flow and oxygenation in the brain or body, which indicate the location of increased metabolic activity and energy levels. The machine, however, is not unobtrusive nor are the results instantaneous. An fRMI machine is room-sized device with powerful magnets that make loud banging noises while they spin around the body part of interest (not a particularly pleasant experience!). One set of readings can require 30–60 minutes. Subjects wear ear plugs and can only see out of the machine via a series of little mirrors. Despite its drawbacks, fMRI imaging has led to a much deeper understanding of where functions are located in the brain.

Once scientists started using fMRI machines to study attention, they noticed some peculiar goings on. Their initial goal was to locate the brain structures where particular skills or cognitive capabilities were processed. The researchers would have cooperative healthy adults lie down in an fMRI bed, and then give the subjects a mental task to perform, such as a series of math problems, or reciting a poem. The researchers would then record which parts of the brain lit up, hopefully indicating the centers where that particular task was processed.

First the researchers noticed that for any given type of task, brain activity was rarely limited to one precise location; rather, many areas of the brain would all light up simultaneously. Therefore, rather than looking for particular locations, they started looking for patterns and how the patterns shifted with different types of tasks. And then, secondly, they began to recognize one pattern of brain activity that occurred frequently and repeatedly during all the tests, universally across all types of task assignments. This brain activation pattern was named the default mode network (DMN), since it was initially hypothesized that it was some kind of resting or idle mode that the brain returned to in-between working on the task assignment. However, that hypothesis was put to rest, so to speak, once researchers discovered that the default mode network used at least as much, if not more, energy than any of the task-specific activity patterns.

So, the mystery deepened: what was the brain doing during this very common pattern? First identified in 2001, research on the DMN exploded exponentially after 2007 when more standardized analytic tools and simpler test procedures became available, allowing the study of less cooperative subjects, including clinically ill patients, children, and even some animals. It was noted that the DMN was 'antagonistic' to attention, such that it switched off whenever the subject started paying attention to the assigned task. Study subjects often confirmed that their minds had indeed wandered off-task just when the researchers had started to observe the DMN pattern light up on their screens.

Subsequent research has confirmed that mind wandering is strongly associated with the default mode network. Furthermore, it can be consistently detected with both self-reports and objective observations. Interestingly, in addition to observing changes in EEG and fMRI readings, mind wandering can also be observed directly, via increased eye movement, greater pupil dilation, and more frequent eye blinks.[10] Thus, the many types of eye movements that we discussed earlier in relationship to eye health are also associated with mind wandering.

Then in 2010, a set of researchers from Harvard University reported on a large experience-sampling study which asked people when and where they found themselves mind wandering.[11] Their specific research goal was to determine if mind wandering made people unhappy, or if vice versa, being unhappy made people more prone to mind wandering. However, their large 'ecologically valid' data set tracking the daily activities of 2,250 American adults allowed them to quantify where and when the most mind wandering occurred in everyday life, instead of in a laboratory setting or locked inside an fMRI machine. Even though they noted that pleasant and neutral topics predominated the daydreaming, with negative topics constituting only 27% of their sample, they still reported that, per their original hypothesis, mind wandering made people unhappy! They found, not very surprisingly, that mind wandering was reported most commonly when people were at work, and least often when they were having sex or meditating.

However, their most noteworthy finding was that *everyone* was mind wandering, for almost half (47%) of their waking hours, and during every possible activity of the day. The surprising findings of this large study got widespread attention, and mind wandering quickly came to be recognized as a normal cognitive activity of all healthy adults, as suggested by Singer, rather than a problem associated with disability or unhappiness. Other researchers started to ask a pivotal question: "*If everybody is mind wandering, for half of their waking hours, perhaps it also has a positive aspect, or at least some necessary cognitive function?*"

Jonathan Schooler and Jonathan Smallwood, both at the University of California Santa Barbara, became leading researchers investigating both the possible negative and positive attributes of mind wandering. In 2012 they published a provocative paper titled *Inspired by Distraction: Mind Wandering Facilitates Creative Incubation.*[12] In a rather simple yet elegant experiment, they asked subjects to provide as many answers as they could to the Unusual Uses Test (UUT), such as "*How many uses can you think of for a paperclip?*" Then they gave the participants a little ten-minute break period. During the break period various groups were assigned a series of simple mindless tasks (such as, what is 2 + 2?), demanding tasks (such as, what is 7 x 128?), no task, or allowed no break at all. They found that "*Performing an undemanding task during the incubation period improved creative performance on the UUT to a greater extent than performing a demanding task, resting or taking no break.*" The improvement was actually quite dramatic, on the order of 40% better. The researchers also recorded the frequency of mind wandering for all the test subjects and found that *"Importantly, the undemanding task condition was likewise the condition with the highest incidence of mind wandering."*

After the break, the researchers also asked a second UUT question (such as, how many uses can you think of for a brick?), for which the subjects did not get the benefit of an incubation period. In this case, the type of previous break-time activity did not influence the quantity or quality of responses. However, the researchers did find that people who reported that they daydreamed very frequently in general, also did noticeably better on this second test. Based on this finding, the authors concluded that *"This last result suggests that individuals who mind-wander more frequently in their daily lives may also be more creative in general."*

Schooler and his colleagues continued with a range of similar experiments, and in 2014 wrote an overview[13] summarizing findings in the field in the previous decade. Great advances had been made in finding objective indicators of mind wandering, including behavioral markers such gaze duration, reaction time, and performance errors; physiological measures such as pupil dilation and heart rate; and brain activity as measured by fMRI and EEG. While acknowledging that mind wandering is associated with disruptive effects on external tasks, such as poor reading comprehension and reduced vigilance, which they call 'experimenter-defined tasks,' they also note that: *"Mind wandering is associated with rich internal activity that often entails contemplating future goals and/or thinking about the self."*

The suggestion is that mind wandering is key to self-awareness, that it provides a mental break in task-oriented activities for the brain to assess internal states, needs and desires. Thus, they conclude: *"One possible function of mind wandering lies in the anticipation and planning of personally relevant future goals, otherwise known as 'autobiographical planning.'"* Kieran Fox, at the University of British Columbia and his colleagues, also published a meta-analysis of other mind wandering studies, with the important observation that all studies seem to point to a similar conclusion, that mind wandering was an essential function of the 'autobiographical self,' the bits and scraps of time when an individual's brain takes stock of his or her needs, concerns, and goals, and figures out next steps.[14]

Insight and Mental Time Travel

In agreement with Singer, Schooler proposes that mind wandering *management* is a learned skill, observing that some people can decide when mind wandering is least disruptive or most productive, especially those able to recognize when their mind wandering could be useful by providing insight to a problem they wanted to solve. Based on these observations, Schooler and his colleagues conclude *"The default mode network is related specifically to solving problems with insight."*

Insight is a very interesting word. It implies a vision into the inner workings of the mind, just as fMRI studies suggested that the default mode network was activated when attention shifted to internal information rather than externally-generated tasks and sensory information. Insight is often claimed as one of the key elements of creativity. But it is not a cognitive process that is under conscious control, nor obviously a function of improved focused attention. Indeed, Schooler suggests that focused attention might be antithetical to insight. So instead of being a problem, mind wandering might be the key to solving problems, especially those requiring insight or self-awareness. In this theory, rather than consciously directing our attentional resources at a given task, mind wandering supports mental function by allowing our brains the time they need to do work behind the scenes, below the level of consciousness.

Some researchers have started talking about mind wandering episodes as 'mental time travel,' when our thoughts project forward in the future or dip back into past memories. Interestingly, both Schooler and Fox reported a relationship between mind wandering and time perception: whereas an individual will consistently overestimate the amount of time that has passed while they were doing boring tasks, the opposite is true while mind wandering. In other words, time seems to pass more quickly while you are daydreaming then when you are working on task, and most slowly of all when you are bored. How often have you caught someone daydreaming, who then exclaims: *"Forgive me! I lost track of the time!"*

With mental time traveling there is a need to quickly anchor our sense of time in the present. Many examples of this need for a mental anchor were articulated by the people interviewed by Matteo Pericoli for his books (see discussion especially in Chapter 13, the Value of View). These writers and artists often relied on their window views both to help launch them out into the imaginary world of their creative endeavors, and to quickly bring them back to a day-to-day reality. Thus, this need for attentional switching may have interesting implications for building design. For example, it might be useful to have a familiar, non-threatening view to look out upon when the need arose to switch attention inward, yet one which can also help us quickly jump back into the present tense. It reassures us that nothing alarming is happening and thus it is safe to disengage momentarily and allow our inner processes to attend to their own needs: *"Are we hungry? Tired? Is there information that needs to be sorted and stored for later long-term memory formation? Is there a problem that needs to be solved?*" I know that, personally, when I am looking out my office window, there is a 99% chance that my mind is wandering: I stare, let my mind blur, and answers to all kinds of unasked questions just bubble up unbidden.

Many people, if not most, seem to be somewhat unconscious of their engagement with a window view. This may because their thought processes are not fully conscious when looking out a window. I observed a dramatic example of this once when working in Portland, Oregon at the home of a friend for a few hours. We both sat at the dining room table working diligently on our laptops, my friend with her back to the window, and I sitting perpendicular to her. She was writing a report, and as an excellent typist, was tickling the laptop keys with great speed and focus. However, every few minutes, she slowed her typing or paused briefly, and then glanced over her left shoulder out the window, up at the great maple trees lining the street outside. With a quick glance, lasting no more than a few seconds, she was back at to work, typing again at great speed. This pattern was repeated over and over again. I decided to try to time it surreptitiously, and observed the pattern repeated every one-to-five minutes. When we took a break for lunch, I asked her why, and when, she choose to look out the window. She looked at me in disbelief and replied that she purposely sat with her back to the window so that she would not be distracted! When I pointed out that I had just observed her glancing out the window every few minutes, she was flustered, and made some excuse about the postman making a strange noise. This was obviously a one-time event that could not explain hours of repeated glances. I concluded she had no conscious intent, and no memory of, looking out the window while she worked.

We learned from the Harvard study discussed earlier that the average person's mind is wandering about half of their waking hours. Another research group, led by Myrtle Faber from the Netherlands, conceived of a study to observe how frequently people's minds wandered, especially relative to concurrent events.[15] They used a semi-naturalistic setting, asking their undergraduate subjects to watch an old movie, the *Red Balloon*. The researchers tracked both changes in visual and auditory stimulus created by the movie, along with the timing of 'narrative events.' They found that, on average, while watching the movie the students' minds wandered every 2.5 minutes. This timing was independent of whether they had previous knowledge of the story or not. It was also independent of how much action there was on the screen. The main predictor of reduced mind wandering was whether a new narrative event was anticipated. In other words, the students' brains were paying more attention to the outward stimulus of the movie when they anticipated that something new might happen.

This observation takes us back to the predictive model we discussed at the beginning of this section on the brain. When the students watching the movie thought that conditions might change, their brains paid more attention to the movie, searching for informational clues to predict what might happen next. When the rate of change promised to decline, their brains went back to mind wandering, switching back and forth about every two or three minutes.

This switching back and forth had already been noted in studies of attention and the default mode network. One study examining the relationship between mind wandering and bodily self-awareness explains: "*The attention network and the DMN participate in functions that compete with each other for control of information processing, and this is why they are antagonistic: as activity within DMN increases, activity in the attention network decreases, and vice versa, in a shift between these two distinct modes of information processing.*" These researchers, specifically looking at how proprioception and interoception related to the propensity to mind wander, hypothesized that the brain needs to disengage from outward stimulus in order to momentarily direct attention inward.[16]

A steady rhythm of mind wandering implies that it is a basic function of the brain, very much like sleep, where internal processes are attended to, in preparation for the next round of outward sensing and activity. Thus, the popular term 'daydreaming' may indeed be very apt, in that it describes a mental process that shares many commonalities with sleeping. Indeed, the literature review by Fox[17] comparing the known characteristics of mind wandering and REM sleep found numerous similarities, from both subjective accounts and objective measurements of brain activity patterns, and thus concluded: "*We argue that dreaming can be understood as an 'intensified' version of waking mind wandering.*"

One of these commonalities might be the concept of 'sleep pressure,' indicating an increasingly urgent need to sleep the longer one stays awake. If so, then the longer time period that one must endure without mind wandering, then the greater the pressure there may be to allow one's mind to disengage for some much needed DMN time. Our society has come to recognize that nighttime sleep is essential to optimum cognitive performance. It may be that daydreaming performs a similar restorative cognitive function on a microlevel, and that our brains are continually urging us to take little snippets of time to accomplish our necessary mental housekeeping.

Brain Rhythms and the Binding Problem

Ultimately, the brain has a key challenge of coordinating all of its sensory input and cognitive processes into an optimum rhythm that correctly represents reality and creates a successful predictive model. Cognitive scientists have called this challenge the 'binding problem,' meaning *"How are all these disparate streams of information merged together in order to form a holistic and coherent understanding of reality?"*

Researchers at UC Berkeley, Princeton, and Stanford led by Randolph Helfrich recently used a highly sensitive version of EEG, involving sensors placed directly on the surface of the brain, rather than outside the skull, to detect very fine levels of brain rhythms. They believe that their findings, first published in 2018, may result in a paradigm shift in our concept of attention, *"suggesting that rhythmic perceptual sampling is an inherent property of the ... attention network. Collectively, these findings support the notion that the functional architecture of top-down attention is intrinsically rhythmic."*[18] In 2019 the team became even more confident, publishing *A Rhythmic Theory of Attention*, in which they claimed: *"Recent evidence has demonstrated that environmental sampling is a fundamentally rhythmic process ..."*[19]

They found that this sampling, first inward then outward, proceeds at about four times per second, i.e. a four Hertz rhythm. This is about as fast as you can say repeatedly *"one-two-three-four, one-two-three-four, one-two-three-four."* Other researchers similarly have found that eye saccades are synced to this rhythmic attention sampling, such that a new saccade is always initiated in sync with other outward environmental sampling. This is like an attentional metronome, of about four beats per second, similar to the way a drummer might keep a rock band in sync, by emphasizing one beat out of four.

For any rhythm to have a useful role in the body or any biological process it needs to be synchronized with the other relevant rhythms that it communicates with. This four Hertz rhythmic sampling is the most fundamental rhythm of attention that has yet been detected.[20] Other cognitive and bodily rhythms are coordinated on top of this steady underlying beat, creating the longer rhythms of perception and mind wandering, breathing and blinking, walking, talking, and eventually into the master 24-hour circadian and yearly seasonal rhythms that keep us in tune with the rhythms of our planet.

Schooler, the UC Santa Barbara psychologist, anticipated this recent finding when he began his essay on mind wandering with the observation that: *"Consciousness not only flows like a stream, continuously moving with ever-changing content, but also ebbs like a breaking wave, outwardly expanding and then inwardly retreating. This perennial rhythm of the mind—extracting information from the external world, withdrawing to inner musings, and then returning to the outer realm—defines mental life."*[21]

Looking for Inspiration

Truly productive writers and thinkers have often described their need for just the right balance of input and output, focus and blur, connection and isolation to fuel their work. As Schooler suggested, they strive to carefully manage their daydreaming for productive effect.

Michael Pollan, a professor of Journalism at UC Berkeley and prolific author of popular books such as *The Omnivore's Dilemma*, contemplated the importance of daydreaming when he was first preparing to design and build his own 'writer's hut' in upstate Connecticut.[22] As described in his first book, *A Place of My Own*, he quit his day job as a magazine editor in Manhattan and began his transition into a newly independent career by reading and digesting many theoretical works on building design, including Gaston Bachelard's thoughtful set of essays called *The Poetics of Space*. Bachelard wrote: *"If I were asked to name the chief benefits of the house, I should say: the house shelters daydreaming, the house protects the dreamer, the house allows one to dream in peace."*

Pollan responded: *"An obvious idea perhaps, but in it I recognized at once what it was that I'd lost and dreamt of recovering"* by deciding to handcraft his own writer's studio. Pollan noted *"Daydreaming does not enjoy tremendous prestige in our culture, which tends to regard it as unproductive thought."* However, he came to the conclusion that: *"Daydreaming is where we go to cultivate the self, or more likely, selves, out of the view and earshot of other people. Without its daydreams, the self is apt to shrink down to the size and shape of the estimation of others."*

Oliver Sacks, a professor of neurology at Columbia University and another prolific author who spent a lifetime observing the peculiarities of other people's brain function, made some interesting observations about his own mental balance. He reflected on the significance of a rather prosaic view from his third-floor apartment looking out onto a street in New York's Greenwich Village. He felt that view importantly supported his own cognitive function as he wrote his numerous best-selling books: *"My typewriter desk sits in front of the window, so this is the view that faces me whenever I sit down to write. I think I need the ever-moving flow of city life as a counterpoint to my own thinking and writing."*[23]

Sacks was an expert in music therapy, and author of the book *Musicophilia*, about how the brain responds to music, so he chose the word *counterpoint* very carefully. In music, counterpoint is a means of creating a contrast to the main element of a composition, with harmony, rhythm, pitch, or pacing. The many forms of musical counterpoint can involve a second and or third melody played at a different pitch, played upside-down or backwards, slower or faster, yet harmonically interdependent, always providing a richer context to the main melody. Thus, for Sacks, the outward view of city life was a desirable *counterpoint* to his own internal thinking.

Sacks also choose the modifier *ever moving* to describe the *flow* of city life outside his window, stressing that this activity is *always* there, always available as a counterpoint, helping to maintain the flow of his work. As mentioned earlier, this desire for a careful balance between interior thoughts and an exterior reality is a recurring theme of many creative people.

Another expert on the value of daydreaming, no less than Leonardo Da Vinci, adds to the perspective. In one of his codices, Leonardo is talking to his reader, whom he might have assumed to be one of his young workshop assistants during his life, and yet, because he wrote it down, and many hands have preserved the text over the centuries, he is now talking directly to us, and telling us where to find inspiration for paintings or new ideas: "*You may discover in the patterns on a wall a resemblance to various landscapes, adorned with mountains, rivers, rocks, trees, plains, wide valleys and hills in varied arrangement; or again you may see battles and figures in action; or strange faces and costumes and an endless variety of objects ... it should not be hard for you to look at the stains on walls, or the ashes of a fire, or the clouds or mud, and if you consider them you will find marvelous new ideas because the mind is stimulated to new invention by obscure things.*"[24]

Here, one of the most creative individuals in the history of humanity is giving us advice on where to find inspiration, based on where his best ideas have come from: by staring, somewhat mindlessly, at random organic patterns, which allowed his mind to solve the problem at hand. Leonardo was striving to arrange the figures in a grand battle painting, or to solve the mechanics of a new invention. His recommendation to look at the ashes of a fire, at patterns of stain on a wall or diaphanous clouds, is not so different than the ancient priests and prognosticators who looked at random objects like tea leaves or animal entrails to gain insight into the future. Or alternatively, in a more modern vein, his suggestions can be interpreted as a mental break with an 'undemanding task,' similar to the creative problem-solving incubation tests conducted by the Schooler team in Santa Barbara. I would interpret Leonardo's advice as: go look at something where your mind is free to wander, that will not constrain you with pre-conceived solutions, but rather will offer random new patterns and connections that may "*stimulate your mind to new invention.*"

Part 2: Perception

6. Learning to See

Unlike kittens and puppies, human babies are born with their eyes open, ready to start making sense of the world. Babies can already hear and feel in the womb, and as soon as they are born, they are making judgments about good and bad smells and tastes. But they must learn to see once they emerge. As it turns out, we are continually learning to see, and re-see, throughout our lives.

Within their first week, full term babies can start to recognize faces within one foot, or 30 cm, i.e. the distance from a nursing baby to its mother's face. The rest of their vision is quite myopic, 20/200 to 20/400; so near-sighted that everything is fuzzy in the distance. Newborns' eyes often move independently, which can be very disconcerting for new parents. Slowly, their eyes learn to focus on objects that are farther away and track objects that are moving.

Vision researchers believe that infant vision first begins to focus on high contrast objects, searching for clear edges to objects, and then starts to track motion of objects. Depth perception starts to develop from 4–5 months, such that by six months an infant's heart rate will rise, with presumed anxiety, when placed on a glass floor a foot or so above the real floor.

Faces and Objects

Human babies come programmed ready to recognize faces first and foremost, especially their parents' faces. Studies have shown that human and monkey newborns are pretty good at recognizing each other's faces, but by at least six months, they have started to specialize on their own species. With practice, humans become supremely sensitive to recognizing individual faces, especially those of their family, friends, and neighbors. Many people pride themselves that *"I never forget a face,"* speaking to the primacy of facial information over names and other personal attributes. However, we are not as good at recognizing the faces of foreigners, especially those of another race with whom we are less familiar, often claiming *"They all look alike."* Studies have confirmed that people are best at differentiating faces of their own 'group,' largely defined by whomever they grew up with, and rely more on broad feature differences for 'other' groups, using simpler stereotypes.

We are so tuned to look for faces that we even tend to see faces in random information, like wood grain or clouds. Indeed, neurologists have discovered that there is one area of the brain, referred to as the fusiform face area, or FFA, that is highly specialized in differentiating between human faces. Interestingly, it has been shown that experts also utilize the FFA in making subtle distinctions between visual categories of some other objects, like automobile vintages or Chinese characters. Research has also shown that this ability is not unique to humans: sheep, horses, and birds have been shown to use similar abilities to differentiate between members of their own species, and human faces too!

Eyes have special fascination for us. I remember my newborn daughter, propped up on the kitchen counter, staring lovingly at our knife rack. Then I realized that the knife handle had two metallic rivets, which I'm sure she thought were 'eyes' shining back at her. After babies have mastered finding a meaningful pair of eyes, they begin to add mouths, then noses, eyebrows, and ears to their visual search. One of our greatest visual achievements is recognizing the subtleties of emotions expressed by a human face. Great movie actors are especially skilled at conveying emotions in close-up images of their faces, with just the subtlest glance of the eye or twitch of the mouth. Removing one key feature from a face—the nose, mouth, or eyes—may also reduce our ability to 'read' the person's identity and emotion. Thus, when looking through a window, a small imperfection or line of frit may cause a disproportionate level of frustration for someone looking at faces beyond. In a similar vein, an especially meaningful test of clarity through a window might be the ability to see a face clearly enough to correctly see the eyes and read emotional expression of a person outside.

In addition to deciphering people and their faces, our visual system is especially interested in identifying specific objects, something we can name. At two years old, my granddaughter was working at mastering the shape and the naming of things. She could identify surprisingly small objects and unusual placements. She noticed a tiny black cat hiding in a painting on our living room wall. With great excitement, she spotted airplanes which might show up anywhere in the sky. It seemed an outdoor vista was merely the canvas in which she might be able to spot familiar objects, and then point and name them with delight and glee. My little granddaughter's thrill at correctly noticing a distant bird, exclaiming *"Birda! Birda!"* likely parallels the excitement of an experienced 'birder' spotting a new species for the first time: *"Look, a downy woodpecker! Downy woodpecker!"* Thus, being able to identify objects, especially those that are rare or novel, becomes an important and satisfying visual task. Staring out into the vast ocean from the Santa Cruz jetty is always interesting for me, because at any given moment, I might see a very distant whale spout, a momentary sea lion jump, or an armada of pelicans tracing low across the horizon. The pleasure of seeing and identifying even very tiny objects will become a recurring theme when we later discuss the content of views.

Our visual system looks to detect many properties—contours and edges, foreground and background, shading and colors, and especially, consistent movement—that all help us identify a singular object as distinct from its surrounds. The computational difficulty of this task is evidenced by the challenge of training computerized vision systems to recognize objects: after decades of trying, it is only very recently that artificial intelligence systems are beginning to approximate rudimentary human visual capabilities.[1]

Motion

Visually tracking the movement of a person around a room is one of the first signs that a baby's brain is developing well. It is a great cognitive achievement: a face has been recognized as a person of interest, and attached to a body, which has been recognized as a distinct and unique object, one which moves independently of all the other visual stimuli in the field of view. In addition, the muscles of the eyes are now coordinated enough to maintain focus and smooth tracking as that person moves around. Human babies can't yet move much on their own, but by watching other objects move around, they begin to understand the three-dimensionality of their world. (Contrast this with the visual development of a baby mountain goat which can scamper up and down a hillside and leap from rock to rock, within a day of birth!)

Once a human baby, or any animal, starts to move, it is confronted with another challenge: how to determine if the visual perception of movement is due to the movement of the object or the self. A familiar example of this mental quandary occurs when you are sitting in a train, waiting for your coach to start moving. When the train on the next track appears to start moving outside the window, does that mean that your train is now moving, or that the other train has started moving? It is often impossible to tell without other sensory clues, like feeling vibrations or hearing sounds.

When the movement is our own movement, due to our own muscles directed by our own brain, we have our proprioceptive feedback system that accounts for those self-induced movements, and subtracts them out from our visual perception of the movement of other objects around us. It would be very frightening if, as we walked, we perceived walls to be headed towards us. Indeed, as discussed earlier, proprioceptive feedback may be a key element of our sense of self.[2] It is essential to be able to distinguish between the apparent visual movement we cause ourselves and that of the physical world moving around us. Once this capability is finally honed, amazing athletic feats are possible, such as a baseball player leaping sideways to catch a ball traveling at 100+ miles per hour (or 45 meters/second).

Correctly predicting the trajectory and speed of objects is one of the primary objectives of our visual system. Indeed, our brains are so primed to decipher movement that they will often assume movement even when there clearly is none. This can be demonstrated with a wide variety of optical illusions, widely available online.[3] Optical illusions can teach us a great deal about how our brains process visual information, and especially about the default assumptions that we tend to make about our visual environment.

Visual Illusions

As an infant's brain struggles to make sense of input from their eyes, it begins to take shortcuts to aid in understanding, it leaps to conclusions that may not always be correct interpretations of reality. Given the primacy of recognizing faces, and fertile imaginations, children are especially prone to seeing imaginary faces (and monsters!) in random shapes. However, seeing faces in random images is so common, even in healthy adults, it has its own psychological term, *pareidolia* (from the Greek for 'wrong shape').

The brain strives to make sense of ambiguous information by picking just one interpretation. Classic visual illusions, like the silhouetted vase whose outlines also look like two silhouetted faces looking at each other, or the rabbit which also looks like a duck, illustrate that our brain chooses to recognize one or the other, occasionally switching back and forth, but unable to perceive both simultaneously.

Regular patterns such as grids and parallel lines are especially suspectable to illusions, since it is easier for the brain to assume that a small sample of the image will replicate indefinitely. One illustration of this tendency may be the 'extinction illusion' illustrated in Figure 6.1. Black dots wink in and out at the intersections of the gray lines, even though the physical image includes no black dots. The psycho-physical explanation for this visual effect is still under debate,[4] but these types of visual illusions all help illustrate where and how our brains are making their 'best guess' about reality and filling in details based on default assumptions. What is important to note here is how easily, and persistently, our brains can be fooled.

Two common visual assumptions that are especially relevant to daylight design are that there is likely to be: A) only one light source, i.e. the sun; which is B) overhead. As a consequence, concave surfaces (dimples) highlighted from *below* will commonly be interpreted instead as convex bumps, highlighted from *above*. Daylighting technologies that change these basic principles, such as by reflecting sunlight

Figure 6.1: Extinction illusion—there are no black dots

upward, thereby turning shadows upside down, may also interfere with these underlying assumptions and distort our perception of reality.

Perspective is one of our most common and best understood visual assumptions, helping us to judge relative size, distance, detail, and movement. However, perspective apparently needs to be learned from childhood experience with distant views. Yi-Fu Tuan, in *Topophilia* recounts the story told by Colin Turnbull, the anthropologist, about Mbuti Pygmy people who lived only in the jungle, with no distant views, and who seemed incapable of reading the cues for perspective. Turnbull describes the bewilderment of the Mbuti man, Kenge, when he was taken to the open grasslands of Lake Edward. A flock of buffaloes grazed several miles away, far below where they were standing. *"Kenge asked Turnbull: 'What insects are these?' Turnbull replied: 'When I told Kenge that the insects were buffalo, he roared with laughter and told me not to tell such stupid lies. "*[5]

Western artists first mastered the rules of constructing perspectives in the early Renaissance, and once having mastered the mathematics they proceeded to play around, finding new ways to trick the eyes. Francesco Borromini, a baroque architect from the seventeenth century, is famous for creating a masterful sculptural illusion in the private gardens of Cardinal Bernardino Spada, now preserved in the Galleria Spada in Rome. A grand arched Roman colonnade, seemingly over 100 feet long, leads to a *huge* sculpture of the god Mercury at the far end of the garden. Sunlight, scaling perfectly, poured through the colonnade, adding drama to the view. However, since Borromini had only

25 feet to work his magic, he distorted all elements of the view. The columns quickly diminish in actual size, while the tiled floor rises up and the coffered ceiling descends towards the exit into the garden, where the final statue is diminutive, only two feet tall.[6]

Many visual illusions fool our brains via the rules of perspective, such as the 'Ponzo illusion' and almost all etchings by MC Escher.[7] The Ames Room is a modern 3D visual illusion which uses similar principles to make the occupants themselves enlarge and shrink. The Ames room appears to be a perfectly square room, reinforced by the presence of checkerboard floor tiles, and a corner entrance door next to two walls meeting at 90 degrees. But the back two walls meet at less than 90 degrees, while the floor slopes upward and the ceiling slopes downward, both made of quadrilaterals with no parallel sides. As a person moves upward toward the back wall, they appear to enlarge. In the other direction they grow ever smaller. Children who are running, or even more fun, rolling, around the room grow and shrink continuously. While there are many online videos you can watch explaining the Ames room, even better is a visit to one of the many physical examples available in science museums around the world, since this environment creates such a profound out-of-body experience. Andrew Glennester, a visual neuroscientist at the University of Reading in England explains the mental quandary created by the Ames room: *"When you watch someone walk across, your brain is faced with two contradictory concepts: rooms have 90 degree corners, and people don't change size when they walk across them. What's most peculiar is that for some reason, our brains choose to throw out the 'humans don't change size' standard in favor of the 'rooms have right angles' standard."*[8]

Thus, the Ames Room is as much a cognitive illusion as a visual illusion. Our visual processing centers are forced to make a choice between two common assumptions, and so they pick one: rectilinear shapes. Daniel Kahneman, the Nobel prize winner who is credited with being one of the fathers of behavioral psychology, made a career of studying cognitive illusions, where our brains quickly leap to erroneous conclusions. Kahneman differentiates between the brain working 'fast and slow' (the title of one of his books), whereby quick, default processing uses stereotypes and rules of thumb to jump to easy conclusions, while a slower, more analytic mental process may arrive at a different, more logical conclusion.

It turns out that since many visual and cognitive illusions are a result of higher-level brain processing, that children with less developed brains, and adults who are inebriated or have some forms of brain damage, are less susceptible to these type of visual illusions.[9] Their assessment of the world is more literal, less biased by pre-existing assumptions, and therefore less subject to being fooled by intentional distortions.

Temporal Illusions

In addition to visual illusions, of course, there are also auditory illusions, tactile illusions, and perhaps most interesting, temporal illusions. Interesting because vision and our sense of time are tightly bound together. David Eagleman, a neuroscientist at Stanford University who has extensively studied temporal illusions, writes: *"Like vision, time perception is underpinned by a collaboration of separate neural mechanisms that usually work in concert but can be teased apart under the right circumstances."* He concludes: *"Time perception, just like vision, is a construction of the brain and is shockingly easy to manipulate experimentally."*[10]

One important time lag built into our visual perception is called chronostasis, which is the perception that no time has elapsed between the rapid eye movements called saccades, discussed earlier. As our eyes scan a scene to gather visual input, our brains stitch the information together into a smooth continuum, deleting the small amounts of time between focus events. You can experience this by looking at your own face in a mirror, and switching your focus between your left and right eye: you can't see your own eyes move, whereas you can easily observe a friend's eyes moving.

Our retinas can differentiate light flashes down to five milliseconds apart, and our visual systems can correctly judge temporal sequences of down to 20 milliseconds. However, not all sensory signals are as quick to arrive. Eagleman explains the implications of this temporal binding problem, whereby disparate streams of information need to be blended into a unitary experience: *"So if the visual brain wants to get events correct timewise, it may have only one choice: wait for the slowest information to arrive ..."* He continues: *"To accomplish this, it must wait about a tenth of a second. In the early days of television broadcasting, engineers worried about the problem of keeping audio and video signals synchronized. Then they accidentally discovered that they had around a hundred milliseconds of slop: As long as the signals arrived within this 1/10th of a second window, viewers' brains would automatically resynchronize the signals."*

Recalling our earlier discussion of rhythmic sampling in the brain, whereby the brain is alternatively paying attention first to inward sensations then external sensations at a four Hertz rhythm, i.e. every 1/4 of a second, then sensory streams that are within 1/10 of a second have a very good chance of being included within one sampling period, and therefore being perceived as simultaneous.

Thus, that early television editors' rule of thumb is now substantiated with specific neuroscience findings. I once watched a World's Cup soccer game live on TV, but with a slight broadcast time delay. The announcer's voice-over was just slightly advanced, by perhaps 1/4 of a second. He could strangely predict every pass, every bounce of the ball, every goalie's save, as if he knew the future. Just that tiny visual time delay ruined the game for me.

Eagleman's experiments have gone on to show that our sense of time can be manipulated, and trained to accommodate consistent delays, such that cause and effect can be perceived to be nearly simultaneous. When researchers trained people to push a button to make a light flash 150 milliseconds later, the subjects gradually accommodated the delay and perceived the button push and light flash to be closer together in time. However, when the researchers subsequently set the light to flash simultaneous with the button push, the participants then perceived the light to flash *before* the button push. Thus, our sense of time can wander, or even be suspended, as during sleep. Indeed, temporal distortions are more common with fatigue, aging, some diseases like Parkinson's, and due to various drugs. It is hypothesized that temporal distortions may be an underlying factor in the hallucinations common in schizophrenia and dementia, and various disfunctions seen in stroke and dyslexia patients.

One of the key strategies that the brain uses to keep in tune with reality, in order to decide what is 'before' and what is 'after,' is by recalibrating its sensory input relative to your own bodily actions, the proprioception we discussed earlier. For example, the sound and sight of a hand clap are judged to be simultaneous with the physical movement of your hands. Eagleman writes: "... *the best way to predict the expected relative timing of incoming signals is to interact with the world; each time you kick or touch or knock on something, your brain makes the assumption that the sound, sight and touch are simultaneous.*"

Other researchers have found that when subjects physically control a visual stimulus, they can better estimate its speed than if they are just passively watching it.[11] In related research, Michael Hausser, professor of neuroscience at the University College London, recently identified the location of 'speed cells' in a rat's brain that contributed to the rats' cognitive maps, such that the rats judged elapsed time and distance by how fast their muscles were moving.[12] This finding suggests that our judgment of time, and therefore perception of reality, is closely tied in with the movement of our own muscles, both big and small. Thus, even eye muscle movements, all those blinks and saccades, may also influence our sense of time. In that case, simply moving your eyes to follow the bees buzzing about or leaves moving in a breeze may be a form of muscle engagement that improves our estimates of elapsed time.

There is another form of temporal distortion, that has to do with perceiving things to take more time, or less time, as measured by a clock. As most people have experienced, when you are bored, time seems to move very slowly, as expressed in the common phrase "*A watched pot never boils.*" In contrast, when you are daydreaming, or working on a deeply engaging problem, time tends to pass very quickly. Researchers have started to use time perception as an easily quantifiable measure of emotional state, cognitive load, and attention quality.

Interestingly, some recent studies have shown that exposure to 'nature' may change both the perception of time and effort.[13] Such studies raise questions about how our sense of time, and reality, might shift depending on the kind of visual environment in which we are immersed. For example, does having a window view change one's sense of time, compared to an equivalent photographic poster or video screen? Can visual simulations interfere with our perception of time and reality, of the 'nowness of the moment,' by limiting the channels of sensory input? These become key questions in Chapter 18, Biophilia and Technophilia, where we consider uses of virtual reality and biophilic illusions as substitutes for daylight and view.

As discussed earlier, the visual system of our brain is constantly at work trying to form a coherent understanding of world around us and prediction of what is likely to happen next. Once that sense of durable reality has been achieved via childhood explorations, our brains also work equally hard to preserve that capability, even as we age, and the clarity of sensory input diminishes.

Aging and Low Vision

At about age 40 most people start to notice the effects of presbyopia (from the Greek, for 'old eye'), which makes it more difficult to focus on near objects. About this time, many people acquire reading glasses for the first time. The American Academy of Ophthalmology explains: "*When you are young, the lens is soft and flexible, easily changing shape. This lets you focus on objects both close-up and far away. After age 40, the lens becomes more rigid. It cannot change shape as easily. This makes it harder to read, thread a needle, or do other close-up tasks.*"[14]

Joan Roberts, who researched eye health at Fordham University, was fond of introducing presbyopia in her lectures with the quip: "*Like it or not, Mother Nature thinks that you are getting old around age 40, or at least that your eyes are.*"

Unfortunately, presbyopia is just the beginning of age-related declines in vision. The muscles that control pupil size and reaction become less responsive. Dry eye and computer vision syndrome become more common with age, especially for women past menopause. Aging also results in a normal loss in peripheral vision, of about one to three degrees per decade, such that by the time people reach their 70s and 80s their peripheral vision may have narrowed by 20 to 30 degrees.[15] In addition, by age 60 or 70 most adults are developing cataracts which yellow and fog the lens, reducing color perception and increasing the amount of light that is needed to see details. Together, these changes result in most people past 60 needing three times more ambient light for comfortable reading than those in their 20s.

These common aging-related changes in the eye, especially cataracts, also take an emotional toll. In a 2014 study in China, a study of nearly 4,600 older adults found that depression was strongly correlated with the presence of cataracts.[16] Jennifer Finney Boylan, a writer for the New York Times, recently wrote a personal account of how her outlook on life changed as cataracts interfered with her visual perception: *"But sadness crept up on me now and again, especially as I got older. For a naturally gregarious person, I found it hard to talk to people sometimes. I had the feeling that the universe I lived in was getting smaller, and darker ... I'm describing my emotional state, but I'm also talking about my actual experience of looking at the world. Everything seemed draped in shadows."*[17]

Happily, cataract surgery can now reverse these effects by replacing the aging lens with an artificial lens. While such surgery is increasingly common in wealthy countries, cataracts remain the primary cause of blindness worldwide, especially in developing countries.

In addition to normal aging-related changes to the eye, there are many diseases that cause blindness or poor vision which become far more prevalent as we get older, such as macular degeneration, glaucoma, and diabetic retinopathy. As a result, most people (but not all) with low vision are elderly, and furthermore, most people with low vision once could see well. Now, later in life, people with reduced vision must 'learn how to see' once again, accommodating all these incremental changes to their eyesight.

This new need to accommodate worsening vision is not just a problem at home, but in workplaces as well, since the employment of workers over 65 has been increasing steadily. Thus, the issue of low vision in the workplace should be a growing concern of every designer and building manager. However, current building codes and design standards are predominantly based only on the needs of younger people with normal eyesight.[18]

Furthermore, most people responsible for designing those buildings are also young and have very good vision. Not having experienced vision problems themselves, it is often hard for young designers to understand the little struggles that people with low vision face on a day-to-day basis. For example, it becomes harder for older people with a loss of color vision to notice little changes: *"Are those flowers still fresh? Is that cup dirty?"* It takes longer to read signs and process details: *"Which way am I supposed to go?"* Visual contrast is reduced, making the edge of objects harder to see, and also interfering with depth perception, which may cause fumbles, stumbles, and falls. Many behaviors which might be attributed to mental confusion or poor balance in older people may be simply more a consequence of aging eyesight.

In order to experience how the world looks to someone with aging eyes, try dimming an incandescent light bulb in your room at night. Lowering the ambient illumination levels while also decreasing the percentage of blue wavelengths somewhat simulates the loss of color perception of the aged. Another simple experiment is to wear sunglasses indoors, especially those with yellow/amber lenses. In either case, your brain will gradually accommodate the changes, until at some point you may no longer notice them.

The loss of color perception is not just a function of cataracts and the yellowing of the lens, but also a loss of sensitivity of the photoreceptors in the retina. Decline in color sensitivity in our retinas begins very gradually as we age, but greatly accelerates as we enter our 80s and 90s. The green (M) and red (L) cones require about 50% more stimulus in order to fire at age 80 compared to age 20, whereas the blue (S) cones require 100% more, or twice the stimulus. As a result, the perception of color contrast also lessens over time. Certain color combinations became especially difficult to distinguish, such as light yellow versus white, blue versus green, dark blue versus black, deep purple versus dark red, and pastels versus grays.

However, in spite of this loss of retinal sensitivity, Sophie Wueger and her fellow vision researchers at the University of Liverpool have shown that, over time, older people manage to maintain remarkably better color perception than the measured physical changes to the retina would predict.[19] Her assumption is that, through neural plasticity, older people's brains are gradually recalibrating their color perception, making do with ever less information from the senses, while continuing to make consistent color judgments!

The steady yellowing of the lens, combined with the lower sensitivity of the blue cones, also suggests that blue rich light, especially from daylight, becomes increasingly important for older people, helping them to maintain both color discrimination and circadian entrainment. A group of British researchers concur that circadian stimulus can diminish in the elderly due to changes in the eye: *"By 45 years of age, crystalline lens yellowing and pupillary miosis reduces circadian photoreception to roughly half that of a 10-year-old. People in their eighth and ninth decades retain only 10% of a 10-year-old's circadian photoreception, so they need 10 times more light for equivalent circadian photoreception."*[20]

There is an additional concern that, with aging, the number and sensitivity of the ipRGCs is also likely to diminish. This means that whereas a brief glance out a window may suffice for a young adult to maintain their circadian rhythm, an elderly person may need to be bathed in daylight for an extended period in order to accrue an equivalent physiological response.

I remember my mother in her 80s, with cataracts and macular degeneration, sitting in her garden and mentioning that some flowers were often more difficult for her to notice, especially the blue and violet ones. She typically kept all the shutters in her house closed so as to avoid the high contrast that came with sunlight pouring in through a window. And yet, she happily spent hours sitting on the porch, looking out into her bright sunlit garden, because ambient light levels were uniformly high there and so avoided the extreme visual contrasts which inhibited her visual comfort and navigation indoors.

My mother was fortunate to live in Los Angeles, where she was able to receive good daily exposure to blue-rich daylight year-round by going outside. In less hospitable climates, access to a brightly skylit dayroom, atrium or winter-garden can help the elderly to maintain daily exposure to natural daylight's colors and rhythms. More implications for including daylight and views in elder care facilities are discussed in Chapter 15, Healing Daylight.

While exposure to more daylight may be useful for elderly vision and circadian health, glare also becomes much bigger issue. My aging mother discovered she was most comfortable in spaces that were either uniformly bright or uniformly dim. She avoided high contrast environments, because her eyes could not adjust quickly enough between bright and dim views. Indeed, older eyes take significantly longer to adjust to new lighting conditions. While a source of glare might be temporarily annoying to a younger person, for an elderly person its disabling impact can easily be *ten times* worse, and last *ten times* longer!

This aging related intensification of glare happens on multiple levels: first of all, the pupil is less responsive; second, the rods and cones are more readily saturated, i.e. bleached out, and cannot restore function as quickly; and third, the chemical adaptation process between daytime and nighttime vision is much slower. In addition, the gradual clouding of both the lens and vitreous fluid that fills the eyeball results in more stray light scattered about the retina, creating halos around bright sources, and obscuring details in the surrounding area.

Understanding glare is essential to good daylight design. It will be discussed in greater detail in the next chapter. However, first it is useful to take a step back and consider more of the physical properties of sunlight and daylight before we delve more deeply into perceptual qualities, such as color and contrast.

7. Patterns of Daylight Illumination

Our experience of daylight versus sunlight, both inside and outside of buildings, are quite different.

The term sunlight is used for the beam of light traveling in parallel rays directly from the solar disk. Sunlight is intense. It casts crisp shadows. Its reflection off shiny objects creates highlights that are almost as intense. Our eyes are adapted to noon sunlight as our evolutionary reference for pure white light, and thus sunlight also serves as a scientific reference for a 'full-spectrum light source,' offering the truest perception of all colors.

Sunlight also brings in an element of radiant heat, also known as infrared radiation (IR), which may be welcome or a cause of discomfort, depending on the climate. Via our skin sensors, we can feel very small amounts of solar heat. Try this: someday when the sun is shining outside, with your eyes closed, first turn the back of your hand and then the front toward the sun. How quickly can you perceive the difference? And how accurately can you orient your hand to receive the maximum amount of heat? Now that you are more aware of your skin's radiant sensors, try the same experiment indoors, near a window, or near a stove, feeling for radiant heat.

The visible light portion of solar radiation is less than one half of the total energy that we receive directly from the sun when we are outside, as shown in Figure 7.1. The graph shows the difference in solar radiation intensity (by wavelength in nanometers) found outside the atmosphere versus the resulting spectral profile at sea level after passing though the atmosphere. Note the peak

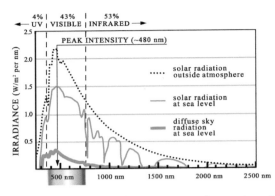

Figure 7.1: Solar radiation: spectral intensity of sun and sky

intensities for both are in the blue wavelengths, at about 480 nm (not coincidentally, also the peak sensitivity of the ipRGC in the retina). Those blue wavelengths are predominately scattered through the atmosphere to become the blue of the blue sky. The resulting diffuse radiation from the sky, minus direct sunlight, is the thick blue line at the bottom of the graph, also peaking at about 480 nm.

The actual profiles are highly dynamic, since the intensity and color content of sunlight also change continuously according to solar angle, and atmospheric and weather conditions. The spectrum of sunlight inside of our buildings is further modified, as it is filtered through various types of glass and reflected by other surfaces, as discussed further below.

Daylight is sunlight's gentler cousin. The term daylight refers to light from the sky, i.e. that sunlight which has been scattered by particles in the atmosphere and travels every which way. Because its light is diffuse, daylight casts soft shadows, or none at all. Because little UV or IR is scattered by the atmosphere, daylight is almost pure light. The softer shadows and bluish light of daylight create a gentler ambience, especially favoring the rendition of cooler colors.

When sunlight enters a room via a clear window, it can be easily ten times brighter, and contributes more than ten times as much energy into the room per square foot of window area than daylight. In addition, any patch of sunlight in a room is also in constant slow motion, tracking the arc of the sun in reverse. The patch will gradually enlarge or shrink depending on the geometry of the building and other obstructions. Thus, given both its intensity and variability, sunlight always has a dynamic presence in a room, making the room seem more vivid and lively.

Figure 7.2 illustrates the range of illumination levels that can be expected at different times of the day, for three seasons, and four window orientations, on clear and sunny versus heavily overcast days. The unit of measurement here is lux, i.e. just the visible light portion of the spectrum, normalized to the sensitivity of the human eye. These graphs are based on data for San Francisco, California, at 38 degrees north latitude. The relative magnitude of

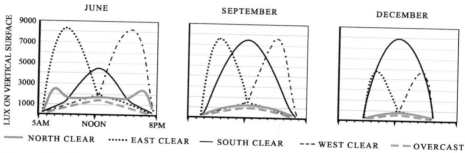

Figure 7.2: Vertical illuminance at a window, by time of day, season and orientation, San Francisco, California

the patterns will, of course, vary by location. But you will note that at fall equinox (September) the east, west, and south-facing windows all produce similar levels of illumination whenever the sun is within view. The relative illuminating power of south versus east and west windows, however, shifts dramatically between summer (June) when sunlight on southern windows is minimized, and winter (December) when it is at its maximum. Also, on an overcast day, all orientations of windows perform similarly to a north-facing window on a clear blue day. Managing sunlight should be a key determinant in choosing daylight design strategies, as discussed in the next chapter.

Together, sunlight and daylight create a vast array of illumination patterns. Variations in colors, shadows and highlights all contribute to our perception of daylit spaces. Designing buildings where sunlight and daylight are the primary illuminants benefits from an intuitive understanding of how the light in a space will change throughout the day and across the seasons, how it will vary by location, weather conditions, and according to the shape of the space.

The more a designer understands about the physics of daylight, the biology of human perception, and how the two interact, the greater the potential to turn science into art, and vice versa. Glare, in particular, has been a recurring concern of daylight design, but we currently lack good methods to really understand and predict it. As you read the following chapter, think carefully about your own experiences with daylit spaces and how you might contribute to this discussion.

Colors

Color is one of the great joys of vision, and yet is perhaps one of the most complex, and even mysterious, aspects of vision to understand. This is because, while color is rooted in complex physical phenomenon, it also does not exist independent of our perception of it. The colors of a landscape are ever changing, and our effort to understand those colors, and the implications of those changes, creates a fascination for landscape that is unlikely to be replicated by any artificial means.

There are times when I have found myself drawn into staring at blue-blue. Crater Lake, Oregon, as its name implies, sits in a deep volcanic crater. The lake is high in the mountains, at 6,000 feet above sea level, and very deep, measuring almost 2,000 feet at its deepest point. Its waters are the bluest blue I have ever seen. I visited the lake years ago and found myself completely mesmerized by the very blue-ness of the water. I couldn't look away, as if I had some deep ancestral hunger for this bluest-of-blues.

The intensity of colors in the desert around Sedona, Arizona can also have a similar captivating effect. On crystal-clear days, the deep green of pine trees dotted about the buttes vibrate against the surprisingly red rock formations, and the clear blue sky frames brilliantly white clouds receding towards an infinite horizon. When people speak of landscapes they love they often mention the joy of perceiving layers and layers of color disappearing into the distance. Why are the intensity and subtly of those colors so fascinating? I would suggest that often we take greatest pleasure in doing things that we are really good at. And for a mammal, humans are remarkably good at detecting colors.

Our perception of color is a function of at least five very different contributing factors. First, it is dependent upon the wavelengths contained in the source of light. Second, it is determined by the reflective, absorptive, and transmissive properties of the surface of the material we are looking at. Third, it is a function of the sensitivity of our retina, and other eye structures. Fourth, it is determined by cognitive processing, i.e. how the signals from our retina are processed by our brain. And finally, it is also a function of our cultural context, how we have been trained to perceive color. We will discuss each of these five factors in turn and consider some of the lessons they might suggest about the design of daylit buildings.

Spectrum

Most people learn in elementary school about how, as a young man, Sir Isaac Newton discovered that sunlight is composed of 'all the colors of the rainbow,' by placing a glass prism in the path of a beam of sunlight. To confirm that the rainbow was a property of the light and not the glass, he then placed a second prism in the path of the rainbow's light and turned the rainbow back into a beam of white sunlight. Newton's discovery dramatically opened up the field of physics and the study of light. Today we have spectrometers, sensitive instruments that can measure the intensity of each band of electromagnetic wavelengths that are contained within a given light source. The readings from a spectrometer are called the spectral power distribution (SPD for short). An SPD graph shows the intensity of each wavelength contained in a source of light or the reflection of light from an object, which is key to understanding the color properties of various types of light. Together, Figures 7.3 and 7.4 allow you to compare the color content of daylight and candlelight to three common electric light sources. We have

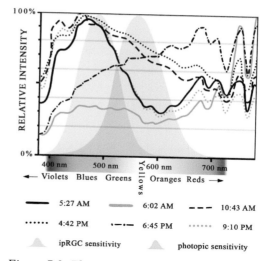

Figure 7.3: The colors of daylight: spectral power distribution of the sky in Como, Italy, May 28, 2016

also added the standard photopic response curve (shaded gray), which is used to transform these SPD graphs into lux values, and the ipRGC, or melanopic, sensitivity curve (shaded blue) to compare circadian stimulus potential.

Figure 7.3 illustrates the variety of daylight spectral power distributions of daylight all recorded outdoors within one day in Como, Italy.[1] Whether we are consciously aware of it or not, there is a constant parade of colors within the flux of daylight. The color content and the intensity of daylight can shift dramatically within just a few minutes. It varies considerably depending on atmospheric effects, the position of the sun and the position of the viewer.

The color content of the ambient light *indoors* is a function of the relative intensity of illumination from all available sources. Depending on the time of day, the daylight from a window might provide more or less illumination than an electric light source, and so one or the other might dominate. Sunlight, on the other hand is so intense that just a little bit of sunlight goes a long way in brightening up the colors in a room: a small patch of sunlight can easily contribute 10 to 100 times as much to the color balance in a room as all other light sources.

Manufactured Light

Another common source of light for early humans was fire, and eventually also oil lamps and candles. All these incandescent (from the Latin word for 'to glow') light sources emit most of their light in the red and orange wavelengths, with little, if any, in the shorter wavelengths of green and blue, as shown in Figure 7.4. The fleeting rosy glow of a sunset can be very similar in intense red wavelength content to a glowing fire. Humans seem to be naturally attracted to this 'warm' colored light, which emphasizes red colors and enhances our complexions. We might hypothesize about how early evolutionary experience influenced humans' fascination with firelight, but centuries of poetry also speak to the pull it has on our imaginations.

Once the incandescent light bulb was invented, it also emitted a similar color spectrum, rich in the reds and oranges and deficient in the blues and greens. If an incandescent light bulb is operated at a very high temperature, such as a tungsten blub at full power, more of the shorter wavelengths show up in the light it emits, with a color balance closer to that of sunlight. (See also color temperature discussion on page 43 and Figure 3.4.) However, as power is reduced and the bulb is dimmed, the color balance shifts back down toward the warm reds and oranges, which remind us more of candlelight, but without the flicker and movement of an actual flame.

Some artificial light sources have very large spikes of spectral power intensity in only a few wavelengths, but have been carefully engineered to produce the sensation of 'white light' for the human eye. Manufacturers of early fluorescent tubes tried to scrimp on the expensive phosphors that could be used to spread out the spectrum emitted by the lamps more evenly, and so got a bad reputation for the quality of colors perceived under 'cool white' fluorescent lamps. More recently, lamp manufacturers have been toying with formulas that give improved perception of color under certain conditions, such as making packaged meat look redder at the grocery counter, or making housewares and clothing appear brighter white. But the biggest revolution in electric lighting has come as a result of the transition to digital lighting with light emitting diodes (LEDs). Although first invented in 1962, LEDs started to enter the market for artificial light sources around 2010, and then rapidly changed our understanding of what was possible with electric lighting. It is interesting to compare the many SPD patterns of daylight shown in Figure 7.3 with four examples of manufactured light sources—candles, a standard incandescent light, a compact fluorescent lamp (CFL) and a newer LED—all shown in Figure 7.4.

LED light sources can be tiny, and thus can be located almost anywhere. They can easily be dimmed with digital controls, so the intensity of the light output from a fixture is no longer a binary on-off. And also via digital controls, the relative output of different wavelengths can be dynamically adjusted, allowing some LED light sources to change their spectral power distribution patterns over time, and thus the color balance of their light. It used to be that dynamically changing the color appearance of artificial light was limited to theatrical design, where an elaborate system of gelatin filters, or 'color gels,' were used to change the color of spot lights, perhaps from bluish for an outdoor scene to an orange glow for an indoor scene. Suddenly, with the ability to easily change the color of the LED light sources, lighting designers began to experiment with decorative color-changing options, especially outdoors. Bridges and building façades were illuminated with a rotating sequence of garish colors—pink,

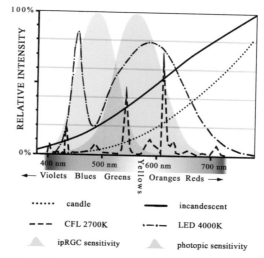

Figure 7.4: Spectral power distribution of four light sources: candle, incandescent bulb, CFL, and LED

red, orange, yellow, green, blue, purple, and back again. Why? Just because it was possible. It seemed fun and novel: a lot like lava lamps in the 1960s.

Now we live in a world where color-changing LED light sources are being actively promoted indoors too, as the next best thing to Mother Nature's daylight. Whereas previously it was only the natural light sources—daylight and firelight—that varied in intensity and color content over time, now LED light sources can be programmed and controlled to do almost any color-changing pattern desired. The key questions are: What is desirable? And why? Just because we can, should we? These questions should be part of a larger exploration about the design of our visual environment—trying to sort out what we, as humans, really need and want, versus merely whatever is possible.

Reflection, Absorption, and Transmission

After light is emitted from a light source, the next step in our visual perception is the reflection, transmission or absorption of that light by the object or material that we are looking at. Solid opaque objects absorb some wavelengths of light and reflect others. We see the color of an object as the color of the light which it reflects. Thus, a red apple absorbs most of the visible wavelengths that strike it, except for red. Black objects absorb all most all wavelengths, leaving very little light to reflect back to us. Likewise, if sunlight first strikes a red surface before bouncing into a room, most of the color content of the reflected sunlight will then be red. For example, my neighbor to the south has a red patio umbrella that she puts up in the summertime. Sunlight bounces off the umbrella upward through the windows of my house, creating a surprisingly bright red smudge of light that daily travels across my white ceilings.

In contrast to opaque materials, transparent materials allow all of the light that strikes them to pass straight through without absorption, reflection, distortion, or filtering. But no material is perfectly transparent. Pure water, which seems very clear indeed, still bends some the light as refraction, selectively absorbs some wavelengths such as red and UV more than others, and scatters other wavelengths, especially the shortest-wave blue light, which explains the deep blue of the deep-blue sea. Another very transparent material, the glass we use in windows, has a similar range of properties, slightly refracting the light, absorbing some wavelengths, reflecting others, and transmitting the remainder. Tints and coatings all change the recipe for which wavelengths will pass through the glass and which will be reflected or absorbed. Furthermore, some wavelengths are reflected more at shallow angles than when perpendicular to the surface of the glass. One of the key decision points in selecting glass for a daylit building is understanding how the glass interacts with the full spectrum of sunlight, from ultraviolet and all the visible wavelengths through infrared radiation.

Simple clear glass, manufactured since Roman times, filters out most of the UV and some of the IR in sunlight, while allowing almost all the visible spectrum to pass through. Low-emissivity glass (low-E) reduces the amount of infrared heat that can pass through glass. 'Selective' is a term used for glazing material that has been formulated to specifically optimize the amount of illumination measured in lux that passes through a window while reducing all other wavelengths. As a result, many selective glass windows tend to look greenish, since they optimize for those wavelengths to which the human visual system is most sensitive.[2]

Filtering the color of light transmitted through glass is not just an issue for the energy balance of the building, but also for the visual perception of the occupants of the building. Tinted glass, especially, can change the color balance of all the ambient daylight inside of the building, and filter out some wavelengths from our view of the outdoors. Blue-tinted glass will make the interior of a building appear more blue, while bronze-tinted glass will do the opposite, increasing the relative intensity of warm colors. I once toured an atrium on the campus of SUNY Albany that was completely sheathed in blue tinted glass, giving the building a distinctive blue-ice-cube look from the outside. On the inside, however, people's skin tones all looked ashen and sickly, because all the warm colors of the daylight spectrum had been filtered out by the blue glass. Not a good look for a medical research facility!

Even glass that appears to be a neutral gray can still have unexpected impacts on how we see things. My old office in Sacramento, California, had, I thought, a fabulous view, looking out onto an interior courtyard featuring a lovely Japanese garden planted with a constantly changing palate of seasonal colors. Late one afternoon after a rain shower I noticed a group of people gathering outside my window, looking up at the sky. I could see nothing but more dark rain clouds, so I went outside to investigate. The sun had broken out at the end of the day under the clouds, creating the largest possible double rainbow arching brilliantly across the sky. But I couldn't see it from inside my office, because my neutral gray tinted windows blocked enough of the critical wavelengths of the rainbow. Who would want to miss a rainbow of such magnificence? Not I.

Some colors seem to have only a fleeting existence, because our perception of them is not tied to the color of the object, but rather to our angle of view. These are the iridescent colors that we see in an opal or a pearl, or on the shimmer of an oil slick. The color does not exist as a pigment. Rather it is formed by the structural interference of a micro-structure with the wavelengths of light, like the varying thin film of a soap bubble. Similar 'structural' colors can be created by the feathers of many birds, like a peacock, as well as some butterfly wings and beetle shells, creating an illusion of brilliant blues and greens, but which disappear when you look at them close up. Dichroic glass has similar properties, reflecting different colors at different angles of incidence. Some architects and artists have used dichroic glass to emphasize special windows, sculpture or whole building façades that play with daylight and color.[3]

The scattering of sunlight in the atmosphere is another form of structural color, whereby sunlight is differentially scattered by random molecules. The short blue wavelengths are scattered the most, resulting in the blue color of the sky, while longer-wave yellow and red wavelengths travel farther and are scattered less. This scattering of sunlight partially explains why the sky is so variable in color, appearing deepest blue highest up in the mountains, and when we are looking away from the direction of the sun, and becoming whiter/brighter, then yellow and reddest when looking towards the sun, especially at sunrise and sunset. Thus, in this sense, the color of the sky is itself an illusion and varies importantly with your point of view relative to the sun.

Leonardo Da Vinci was fascinated by the color of the sky, and tried over decades to capture all of its effects in his paintings. As a young man he had hiked in the Italian Alps and noticed that the sky got bluer and darker as you hiked up a mountain, and appeared whiter and brighter as you looked down at the horizon. From his notebooks we now know that he conducted a number of experiments to determine if 'air was blue' or if the blue of the sky was an illusion. He also noticed that colors of objects were most vivid close up, and dulled as the objects were farther away. He famously captured this 'atmospheric perspective' of the dulling of colors in his famous paintings, such as the Mona Lisa.[4] (While he may have been the first of the great European painters to do so, many Chinese painters had mastered this technique centuries earlier.)

Retinal Sensitivity

The third factor in our perception of color is the sensitivity of our eyes to receiving and processing those colors. 'All the colors of the rainbow' is a favorite phrase to describe the range of colors we see in the world. However, not all people see the same rainbow, and our human perception of a rainbow is quite different from that of other animals. As we discussed earlier, people with cataracts or yellowed lenses receive substantially less stimulus in the blue and violet ranges. Very young children whose lenses are especially thin and clear can see the widest range of blues and violets, and may even have a hint of UV perception that adds to the intensity of those blues and violets. If so, UV perception might explain some of young children's fascination with rainbows and flowers!

A dog or other mammal, with only two types of cones—blue and yellow—sees a narrowed rainbow, ranging only from blue through green to yellow, fading into browns. A bird such as a pigeon, with four types of cones, sees a much broader rainbow then any human, starting with the ultraviolet bands that we can't see and continuing into deeper hues of red that are also invisible to us. Some butterflies have five or six types of cones. Mantis shrimp are the current world color champions with 16 (!) different types of cones. Perhaps not coincidently, they are also some of the most colorful creatures on the planet.[5]

The sensitivity of our retinas determines how we perceive colors. For example, a spectrograph of a healthy green lawn shows most of its reflected light is in the reds and deep reds, with just a little bump of light intensity in the greens and yellows. How could this be? How could we be perceiving this grass as green, when a spectrometer clearly shows that most of the light reflecting off of the lawn is predominantly red? The explanation would seem to be that our color vision is extremely sensitive to green wavelengths and much less to the reds, so the green sensation predominates, and we call the grass green.

Some people are termed 'color blind,' when in reality a better term might be 'color limited.' Sometimes they just have fewer cones, or less sensitive cones of one type. Others, genetically color blind, have two types of cones instead of three. They still see a range of colors, but with a limited pallet, similar to non-primate mammals. The most common forms of human color blindness, found in about 8% of males with European ancestry, and about 0.5% of women, results from a deficiency of either the long-wavelength (L) or the mid-wavelength (M) cone receptors that help to differentiate between shades of green and red. Instead of greens, yellows, oranges and reds, they tend to perceive variations of yellow and brown, from bright yellow to beige and khaki.

Indeed, as mentioned earlier, there is a surprising amount of genetic variation in humans' long-wavelength (red) L-cone. The ratio of red to green cones varies considerably in any normal population, from 2:1 to 4:1.[6] Furthermore, there are some women who have activated two different versions of (red) L-cone gene. These rare women see an even greater range of reds and oranges, resulting in a world that has many more vivid and subtle colors, closer to the perceptions of birds and butterflies.

Color Constancy

We humans have an amazing ability to maintain our perception of the color of an object, even as the color content of the light source changes substantially. We call this color constancy. A red apple is perceived as the same color red even as you move it from sunlight to shade, whether you look at it outside for a picnic under daylight or inside for dinner under electric light. Physically, in terms of the measurable wavelengths reaching our eye, the color content of our view of the apple is changing dramatically, but we perceive it to be the same red apple. Basically, as the colors of the light reflecting off an object change, our brains have to make a perceptual choice: is the light changing or is the object changing? Our brains seem to prefer to assume that the color properties of the object are remaining constant and that the color content of the light source is changing, rather than vice versa. That assumption is certainly consistent with millennia of evolutionary experience with the outdoor world, where the color balance of daylight is constantly changing, and where there is only one dominant light source—the sun—for almost all of our visual experience. Color constancy gives us the ability to make quick judgments about natural objects: do those green leaves look different because they are in shadow, or because they are sickly?

With the advent of electric lighting, where the color content of a light source could be changed at will, the issue of color constancy became an interesting research subject. It was discovered that humans recalibrate their color perception based on the current ambient conditions. For example, if you step into a room illuminated only by pink lights, at first everything in that room will appear weirdly pink to you. But gradually your brain will adapt to the new environment, and start to normalize the pinkness, such that the whitest object in the room will appear ever whiter, gray objects will start to take on shades of other hues, and your perceived skin color will start to return to an expected norm for skin color. When you step out of that room 20 minutes later your brain has to go through the process all over again: the world will appear weirdly greenish until it recalibrates.

One way that our brains do this color calibration is by identifying the whitest object within view as a reference against which to judge other colors. In the natural world, clouds and snow are some of the whitest objects we normally experience, because they are simply diffusing and reflecting pure white sunlight. White has been called 'achromatic,' as in 'the absence of color.' In reality, white objects are reflecting all colors equally, and in seeking to identify the whitest object in view, our brains are essentially looking for the object which reflects the most amount of source light with the least amount of color distortion.

Similarly, people who are color blind can often learn other cues that help them differentiate colors according to cultural norms, such as "*If it is associated with plants, it is probably greenish*" or "*If it is a toy, good chance it is red.*" My own father was color blind, but I never knew this until late in his life. He was an excellent watercolor painter in his free time, and dealt constantly in color in his job as a television art director, an odd job for someone who is color blind! (Although, when he started work in the 1950s, all televisions were black and white, so color choices had little relevance at the start of his career.) Finally, one day he told me a sad story about how he had wanted to become a pilot during the Second World War, but failed the pilot training test because he was color blind. He had no idea. He thought the test was silly, because of course the world looked perfectly normal to him. However once he told me, I began to notice a few peculiarities in his behavior and color choices which could then be easily explained by color blindness, such as poorly matched khaki clothes and touches of turquoise paint added to an otherwise blue sky.

Naming Colors

Colors largely exist in our perception because we have given names to them, and there is good evidence that without a name for a color, people have difficulty perceiving it. This is the fifth, culturally-driven component of color. Tests by various anthropologists in pre-industrial tribes find that without a word for blue, for example, a blue card is not perceived as any different from a sample of green cards. In that case 'blue' is not recognized, it is a 'nothing' color. In contrast, the very elaborate vocabulary of colors that has evolved recently from the paint, fashion, and cosmetic industries has enabled people to differentiate, and remember, ever more colors. The company Pantone makes a business of officially naming and indexing thousands of standardized colors for industrial use around the world. Should that shade of pinky-orange be called salmon, apricot, peach, copper, coral, or light terracotta? Should that bluish-green shade be called teal, turquoise, aqua, or cyan?

One theory is that the naming of colors followed humans' ability to manufacture the color for painting—think charcoal and chalk on cave walls, and burnt clays for red markings on skin. Strangely, linguists have discovered that the color blue is one of the last color words to enter most languages.[7] The first written mention of a word for blue seems to be by Egyptians who made much use of a blue semi-precious stone, lapis lazuli, around 5,000 years ago. They later discovered how to manufacture a similar blue pigment, calcium copper silicate, now known as 'Egyptian blue' as glazes for their pottery, which increased their use of a term for 'blue.' Eventually other manufactured blue pigments became available, but remained very expensive and rare. During the Renaissance, artists learned how to transform the stone lapis lazuli into a new pigment called ultramarine blue, which was so prized it was reserved primarily for paintings of the Virgin Mary's garments, or the celestial blue heavens painted high in the cathedral vaults.

It is interesting to reflect that much of our understanding of color and perception may have been driven by technology: long ago by artists looking for mixes of pigments that best reflected what they saw in the world, and more recently by research into digital technologies, with the end goal making digital media appear more life-like. We have made amazing advances in color science for computer screens, cell phones, and movies, even establishing a sense of hyper-reality where colors are always more saturated than we normally experience. An extreme example of the disconnect between digital images and natural experience might be that of the northern lights, the Aurora Borealis, where human eyes see predominately greenish-yellow curtains of light, but tourists' cameras record dazzling blues, purples and reds to show to folks back home. In such a case, reality can become a disappointment compared to the brilliant colors we come to expect from of our digital devices.

It may be that the subtle colors, such as those found in a landscape, are most deeply fascinating to an artist or technologist who is trying to replicate them. I have studied color as an artist, an architect and a lighting professional, and have mastered many technical ways to describe color, but I have never figured out how to describe the transitional color of the sky at dusk and dawn, as it transitions from blue above to a yellow-orange glow on the horizon, nor can I capture it on a camera. I've been told many times that there can be no such thing as bluish-orange, since blue and orange are perceptual opposites, and yet somehow the sky seems to smoothly transition between the two colors, without ever becoming either white or gray. I think my cultural vocabulary is simply missing the word which describes this. This is another 'nothing' color, waiting for an artist or scientist to give it a cultural meaning.

Khaki is another strange color term, originally borrowed from the Urdu word used in India for 'dusty.' It is a good color for camouflage so it is often used for army uniforms; an indeterminate mix of many colors blended into a drab reflection of its dusty surrounds. There are other words, such as gray and beige, that also try to capture an indeterminant color mix, those which we have a hard time understanding as a mixture of the primary colors seen in a rainbow, the opposite of vivid. Grays have a huge range of color balances, from warm grays to cool grays; basically, any color can be desaturated until it appears grayish. Gray is thus a word indicating a lack of color. Indeterminant color terms may also indicate other color deficiencies: in the spectrum of the light source, in our vision, or our inability to place the color in a larger context. When our world turns beige and gray, when vibrant colors disappear, it is a good indication that something is deficient. In the world outside of our buildings, colors are most intense in full sunlight. As Leonardo Da Vinci discovered, they fade in the distance, they fade in the shadows, and they fade at night.

Shadows

Shadows are key to our understanding of three-dimensional space. In daylight conditions, the angle and length of the shadow tells us much about the position of the sun, high overhead or low on the horizon. But it also gives us information about the position of the object casting the shadow, and the terrain against which the shadow is cast. Have you ever stood on top of a building or bridge and waved, to see if you can identify your own shadow waving back at you?

Shadows may seem flat, like a two-dimensional shape applied over a surface, but in reality, a shadow is a three-dimensional shape, a void of light, that we only see when it intersects a surface. But even this is not completely true, for there are shadows of clouds within clouds, shadows of trees upon trees, and shadows of mist, and steam, and even shadows of heat waves that we can see shimmering across a surface.

When shadows behave in strange fashion, they can create cognitive dissonance, as our brain struggles to make sense of the unexpected situation. For example, shadows are expected to be underfoot, not overhead. A shiny floor in the sunlight, or sunlight-redirecting devices in a window, can cast shadows in the reflected light up onto the ceiling, creating an oddly spooky effect if you can't immediately determine the source of the shadow. I remember once watching long shadows rapidly fluttering on the ceiling of an office, wondering what giant was moving outside, only to realize that they must be the upside-down shadows of the trees outside blowing in the wind, reflected upward via reflective louvers in the windows.

If you see two shadows when you are outside during the daylight, or a shadow within a shadow, it's a good chance you are deep in an urban canyon on a sunny day with window reflections casting shadows every which way, or near a building with reflective windows, mirroring the sun back in your direction. A reflection powerful enough to cast a shadow in broad daylight (!) is also likely to be an intense source of glare when facing the other direction. Buildings with reflective glass, especially those with a concave surface that can focus those reflections, are becoming a major urban menace. In 2013 a new skyscraper going up in London at 20 Fenchurch Street made international news[8] due to a focused solar reflection that melted the plastic parts of an expensive car parked out front. Similarly, daylight consultants were called in to fix major problems created by the Wynn Hotel in Las Vegas and the Disney Concert Hall in Los Angeles, which also have reflective façades with concave surfaces. These consultants have started to speak in terms of the 'number of suns' which can be reflected by a building. Double suns create intense heating, sunburns, and material deterioration. Triple suns can melt plastic and kill birds flying by.

Deep shadows are the result of two factors, our own visual adaptation and the physical interreflections of light within the shadowed space. In very bright sunlight, the high contrast conditions may put a shadowed area outside of our perceptual range. In other words, *"The brighter the light, the deeper the shadows."* As we approach a shadowed space so that it fills more of our field of view, our eyes start to adapt to the lower ambient light levels, a process which can take seconds or minutes to complete, until we can see more details within.

On the other hand, the darker the surfaces around and within the shadowed space, the less light will be reflected back out, and the deeper and darker the appearance of the shadow. It is very hard to see a shadow on a black surface, because so little light is reflected back to the viewer. In comparison, white or light colors, which reflect light back to the viewer, do a better job of capturing the subtle shape and movement of shadows, and thus conveying information about the shape of a space and objects within the space.

Colored Shadows

As any good impressionist painter knows, shadows also have colors. A shadow is the absence of light, so if the light source has a predominate color, the shadow will appear to have the opposite color. This principle is conveyed to young artists with the mantra *"Warm light, cool shadow, and cool light, warm shadow."*

I often show a photograph of a white marble bust displayed in the Getty Museum in Los Angeles in order to illustrate this principle to an audience. The right side of her shoulders has a sharply edged, bluish shadow of her head and neck, while her left side has a fuzzy edged orangish shadow (shown as gray in Figure 7.5). Based on the photograph, I then ask the audience to tell me the source and location of the light on the sculpture. The incandescent point-source spot light, up to the left, casts a hard-edged shadow, which appears bluish, in the absence of the warm incandescent light, while the skylight, up to the right, casts a soft edged shadow, which appears more orangish, in the absence of the blue-infused daylight.

Figure 7.5: Marble statue with two shadows

The fact that in the image these two shadows appear to have about equal density suggests that the two light sources—skylight and spotlight—are contributing equally to the illumination of the statue. If one light source were much less powerful than the other, then its shadow would appear much fainter, perhaps only a hint or blush of color.

Shadows not only capture the color of the direct light sources, but also any indirect light reflected off nearby surfaces. And here is where shadow colors start to get really interesting, because the reflected light is filtered by the color of the surface from which it reflects. Thus, like my neighbor's red umbrella which reflects only the red portion of sunlight up onto my ceiling, a wooden floor will reflect only warm-hued light upwards, creating a warm-colored ambient glow.

In this way, colors intensify within a space. For example, three walls painted pink will appear as more intensely pink than just one wall painted pink, due to the inter-reflected pink light among them. (This is one of the reasons that it is so difficult to pick paint colors for a room, because it is hard to visualize the effect of interreflections.) While inter-reflected colors get washed out in full sunlight, they start to dominate in the shadows, where they contribute proportionately more of the ambient light.

Reading the Shadows

Our brains' default assumption is that there is one primary source of light, somewhere over head. But sometimes, especially inside of buildings, we may have multiple shadows, as daylight streams in from more than one direction, and electric lights cast their own set of shadows. Looking carefully at these shadows can tell you a lot about the direction, intensity, and color of the source of light casting each shadow.

I have often used what I think of as the 'finger method' to assess the directionality and intensity of light sources in a room. I touch my index finger to a surface—the wall, a desk, an open book—and study the resulting shadows. A smooth white surface works the best. Wiggling the finger around a bit helps to clarify the relationships of the various shadow directions. A handy pencil or stick can work even better. You can more easily see which shadow is strongest, and which are secondary, or just barely there. The strongest shadow points directly to the brightest light source. You can see where the shadow directions overlap, and how the colors of the shadows shift if there are multiple light sources. Often these colors become most apparent when two shadows overlap. Is there a hard-edged shadow? And maybe a very subtle smear in another direction? Try putting down two or more fingers and see how your perceptions change.

As described earlier, when two shadows have equal intensity, it is an indication that the two light sources casting the shadows also have equal intensity, i.e. are contributing equally to the ambient light at that location. This is a quick and easy way to tell how much light in a room is contributed by daylight, and how much by electric light: just look at the shadows. Carefully observing shadows is a game you can play while visiting any daylit building, asking yourself: Where is the light coming from? Which source is the most powerful, and which are secondary? Where are there upward reflections from the nearby paving or a roof? And how are the colors of the light sources and reflecting surfaces changing the colors of the shadows?

Dappled Light and Highlights

Some of the most attractive daylit places have a gentle, dynamic mix of shadow and sunlight, as is found under a leafy tree in midsummer. The subtle movement of spots of light and shadow also conveys the movement of a breeze moving the leaves. Intuitively, most people recognize this interplay of light and shadow as indicating a fresh and healthy environment. In such a dappled light, the shadows are brighter, filled in with reflected light, and the spots of sun are a bit diffused and fuzzy. Dappled sunlight is the perfect condition for a picnic bench, or a café table set out under a shade tree. Bright and lively, but shaded: an in-between spot between sun and shade.

The shadows of a tree cast against a window provide that element of a living shadow to a room. Likewise, watery surfaces may create reflections and refractions that transform uniform sunlight into complex patterns, such as seen at the bottom of a swimming pool on a sunny day. These liquid patterns are called 'caustics,' from the Greek word for 'burnt.' A caustic chemical burns organic material because it is so harsh. But a caustic sunlight pattern could burn by concentrating the light so intensely, like with a magnifying glass. Much gentler, and more intriguing are the complex patterns of refractions and reflections that result when sunlight passes through a wine glass, or other complex curved surfaces. Some architects have played with these optical complexities, passing sunlight through or across shallow planes of water to add a dynamic element to daylit spaces.

Kevin Nute, professor of architecture at the University of Oregon, is especially interested in finding ways to bring the experience of nature indoors, and to do so in a way that is inherently natural itself. He produced a video book *Naturally Animated Architecture* that illustrates a variety of techniques for generating visual movement inside of buildings. It features design techniques that take advantage of sunlight movement, shadows, and liquid caustic patterns. In one of his experiments, he reflected caustic sunlight patterns upon to a ceiling via light shelves covered with wind-rippled water. He found that: "... *this kind of wind-animated light not only lowered occupants' heart rates but was also less distracting than similar, artificially generated moving patterns. Importantly, adding wind movement did not reduce the amount of light the shelves transmitted. However, it did make the shelves much more visible to people using the space.*"[9]

Dappled sunlight can also be an intentional design choice, as evidenced in a stylish hotel designed by the Spanish architect Javier Mariscal, located near the main architectural attraction in Bilbao, Spain, the Guggenheim Museum. The eight-story hotel features a dining terrace up on its roof that overlooks its famous neighbor to the north. In the sunlight, the view of the Guggenheim is resplendent, but can occasionally be overwhelming, as the curving metallic skin focuses the light. The open-air part of the terrace, along the balcony wall, can be a pleasant place to sit when the sun is not too strong, or later in the evening, once shadows lengthen. The back half of the terrace provides a roofed area to keep out the rain, with floor-to-ceiling glass doors that can close in inclement weather, while still allowing a full view of the Guggenheim for the diners. The architect clearly envisioned this sheltered terrace as more like a perfect picnic spot, with dappled sunlight filtering from above. A glass roof overhead is shaded by woven metal strips, replicating the pattern of palm fronds over a beach hut, with little one-inch holes that allow sunspots to dance across the tables and chairs. The faces of diners and waiters are struck with bits of sun sparkle as they talk and move about the terrace, further animating the space. The dappled sunlight filtering down through the faux-fronds overhead makes this a very unusual and evocative daylit space.

Sparkle

Sparkle and highlights are the other half of the equation, balancing shadows, that help our eyes to understand the three-dimensional shape of static objects. The location of a highlight on a stationary object pinpoints our geometrical relationship to a source of light, based on our understanding of the shape of the object. That highlight location will then move if we move, or if the object moves. (Generally, our brain will make a default assumption that the light source itself is not moving.) Artists have learned how to carefully place little dots of white as highlights on faces and other shapes in their paintings to 'bring them to life,' and to better represent how we see the three-dimensional world as depicted on a two-dimensional surface. Before the advent of photography, palaces were often decorated with landscape paintings using an artistic technique called *tromp l'oeil*, a term borrowed from the French, meaning 'to fool the eye,' such that, with the careful use of shadows, highlights and perspective, a flat mural was made to look vividly three dimensional.

The importance of highlights and sparkle in understanding three-dimensional space came to me one day when I was visiting a classroom in one of my early studies of daylight in schools. This particular classroom had very little daylight coming from one tiny window off in a corner. It also had a standard grid of surface-mounted fluorescent troffers with aging acrylic diffusers on the ceiling.

The fourth-grade class had just let out for the day, and the teacher noticed that I was taking light-level readings with an illuminance meter. She came over to ask for my help: would I *please* tell the administration that her room lighting was dim, noticeably darker than all the others, and that she needed more light! Unfortunately, I told her, the light levels in her room were essentially the same as all the rest of the school, and remarkably uniform. I showed her my readings, 300 lux more or less everywhere, horizontally on every desk, and even vertically on all the walls.

She paused for a moment, then said: "*Wait! Look what happens when I open my door!*" She opened the door to her classroom, which looked out onto the adjacent playground. The late afternoon sun glinted across the black asphalt. "*There!*" she explained, "*See how much better that is! I need more light, like that!*" I went around the room again and repeated my measurements: a few readings might have changed from 300 to 310 lux, certainly not enough that any human eye could perceive the difference. I was about to give her the bad news, when I looked around and noticed that now the desks in the classroom cast very slight shadows, whereas before the highly diffuse overhead lights had created none. The aluminum chair frames had little highlights on their corners, reflecting the brighter daylight from the open door.

I realized that the teacher was not responding to the amount of illumination in the room, but rather the quality of the light. Her use of the word *dim* really meant *dull*, rather than dark. The added shadows and highlights from the open door made every object in the room a bit more vivid. These very small additions to the room lighting made a big difference to the teacher who worked in there every day. Her passionate request for help to procure 'better lighting' has never left me. In addition, the experience taught me to always question people's use of words to describe light, which are often used very differently than seemingly similar professional concepts.

Our eyes (and brain) naturally expect to see a bit of sparkle during the day wherever we go, given the three-dimensional nature of our world, and an evolutionary default assumption that there is one sun moving about overhead providing intense directional light. Thus, most indoor settings benefit from the addition of a little sparkle. This can be done by adding a few shiny surfaces to enhance natural highlights, or curved surfaces that tend to focus the ambient light via interreflection, or even little bits of light provided by an electric light point source.

Richard Kelly, one of the early lighting design educators in America, coined a term 'the play of brilliants' to describe various forms of sparkle that can be used in lighting design. The term captures both the lighthearted nature of sparkle, and perhaps the design genius that inspired him to add them into a design. Windows that let in just enough spots of direct sunlight into a space, or reflections from the brilliant sunlight outside, can serve this purpose of adding highlights to a space.

Long ago, I developed a rule of thumb for retailers that one clear skylight for every nine or ten diffusing skylights, or 10% of the overall skylight area, would add just the right element of sparkle to their displays. William Bruder, the architect of the Phoenix Central Library, played this sparkle game with the special skylights he designed for the reading room at the top floor of the library. A diffusing skylight sits above each column that supports the space frame structure spanning the vast space. However, set into each skylight dome there is one small circle of clear glazing that lets a small beam of sunlight into the space. The location of this clear circle is such that at exactly noon on the summer solstice, the sunbeam strikes the top of the column, making it seem to burn with the intensity of the sun. At that moment, the reading room lights up with more than the usual delight, and transforms into an observatory for our place on Earth and in the larger solar system.

In the absence of direct or reflected sunlight, small electric lights can also add bits of sparkle to an otherwise uniformly daylit space. They can be tiny point sources in a chandelier, downlights, or string lights that add both an interesting visual and a small source of directional light, greatly brightening our perception of the space. Often adding only a few watts of LED sources to a uniformly lit space will change the perception of it from dim, i.e. dull or gloomy, to interesting and bright.

The Jeppesen Terminal at Denver International Airport, designed by Fentress Bradburn Architects and opened in 1995, provides an interesting example of the use of artificial sparkle to enliven a daylighting design. The terminal is roofed with white fabric suspended from an array of poles, a tensile structure whose shape mimics the snow-capped peaks of the nearby Rocky Mountains, or perhaps a cluster of Native American tepees pitched out along the high prairie. The huge fabric roof is translucent, and so during the day all the upper floors are bathed in a very uniform ambient daylight. The daylight emanating from this diffusing material is ample, but rather flat. At some point the designers decided to add narrow tubes of neon lights around the edges of things to add small lines of more intense light to the scene. This simple addition does the trick, brightening up our sense of the space.

Sparkle versus Glare

Allowing in 'just enough' sparkle from sunlight is easy to say, but difficult to specify. Sunlight is most welcome when it has been rare, and least welcome when it is in over-abundance. Sunlight after a big rainstorm is a welcome sign that the weather is changing. Sunlight on a cold winter day is a sign that spring will be along eventually. Sunlight, pouring through a window during the peak of summer's heat can be oppressively bright and hot, and an unwelcome reminder that summer's heat will not be leaving anytime soon.

Sparkle is an interesting word in the English language. A spark is a momentary event, it is a tiny thing, a small bit of energy, but of unusual intensity. Sparkles come from many intermittent sparks. Synonyms for sparkle include *glitter*, *glisten*, *twinkle*, *flicker*, *shimmer*, or *iridescence*: all words that imply movement, variability, or impermanence. Making an analogy to our sense of touch, there is a lightness to sparkle, like a tickle, or a gentle caress. A person with a sparkling personality is lighthearted and witty, even fascinating, certainly not a threat or annoying.

The extreme form of 'to sparkle' might be 'to dazzle,' implying momentary blindness. Someone who is bedazzled is still fascinated, but perhaps also slightly blinded to some important details. To be dazzled by someone's performance implies a sort of pleasant confusion, where the outcome is positive, but the process is slightly mysterious or overwhelming. It is perhaps no surprise that many stage performers, especially for circus and magic acts, wear sparkling costumes covered with sequins and shiny fabrics. Likewise, many rock concerts use moving stage lighting focused more on the audience than the performers, to bedazzle, and hopefully heighten the excitement of, the audience.

Those little points of sparkle can, however, become more of an annoyance than a delight when there are far too many of them, or they are too intense, or we are forced to look at them for too long. For example, the lighthearted sparkle of bits of sunlight dancing upon a wind-rippled pond at midday can become blinding later in the day as the sun lowers in the sky and the occasional sparkles consolidate into a continuous path of reflected sunlight. When those bits of sparkle prevent us from seeing or understanding something that interests us, we give them a negative term: 'glare.' Glare is when dazzlement stops being fun and lighthearted, and instead becomes tiresome, distressing, or even painful.

Glare

The English word 'glare' also has an interesting entomology. The noun 'glare' can mean a fierce or angry stare, like from a disapproving or unforgiving fellow human. Such a glaring stare is steady and unrelenting. Similarly, the sun can also glare at us, as if it were unforgiving, an unrelenting brightness that we seek to avoid. Thus, glare has the implication of being steady, unblinking, inescapable. Whereas sparkle and dazzlement have a suggestion of attraction, glare is something we seek to avoid. While we tend to look towards the direction of sparkles, we tend to look away from the direction of glare, shielding our eyes from the discomfort of too much blinding light.

In addition to looking the other way, we have other defenses from too much glare. A carefully positioned sunhat or umbrella can keep our eyes in shadow from the sun. Likewise, architectural solutions include roof overhangs and awnings to shade windows from unwanted sun. Tinted sunglasses reduce the intensity of the sun, and especially its reflections, and similarly tinted glass can help mitigate the excessive brightness of too much sunlight bouncing around a landscape outside a window. However, fundamentally, as our eyes adapt to the lower overall illumination through the tinted glass, the contrast ratios between the brightest and darkest areas remain, still stressing our ability to see well.

Glare has long been a subject of much study and controversy in the world of illuminating engineering. In the early days, the primary goal of the profession was to learn how to best specify the design of electric lighting in the workplace. Studies of glare were concerned primarily with how glare sources interfered with visual tasks at work, such as reading words written in pencil on paper, proofing typewritten documents, or detecting the caliber marking of metallic instruments. In other words, the 'motivation to look' was assumed to be achieving acceptable accuracy on a required, workplace visual task. Furthermore, workplace design dictated that the task would be performed in a fixed location, such that looking the other way was not a viable option.

When designing to reduce glare problems in such an environment, there were two primary concerns: avoiding overly bright electric light sources within the field of view, and avoiding reflections on shiny surfaces that would 'veil' the desired information.

Illuminating engineers quickly learned that visual task performance could be improved if excessively bright light sources were shielded from direct view. Thus, instead of a bare electric light bulb dangling from the ceiling, a simple hood over the bulb helped to direct more light to the task location while also shielding the eye of the worker from the glare created by an overly bright bulb. The term luminaire became the preferred way to designate a more sophisticated light fixture that was carefully designed to distribute light where needed, while lessening glare. Fluorescent tubes were enclosed behind grills, grates, and lenses to redirect and diffuse their light, while preventing a direct view of the tube itself.

An analogy can be made to the design of a room, with the sun as the light source, and the window enclosure and its attachments as part of the 'daylight luminaire.' Exterior awnings, overhangs, fins, and louvers can serve to shield the eyes of the room's occupants from direct sunlight, while also reflecting and diffusing it in useful directions. Operable interior blinds, shades, and curtains provide an even more fine-grained level of control, somewhat similar to the lens of a luminaire, allowing occupants to either block or redirect sunlight when needed and also to adjust the overall brightness of their view through the window. Obviously, pulling a shade over a luminaire will reduce its optical efficiency in delivering illumination; and so too, pulling a translucent shade over a window greatly reduces its transmission of light. The design challenge is how to balance the entire visual environment, so that occupants can achieve their visual objectives while maintaining visual comfort. One of the visual objectives may be performing a work-related task, but another visual objective may be looking out the window at the view.

Far too often, enthusiastic architects design buildings with lots and lots of glass, with the intent of providing ample daylight for the interior and sweeping views to the outside. Yet the result is an intolerably glaring environment, where the owners or occupants end up taking action to block the windows, thereby thwarting all the potential benefits of daylight and views. In addition to blinds and shades left permanently closed, I've seen offending windows blocked with bookshelves, cardboard boxes, or aluminum foil. If we are going to avoid the extreme irony of blockaded windows, designers need a much better understanding of how and when daylight can cause glare inside of buildings, and how to create high-quality visual environments where occupants can continuously enjoy the benefits of daylight and views.

Evaluating Glare

Unfortunately, currently available daylighting glare analysis does a poor job of predicting occupant comfort or satisfaction. While mathematical and theoretical models of glare for electric sources have been quite successful at helping to improve the design of luminaires and electric lighting design in spaces, the corresponding models of glare for daylighting have generally been an abysmal failure. To explore why, first we will take a brief detour to look at studies and models of electric lighting glare, and then consider a few prominent studies of glare in daylit spaces.

Originally, glare analysis tools were developed to evaluate electric lighting designs. Early glare researchers found it useful to distinguish between two types of glare. The first was termed 'disability glare,' a form of glare that resulted in measurable loss of performance on visual acuity tasks. Researchers tested various luminaire designs in laboratory settings, to see how much they interfered with easily repeatable tasks which served as a proxy for standard office work, such as how quickly and accurately can you count the 'C's in a field of 'O's.

Here, you can give disability glare a try yourself under different lighting conditions:

CCOOOCOOCCCOCOOOOCCCCOCOOOOOCCOOOO.

The fact that the intensity of disability glare was measurable, based on performance of standardized tasks, and thus objectively quantifiable, gave it a certain stature within the field of illumination engineering. Furthermore, disability glare could be dangerous, even life threatening, if it interfered with your ability to operate a machine or resulted in misreading instructions.

Direct beam sunlight seemed an obvious cause of disability glare, as sunlight is generally brighter than any electric light source. If the orb of the sun is in your field of view, you probably need to look away. If part of your visual task is in sunlight and part is in shade, good chance your performance on that task will suffer, as your eyes will tire from adjusting back and forth between the two extreme light levels. Thus, the solution for disability glare from sunlight was fairly simple: keep direct beam sunlight out of people's eyes and away from the visual task.

The second type of glare was termed 'discomfort glare,' a milder form of glare that did not immediately interfere with visual performance on discrete tasks, but instead resulted in people complaining about visual discomfort. Discomfort glare has always been much more problematic for study and analysis: no objective tests were developed for detecting discomfort glare. Instead, identification of discomfort glare was based on subjective assessment. Studies of discomfort glare commonly asked individuals to identify their personal borderline between 'just acceptable' and 'just unacceptable' in the various scenes being tested. Researchers consistently found a wide variation in responses, i.e. that some people were much more sensitive than others.

Mathematical models developed to predict *discomfort* glare tended to follow the same format as those used for *disability* glare; that, for a given ambient lighting level, the brighter and the larger the sources of glare, and the closer they are to the direction of gaze, the more people will find the scene visually uncomfortable. Discomfort glare *from daylight* was assumed to involve the same principles, but just with bigger and brighter sources. Visual tasks were assumed to be the same type of workplace tasks tested earlier, and the glare sources—i.e. either patterns of sunlight reflected about in the space or the bright windows at the periphery of the room—were assumed to be as static and utilitarian as the electric light sources tested in the laboratory. Many competing equations were developed, all following similar methodologies.

However, in all these efforts, the positive visual *comfort* end of the scale was missing. Only negative experience was measured. There was no visual interest or motivation other than successful performance of the standardized experimental task, no other basis for evaluating visual comfort, let alone visual delight.

And yet, daylight in itself is inherently interesting. Unlike patterns of luminaires mounted on a ceiling, people enjoy looking at patterns of sunlight on a surface (as discussed further, below). The variability of daylight in a space provides useful information about time and place. Views out of a window are also inherently interesting, and tend to attract an occupant's attention.

In the following discussion about various studies of discomfort glare in daylit spaces, a recurring theme will be that people's aversion to temporary glare from daylight sources is often counterbalanced with their enduring attraction to window views. In other words, there is another important 'motivation to look' at play beyond the standard workplace task.

Field Studies of Glare

A large field study of discomfort glare in daylit buildings was published in 2013 by Michael Hirning and his collaborators. They collected detailed comfort surveys from 468 people working in large, open plan offices in five certified green buildings in Brisbane, Australia. These buildings were chosen because they had been *"specifically designed to include daylight as a significant lighting component as well as provide occupant comfort."*[10]

However, all was not well with the daylighting design of these buildings. The survey showed that half of the people reported that glare was a significant issue for them. This was in spite of the fact that *"Three of the five buildings already had new blinds or shading controls retrofitted to reduce the impact of glare in these buildings. Two had disabled their automated blind systems, which is a common occurrence within green buildings."*

The researchers also collected high dynamic range (HDR) luminance map images that were taken at each workstation representing the normal view of the surveyed occupant. These HDR images were then analyzed for input into a variety of competing discomfort glare equations, in order to determine which equation might best predict the occupant discomfort. From the analysis of these images the researchers found that *"Over ten times more glare [sources] occurred from daylight (222) than electric light (21), with the majority of daylight glare originating from the window. (167).*" In other words, based on the glare equations, the windows were the primary suspect in creating this glare problem.

The Australian team tested five of the leading discomfort glare indices and they found that none of them adequately predicted the occupants' reports of discomfort glare: "*All glare indices tested in this investigation severely underestimated discomfort.*" The authors proceeded to lay out a blunt critique of the existing knowledge on daylight glare: "*Large studies of discomfort glare are rare. Much of the research into discomfort glare involves very small sample sizes, comprised largely of students from the researching institutions ...*" They continued: "*Traditional glare research involves laboratory setups with simple lighting distributions from artificial windows (fluorescent lights behind a diffusing screen) ... This type of discomfort glare research has proven inconsistent in the field situations where there are real tasks to perform and interesting visual background stimuli.*"

In the process of collecting data in their five buildings, they discovered an important limitation of their field-study methodology, which was that occupants tended to abandon their desks during the times of highest discomfort glare. "*Employees in these buildings had flexible working hours and a majority of the occupants had worked under their lighting conditions for over six months. Occupants have an acute awareness of the time of day when glare becomes intolerable. At these times occupants simply make sure they are not required at their desk.*"

Thus, those occupants who were in the worst conditions, or most sensitive to glare, were most often excluded from the study.

However, even in spite of the occasional glare, the researchers realized that: "*Almost all comments on window view were positive ... [and] those occupants who indicated discomfort ... often mentioned that even though at times they found their workspace too glary, they still enjoyed the window view.*" The researchers concluded their paper with the statement that: "*... in a real environment, the evidence suggests occupants are willing to compromise personal comfort for short periods, in order to experience daylight and interesting views most of the time.*"

Kevin Van den Wymelenberg, in his PhD thesis, had very similar findings. In a detailed laboratory study, he compared the ability of a wide range of glare metrics to predict visual comfort and found them all more or less wanting.[11] His methodology had 18 college students performing computerized and paper-based tasks in a single occupancy office with a large south-west-facing window a few feet away to the left of their desk. The subjects filled out evaluations of their visual comfort under a wide variety of daylight and electric light conditions. Automated HDR photography captured the scenes for later analysis, testing dozens of candidate visual comfort and glare prediction metrics. The study subjects were also asked to adjust the louvered window blinds to their preferred setting.

Somewhat surprisingly, Van den Wymelenberg found that in 92% of the tests, *"participants preferred to allow sun into the space when it was available."* He noted that the *"most preferred blind setting included allowing bits of direct sunlight into view on the worktable and walls."* It is possible that this finding was influenced by the colder mid-winter weather when the tests were conducted in Idaho, or the short time span of the tests. However, the findings also run counter to almost all advice given to daylight designers, which is that they should attempt to exclude direct sunlight from an office space as much as possible.

Nuanwan Tuaycharoen and Peter Roy Tragenza tackled these questions by comparing measured and subjective discomfort glare from a window to its view characteristics. They had one group of students grade a variety of windows in a campus building for the quality of the view, while a second group of students ranked the same windows for their level of discomfort glare. They also rated the very same windows a second time, covered with tracing paper in order to provide similar luminance patterns, but with no view. Overall, they found that the students' subjective visual comfort was best predicted by the ranking of 'view interest,' not by physical measurements of luminance or discomfort glare metrics.[12]

With these studies and others,[13] we have fairly consistent evidence that occupants have visual preferences in daylit spaces that are not captured in traditional glare equations. Robert Clear, a statistician at the Lawrence Berkeley National Laboratory, published a meta-analysis of studies used to derive the many discomfort glare models then in use around the world, hoping to untangle all the various approaches used to predict discomfort glare. He found them wildly inconsistent and noted a number of structural flaws.[14] For example, a duration factor was missing in all the equations. How did tolerance change from a quick glance to a long stare? Did longer exposure result in adaptation or less tolerance? There have also been hints that sensitivity to glare may be time of day or seasonally dependent. It is certainly age dependent. All this suggests we may need a different paradigm to successfully predict glare under real-world daylight conditions.

Glare and Noise

Perhaps glare could be studied similar to the way noise in the acoustic environment is studied. Glare could be considered to visual comfort what noise is to acoustic comfort: glare results from annoying patterns of light that get in the way of looking at what you want to see, just as noise results from annoying patterns of sound that get in the way of listening to what you want to hear.

And they both have a temporal component. We all know that the presence of noise gets progressively worse over time. Noise is stressful, and stress tends to accumulate. So too with glare, whether from an unrelenting fierce stare or unavoidably bright light. It can be ignored temporarily, but there are limits for how long we are willing to put up with it. An unacceptable duration of glare is likely determined not only by the intensity of the immediate glare source, but also by context, such as how tired or stressed we are, and how motivated we are too look.

Noise became an important concept in the early days of telephone development, as a problem that interfered with speech recognition. Without the additional visual information of a face to lip-read, people had more difficulty understanding speech over a telephone wire, and a little bit of random noise at the wrong time could degrade communication quickly. When we began to transmit digital data over the same telephone wires, the concept of noise was redefined to mean an 'error in the system,' i.e. random fluctuations of data that interfered with the perception of a meaningful signal.

The concept of the 'signal-to-noise ratio' became a common metaphor, and it clearly suggests that there are two choices to improve communications: either reduce the level of noise, or amplify the signal. It turns out that our brains are very good at doing that internally. This is the 'cocktail party effect' described earlier, where a partygoer can focus all of their auditory attention on a single conversation in a noisy room. The brain has remarkable ability to selectively focus on the stream of information that is most meaningful at the moment, discounting all other stimuli; 'tuning in' on a single voice and 'tuning out' all others.

Thus, a key question in evaluating noise is 'what is meaningful?' What one person considers to be noise, another may find meaningful. Acousticians have developed a concept of an environmental 'soundscape' which describes all elements of the acoustic environment, including human-generated sounds, mechanical and natural sources. But crucially, the concept also includes the listener's perception of the sounds, which adds the aspect of meaning, or saliency, to understanding the elements of a soundscape. Similarly, the visual environment might be understood as a 'view-scape,' including everything within view, but also identifying the visual information of greatest interest.

To summarize, the concept of noise cannot be understood without an understanding the motivation to listen. Similarly, glare cannot be understood without an understanding of the motivation to look. So, the question naturally arises, what motivates us to look out of a window? And, are some views more motivating that others?

Glare Illusions

Mark Changazi, a theoretical neurobiologist who has written about visual perception in his book *The Vision Revolution*, proposed a very different approach to understanding discomfort glare.[15] He hypothesized that discomfort glare maybe largely a learned conditioned response to a type of visual image; in other words, a Pavlovian response. He illustrates this by showing a picture of a cityscape with a hazy sun in the sky. Part of the image is washed out around the sun, as if that area of our vision were bleached out. The photograph is indeed discomforting to look at, even though the image of the sun and its glaring halo is physically no brighter than the rest of the white paper surrounding the photograph.

Some other researchers at the Vision Sciences Laboratory at Harvard University[16] took this idea a step further in a lab study and gave their study subjects a variety of slide images to look at while they measured instantaneous changes in their subject's eyes, such as pupil diameter. Images included photographs of a romantic couple looking out towards a glowing red sunset, with and without the orb of the sun present. The study subjects' pupil diameters immediately constricted within a second of exposure to the images with the sun in view, and then gradually recovered over the next two seconds. The response was much less pronounced for the other image without a sun, as might be expected in an unconscious response to the threat of glare. They tried the same sequence with a set of very simple line-drawing cartoons, with and without the sun in the picture, and found a similar, through reduced, pattern of response. Clearly an image of the sun was causing an automatic glare response, even when the picture was not realistic.

The Harvard group then used a technique common to vision science researchers who are trying to understand cognitive processing: they tested with same images, but presented upside down, in order to see if orientation influenced the pupillary response. The simple answer is that it did: there was very little response, if any, to the upside-down images, even though the luminous patterns were statistically the same.

The Harvard researchers noted it was clearly not the overall brightness, nor the pattern of brightness in the image, that was eliciting the pupil response, since the inverted images had the same illuminance statistics as the upright images. *"This difference in luminance predicted that image onsets would trigger pupil dilations, but we observed the opposite pattern,"* they wrote, and went on to conclude that *"high-level [cognitive] visual processing of scenes underlie these findings"* and *"the sun and inversion effect point to a high-level influence of scene perception and object processing."* In other words, the content of the image matters greatly, and is being processed very quickly, at a subconscious level, as indicated by the instantaneous pupillary response.

On the one hand, we might think of these experiments as demonstrating 'glare illusions,' i.e. our brains are reacting to an image as if it were glaring, when light measurements indicate it should not be glaring according to accepted equations. Why should the orientation of an image influence our glare assessment? But, if instead, glare is a function of our interest in the image, then it makes sense that the more interesting the image, the more *salient* the content, then the more glare is an issue. Just as with noise at a cocktail party, glare might be less or more annoying, depending on how interested we are in looking.

Gaze Direction

So, we might ask, *"How interesting is a view?"* That question can be partially answered by observing how much time people naturally spend looking out a window, as opposed to other possible directions. A group of researchers at Switzerland's EPFL and Germany's Fraunhofer Institute set out to observe where study subjects looked within a simple daylit office setting while performing a sequence of common office tasks. One of their study objectives was to test if a prediction of discomfort glare should include a factor for gaze direction, such that people might be less likely to look towards a more glaring window. In order to monitor the direction of people's gaze within three-dimensional space they used a wearable head and eye tracking system which *"minimally limits the participant's movements and allows for natural exploration of the scene."*[17]

The Fraunhofer test room was outfitted to resemble a small single-person office. The test subjects sat in a standard mobile office chair facing a computer screen on a desk set perpendicular to a large window on their left. The window view looked out over a mixed-use urban environment, with some trees in the midground, and sky occupying the upper two-thirds of the view area—an exceedingly normal urban view. The windows were double-glazed with a medium tinted glass. The tests were conducted during the spring months in Germany, with many overcast days. Furthermore, the Fraunhofer test room, up on the roof of a building, could rotate! So, for the first study, the window orientation was rotated as needed to avoid any direct sunlight into the space. Therefore, for this study, glare from direct sunlight was never an issue, and no blinds or shades that would encumber the view were used during the tests.

A group of 23 participants were asked to perform a series of three tasks, given in random order. One task was completely computer-based, one was paper-based, and one was conducted over a telephone. Each task involved four phases: one minute was allotted to explain the task; two minutes to think about the task; one minute was allotted to learn about the task; two minutes to think about the task; one minute to perform the task; and three minutes to provide an evaluation of the task. The researchers wanted to know precisely wherein the room people would spend the most time looking during each phase of the tasks.

Overall, the head and eye tracking showed that the participants spent just over half of their time looking straight ahead, i.e. towards the wall perpendicular to the window and within 15 degrees of the center of the computer screen. Using round numbers, they also spent about half of their time looking away from that center line, of which 40% was looking more towards the window and 10% was looking in the other direction, away from the window. Notably, the subjects were almost always looking straight ahead during the computer-based tasks, whereas the phone-based task was the most variable in view direction, and the paper-based task was somewhere in between. The most striking exception to this observation occurred during the 'thinking' phase of the computer-based task, when more than half of the view directions were out towards the view, and none were in the opposite direction.

The research team then conducted a second set of tests, this time with many more subjects, and also while sometimes allowing sunlight into the space. Again, they found the data during the thinking-phase of the computer-based task was most interesting, when people were processing information but not tied to performing a visual task with a fixed location. During this thinking phase, people oriented their gaze towards the window in 82% of the trials, on average about 20 degrees off of the center line. And in 36% of those trails participants' heads fully rotated towards the window. Similarly, in all four phases of the telephone-based task, the patterns of gaze orientation looked very similar to the 'thinking' phase of the screen-based task. In other words, despite the constraints of the tasks, people tended to look out the window whenever they could.

The researchers were not able to confirm their original hypothesis that discomfort glare metrics should include a factor for gaze direction. Instead, they noted that: *"The results show that the 'view outside the window' is the main determinant of gaze direction whenever the participant is not focused on a cognitive or visual office task procedure.*" They did notice a slight effect of sunlight on the direction of gaze: when the orb of the sun was in the field of view, people tended to avert their gaze slightly, looking more straight ahead and glancing out of the window less. However, even when sunlight illuminated the view, brightened the opposite wall, or fell on the desk surface, it had little effect on people's gaze direction: they still tended to look out of the window more often than not. Not unlike the mind wandering studies discussed earlier, people were observed to spend much more time gazing out a window then initially expected.

There are many other interesting details to be learned from this method of study, of simply observing what humans naturally do under a wide variety of design conditions. It may be that such observational studies can provide better insight into how we react to our visual environment, and thus help to develop a better theory about glare and visual comfort, correlated to task, motivation, attention, cognitive function, and perhaps also daydreaming.[18]

Now that we have a wider vocabulary to discuss sunlight and daylight, color, shadow, sparkle, and glare, let's take a deeper dive into the dynamics of daylight as a source of illumination, and the many different ways that daylight can be used as a fundamental design element in the design of buildings.

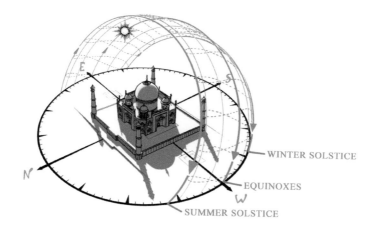

WINTER SOLSTICE

EQUINOXES

SUMMER SOLSTICE

8. Designing with Daylight

Utilizing daylight to illuminate our buildings is one of the most locally appropriate things we can do, intimately connecting the experience of the inside of the building with its geographical and cultural location. Learning to design with daylight should begin with mastering solar movements, understanding how seasonal changes impact the angle of sunlight and shadows, the timing of sunrise and sunset, and the duration of twilight. But the designer should quickly progress to an awareness of regional weather patterns, such as how cloud formations and humidity influence daylight quality, how nearby bodies of water, mountains, forests, and deserts change the mix, and how local traditions of building form and materials also modulate people's experience of daylight, and thus their sense of place. Together, this is a powerful well of knowledge that designers can bring to their work, whether it is at the scale of urban planning, building design or interior furnishings.

There are many wonderful books written about lighting design. They are mostly written for interior designers and electrical engineers, in order to help them learn how to select, place and control electric lighting fixtures. In general, these books assume that the architecture of the place—its volumes, its surfaces, the spatial organization of tasks and activities—are predetermined. This is because lighting designers and electrical engineers are often the last professionals to join a design team, and thus, their work primarily responds to the work of others who have already 'set the stage,' so to speak. Indeed, many lighting designers first fell in love with lighting design as a profession via the theater, where working inside the completely black-box of the theater building, they were asked to imagine a lighting scene that would bring to life the playwright's fictional worlds, full of drama, surprise, and emotional power.

In the vast majority of lighting design books, daylighting is an afterthought, at best deserving a chapter, more often just a few paragraphs. It is most often portrayed as a *problem* to be addressed by the lighting designer, especially to avoid glare or too much energy waste, rather than as an opportunity. Daylight is very rarely portrayed as a design element that the lighting designer can purposefully manipulate to improve the lighting quality of a space.

There are far fewer books to date that attempt to teach the art of daylighting to designers. Daylight is not as easy to control as electric light—it cannot be turned on at will. Daylight is like a wild animal that follows its own whims, caring nothing for our schedules and habits. If we want to work with daylight as a design element, we must understand its native habits.

I think one of the most basic design concepts to understand about daylight is that it is big. VERY BIG! We can choose to let little bits of daylight permeate our buildings, but there is always more outside, waiting to come in: an atmospheric ocean of light. By adding more holes in our buildings, like a colander, daylight will fill the space within, as big as we want it to be. Actually, the bigger the volume of a space, the easier it is to daylight.

One of my early introductions to daylighting design was via William Lam. I was freshly graduated from architecture school, and had the privilege of interviewing him for a 1980 magazine article on how daylight, as one form of solar energy, could be used to save energy.[1] At the time, Lam was already a famous electric lighting designer in Cambridge, Massachusetts, but in the spirit of the times, he had recently become an outspoken advocate for restoring the primacy of daylight in our buildings.

Working with physical models, long before the age of computer visualization tools, he took these scale models, built of white foam core, outside in order to use real skies and real sunlight as the light sources. A little sundial mounted on the base enabled the model to be physically rotated in space to create the correct solar angles for any time of year. A small porthole in the model let Lam and his team directly observe, photograph, and measure the resulting illumination patterns. Because light scales perfectly, this worked well, and will still work well for anyone who wants to try it. Eventually, he summarized his investigations in a wonderful book, *Sunlighting as a Formgiver for Architecture,* full of case studies, details, and tips.[2]

In his book, Lam argued that the *form* of the building should be the essential determinant of lighting quality. This is a challenging paradigm shift for thinking about daylighting design. What if light determined the form of the building, rather than vice versa? What if electric lighting was considered merely supplemental to daylight? It would be as if you were designing an outdoor patio for family parties—logically you would not expect electric lighting to be used outdoors during the daytime! Rather, electric lighting would be a system that could extend the use of the patio at the end of twilight and through the night, however long the party lasted. Interior spaces can be similarly conceived, with the presumption that they will be awash in a sea of atmospheric daylight while it is available, and then supplemented with electric light when needed to extend the period of human activity.

Solar Geometry

Lam's 'sunlighting' design approach relied on a deep understanding of solar position in relationship to building form and openings. Most children gain an early intuitive understanding that the sun moves around, a lot! However, they generally have to be taught that it always rises in the east, sets in the west, and it is overhead at noon. Beyond that, few people learn the fundamentals of solar movement, even though the hourly position of the sun in the sky is absolutely predictable. Indeed, solar geometry was originally mastered in Neolithic times!

Every window and skylight in a building creates an opportunity for a form of sundial, defining a discreet sun patch that will move about the room in a completely predictable pattern. You could paint lines on the floor that point out: "*The edge of the sun patch will be right here at 3:30 pm on my birthday!*" In my own house, I have a west-facing window at the top of the stairs. Twice every year, there is a magic hour when the sunlight perfectly aligns with the angle of the stairway, highlighting the edge of each oak tread and setting the whole stairwell aglow in golden light.

Understanding the geographical relationships between season, time of day, orientation, and altitude of the sun can help inform a designer's decisions about where to put windows, or when to choose skylights over windows. A designer can know exactly when a window will let sunshine into the building, or instead enable building occupants to look out onto a sunlit landscape. The quality of a given view is hugely dependent upon the quality of daylight outside, and especially the angle of the sun. Although a north-facing window (in the northern hemisphere) receives little sunlight, it will usually look out onto a brightly sunlit landscape. In contrast, a south-facing window may receive a great deal of sunlight, especially in the winter, but its view will be primarily out towards shadows and silhouettes. East- and west-facing windows take turns acting like north or south-facing windows: half the day they receive sun while looking out at shadows, then for the other half they are protected from the sun while looking towards a sunlit landscape. (Figure 7.2 illustrates the timing of illumination from the sun versus from the sky, by window orientation.)

On just two special days per year, once at spring equinox and once at fall equinox, the sun rises directly to the east and sets directly to the west, *everywhere* in the world. Other than those two days, the apparent direction of sunrise and sunset depend primarily upon where the observer is located on the planet between the north and south poles, i.e. the latitude above or below the equator. This angle of the sun, relative to true north across a horizontal plane, is called the solar azimuth angle. The other half of the equation is solar altitude angle, how high the sun is above that horizontal plane. From this information, we can easily predict, at any location at any given hour, how much sun could strike the surface of any window or skylight (weather permitting). Fortunately, we now have wonderful graphic tools and even animated aides, that are widely published in books and online to help people predict exactly where the sun will be in the sky on any given hour of any given day.[3]

While solar geometry can be calculated with great precision, it is also useful to develop an *intuitive* understanding of where the sun will be throughout the year. Try this exercise from your home, and then a few other places around town, and you'll soon be able to approximate solar locations throughout the year.[4]

Start by facing true south (or true north in the southern hemisphere), and stretch your arms out due east and west. Now point your right hand due south and up towards the position of the sun at noon on equinox (90 degrees minus your latitude). Bring your left hand up to the same position and then let your right hand return to pointing due west. You have just traced the arch of the sun on equinox.

Repeat the process for winter (and summer) solstice: the noon altitude will be 23.5 degrees lower (higher) than equinox noon. Winter sunrise and sunset locations depend on your latitude, both equally closer towards (farther from) the equator. (For example, in San Francisco at 37 degrees latitude, the sun will rise and set 30 degrees farther south at the winter solstice, and farther north at the summer solstice). While you do this exercise with your arms, note some landmarks on your horizon. Then over the course of the coming year, observe how daily sunrise and sunset locations progress around those landmarks.

I like to simplify the consideration of solar altitude into three sky bands: a low range from 0 to 30 degrees above the horizon, the mid-range from 30 to 60 degrees, and the highest range from 60 to 90 degrees. (A simple mental trick to imagine these angles is to visualize a 90 degree right angle, then divide it into three equal parts, each 30 degrees.)

When the sun is below 30 degrees of altitude it can be quite bothersome. It is usually below the brim of a hat, and likewise, it is difficult to shade a window from such low sun angles: any shading device would have to be more than twice as long as the window is tall. For example, a four-foot high window would need more than an eight-foot deep overhang! Thus, solar altitudes below 30 degrees are extremely problematic for glare-free window design. Often the best solution for these low solar angles is a vertical obstruction, such as another building, a fence, vegetation, or steeply angled awning or louver blocking a direct view of the sun.

The opposite is true when the sun is above 60 degrees, where the reverse formula applies: a four-foot high window only needs a two-foot wide overhang or less. Furthermore, for most people, the sun at 60 degrees above the horizon is outside of their normal field of view, with their eyebrows shading their eyes from the sun high overhead.

The middle sky band, between 30 and 60 degrees, in between these two conditions, constitutes the majority of the architectural design challenge, of how to take advantage of sunlight while avoiding its discomforts. We will delve more deeply into strategies for this middle band later in this chapter in the section on curtains, blinds, shades, and shutters.

Twilight and Nightfall

Solar geometry and timing also determine the duration of twilight and the qualities of shadows. In the tropics, sunsets are brief, ten minutes or less, and twilight does not linger long. The walls of a building are illuminated by low sun for only a few hours in morning and evening. Throughout the middle of the day, shadows are compact and directly underfoot: hats, parasols, and overhead shading work very well to protect people from the glare and heat of the sun. The contrast between sun and shadow is intense. Shadows are not filled in with much reflected light, since reflections primarily bounce upward, from paving and other horizontal surfaces, and either quickly hit another built surface or return to the sky.

Farther north (or south), on the other hand, twilight has a major presence. In the temperate climates of Southern Europe and most of the United States, at 40 to 50 degrees latitude, twilight, i.e. from sunset to the full darkness of night, lasts for two hours. In many Northern European cities, above 60 degrees latitude, twilight can last from 3.5 hours in the winter to literally all night long in the summer. Colors shift as twilight deepens, but ever so gradually.

Those long, slow mornings and evenings of Northern Europe are also accompanied by lots of low, slanting sunlight, highlighting vertical tree trunks and building façades, and very long shadows, that reach far down the block, or even out of sight. The low sunlight grazes horizontal surfaces, highlighting the textures of fields, isolating a few feathery grass heads in the light, and silhouetting distant trees against the bright horizon. The very low angle sunlight can also reflect off of wet roadways or snow fields, creating vast glaring surfaces. But these glancing reflections also provide a great deal of inter-reflected light, softening shadows and adding complexity to the color of light as it bounces off so many different surfaces. The daylight progression in these regions, from long afternoon shadows to soft twilight glow, is a long drawn out affair. Our eyes have far more time than their necessary 40 minutes to adjust to full night vision.

In my own experience, operating a daylit office building for my consulting company, many of my employees would continue to work under the fading light of twilight, with no additional electric lighting, long after interior illumination levels had plunged far below any levels recommended in standard practice. The slow progression of twilight seemed to aide their adaptation to ever lower illumination levels. Finally, making a move to turn on the overhead lights was a critical decision point, usually perceived as a commitment to keep working for another hour or so.

The so-called 'magic hour,' when indoor lighting and outdoor daylight are nearly balanced is a favorite of architectural photographers. They can then take pictures where building interiors and exteriors are both illuminated within the dynamic range of the printed image. Electric lighting is seen to sparkle and add a presence beyond sky and shadows. Because of this visual balance, many published photographs of daylit buildings are taken at this time, but if so, they do not fully represent the qualities of daylight in the buildings. Humans seem to be especially drawn to images of sunsets and twilight, as if the ineffable shifts in the color of light add a living quality to each image.

The experience of daylight is certainly enhanced by its opposite, the darkness of night. However, in most modern cities, as the daylight dims, the electric lights gradually increase their presence, almost like the stars coming out for the nighttime. Over the past century, just as we have erased the presence of daylight in our buildings, we have erased the presence of moonlight and starlight in our cities. Generations of modern urbanites have grown so accustomed to the omnipresence of electric lighting that they have difficulty noticing the phases of the moon. On a full-moon night, the illumination from the moon can extend twilight conditions through the night, even in the tropics. However, the difference between a night with a full moon versus a new moon will be lost on someone walking in a brightly lit city, where the streetlights are far brighter than the moon. The full moon, alone up in the sky, casts crisp singular shadows, but the new LED streetlights can shatter shadows into dozens of overlapping bits, challenging the congruity of an outdoor nighttime experience. (One wonders if all those romantic songs, about a lover's face lit so brightly by the 'Moon in June,' will make any sense to future generations.)

Regional Light

In addition to the timing of sunrise, sunset, and twilight, and the relative angles of the sun, there are many other factors that contribute to a regional sense of light. Every region has specific weather patterns, humidity, turbidity, thermal inversions and stratifications, and sources of reflection that make the quality of its daylight unique, and uniquely memorable for its residents.

The snow and ice in the wintery north increase solar reflections, and create a stark visual contrast between the bright white ground and everything else. The cold air squeezes out most humidity, adding crispness to the sunlight. On sunny days in the far north, or high up in cold mountains, the sky opposite the sun is the deepest blue, with little atmospheric turbidity to return reflected light.

In the warm summertime, and near the ocean, higher humidity layers tend to soften the sunlight, while simultaneously brightening the diffuse light from the sky. More daylight is returned from the sky opposite the sun, adding highlights in the shadows and softening the shadow's edges. Adding the sun's heat to humid air creates active cloud formations that rise and fall with the day's weather. The clouds throughout the narrow Italian peninsula, framed by oceans on two sides, are some of the most beautiful I have ever seen, lofty and billowing, misty and amorphous all at the same time. Tall clouds can add a new directionality to daylight, creating a huge white wall reflecting sunlight back in the opposite direction. These Italian masterpieces of clouds were clearly an inspiration for the work of so many renaissance painters.

In drier southern climates, the air may alternate between intensely clear, or filled with dust kicked up by windstorms. The deserts of the American Southwest are legendary for the clarity of their daylight: there are the crystal-clear days where landscape details and colors are just as intense far away as they are close up. On such days, atmospheric perspective has no hold: distant mesas are just as red as those nearby, distant trees vibrate with color and detail, and layers of precisely defined clouds recede towards an infinite horizon. The American painter Georgia O'Keefe beautifully portrayed the colors and clarity of these Southwestern landscapes.

On the other side of the world, architect Davidson Norris meticulously studied the 'light of place' in Jerusalem, Israel.[5] Norris realized that Jerusalem sits right at the intersection of a humid body of air influenced by the Mediterranean Sea and the dry Arabian desert to the east. Clouds often roll in from the sea to the west, and quickly evaporate, disappearing directly overhead, as they encounter the dry desert air from the east, sometimes creating a high wall of dramatically lit cloud banks right at the edge of the city.

With the eye of both a technician and an artist, he described the impact of this collision of atmospheric effects on the perception of the humans below: in the morning the sun rises unambiguously, but tinged a soft gold, through a slightly dusty horizon, "*a perfect white gold circle at the center of a radiating red/yellow gold field ... In contrast, the white light of the midday sun is intense, relentless, and inescapable.*" The brilliance of the sun is partly amplified by the dust particles suspended in the desert air, which: "*scatter incident noonday light forwards and backwards, creating a diffuse light that is omnidirectional, uniform and shadowless. This scattered and intense light fills space around Jerusalem volumetrically, delivering ... overlapping veils of light. These confound the edges of things, making it difficult to perceive form, discern color and judge depth.*"

Norris divided his study into two concerns, which he called primordial light and anthropogenic light: "*Primordial light was a product of the sun and the sky, atmospheric and optical interactions with the climate, geology, landscape and vegetation that define the city's broader natural environment. Anthropogenic light resulted from interactions with the city's public space, buildings, streets and building materials, all products of human enterprise.*"

Thus, he found that it was not only weather and landscape, but also the physical shape and materials of the city that generated the unique daylight qualities of Jerusalem. The blue-gray paving stones of the old city reflected the sky upwards, while the ubiquitous golden stone of the city walls intensified the horizontal component of the warmer-colors of sunrise and sunset.

The distinctive daylight conditions of the American Pacific Northwest region are wonderfully documented in a book by Kevin Van den Wymelenberg and Christopher Meek, wherein they also discuss case-study buildings that take full advantage of the region's light.[6] Because of the region's dramatic topography, with multiple high mountain ranges and huge inland bodies of water, the weather conditions of the Pacific Northwest vary dramatically and can change radically within a few miles. Locations around the coastal waterways tend to have a high percentage of overcast skies, while 'rain shadows' are created east of the coastal mountain ranges, resulting in more sunny days and drier weather inland.

a letter, most likely from a suitor, in the light near a multi-pane window. The artist faithfully portrayed the illumination provided by the windows, set into thick masonry walls, typical of an old Dutch home. The horizontal flow of light first highlights vertical surfaces, such as the girl's face, the wall behind her, and the curtains hanging between her and the viewer, and then reflects around the room, softening shadows. The shadows are deepest around the window.

Contrast Glare

Vermeer's painting illustrates the common problem of contrast glare. In the very same scene, had the artist been looking perpendicular to the window, rather than parallel to its surface, the girl would have been in deep silhouette and the bright window would have created strong visual contrast with the shadowy wall around it. The window enclosure, its sill and jambs receive the most daylight, while the wall adjacent receives the least. Any illumination from the window has to first bounce all around the room and its furnishings before returning to that wall, greatly diminished in power. Thus, a single window, one hole in a wall, can be a source of visual discomfort, a.k.a. glare, due to the visual contrast between the bright opening and the darker wall surrounding it.

Electric lighting designers fret a great deal about this problem. They tend to think of windows as the source of the problem, rather than the solution to the problem. I have seen far too many electric lighting designs where additional light sources are placed on or above the wall next to the windows to try to combat this excessive contrast. The hope is that the additional electric light will brighten the shadows and reduce the contrast and visual discomfort. The reality is that when the window is at its brightest, creating the most contrast with ambient lighting conditions, it can overpower any electric light source, which looks simply feeble in comparison.

The problem of extreme visual contrasts created by punched windows, i.e. those set into the middle of walls, is especially common in sidelit office spaces, where deep spaces and low ceilings reduce the amount of interreflections and further decrease the amount of daylight which returns to brighten the wall holding the windows. One commonly employed solution, which involves changing the design of the windows, not the electric lighting, is to make the windows bigger. Strip windows, i.e. those that run continuously along a wall, avoid the dark corners, since there is no longer any opaque wall between each window opening, as there is with punched windows. Curtain walls, i.e. floor to ceiling window systems that fill in the entire exterior wall, reduce the problem even more, not only by removing all the opaque wall area that would remain in shadow, but also by bringing the daylight from the window to the very edges of the room. The perpendicular walls at either end of the curtain wall, plus the floor and ceiling surfaces, now act like a giant sill and jamb, reflecting the daylight deeper into the space and reducing the visual contrast of the window surround. The huge glazing areas of curtain walls can create other building performance problems, but they do help to solve the visual contrast problem that punched windows create.

However, there are also many more economical daylighting strategies that take advantage of daylighting's power to solve the problem of contrast glare. I encountered a classic sidelighting visual discomfort problem in one of the classrooms we studied as part of our daylight evaluation project. As part of a project to develop a new set of daylight metrics, I arranged for a troop of daylighting experts to travel around the country evaluating the daylight quality in a wide variety of daylit spaces.[8]

There was one classroom that got the worst visual comfort ratings of all the 61 spaces that we evaluated during that trip. It was a very typical portable classroom, with the teaching wall in the center of the long south wall. The narrow east end had one door and a small window looking out to the paved playground, and at the west end was another small window, looking out to some tall evergreen trees. The classroom had absolutely standard overhead fluorescent lighting, which provided decently uniform lighting at prescribed levels throughout the classroom.

It was the little windows that were the problem. In the morning, the east-facing window brought in sunlight and glare bouncing off the pavement, and in the afternoon, the west window brought in streaks of sunlight that made it through the trees. At the same time, the non-sunlit window looked out onto a bright sunlit landscape. Either way the windows were too bright for the ambient levels in the room, and they made the adjacent walls seem dark and dingy in comparison. My troop of experts all agreed that our eyes would get very tired adjusting back and forth between the bright windows and the darker walls.

A common solution might have been to try to make the walls brighter, with more electric lights directed at the two side walls, or to make the windows darker, with a tinted film or screen, or to block them completely with curtains or artwork. But a far better solution was available for study right next door. This school, in Auburn, California, had recently agreed to be a study site for an experimental daylighting retrofit, where six small tubular skylights (14" in diameter) had been retrofitted into the ceiling with optical diffusers which spread the daylight broadly. Under overcast conditions, these six skylights provided uniform daylight illumination levels similar to the electric lighting, and in sunlight they provided even more. Nothing else in the classroom was changed, so the two sister classrooms made a perfect side-by-side comparison.

When the group of daylighting experts went next door into the classroom with skylights, they gave it an excellent rating, with very little probability of glare; and yet the window configuration, the source of the glare in the first classroom, were identical! The key difference was that, when the windows were very bright, so were the skylights. The skylights allowed the illumination in the room to rise and fall with the outdoor daylight conditions, naturally adjusting ambient illumination levels. The essential problem with the glary windows in the first classroom was not so much that the windows were too bright, but rather that the room was too dark.

The two teachers, when interviewed, agreed that the classroom with the retrofitted skylights was superior. The teacher with no skylights had requested they be added to her classroom too. The teacher with the skylights reported that since the retrofit she rarely turned on the electric lights; that she and her students had become used to the fluctuating daylight levels throughout the day; and they found the dynamics of the daylight both calming and invigorating.

It turns out the best way to balance the visual conditions in a daylit room is usually with more daylight. That is because the daylight is always in sync with itself.

Light from Two Sides

Christopher Alexander, the architectural theorist who wrote *A Pattern Language*, gave each one of the many patterns in his book a succinct and descriptive name. One of the most memorable patterns, one that many people have quoted back to me, is called "*Light from Two Sides*," which postulates that to be successful, a well-daylit room should have windows positioned on at least two different walls.

Alexander explains his rationale for this pattern: "*This pattern, perhaps more than any other single pattern, determines the success or failure of a room. The arrangement of daylight in a room, and the presence of windows on two sides, is fundamental. If you build a room with light on one side only, you can be almost certain that you are wasting your money. People will stay out of that room if they can possibly avoid it. The importance of this pattern lies partly in the social atmosphere it creates in the room. Rooms lit on two sides, with natural light, create less glare around people and objects; this lets us see things more intricately; and most important, it allows us to read in detail the minute expressions that flash across people's faces ... and thereby understand, more clearly, the meaning they are after. The light on two sides allows people to understand each other.*"[9]

A classically trained photographer would translate this concept into 'fill light,' meaning that the second window, like a photographer's secondary light, provides illumination from a different direction, gently brightening the shadows created by the first. The magic of daylight is that this always works, because the intensity of the light from the two windows rises and falls in relationship to each other as the day progresses.

There are other design strategies that also involve taking advantage of the power of daylight, rather than trying to fight it. For example, a three-dimensional object placed next to a punched window—not in front of it, but next to it— will pick up and reflect some of the daylight spilling beyond the width of the window. The object, which could be a potted plant or a sculptural form, is then also more interesting to look at and a bit brighter than the shadowed wall behind. Therefore, the eye sees less contrast, and the window becomes less glaring.

Another trick is to visually soften the edges of the window, with elaborately shaped moldings, gauzy curtains, or perforated vertical blinds. If the surfaces immediately adjacent to the window are painted white, they will both help to redirect more of the daylight in multiple directions, softening the shadows in the room, and also create a brighter and wider visual frame around the window. A white visual frame around a window view is much like a traditional white matt around a photograph, or the white margins around the edge of a printed page, providing the eye with a place to rest before returning to consider the information embedded in the view.

Blinds and louvers can also help to redirect some of the daylight, creating a secondary direction of daylight within the room. With vertical blinds, some daylight can be redirected sideways, while with horizontal blinds, some daylight can be redirected upward or downwards. All of these design strategies work to improve the daylighting conditions and visual comfort within a room without significantly reducing the amount of daylight illumination.

The simplest rule of thumb for lighting design is: "*Put the light where you want people to look.*" People are naturally phototropic. Their eyes are drawn to the brightest object in sight. Thus, an electric lighting designer will often focus spotlights to highlight a painting, a sculpture, or a gorgeous vase of flowers in a room. In a well-daylit room, it is often the window view that is the most attractive thing to look at. Thus, allowing the window view to be brighter than other surfaces in the room is not just acceptable, but is expected by occupants who want to look at the view. A well-daylit space with a gorgeous view will bathe the view window in a balance of daylight that perfectly frames it, while allowing the view to shine as the key visual feature of the space.

A Well-Daylit Space

The question naturally comes up, how to describe a well-daylit space? Christopher Alexander thinks that it must have 'light from two sides,' which indeed will certainly help to balance the patterns of daylight and shadows in a room. He describes a space where people naturally prefer to be. In the daylight metrics project mentioned earlier,[10] undertaken to help inform a new generation of daylight performance metrics for the Illuminating Engineering Society, our study team visited a wide variety of daylit spaces and asked the occupants a number of questions to describe their visual comfort. Similar to Alexander, occupants were asked to agree or disagree with the holistic statement "*I enjoy being in this room.*" But we also asked them to rate statements like "*I find this room visually attractive*," "*I like the view I have from the window*," and "*The lighting conditions are always comfortable.*"

Part of the study protocol was to observe each room under purely daylight conditions, with all of the electric lights turned off, and preferably, with the occupants still actively at work. Turning off the electric lights was often one of the most challenging parts of the site visits. One of the early site visits was to a lovely Carnegie Library in San Francisco, built in the Classic Revival style of the 1920s. It had a large reading room with huge arched windows on all four sides. The famous fog of the Sunset District, and some tall neighboring buildings, kept those big windows free from direct sunlight for much of the year, but operable shades could also be lowered when needed.

On the midweek afternoon of the site visit, the reading room was full of library patrons, searching the stacks for books and occupying almost every table and cushioned chair provided. Our traveling study team wanted to observe the reading room under purely daylight conditions and to take a few illuminance measurements and HDR photographs, but the three librarians were adamant that they did not want to disturb the occupants by turning off the electric lights. We asked if they had ever worked in the library under purely daylit conditions, and interestingly, the librarians reported that just the previous week, while the library was full of patrons, there had been a series of power outages that lasted for an hour or more. The librarians had been flustered that they could not use their computers to check out books and had to revert to writing everything down by hand. "*But,*" we asked, "*did the patrons have to leave the library?*" Oh, no, they explained, there were no immediate safety issues and there was still plenty of light. So, thinking quickly, we suggested that we conduct a little experiment: we could briefly turn off the lights and just pretend that the library was having another power outage. We would turn off the lights for a maximum of ten minutes, and if anyone complained, we could turn them back on sooner.

Our team of eight daylighting experts dispersed through the reading room, ready to take light-level readings and observe patrons' reactions as the overhead lights were switched off. When we switched off the electricity, the horizontal illumination levels instantly dropped from about 500 lux to 200. But none of the patrons seemed to notice. No one paused what they were doing, or looked up, or looked concerned in any way. It was a remarkable lack of response. The librarians were impressed, but still feeling insecure, were happy to have their lights turned back on quickly as promised. Again, no one commented or seemed to notice. I've since come to consider this the acid test of a fully daylight space—if you can turn off the electric lights and no one complains, or seems to even notice, you can probably consider that space well-daylit.

The search is still on for quantitative metrics that can capture all the qualities of a well-daylit space. Jan Vermeer did a good job of visually rendering the feeling of a well-daylit space in his painting of the *Girl Reading a Letter at an Open Window*. However, today we also need quantitative metrics that will help guide computer analysis and set performance criteria for codes, standards, and product development.[11] So, for example, the Illuminating Engineering Society has a standing committee that is tasked with developing a suite of metrics that eventually will fully describe the qualities of a well-daylit space.

Electric Lighting for Daylit Spaces

Even the most beautifully illuminated daylit space will still need some electric lighting if it is to be used at nighttime. It makes perfect sense to design an electric lighting system that can function independently when there is no daylight available. However, such a lighting design might be very different than one conceived for a room that is used only during the day. Task and timing should determine the design. For example, imagine a family room that is used for many purposes at different times of the evening and night. For hosting a party, when company is visiting, children are playing and conversations are lively, you might want to have lots of electric lights on to make the room almost as bright as daytime, but later on, for a private conversation between two people, a soft warm light from a single lamp might set a better ambience. Even later, after bedtime, a minimal amber glow of a night light might be sufficient to allow safe navigation through the room. It is not hard to imagine many other purposes—watching TV, reading a book, playing a board game, sewing a quilt— that might benefit from very different illumination conditions within the same room.

Electric lighting is extremely good at providing this degree of variety via different types of light fixtures, in different locations around the room, each of which can be switched on or off at will. Newer LED lighting adds even more advantages—tiny sources that can be tucked away in unobtrusive locations, such as underneath a cabinet, or a tiny book light that moves with the book. LEDs can be so small that they can easily be powered by a long-life battery, untethering them from the electric wires in the walls. LEDs can also be easily dimmed, allowing the user to adjust the light output to just the right amount needed. This kind of mobile light source is often called 'task lighting' because it is used only when and where needed by a particular task. My favorite task light is on my sewing machine, providing a tiny spot of bright light exactly where I need it to keep my stitches aligned. What a wonderful invention!

Perhaps the ultimate example of task lighting for my generation was the refrigerator light: that little light which was magically always on when you opened the refrigerator door. As children we deeply pondered the mysterious question: "*Does the refrigerator light stay on when the door is closed?*" Short of trying to climb inside of the refrigerator, which was fortunately too cold and too small, we could not think of a good way to find out. Of course, there was a simple mechanical switch controlled by the movement of the door. Now we have remote sensors that detect our presence via heat, sound, motion, or a Bluetooth signal, and which can then be programmed to turn lights on or off as needed. In the future, smart electric lighting will surely continue to evolve, allowing us to have infinitely responsive electric lighting, always just the right color, intensity, and timing for our varied needs.

I gave some thought to how daylight might be similarly responsive, and realized that daylight is really the antithesis of electric lighting and that the two should be appreciated for their differences. Whereas LED light sources can be tiny, daylight is always big. Whereas LED light sources can be aimed where needed, and turned on and off at will, rather like a flashlight, daylight follows its own planetary schedule. Whereas a person can position a little LED light wherever it may be needed, with daylight people need to move to where the daylight is available. Another important distinction is that, while daylight cannot be *turned on*, it can be *dimmed or turned off*. We often use sunglasses, hats, umbrellas, black-out curtains, blinds, or shades to control daylight. Thus, while we don't have something called task daylighting, we do have lots of forms of task shadowing.

This train of thought presents a slightly different way to think about electric lighting and daylighting design: electric lights are something that you can turn up when it is too dark, and daylight is something you can turn down when it is too bright. Electric lighting is a light source that you can move around within a space, bringing it as close as needed for highlighting one area or task. The source of daylighting, on the other hand, is always far away. Instead, we move things and ourselves into the daylight. While electric lighting may enhance the quality of a space, the quality of daylight is determined *by* the design of the space. Where are the apertures? How high is the ceiling? The daylight design of interior space is a uniquely architectural creation.

Daylighting as the Default

One modern architect who has mastered artful daylighting is the Spanish architect, Salvatore Calatrava. I first experienced one of his designs at the airport in Bilbao, Spain. What struck me initially was the exuberance of structural elements shaping great vaulting roofs and colonnades. It took me a while to notice that there were no electric light fixtures in sight. Not one! Vast volumes of the terminal were all completely daylit, feeling as natural as a breath of fresh air. Calatrava has since completed many daring designs in Europe and America, such as the skeletal Oculus at the World Trade Center in New York City, and the bird-like Milwaukee Art Museum pavilion (see page 185). They all use repeating structural elements in a virtuoso symbiosis with daylighting design: the structure channels and diffuses the daylight, while the daylight reveals the beauty of the structure.

Today, electric lighting has become so pervasive that it is now used as a metaphor for human activity. "*We need to keep the lights on!*" people cry when economic activity weakens. "*Time to turn on the lights!*" is a metaphor for time to start the show, whether it is a private party or a public concert. Imagine instead a world where daylighting is the once again the default for the design of all spaces, just as it was not so very long ago, before the advent of the electric lighting. In such a world, people would expect days to be bright and nights to be dark, just as our circadian health requires.

If daylighting were the default condition for the interiors of buildings, it would be obvious to all that light is indeed a very dynamic environmental condition. Control of interior illumination would be far more subtle, not simply *on* or *off*, a dualistic 'yes/no' condition. Mechanisms for making adjustments for a little more task shadow, or a little more task lighting, would be so intuitively obvious that even a small child could easily understand how to do it.

Curtains, Blinds, Shades, and Shutters

I have always been fascinated by how many layers of daylight control are available for traditional windows in European cities, with five, seven, or even nine layers! Starting on the outside, there is often a balcony at each window, providing a carved balustrade or ornamental railing around the base of the window and an overhang above, plus there is likely to be an awning overhead and shutters to the side, or a security shutter that rolls down from the window head. Then paneled glass windows or doors swing out, with a secondary layer of storm sash or insect screens hinged separately inside. Then there might be a set of Venetian blinds and/or a gauzy curtain to provide some solar control while still allowing ventilation. Finally, a set of heavy velveteen drapes can be pulled to keep out unwanted light, or to add insulation at night. These traditional residential window coverings illustrate the huge array of filtering systems that might be considered for a window, impacting many dimensions of window performance, including blocking or redirecting sunlight, filtering daylight illumination intensity and color, view preservation and visual clarity, ventilation, air filtration, acoustics, privacy, security, ease of operation, and of course, aesthetics.

Over my career I have witnessed generations of new technologies, introduced with great fanfare, that promised to single-handedly meet all the diverse window performance needs. Durable and maintenance free! Privacy and transparency! Variable solar control! Automated operation! Dynamic windows which can change their properties as needed have been a holy grail for the window and glass industry for decades. We now also have companies striving to be the first to integrate novel electronics into windows, including photovoltaic solar electric cells, self-activated shading controls, integral illumination, decorative night lighting, and even exterior signage.

User Experience

Those small children we should use as our building beta-testers can quickly learn how to open a window or pull a curtain closed. On the other hand, it may require an expert programmer to fine tune the automated operation of an electrochromic window. All of these operations are included under the rubric of window management, i.e. operations that change the properties of a window or skylight, allowing in more or less sun, providing more or less privacy, ventilation, or view. Any window system than can be purposely changed over time needs some form of *user interface*, whether a simple manual device or a programable electronic control. Each type of interface facilitates some types of actions, by some groups of occupants, but may make others more difficult.

For example, my consulting company once did a side-by-side comparison, trying to understand user preferences for various types of window blinds and shades operation. We found an almost perfect study site—two office suites on the third and fourth floors of a building in San Francisco, with identical windows facing the same view of the harbor to the southeast.[12] We installed five different types of window treatments, each across multiple windows, and monitored their operation for six months. These included three types of mesh roller shades and two types of horizontal blinds. The mesh roller shades were either manually or automatically deployed downward from the top of the window (top-down), or manually pulled upwards from the bottom (bottom-up). The horizontal blinds were both manual, one a typical mini-blind with micro perforations, and the other had wide inverted slats, designed to reflect sunlight upward towards the ceiling. Even though the setting, windows, and climate were essentially identical, we found the operation of the five different systems were quite different, resulting in different energy impacts, and daylight and view availability. Most notably, the occupants left the bottom-up roller shades *open* more often than any of the top-down options. Why? One theory was that it took just a little more time and effort to pull the shades up than to let them down, and so the lower work-effort option prevailed.

Another key difference observed was between the occupants' view preferences on the two floors. One housed an architectural firm, with many visually oriented people. They generally loved their view and favored having the shades open as much as possible. The other housed a software company, full of computer programmers and administrators. The software engineers, especially, had no interest in the view. They kept their blinds closed at all times, and expressing annoyance when little bits of sunlight peeked through. Clearly, although the physical conditions were directly comparable, the social conditions were not.

Julia Day, of Washington State University, has conducted a number of field studies that explored the impacts of window management options, and how they determine occupant choices, behavior, and satisfaction. She made a few glaringly simple observations: if people can't easily reach the wand that controls the blinds, they will never adjust them.[13] She also studied three different types of automated window management systems—a horizontal louvered system, a mesh roller shade, and electrochromic glass, all with slightly different control algorithms and occupant override options. While all occupants complained somewhat about the automated control, in general, the closer they were to the windows, the happier they were, regardless of control type. The electrochromic windows notably had the most unhappy occupants, who complained of gloominess and a perpetual sense of an overcast sky. The other two systems were comparable at the front of the rooms, but the folks at the back of the room with mesh shades were happier.[14] (I would hypothesize this was because, from the back of the room, the sunlit mesh created a brighter upper horizon than the opaque inverted blinds.)

Long ago I postulated in the book *Thermal Delight in Architecture* that people tend to best understand and appreciate those aspects of a building which they can directly observe functioning and operate themselves. Drawing the curtains at a bedroom window is a very personal and expressive action, which may have many motivations, but will always put a person in a direct relationship with the window. Watching automated window shades lower, or electrochromic glazing slowly adjust in an office suite, may only reinforce a relationship with the window if that automated action is noticed, understood, and appreciated for improving comfort.[15] However, if the automated system is programmed to execute functions for which an occupant does not feel a direct need—such as improving the efficiency of the heating ventilation and air conditioning (HVAC) system or increasing corporate security—then the automated system may be perceived as more of an annoyance than a friend. Perhaps most critical to occupant acceptance is whether the control systems are perceived to be enabling greater choice and comfort, or perceived to be restricting choice and imposing discomfort.

Automobile designers and computer programmers have developed an entire research field called 'user experience' to optimize how a person interacts with the vehicle or software. Building designers are much further behind, rarely giving much thought to the subtleties of how an occupant could or should interact with an operable system. Imagine if some types of interactions were intentionally more intuitive and pleasurable than others, or if subtle feedback suggested if the occupant had made a wise or questionable choice. Learning how to operate each new programmable system has become a major challenge. In my own newly-constructed home, my husband and I must deal with a plethora of automated control devices that have wildly different and confounding user interfaces—the radiant floor slab, the mini-split heat pumps, the motorized skylight, the on-demand hot water heater—to the point where we are forced to provide a tutorial for all our house guests. I now dream of a day when operating a building will be as simple and self-evident for any new occupant as driving a new rental car.

Lazy Occupants

There is a great debate within the building science research community about the value of highly integrated automated controls versus simple and direct manual controls. Building managers and energy efficiency program managers tend to favor the use of automated systems that can guarantee a desired performance outcome, such as reducing solar heat gain via objectively measured inputs like air temperatures and solar position. Occupant use of manual controls is considered unpredictable and unreliable.

For example, there is widespread presumption that, due to 'lazy occupants,' window shades and blinds will be left closed more often than not, defeating all of the advantages of daylighting and view. However, when Day surveyed recent studies comparing automated versus manual systems, she found that manual systems frequently improved overall energy savings. Manual control options also helped prevent complete failures of the automated systems, and resulted in higher occupant satisfaction: "*Human subject research has consistently shown that occupants not only want control of their environments, but they will get grumpy, and increasingly inventive if their attempts at control fail. Indeed ... occupants will find their own ways to gain control of their buildings, when it is not available otherwise.*"[16]

Day proposed a more systematic approach to understanding the options and consequences of window management systems by thinking through all the attributes of a control interface, and considering its implications: the 'who, what, where, when, how, and why' of each device. Together these attributes create a device's 'behavioral profile' that can quantify both potential energy savings and occupant satisfaction. Ultimately, she recommended finding an appropriate marriage of automated and manual controls. For example, automated controls can create a default operation, programmed to maintain baseline efficiencies and avoid worst case scenarios, while manual overrides allow occupants to tailor the system to immediate needs and personal preferences. As Day explains, this approach can reduce the downside and increases the upside potential for both types of operation: "*This way the automated system reduces the behavioral risk, by bounding the problem, while the occupant adjustments increase comfort, satisfaction and energy savings due to more tailored use.*"

As we will see in the following chapter, people often develop intensely personal relationships with their window views, whether at home or at work. Supporting that relationship with appropriate controls for the many services that a window provides—daylight, view, ventilation, privacy, security— should be a key objective for any designer. It may require considering occupants' needs at all levels considered in this book— physiological, sensory, emotional, and cultural—in order to do a better job of designing for visual delight.

Framing a View

The placement of a window, or more generically, an aperture, determines not only the flow of daylight *into* a building, but also the view *out of* a building. Not many other architectural elements have such distinctly dualistic, and sometimes contradictory, purposes. Where we might want the most daylight illumination in a room may be quite different from where we want to look out. Composing a symphony of daylight illumination inside a building could potentially be at odds with which perspective we desire of the world outside. Resolving this discrepancy is certainly one of the challenges of artful daylighting design.

Earlier in this chapter we talked about the relative brightness of a view, whether it is sunlit or in shadow depending on orientation and time of day. Later we talked about balancing the luminance patterns within a room, by bringing in daylight from multiple directions and diffusing direct sunlight when it is allowed to enter. Those issues should also influence the placement of a window to frame a view, but in addition, the designer should also consider the likely location and activity of the observer. Will they be standing, sitting or lying down? Far from the window or with their nose at the glass? Looking obliquely past, or frontal to, the intended view?

Michael Pollan's first book (quoted earlier about daydreams), was about his effort to build himself the perfect workplace, a tiny writer's studio on an old farm in Connecticut. Only eight feet wide by twelve feet deep, the studio ended up with five radically different windows, selected both for the quality of light they created within the space and the type of view they offered of the surrounding woods. Each window had a different character and a different purpose in helping him to focus on the work of writing.[17]

First, there were two tiny square windows up near the peak of the ceiling, each admitting just *"a paragraph of sky"* to highlight the wooden framing of the roof. Second, a small casement window located just to the right of his writing desk was only visible when seated, something like a reward for finally getting down to work. This little window, which he compared a pilot's cockpit window, allowing quick communication with the ground crew, also offered close-up contemplation of a huge boulder immediately outside, *"like a blown up-photograph, a detail dwelling on the intricate map of lichens and moss that covered its granite skin."* Third, on the opposite side of his writing room, a double French casement opened outward towards a cedar lattice covered with vines, offering greenery and ventilation, but privacy from the rural road nearby. Fourth, at the back of the room, a "*big awning window looked up the hill toward the meadow*," bringing in soft morning light filtered through the trees.

Finally, the ultimate reason for the location of this building was the view through the largest window that fully spanned the width of his desk, looking out to a pond and garden nestled in the trees just southwest of the hut. The window was custom-built to hinge inward and hook to the ceiling above, turning his studio into an open porch on pleasant summer days. Six feet wide by four feet tall, wooden muntins supported six panes of glass, each two feet square.

Pollan was fascinated with how his experience of the view changed after that window was installed: transforming a raw hole-in-a-wall to a carefully articulated window frame, that imposed a simple grid across the view: "*... the windows had invested the building with a kind of intelligence, a point of view. What had been a single uninflected horizontal view out over the desk was now divided into six discrete square frames. The surprise was just how much more you could see this way, that there were six focal points instead of one, and twenty-four edges composing the scene instead of four ... For someone not blessed with great powers of visual observation, the grid of muntin bars was a lesson in looking, a little like the graph paper art students sometimes use to break a scene own into manageable components.*"

Not only did the grid of the window frame parse the view into discreet images, but it also created a 'frame of reference' which accentuated any movement or change in position: "*I noticed that any movement on my part would radically revise the content of the six frames ... a shifting mosaic of views.*" Thus, the window grid both heightened his awareness of the exterior landscape, and also his position within the room.

The experience prompted Pollan to reflect upon how windows determine our relationship with nature. He thought about the picture window in the house where he grew up. Picture windows were a very popular feature in new homes built the 1950s. "*Only much later did I realize that my parent's picture window contained its own implicit philosophy of nature ... to put nature up on a kind of pedestal, as the picture window does, is to hold it at arm's length, regard it as an aesthetic object—a 'picture.' ... The picture window turns the stuff of nature into a landscape, the very idea of which implies separation and observation and passivity—nature as spectator sport ...*"

Kent Bloomer, a professor of architecture at Yale University, also took up the crusade against the primacy of the mid-century modern picture window. In the book *Biophilic Design*, Bloomer argued that the mere presence of a big glassy view to the outdoors through plate glass should not be considered a 'biophilic element,' as it is too simplistic and too divisive. He did not believe that the perfect transparency of a picture window offers enough emotional engagement to really connect the building occupant with the world beyond the building. He asked: *"Why do we go to such great pains to get clear glass, to sanitize it and make it so transparent that its visual substance disappears and thus virtually dematerializes? Curiously, with such means of viewing we might be looking at nature in a manner similar to the way we looked at animals in early twentieth-century zoos, their dangers held at bay by the slender bars of cages. Through glass, we observe the world outside comfortably and safely and without the challenges of actual engagement."*[18]

Bloomer's recommendation is to add intermediate layers to the window opening via ornamentation, visual rhythm, and a tactile boundary between inside and out. This could be achieved with mullions and moldings around jamb and windowsills that accentuate the visual transition between indoors and out, creating more detailed shadow patterns with a greater range of values between light and dark. He also advocates for tracery and visual patterns in the glass itself, such as the decorative geometric patterns designed by Frank Lloyd Wright or the great Tiffany stained glass window at the Lyndhurst gothic-style mansion in upstate New York.

Bloomer however, ever the architecture professor, focused only on the architectural solutions to the problem he posits. He acknowledged, but only in passing, that such transitional elements could also be achieved with, say, curtains. He ignores all the other *non-architected* elements, such as lace work, blinds, decorative screens, exterior elements like lattice-work or trellises, or indoor and outdoor plantings that could also provide his desired visual tracery and transition. Furthermore, Bloomer was considering only the permanent features of the building, not the changeable qualities of the window's view, in his assessment of how successfully a window could create a biophilic element for the occupants. But our experience of a space includes not only the architectural form, that which we can touch, but just as importantly, all that we can see, both within the space and beyond.

In other words, the content of the view is itself important: which is where we will turn next.

9. Elements of View

What constitutes 'a good view'? In some ways this is a ridiculously simple question, yet in other ways, it is a surprisingly difficult one, perhaps because there is so much complexity. Certainly, we know that people have strong feelings about views. Real estate investors pay millions of dollars for property with the potential for a good view. Landscape artists spend a lifetime painting views that inspire or intrigue them. Landscape architects devote their professional careers to designing views in the hope that others will consider them beautiful, tranquil, or fascinating. There are also a few researchers who have tackled the question, trying to categorize better versus worse, although most would agree that rigorous research on views is in its infancy.[1] The simplest answer is perhaps the most obvious: a 'good view' is the one that people most want to look at.

We will tackle this question at many levels. We begin by considering the more material elements of views that people love to look at, such as skies, birds, trees, people, pathways, landmarks, water, and then move on to progressively more abstract qualities, such as size, distance, complexity, ambiguity, change, and salience. This chapter focuses on these perceptual elements, whereas in later chapters we will examine the deeper emotional, social, and cultural bonds we form with views.

Edward O Wilson, a professor of biology at Yale University, has written extensively about how humans and the environment interact. As a biologist who first studied the complex behaviors of ants and other insects and how they interacted with their environment, he posits that there are also certain types of landscapes and certain types of views that humans naturally gravitate to: "*All mobile animal species have a powerful, often highly sophisticated inborn guide for habitat selection. Why not human beings?*"[2]

Wilson always takes an evolutionary overview, and since he believes that humans evolved for millions of years in the African savanna, he believes that we have a genetic predisposition for that type of visual environment. However, the studies that Wilson cites may have been biased towards northern climates, and European and North American subjects. For example, a recent view of literature on *The Benefits of Interacting with Nature* found that of 57 published studies, 79% were reporting from high latitudes, and none were located in South America or Africa.[3] Thus, we have yet to confirm that view preferences are universal across all cultures and climates.

Over the years, I have interviewed all kinds of people about their attitudes towards their views at work or at home. In general, I find that initially people not are very articulate about their views. While they might have strong feelings— "*I love it!*"—they typically don't have much experience discussing the details. My informal interviews at someone's workplace might follow a sequence such as: "*Is that view important to you? Why? When do you think you tend to look at it the most? How would you rate it on a scale of 1–10? What do you enjoy about it the most, or the least? What would you change about it if you could?*" I find that the answers I receive usually fall into two categories. First, there is the quick answer, that fits easily into stereotypical concepts of what *other* people are likely to consider 'a good view.' Then, if I persist, come the deeper contemplations of what that individual really noticed and enjoyed most about their view.

This two-level response was exemplified by a woman who worked at a shared workspace near where I live. Her preferred workstation was a standing desk looking out a full-height window facing the downtown streetscape and hills to the north. Initially when I asked her to rate the quality of her view on a scale of one to ten, she gave it a low rating: "*Oh, about a three,*" she said. This surprised me, as few workers have access to such a large, layered or complex view. However, when I asked her to describe what she liked and didn't like about the view, her attitude changed dramatically. She first talked about the hummingbirds that visited the bushes in front of the window, and then the changing color of the leaves and the clouds hovering around the hills. Next she mentioned all the people-watching she did, wondering where a festive group of people were headed, or if the bar owner across the street might be changing his hours. Observing these moments, she said, made her feel part of the flow of life and less isolated in her work. Working from this spot for the past two years, she said, made her feel a part of the story of Santa Cruz, creating an intimacy with her town that she hadn't felt previously. When I asked her about her earlier low rating of the view, she replied "*Oh, that was as if it were a picture postcard. But really, I'm very fond of this view. It's the entire reason I choose to work here!*"

Matteo Pericoli is an Italian architect and illustrator who also became fascinated with people's relationships to their window views, and found a unique way to investigate that relationship. While living for a time in New York City, he began to ask people he met about their window views: what the view meant to them, and why it was important, or not. Then, working from a collection of photographs, he made a meticulous line drawing of each person's view, as seen looking out through the window frame. These interviews and illustrations were compiled into a delightful little book called *The City Out My Window.*[4] Pericoli then branched out geographically and invited 50 authors from around the world to contribute similar reflections about their workplace views, spanning every continent and many cultures.[5] As might be expected, those 50 authors were especially articulate about how their particular views interlaced with their working process. Pericoli's two books were a treasure trove for me, as they provided intimate interviews with very thoughtful people from a wide range of perspectives, and provided many kernels of insight that appear throughout the following pages.

Sky

The sky is frequently mentioned as an essential element of view. People often express simple gratitude when they can see the sky. For example, Nathan Englander, a short story writer quoted in Pericoli's collection of New York stories, began his view description with: "*I'm just happy to see the sky. I really never take it for granted.*"

But what is it about the sky that is so important? When I asked people why they value their window view at work, by far the most common answer was "*I want to know what the weather is doing.*" This makes a great deal of sense in places where the weather is highly changeable and unpredictable, where rain showers or snow flurries quickly come and go. However, I have spent much of my life in Los Angeles and Sacramento, California, where the weather literally does not change for months. Every single day can have a clear blue sky, one after another, for weeks and months on end, and yet people in Los Angeles and Sacramento will still claim they want to know what the weather is up to. This suggests to me that 'knowing the weather' may be a code for some other need or desire.

Temporal orientation is a likely candidate. A view of the sky is likely to include an opportunity to see a splash of sunlight enter a room, setting a vivid time marker for the day, along with an opportunity to watch the changing colors of sunrise or sunset, and perhaps the arrival of the moon or a few stars at twilight. Atmospheric dynamics, as we discussed earlier, provide a temporal grounding for the day: we intuitively judge the time of day by the color and luminance of the sky. I once walked into a room with darkened electrochromic glass that had turned the sky a deep blue. My brain quickly concluded that I had somehow lost a few hours, and early afternoon had become twilight. A glance at my watch proved my brain wrong, but emotionally I felt confused by the cognitive dissonance between my temporal expectations and the apparent color of the sky.

Staring at the sky also may be also the most direct way to feed our appetite for circadian stimulus, like my experience at the O'Hare terminal (see page 33). Whenever you feel a need for a circadian boost, try staring at the blue sky for a while and see how that feels. This may also be related to the sensation described by Leila Aboulea, an African writer living in Aberdeen, Scotland, who wrote about her view in *Windows on the World,* Pericoli's second book: "*It is good to write and then look up at the sky, at the uninterrupted view of the tops of houses. When I am on a roll, there is a pressure of meanings clambering to be words, there is a gush that needs to be controlled, or at least manipulated and the respite from this turbulence is always the clean familiar sky.*"

She describes looking at the sky as a cleansing experience, a blank canvas that provides an invitation for more thoughts, more clarity.

A view of the sky can also be an open invitation to daydream. Andrea Levy, an English novelist, wrote: "*When I was young my mum used to complain that I spent too much time daydreaming. That was because I liked to stare at the sky. She thought that while I was dreaming, I could be doing something useful as well, like knitting. Now that I am a writer, I have the privilege of daydreaming as part of my job. And I still love to gaze at the sky. The view from my workroom in my North London house has a lot of sky, and I couldn't work without it. There are never any structured thoughts in my head when I look up. They just come and go and change shape like the clouds.*"[6]

Who has not been fascinated by the subtly changing formations of clouds, and daydreamed while searching aimlessly for some recognizable shape? When my brother, an artist, was looking for a new place to live, I asked him what he most wanted in his new home. "*Great clouds.*" he answered simply. At the time, I thought that an odd criterion for a real estate purchase. But in hindsight, clouds were much of his inspiration to work.

Diane Ackerman, in her contemplative book *A Natural History of the Senses*, describes the sky as far more than something to look *at*, but rather as the vibrant atmosphere we live *within*, the medium of our existence: "*Look at your feet. You are standing in the sky. When we think of the sky, we tend to look up, but the sky actually begins at the earth.*" She continues on, describing the complexity of the phenomenon of sky: "*Without thinking, we often speak of 'an empty sky.' But the sky is never empty. In a mere ounce of air, there are 1,000 billion trillion gyrating atoms made up of oxygen, nitrogen, and hydrogen, each a menagerie of electrons, quarks and ghostly neutrinos. Sometimes we marvel at how 'calm' the day is, or how 'still' the night. Yet there is no stillness in the sky, or anywhere else where life and matter meet. The air is always vibrant and aglow, full of vital gases, staggering spores, dust, viruses, fungi, and animals, all stirred by a skirling and relentless wind. There are active flyers like butterflies, birds, bats and insects, who ply the air roads; and there are passive flyers like autumn leaves, pollen, or milkweed pods, which just float. Beginning at the earth and stretching up in all directions, the sky is the thick, twitching realm in which we live.*"[7]

Thus, another attraction of the sky is that it is so full of other things—clouds, birds, insects, airplanes, and now perhaps drones—going about their business. Let's turn our attention to some of these.

Birds, Trees, and Other Invitations

Birds can be an important part of a sky view. A friend who works near the top of a high-rise office building overlooking Biscayne Bay, with a vast view of sky, says he especially likes to watch the birds soar about his building. At that altitude, it is mostly hawks, seagulls, and vultures who soar on the thermals, often circling within view for long periods before they move on, providing a gently moving focus for his contemplation.

At my writing desk I sit at an upstairs corner, looking out two sets of windows. The lower third of my view is filled with other homes, trees, and telephone wires, while the upper two-thirds is sky. Clouds, in this coastal town, are often lovely and lively, and the sunsets can be riveting. But I realized that it is the birds that really animate my view. We have hummingbirds that are incredible athletes, zipping up and down faster than I can think. The local mockingbirds defend their territory, singing incessantly and putting on repeated aerial displays to scare off competitors. Of course, there are also plenty of seagulls and lots of 'little brown birds' I can't quite identify, but it is the occasional hawk or heron that really stirs up the neighborhood, as the other birds scream and try to chase them away. The trees provide an important perch, and sometimes a huge flock of crows will all settle down on one tree, drooping its branches and likely creating a mess below. But those trees are important bird attractors. I don't think my sky would be nearly as entertaining without the trees, because the birds, and all their avian drama, would just pass by my neighborhood.

Trees are another feature that get a great deal of attention in recommendations for good views. A view of trees is often equated with a 'view of nature.' It may be that trees are indeed a good proxy for a more inclusive definition of nature, since it is difficult to grow trees without exposure to sky, wind and rain, or if birds, squirrels, insects, and other creatures have been excluded. Even an indoor potted tree, with soil, bark, and leaves will establish its own happy little ecosystem with a balance of mites, fungus, bacteria, and other microbes all living in harmony.

It is important, however, to remember that not all trees are green. Deciduous trees in the northern temperate forests hold only bare twigs for many winter months, resulting in an almost monochromatic scene. But, interestingly, although they are missing their leaves, these barren trees allow much more transparent views deeper into the woods, and many more sightings of birds and other animals going about their woodland business. In the limited color palate of the wintery woods, a few spots of color draw our attention: the purple blush of some twig tips or the flash of a red cardinal.

TC Boyle, who lives in the hills above Los Angeles, is a prolific environmental novelist. He explained how he inhabits his view: *"What I'm looking at in this view ... from my desk is a big oak tree just beyond the roofline, and beyond that—oh, maybe three miles off—the high buff ridge of the Santa Ynez Mountains. In between is a whole lot of vegetation, a big scoop of sky, and the hawks that hang there like mobiles ... What do I get from all of this? Distraction and lack of distraction both. I can pause, look up from my work, and see the way the light sits in the trees or observe the woodpeckers and squirrels raiding acorns from the oak, and yet there are no larger distractions in the form of traffic, noise and big-ape bustle. When I'm done with the work I go out into those woods and maintain things in a proprietary way."*[8]

Thus, the woods for Boyle are both an invitation to contemplation and an invitation to future action. He watches other creatures inhabit his woods, and plans his own future activities in those woods. In that sense, the trees are providing a structure, a visual scaffolding, that allows his imagination to easily move outward beyond his desk.

I think trees are just one of many possible visual props that our brains like to use this way. Others include chairs set out on patios, balconies or decks, and umbrellas and picnic tables that invite us to inhabit them, whether we actually do or not. The visual presence of these human-centric objects creates a welcoming invitation, independent of their actual use. Rebecca Walker, writing in *Windows on the World* from Maui, Hawaii, describes her simple view of a balcony outside, with two empty chairs, sheltered from the tropical rain and sun, looking out over a forest of palm trees: "*I have loved my two empty chairs, sentinels awaiting their visitors, open to the promise of more.*"

Maria Endicott, writes from the northern climate of Edmonton, Alberta, Canada about a particular quandary, of a patio that seems visually inviting, and yet does not actually welcome physical habitation: "*I stare out at a suburban patio, a generous and quiet garden ... From the inside the garden looks like a reward: the drink on the terrace that is much more delicious in anticipation ... Early in the morning, I could drink coffee there ... doing some writerly thing with a fountain pen. But in reality, pernicious mosquitoes make it impossible to sit and work outside. It is a vision of the original Garden, and just as unattainable.*"[9]

Thus, for many places, an inside window view can offer more comfort than the harsher reality of being outside. The separation of the window glass between us and the outdoors can filter out unwanted cold, wind, noises, odors, pollen, insects, and other intruders, filtering out so many hardships and threats to our comfort, while still leaving us with an illusion of engagement with life going on outside. In this way, views of trees and wild critters can help to delineate what belongs *outside*, and therefore, provide a heightened sense of safety *inside*.

Emma Larkin, a journalist living in Thailand, tells such a tale from life in a tropical city: "*My study window looks out over an incongruous jungle located in the heart of Bangkok. As the rest of the neighborhood is dominated by high-rises and town houses that have sacrificed yards for concrete parking spaces, all remaining wildlife seems to gravitate to our garden. Myopic fantail birds tap against the window panes, squirrels chew on the frayed corners of the shutters, and neon-green tree snakes sunbathe silently in the rain gutters.*" And yet, she continues, there is another layer to the view: "*There is another type of wildness here, too. The ficus tree on the righthand side ... is where the house spirits now reside ... In accordance with Thai custom, regular offerings of food and flower garlands are laid out for the spirits so that they might be enticed to exist outside the house, rather than inside—a practice that has put a stop to most (but not all) of the inexplicable shadows and footsteps that flit through these old wooden rooms.*" Larkin concludes by describing how her courtyard view helps nourish her writing: "*This scene encompasses both the wild and the urban, the known and the unknown. It reminds me that the dividing line between fact and fiction is less clearly defined here in Thailand and that the boundary between the two is porous. In such a place, stories thrive.*"[10]

The snakes, the squirrels, and the house spirits all provide an element of randomness and wonder that help spark her imagination.

People and Pathways

In more urban settings, people-watching becomes one of the prime pastimes, providing a similar degree of mild fascination, amusement, and imaginative wanderings as can birds and animals. Given enough privacy, most of us have an enduring interest in surreptitiously watching our fellow humans.

Daniel Galera, writing from Brazil, noted that the movement of people and traffic was an essential component of a good view, *"softening the solitude,"* for his preferred working environment: *"Some kind of open view really helps my mood in order to work, but there's a special kind I prefer. A wide and beautiful natural landscape is distracting to me: I feel like going outside and must close the window. A window facing a wall is worse, I feel oppressed. This is just what I need: a square with some trees, people, and noise. Even the traffic noise is somewhat stimulating to me—that way I am connected with my urban environment, with city life, I am aware of people living and doing other stuff around me, and that breaks the continual isolation often required to write, softening the solitude ... Some windows are an escape for daydreaming, but this one kind of keeps me company."*

A window looking out onto a street, or perhaps even better, from a floor above the street level, can provide just the right remove, just the right level of detachment, from the social scene, allowing us to be a little curious and entertained by the lives of those other people going about their daily business, without feeling burdened by too much concern or sense of responsibility for the details of their lives.

It turns out that at a mid-distance, we humans are astonishingly good at interpreting the body language of our fellow humans. The Swedish perceptual psychologist Gunnar Johannson first demonstrated our ability to easily read the intent and emotive content of body movements in 1973.[11] He originated the technique of 'motion capture,' a technique that is now widely used in research, and in the video gaming and motion picture industry to transform human actors' motions into ever more realistic animated characters. He discovered that with just 12 points of light against a dark background to outline body movement, viewers could reliably determine the meaning and intent of a subjects' action, and even their age, sex, and emotional state. This ability to read 'biological motion' develops with experience, and is often preserved even when other areas of the brain involved in object recognition are damaged. Thus, a window view that enables reading the body language of other humans nearby is likely to be highly valued.

During the early days of the coronavirus pandemic in 2020, cities became strangely quiet, as schools were closed, businesses shuttered, and citizens were asked to stay at home to slow the rate of infection. It is during such times that people's hunger for visual contact with other humans becomes most conspicuous. All over Italy, which was one of the most hard-hit countries early on, people took to sitting out on their balconies every evening just to watch each other, and sometimes share a song or dance. The news media filled with poignant photos of residents of nursing homes waving wistfully through their windows to their loved ones outside. Simple visual contact with other humans was the solace most sought.

William Whyte, an urbanist, journalist, and professional people-watcher, was one of the first to make a case for how important people-watching is for the life of cities, as explained in his influential book *The Social Life of Small Urban Spaces* (1980). He mentored many other important urbanists of the twentieth century, such as Jane Jacobs and Jan Gehl, by urging the direct observation of where people tend to congregate in urban settings, and how they behave and interact. One of his important observations was that the most successful people-places were usually right in the middle of other activity: at the entrance to buildings, the crossing of busy paths, or narrow streets where traffic and people intermingled. He observed that small groups of two or three people would often stop right in the middle of the flow of pedestrian traffic to have long, extended conversations. His explanation was that being in the flow of traffic provided an easy excuse to end an informal conversation at any moment. Whyte was also a big advocate for 'seeding' plazas and sidewalks with benches, stairs, chairs, and umbrellas set out for food stands and sidewalk cafes, as a clear invitation for people to stop and gather.[12] Especially for people who love urban life, the more pedestrian activity, the more satisfying the view.

But a pathway doesn't have to include people to be visually interesting. Just like an empty chair on a balcony invites one to come and sit, a view of an empty pathway invites you to consider a future amble down that path. A pathway that disappears around the bend, or into the shadows of a tree, provides a hint of mystery that might be even more motivating to encourage future exploration, whether physical or imaginative. The image of a disappearing path is a very common meme of landscape painting and photography: artists have long known that such an image tugs at viewers' imagination and invites them into the picture.

Kevin Lynch, in his seminal book *The Image of the City,* hypothesized back in 1960 that there are five key types of navigation aids that we humans use in developing a cognitive map of a city: paths, nodes, districts, edges, and landmarks.[13] When he asked people to draw an image of their city, these five elements were common to most peoples' narrative and simple sketches. *Paths* are linear elements where we can move along easily to somewhere we'd like to go, whether a sidewalk, street, boulevard, or dirt trail through a field, connecting all the other parts together. *Nodes* are the crossings of paths, where interesting things happen, where people congregate, locations where certain activities can always be found. *Districts* are larger areas with some form of unified character, which might be comprised of building type, activity type, population, or history.

Edges are the opposite of paths; they are barriers that are difficult to penetrate, or that form mental distinctions between districts. Edges are often comprised of fences or walls defining property lines, or impenetrable lines of buildings or highways that can't be easily crossed. Because edges inhibit movement, they may be less desirable components of views. Unless the fence is protecting us, we are less interested in looking *at* someone else's fence, than *over* it. A low wall or lattice fence can create an edge for directing movement, such as defining the edge of pathway, while still allowing a view beyond, but a high opaque wall or fence that we cannot see over creates a visual void in our cognitive maps. Indeed, building a high wall that blocks others' view is one of the most aggressive actions that neighbors sometimes take against each other, as described in chapter 13's discussion of 'spite walls.' (See page 242.)

Landmarks and Urban Views

Kevin Lynch's understanding of the importance of the fifth type of navigational aide, *landmarks*, is probably his greatest contribution to environmental psychology and urban design. He recognized that, much more than logical maps of street patterns or topography, people remember images of their city, and navigate their way around via singular visual landmarks.

Lynch found that tall, prominent landmarks were important for visitors who were new to a place, but much less so for locals. Local residents, in contrast, relied more on a sequence of modest yet still singular objects or buildings to establish their navigational landmarks. Any characteristic that made it more distinctive, such as the newest building in an old neighborhood, or one set at a funny angle to the street, or local sounds, smells, or history help to reinforce the memorability of a landmark. Lynch writes: "*Historical association or other meanings are powerful reinforcements ... Once a history, a sign, or a meaning attaches to an object, its value as a landmark rises."*

Tourists, by definition, come to see the sights of a new place, and local landmarks are generally at the top of their 'must see' list. Once a landmark has become famous, via references in novels, artwork, or films, tourists want to experience a classic view of it themselves. These landmarks are then reinforced again and again as movies and advertisements use them as a shorthand to establish location. Then, intensifying the landmark feedback loop, tourists post photos of themselves in front of the landmark, to prove that they were there. It is interesting to consider how landmarks progress: when does a local landmark, useful in anchoring an individual's cognitive map, become a local social magnet, then a cultural icon?

Famous landmarks seem to provide important emotional anchors, reminding people where they are, why they are there, and what they love about the place. The many New Yorkers featured in Pericoli's book *The City Out My Window* are especially effusive about their city's landmarks. The writer Nora Ephron wrote: *"One of the things I can see through these beautiful Juliet windows in my office is the Chrysler Building. It's my favorite building in all the world, the absolute epitome of every glittery dream I have ever had about New York."* I would note that, per Pericoli's line drawings, the Chrysler Building was very far away from Ephron's window, constituting just a tiny exclamation point out at horizon, and yet still, it captured her attention. Leila Mizra noted this common distortion of size in her doctoral study of views in New Zealand. She asked her study subjects to sketch their views from memory. In the drawings, cherished places and landmarks were routinely greatly exaggerated in size relative to other elements in the view.[14]

Modernist composer Phillip Glass took a more mechanistic perspective in describing his studio view: *"Water tanks, air-conditioning, and exhaust pipes. The infrastructure of New York in plain view. I love it!"* Tony Kushner, the playwright, quipped: *"I assume anyone who really loves Manhattan must find engineering erotic."*[15] When I once led a group of experts around the country to assess the visual quality of daylit spaces, I was struck by their cultural relativism, especially when in New York City. The experts from the west coast—California, Oregon, Idaho, and Washington State—all gave the highest ratings to distant vistas of trees, mountains, and water. They found the views of Manhattan buildings, streets, and skyline less inspiring, while the local New Yorkers waxed poetic: *"Water towers! Pigeons! Traffic! History!"* The urbanites clearly treasured their knowledge of their city's history and every reminder seen in a window.

Pericoli's illustration of artist Nick Ghiz's view shows the lower half with a rooftop full of HVAC equipment, and the upper half with a few richly detailed buildings and the sky beyond. Ghiz writes: *"When I first moved to this studio, the window was covered with boards. As I removed them and replaced the window, I realized what a marvelous, comprehensive view is this of Lower Manhattan. From the 1760s Dutch church to the most modern buildings, it contains more than two centuries of architecture ... It represents to me the endless activity and hopefulness that is life here in New York City."*[16]

I think that last sentence captures the essence of urban views that some people love—*"the activity and hopefulness"* that generates constant motion, sustained across generations. In one way or another, all these landmarks embody the soul of the place for the observers, providing reassurance that there is continuity from past to present, and perhaps also that the present will be remembered in the future.

It is not just buildings and historical landmarks that engage these urban dwellers, but the people behind the windows, all looking back at each other. David Byrne, lead singer of the Talking Heads, wrote: *"I think of my view as pretty typical for a New Yorker. We look out of our windows at other windows. That, in a way mirrors our lives here—we are constantly looking at each other, millions of us, on the streets and elsewhere."*[17]

Many other people wrote of the enjoyment of watching city lights come on at night, whether in New York, Sydney, or Beijing. We humans used to stare at the sparkling night sky, and imagine that the stars represented gods and mythical beasts inhabiting the sky. Now, we seem to find a similar sense of companionship in views of a city at night, lit by thousands of lights, each representing someone going on about their life nearby.

Distant views of cities at night are among the most desired of all residential views, and yet the light pollution generated by all those lights is causing its own problems. Indeed, nighttime lighting has such appeal to humans that it is now one of the fastest growing industries internationally. Based on analysis of yearly satellite images, NASA has estimated that land area lit by nighttime lighting has been growing globally by 2.2% per year over the past 20 years.[18] At night, the skyglow from the bright lights of Los Angeles and Las Vegas appears like a perpetual sunrise from a hundred miles away. As light pollution grows, stars overhead disappear. As night turns into day, the circadian rhythms are blurred and confused song birds exhaust themselves singing all night long. We may become unwitting victims of our intrinsic love of light.

Water

Water may be the most universally treasured component of views. What is our fascination with water? I would argue that there are many levels of fascination, all operating simultaneously. Water bodies manage to evoke almost every desirable aspect of view content we've discussed. The water's surface reflects the sky and clouds, and those ever-changing colors amplify our awareness of weather and the passage of time. Wind, birds, and insects animate the surface, while fish, and sometimes mammals, pop up at random moments from below. The water's edge provides an especially rich structure where four distinct ecological niches all come into contact: air, water, land, and soil. The water also provides an invitation for many kinds of human habitation, whether we fantasize about sunning at the water's edge, floating on a boat, or heading out to an adventure down a river's path or to distant ports. And the fascination of water continues through the night, as its ripples and waves reflect the sunset, the moon, or lights of a city.

Water provides us with mental connections that few other elements of a landscape can. A river or stream is continuously moving from one place to another. Even brooks and puddles connect us with the recent past, via the amount of rain in past days that has filled them. Migrating birds stopover in lakes and marshes, connecting us to seasons and far away continents. On larger rivers and harbors, boat traffic moves by, slow and stately, reinforcing human links via commerce and cultural connections. On a vast sea or ocean, there is the imagination of the shore on the other side. At a primal level, a view of water may also provide us with evolutionary reassurance that our most basic physiological needs will be met, providing us with sufficient drink and food.

A water body is often a key feature of a cognitive map, creating an edge that restricts our passage, yet also providing an indelible landmark closely tied to the history of a place. Since waterways were the primary transportation pathways in past centuries, and moving water was the primary source of power, waterways also often connect us with the history of a place. Almost every town situated near a body of water has a long history, whether back to the Romans, the ancient Chinese, or Native Americans. If you want to quickly find the historical section of a city, it will usually be near the edge of a waterbody.

Any glimpse of water, almost no matter how tiny—maybe just a fine line shimmering on the horizon, out there behind hundreds of buildings—was mentioned both in Pericoli's books and my own interviews. Indeed, I've had people make comments to me, with great enthusiasm, such as: "*And, you could even see the river, right down there, if the only those trees weren't in the way!"* Thus, even an awareness of *where the water should be* in a view seems to be valued.

Losing a water view was also a surprisingly common recurrent theme. I once had a long conversation with a lawyer living in Connecticut who had previously had a home with a grand view of Long Island Sound. After her husband died and she retired, she decided to downsize and moved to a small townhouse inland, away from the water, with only a small garden view off of the back porch. She immediately regretted the loss: *"It took me about two weeks to realize what a horrible mistake I'd made. I thought I didn't need the water view anymore, that I'd become inured to it, and could make do with a simple view of my garden. But once I didn't have the water view in my daily life anymore, I realized how very much I missed it. So, my new home is back up for sale, and I plan to move back somewhere with a view of the Sound."*

Missing, Negative, or Constrained Views

My lawyer friend had thought she was 'done' with the view, but very quickly noticed its absence once it was no longer available. This raises the question, at what point do we become inured to view? When is our initial interest in a view satisfied, so that it is no longer interesting and we are content to live without it?

Consider, for example, the phenomenon of the view at a vacation hotel, which at first is deeply fascinating. We may have paid extra, maybe $100/night, for an upper floor room with a 'water view' or 'city view.' At first the view is riveting, as we notice all the distant details, the new activity, the changing light. And then gradually, the view becomes less compelling. We just glance at it to reassure ourselves that it is still beautiful, still worth the extra money. Gradually the curtains stay closed longer. Eventually, as we leave, we drink in one last long look, trying to remember the exhilaration of that first moment when we walked in and stood in awe before the window.

Why does the hotel view become less important over time? How long does it take to lose its emotional punch? Could we have been just as happy with a hotel room downstairs, with the curtains pulled, blocking the view of an adjacent brick wall?

There are plenty of scenes that people don't care to look at—a garbage dump, belching factories, prison walls—basically almost any unhealthy, unhappy reminder of the negative side of life. In such cases, avoidance is often an available strategy: close the curtains, turn the chair the other way. One of the most striking examples of avoidance I've encountered were some soldiers

I interviewed at the Twentynine Palms Marine Corps base in California's Mohave Desert. I was there to study some new daylit office buildings. Marine battalions rotated through the base every six to nine months while training for assignments around the world. Thus, everyone I interviewed was a temporary resident.

A handful of soldiers hated the place, and always kept their window blinds closed, specifically to block their view of the desert. These soldiers told me: "*I really don't want to be reminded where I am, how hot and dry it is out there.*" Outside their office windows was a sparse sandy landscape, with a few desert bushes and Joshua trees scattered far apart, yet not without an aesthetic for those who appreciate desert landscapes. However, for a soldier used to green lawns and leafy trees, it was indeed an alien environment, and a daily reminder of their current situation.

Interestingly, I rarely encountered people complaining that a window was too small or a view too limited. The size, perspective, and content of the window and its view all seem to be taken as a given, not subject to analysis or critique. People are generally thankful for what they can see, and rarely complain about what they cannot see (unless they covet a co-worker's view).

The distance to a landmark, and therefore its perceptual size, were also rarely a concern. The Chrysler Building in Nora Ephron's view was very far away and tiny, but still figured as a central feature of what she valued in her view. In Paris, being able to recognize the Eiffel Tower, even at a great distance, is meaningful to visitors and locals alike. There are many other small details that may be of interest in a vista. A tiny dot in the sky might turn into an airplane, or a bird, or a kite. A tiny dot out in the ocean might be a ship, a buoy, or a whale. Living near the ocean, I find I can now identify many marine birds and mammals just by the shape of their splash as they enter the water, even a mile away. I think it is truly amazing how very little information my brain needs to differentiate these very small objects or events, and how I get a tiny moment of pleasure each time I can correctly identify something at such a distance.

Both in Pericoli's stories and my own interviews, big, sweeping views were always described with superlatives. With big, wide views there is just more information, plus more chances to observe any movement, near or far, and the greater the probability that you can see the horizon and the sky, along with all the additional information they may offer. People simply don't complain about views that are too large, or too panoramic. Rather they complain about feeling too exposed, losing their privacy. The recurring theme is always greater opportunity to observe, and less opportunity to be observed by others.

Instead, if people were not happy with their view, feeling that it was too limited, the most common phrase used was *"I feel like I'm in prison."* I have heard this over and over again, in so many contexts, that I've come to believe that judging a view to be poor seems to be related to a feeling of confinement. Rather than critiquing the content or quality of their view, people offer the emotional self-assessment that *"I feel like I'm in prison,"* which may be code for *"My view is too small and makes me feel constrained"* or *"I don't like the decisions that someone else made for me."*

However reticent people felt about critiquing views they did not like, the folks I interviewed felt no compunction about effusive descriptions of views that really made them happy. In addition to 'sweeping' views, clarity, color, detail, change, and movement were mentioned with consistent enthusiasm. Many of the most evocative stories were about views that changed somehow, that invoked a sense of the passage of time, whether short or long.

Time, Change, and Motion

How often do we feel a need to look at a view? This is an essential question to answer, as it then dictates how we design buildings to allow access to views. Can your desire for a view be satisfied with a once-in-a-lifetime event, like visiting Niagara Falls or the Taj Mahal? Is it a view you feel a need to see yearly, perhaps like your home town dressed up for the holidays? Or weekly, daily, hourly, or even every few minutes, like my friend in Portland glancing out the window while she was busy typing? (See page 72.)

I think one key determinant of how often we want to look at a view may be how much it changes, and how quickly it changes. But change has many other characteristics in addition to speed—such as steady versus intermittent, rhythmic versus random, predictable versus unpredictable, permanent versus fleeting—which all influence our desire to look at a view.

An easily discernible type of change is simply a result of daily weather, which is much more entertaining in some places than others. Predictable seasonal changes in vegetation, animal, or human behavior are also of interest. Alternatively, a rapidly evolving vista, such as a construction project transforming from a hole in the ground to a finished building, sustains curiosity in the present and adds temporal perspective in the future. Many other intermittent events—such as street parties, parades, fireworks, or special holiday markets—give extra meaning to a window view, adding both memories of the past event and anticipation of the next.

Unpredictability increases the frequency with which one wants to 'check' a view. Many people who treasure a view of a nearby mountain find themselves checking frequently to see if it is currently visible through the clouds, and if so, how its form and color are changing throughout the day. Mount Hood, a classic conic volcano, is one of the most important landmarks for Portland, Oregon, but it is often hidden behind the region's thick cloud cover. When in view, depending on atmospheric conditions, its appearance varies from a vivid rock-solid presence to merely a faint ghost hovering far off in the sky.

I encountered an extreme example of the importance of intermittent events at a daylighting study site at an engineering building at the Naval Base in Norfolk Virginia. The south-facing façade had continuous, ten-foot high windows, covered with horizontal mini-blinds, which were typically kept fully closed to block the southern sunlight. Only at the very bottom of the window, from about two to four feet above the floor, was kept clear of blinds. We substituted an innovative sunlight-redirecting film for the top two feet of mini-blinds, which brought substantially more daylight into the space. Then we asked the workers, siting in their cubicles, how they liked the change. Instead of appreciating the greater amount of daylight illumination, a number of them complained that the new film *"blocked their view."* I found this very surprising. I could not understand how the film could be newly blocking a view that was previously blocked by closed blinds.

Then one of the engineers took me aside to explain the situation in more detail. This office building faced directly at the practice landing strip where new pilots were being trained to take off and land on a pretend aircraft carrier. Usually, the new pilots did well, but there were occasional mishaps, which were always big news around the base. Even though the mini-blinds were always closed, they did have pin-hole perforations, which were just enough to reveal the shadow of an airplane approaching the field for a landing. The office occupants could see the upper two feet of the windows over the top of their cubicles, and when they noticed a bit of airplane shadow moving across the blinds, they had just enough time to glance around their cubical partition, and look out the clear bottom two feet of the window, in order to observe the landing. The sunlight-redirecting film we had installed blurred the image of the sky and the plane, so they could no longer correctly *anticipate* when to watch a landing. That was the problem.

So here, in this story, we have a very occasional and unpredictable event—a landing mishap—driving the occupants' valuation of the importance of their view. And the prompt for this event was derived from the tiniest amount of visual information—shadows seen through the pin-hole perforations of an opaque blind—from the top two feet of a ten-foot high window. That's when I realized how even the most minimal information provided by a window could still be highly valued as 'a view' by office workers.

Psychologists would describe the tiny moving dots of the airplanes as 'an alerting event,' one that captures our attention and directs the focal area of our eyes to look for more information. Thus, detecting that little bit of movement is the essential first step in gathering the desired information from the window view. This, of course, assumes that the information is 'desired' and welcome. It could also be possible that the 'alerting event' is an unwelcome distraction. Preventing such distractions has long been a justification for creating workplaces and classrooms with few or no windows.

Managing the balance between welcome and unwelcome distractions, balancing outward views and inward privacy, is another piece of the equation in the design of windows and their attachments, as discussed earlier (see page 147). Both the flow of daylight in and the clarity of the view out are hugely determined not only by the choice of window treatments, but also by who has the prerogative to select that system and who has the authority to operate it, as illustrated in the next set of stories. These stories address the question of how filtered or fractured can a view be and still be valued? At what point does a partial or eroded view produce more frustration than pleasure?

Filtered or Fractured Views

Long before the Norfolk study, I had conducted a similar set of interviews with employees of a bank in Vancouver, Canada, which provided some interesting insights about workers' relationships with windows. One manager had a private office with a large window looking north over the strip-mall parking lot. The upper one-third of the window was clear, allowing a view of the sky, while the lower two-thirds had been obscured with a frosted film, presumably for privacy. He received plenty of daylight from both the upper window and the lower frosted section, and he could see vague shadows of people passing by on the adjacent sidewalk. When asked about his window, he said he found it *extremely* annoying, as he "*couldn't see out.*" He wanted to know who was walking by his window: was it his next appointment showing up? And even worse, sometimes he could hear an argument or a crash in the parking lot beyond, and then he felt compelled to climb up on his chair so that he could see what was happening. To him, his big window was just a tease. It provided him with alerting events—shadows or noises—but no resolution. The manager next door had a similar office arrangement, but instead of the frosted film on the lower window she had vertical blinds, which she kept mostly closed. She could easily peek through them if need be. She had no complaints.

Some other workers at the bank had desks arrayed along windows fronting the street, which provided valuable real estate for corporate advertising. Huge framed posters hung in some, filling most of the glazing area. Little four-inch slices of clear glass remained at the sides and bottoms of the posters. All other windows were completely covered with giant images of happy customers, printed on perforated vinyl wrap.

The people working next to the opaque posters reported feeling distracted and annoyed by their little slices of view. Traffic outside flashed by too quickly for them to understand. They generally tried to ignore the windows, even shielding their eyes with their hands. However, they explained, they occasionally did peek outside by putting their nose right up to glass. They appreciated the ability to do so.

The people sitting next to the vinyl wrap were more content with their windows, and less distracted by the movements outside, since they could detect the blurry but coherent shapes of people and cars through the pinholes. They did, however, feel a bit oppressed by the giant faces looming above, and reported that they didn't feel like they were sitting next to a *real* window.

In both cases, understanding the movement of people and cars outside largely determined their satisfaction with the view. The first group, sitting next to the paper posters, had clarity, but no continuity. Because their view was fragmented into little slices, it become incoherent and frustrating. The second group had continuity, but little clarity. While detail was missing, they could still detect big objects and big movements.

The most common form of filtered view is surely just through a dirty window. The gradual accumulation of dirt and grime on a window can be imperceptible, very slowly and uniformly fading its light and eroding the clarity of a view. I personally associate dirty windows with old and forgotten places, attics, and basements that have been uninhabited for years. I have sometimes walked into an old barn or factory and been amazed at the buildup of dust, dirt, and cobwebs that obscure windows almost to the point of opacity. Thus, hazy windows can imply poor maintenance and disrespect for the occupants. In contrast, clean glass has a crisp sparkle that accentuates the immediacy of whatever life is taking place outside.

Films and ceramic frits adhered to the surface of the glass can also create a variety of obscure patterns, and they have the advantage that they are applied in controlled patterns, allowing clear and obscure glass to alternate. These techniques allow a designer to choose the right amount of clarity versus translucence, a balance that allows just enough of both privacy and view without inducing too much frustration. Getting that balance right may require some artistry. If that bank manager in Vancouver had just a few small voids of clear glass in his frosted window, he might have been less frustrated!

Indeed, obscure or frosted films and frits can now be manufactured to create almost any conceivable two-toned, two-dimensional design: a decorative pattern permanently frozen onto the glass surface. Elaborate geometric or floral patterns, logos, maps, even photo-realistic portraits, are not much more difficult to implement than simple stripes or screens. In this case, the design printed on the glass becomes itself both a filter and the intended view, much like an antique lace curtain displayed in a door's window. The scale of the pattern, the regularity of the voids, and importantly, the balance of light on either side of the glass, determines which is seen as dominant: the view beyond the glass or the design printed upon it.

Veiling and Scrims

Theatrical designers have long known a secret of using a scrim, a tautly-stretched, gauzy fabric as a backdrop for their stage sets: an image painted on the scrim, such as a street façade, will seem completely solid when it is brightly illuminated from the audience side. However, as the light balance changes, so that the actors behind the scrim become more brightly lit, then the scrim eventually disappears from view as the audience looks beyond it. Our eyes look through the darker surface and pay attention to the brighter objects beyond. The darker the fabric, the easier it is to see through, as the dark threads scatter less light, causing less interference with the view.

This principle also applies to almost any kind of architectural screen, whether fabric, metal, or printed on glass. When the surface of the screen in front of you is most brightly lit, you see the surface as opaque. Whenever objects behind the screen are more brightly lit than the surface of the screen, it appears transparent. This means that a sunlit mesh shade will mostly block a view to the shadowed scene outside. The effect reverses at night when the room is more brightly lit than the outdoors: then, screens that provide privacy to an interior room during the day become transparent in the other direction, allowing outsiders to look in, while preventing the occupants from seeing out.

Moghul India transformed architectural partitions into a high art form. Beautifully carved wood and stone screens, with elaborate geometric and floral arabesque designs, called *jali* (from the Hindi/Urdu word for 'net') became an integral part of Indo-Islamic architecture. While found in some temples and mosques, jali were most commonly used in the women's quarters of homes and palaces to provide privacy and security, along with ample ventilation and a filtered view of the outside world. Persian artisans preferred geometric designs, while indigenous Hindu artisans created elaborate florals and arabesques. The perforated stone provided enough depth to create shade from the sun overhead, and also increased the surface area for heat exchange, absorbing some of the heat of the day, to cool the ventilation air as it passed through. They were artful, while providing privacy and cool shadows. Thus, the jali were a form of extreme luxury: architectural lace.

Architects have recently been experimenting with perforated metal sheets as solar screens on the outside of buildings: you can think of these as permanent architectural scrims, or jali produced on an industrial scale. Originally the metal screens were created with simple mechanical hole punches that produced regular circle or square voids, but now highly elaborate and intricate patterns are possible using digitally-controlled laser-cutting technology, just as with the films and frits discussed above. Perforation patterns can be reproduced at monumental scales, likely with far more attention to the uniqueness of the design than the quality of the view through it. These buildings are being veiled, hidden behind perforation patterns that create both images and shadows, thin two-dimensional patterns that dominate the definition of a façade.

At what point does the veil create a sense of imprisonment instead of protection or privilege? I have been wondering about that question since one of our early studies of schools found that children in classrooms that had some form of security protection around the windows, such as bars, perforated metal screens, or plastic security glazing (usually scratched and yellowed), made significantly less academic progress over the school year.[19] We were assured by the school administrators that these security measures were left over from previous uses, like last year's computer lab, and did not reflect on the type of students assigned to those classrooms. Other systems of reducing daylight and view, like tints, curtains, blinds, or pictures taped to the windows, didn't have such a consistently negative effect on student performance. Thus, the most likely explanation for our finding was some kind of psychological effect on the students implying constraint or deprivation.

Reflections

Another type of filter that can create even more ambiguity is mirrored surfaces. The first mirrored surface was undoubtedly quiet water, when one of our hominoid ancestors first looked down and recognized her own face, much like Narcissus in Greek mythology, enraptured by his reflection in a pool of water. Clear calm water can allow us to both look down through the water, to see pebbles or fish, and see an upward reflection at the same time. Polished glass is also partially reflective under the right conditions, reflecting best at glancing angles and when the light balance is brightest on the observer's side. Jalousie windows, common in humid tropical climates like Hawaii and India, present an interesting example. They consist of operable horizontal strips of glass shingled downward to allow ample ventilation while shedding rain.. The angled glass differentially reflects light, and can create layered strata of view/reflection/view/reflection that allow the observer to see both inward and outward simultaneously.

Some conceptual artists have been playing with the idea of interlaced views and reflections on a monumental scale, creating mirrored outdoor sculptures that create immersive mazes for people to walk through, experiencing the confusion of fractured views. Imagine wandering through a miniature Stonehenge built of perfectly reflecting mirrors, whose purpose is not to orient you, but rather to disorient you. For example, Danish artist Jeppe Hein's mirrored sculpture *Semicircular space 2016* was described as: "*a nautilus-like labyrinthine ... where the physical space and the mirrored space are experienced in an alternating rhythm.*" As people walk into the spirals, they see both themselves in multiple narrow reflections, along with staccato slices of other visitors as they pass by. The progressively angled mirrors double the apparent motion, and toy with any conception of a cognitive map, as physical presence and reflection become indistinguishable.[20]

I experienced a prosaic version of this mirrored ambiguity in some workstation partitions that we installed in our company's offices. We choose a partition system that was opaque up to four feet, then had glass panels above, thinking that it would increase access to view and daylight deeper into the space. What I hadn't counted on was the partial reflectivity of the glass panels, such that when facing the window, you could also see a subtle reflection of someone standing behind you, and when sitting looking away from the window you could see a transparent reflection of the sunlit trees outside. This was both useful, allowing employees to more easily monitor their surrounds, and enchanting, as the reflected street trees added layers of seasonal color and detail throughout the office.

Reflective glass surfaces, however, can also wreak visual havoc when solar reflections and glare are not properly anticipated. A new government office building in San Francisco had a difficult challenge: optimize daylight and views for offices along a large north-west-facing façade. The designers choose to mount vertical glass fins around windows to both shade the windows and bounce western sunlight deeper into the space. The glass fins had a sanded finish, likely intended to better diffuse the sunlight, but being translucent, they also restricted the view. Furthermore, the redirected sunlight translated into intolerable glare for the office workers, resulting in widespread rebellion and eventually, expensive lawsuits. Extensive retrofits added both tinted films and roller shades to reduce the apparent brightness of the sun. However, a post-occupancy evaluation of this building *after* the retrofits found that occupants were still extremely dissatisfied with the visual conditions, largely because the low angle sun, doubled by its reflection, was both inescapable and disorienting, while the views were fragmented and unsatisfying.[21]

These stories of reflecting surfaces creating partial transparencies, fragmented views and disorienting reflections again raise questions: how filtered or fragmented can a view be and remain satisfying? Where is the dividing line between ambiguity that is intriguing, versus annoying? What is the relationship between size, scale, distance, and movement in determining clarity or continuity? Some insight can be provided via the concept of spatial frequencies.

Spatial Frequencies

The mathematical concept of 'spatial frequency' offers a useful framework for trying to understand how people respond to views—in terms of understanding how scale, detail, distance, filters, and obstructions all interact to impact clarity and coherence. Spatial frequency analysis is derived from Fourier analysis, a branch of physics that studies wave forms and harmonic patterns to describe the distribution, density and interaction of information. Waves, such as sound waves, can be observed to have multiple harmonics, with both big and little waves interacting to form complex patterns.

In the realm of visual perception, spatial frequency describes the scale of details within an image, reported as the number of contrasting cycles per degree of visual angle. Things that we see as very small, whether close up or far away, have high spatial frequency; whereas things that loom larger in our field of view have lower spatial frequency. Because a given object will appear smaller the farther away it is from the viewer, spatial frequency accounts for both the size of the object and the position of the viewer. Thus, a row of identical houses, seen in perspective, will exhibit a full range of spatial frequencies, from very low frequencies for those houses closest to the viewer to high frequencies, for those farthest away.

It has been hypothesized that cells in the human retina and visual processing centers are individually tuned to respond to specific spatial frequencies, such as those which are especially important in differentiating human faces and motion. These systems are happiest when they are all acting in concert. Thus, a view that activates the full range of spatial frequency responses will be found more pleasurable than one with a limited range. If so, then logically, a 'good view' should include a range of fine details, middle sized objects, and big organizing structures.

I would argue that, in general, the most essential information that we gather from our window views has lower spatial frequencies—such as patterns of light, shadow, and colors—that determine the shape, location, and movement of large forms and structures. However, the visual information that we most enjoy are the tiny details—such as identifying faces, the sparkle on a lake, the twigs on a tree, or a bird in flight—which all have extremely high spatial frequency.

Indeed, one recent study conducted at the University of Waterloo, Canada, seems to bear out this hypothesis.[22] Researchers there tested the response of 55 undergraduates to paired photographs of somewhat similar urban and natural scenes, and also manipulated the images to reduce various bands of spatial frequencies. They found that the natural scenes of forests or parkland were judged the most pleasant, and also had the highest spatial frequencies. But when the researchers selectively removed the higher spatial frequencies, the emotional distinction between natural and urban views disappeared.

Intersecting Patterns and Motion

Earlier, in the discussion on 'Framing a View' (see page 151) Michael Pollan pointed out the power of a window grid to segment a view, creating multiple panes of reference *"like an artist's grid."* He described how his own motion changed the perspective between the middle view of the mullion grid and the more distant view of his pond and forest. Any geometric arrangement of window segments is likely to have this effect of emphasizing movement, either indoors or out, by creating a refence grid.

Most windows may also have some type of screens, shades, frits, blinds, or louvers which also create regular patterns of grids, holes, or stripes at a much smaller scale. Horizontal blinds (a.k.a. Venetian blinds) are essentially a pure visual diffraction grate, creating a striped yes/no pattern of view/no-view/view/no-view. Our visual processing centers are remarkably good at filling in the missing information, especially from a regularly spaced grate, by interpolating between the strips of information that are provided. Similarly, we can do a remarkably good job constructing an image from a screen with regularly spaced holes.

Here is where spatial frequency analysis comes in: the larger the holes, and the closer they are spaced together, the more detail (high spatial frequency information) is preserved. Likewise, with horizontal or vertical blinds, the more closely spaced the voids between the slats, the easier it is for our brains to construct a detailed image. The original Venetian blinds made of large wooden slates were three to four inches wide, and created thick slices of the world that were hard to piece together into a coherent image. However, the farther you step back from a window with old-style thick Venetian blinds, the more coherent a view you can see beyond them, as the relative spatial frequency of the slats are increased due to their distance from your eye. The use of aluminum slats to manufacture one-inch mini-blinds greatly improved the overall transparency of horizontal blinds. Even smaller, ½ inch thick micro blinds are barely visible until they are completely closed.

There is a related phenomenon which has to do with motion, both the motion of an object on the other side of the screen or grate, and the motion of our own eyes and body while looking through it. The airplane was easily identified by the office workers in Norfolk because it moved so quickly and predictably, crossing multiple pinholes in a smooth trajectory. When an object that we are looking at moves between the voids of a screen, our brain easily identifies it as a unified object, rather than independent flashes. Vision scientists have done lots of interesting studies about the conditions under which we will perceive flashes of light as representing a continuous object in motion, rather than unrelated events.[23]

The flip side to this equation is that when we move our viewpoint relative to the screen or grate, the screening element becomes more transparent, as our eyes move around it, whether up and down or side to side. Try putting your hand out in front of you on an outstretched arm, with your fingers spread equally apart. Then look past your hand at an object on the other side of the room. First try jiggling your hand a bit, and see how quickly it becomes transparent. Next try jiggling your head instead. Likely, when you move your head, you will have a more difficult time making your hand appear transparent, as your eyes compensate for the movement of your head, trying to stabilize your view. But the reality is that our eyes and our heads are continuously moving. We bob our heads up and down when we walk, we look side to side while we are sitting.

Try the experiment again with your hand out in front of you, this time holding your hand still, with both eyes open and looking past your hand to the far side of the room. First hold up one finger, then two, then three fingers, and note when they are no longer fully transparent. Repeat the experiment with one eye closed, so that you no longer have the advantage of binocular vision: even just one finger remains fully opaque. Thus we've got three things going for us, helping us to see past nearby screens and slats: first, binocular vision; second, eye saccades; and third, head nodding and bobbing.

Your pinky finger, seen at the end of your outstretched arm, is about one degree wide. Your thumb is about two degrees. Four fingers held out at arms-length cover about five degrees of visual field. Using a combination of binocular vision, eye scans, and head movement, our brains can easily knit together images separated by one or two degrees of blank space, such as by a blind slat or a window mullion, but beyond that it gets increasingly difficult, unless our bodies are also moving perpendicular to the openings. Sitting in a moving automobile, picket fences quickly become completely invisible as the vehicle picks up speed. Sitting in a train, you can even see right through an adjacent train moving in the opposite direction, knitting together the view between the cars, if the two trains are going fast enough.

Thus, with movement, we gain the ability to congeal even more information together into a coherent view. The more predictable the view, the more regular the pattern obstructing the view, the more consistent the motion of the object being viewed, and the more quickly we can move our own viewpoint, the easier it is for our brains to knit all this information into a coherent image.

However, there is also a warning here. Because our brains are so primed to try to understand regular patterns, they can sometimes go into over-drive. Some highly sensitive people can react to certain regular visual patterns, especially high contrast stripes and dots, with migraines or even photosensitive epilepsy. Striped stairway patterns can easily induce dizziness and vertigo. I once visited a building that used fritted glass to reduce the transparency of the glass around an interior atrium. The frits were in a regular dotted pattern. When I looked through the glass on one side the atrium to the opposite glass wall, the close-up and far-away dot patterns interacted to create complex moiré patterns, which undulated with slightest head movements. It was very disorienting, and indeed, I learned that many workers had reported migraines and requested reassignment to another building. Arnold Wilkins, a professor of psychology at the University of Essex in the UK, made a career of studying these kinds of visual disfunctions. He recently wrote a plea to those involved in building sciences to pay more attention to the impact of interacting visual patterns. He contends that those patterns which are most different from naturally occurring spatial frequencies cause the most problems.[24]

Fractals

There is another mathematical area that promises to help us better understand the appeal of views: fractal analysis. Fractals are patterns of self-similar shapes that repeat at many scales. The term was invented by the mathematician Benoit Mandelbrot in 1975, to describe shapes that were generated from a formula that he devised, that generated geometric shapes of great complexity, but with infinitely repeating themes at ever smaller and ever larger scales. The original Mandelbrot Set he devised still amazes with its repeating, ever-folding, and flowering complexity. (It is best viewed as a video to observe the continuous transformations.[25]) Artists soon discovered the visual fascination of fractal patterns, and a whole new discipline of fractal art was popularized, facilitated by ever more powerful computer graphics and data analysis.

It was also quickly realized that some of the mathematical equations for fractals generated very naturalistic looking shapes, resembling trees, flowers, mountains, rivers, or coastlines. Thus, scientists suspected that there might be fractal principles at work in the generation of natural forms. Biologists began to look for fractal patterns and found the repetition of shapes and patterns at many scales in the plant and animal kingdoms, from cellular growth to ecological relationships. These fractal relationships were not just in visible patterns, but also in temporal patterns. Indeed, fractal processes have since come to be recognized as intrinsic to the health of biological systems, as explained by Li Ping, a Harvard circadian sleep researcher: *"Fractal regulation is an intrinsic property of many biological systems and are believed to be a hallmark of healthy physiology, indicating system integrity and adaptability. Numerous studies have demonstrated that alterations in fractal physiological fluctuations are associated with aging, pathological conditions, and diseases, in which systems become less adaptive to perturbations and more vulnerable to catastrophic events."*[26]

I recently took a trip to Death Valley National Park in California, set in a desert known for being one of the hottest and driest places on the planet. With very little vegetation, Death Valley offers amazing vistas of mountains and plains completely missing an overlayer of plant life. Death Valley is a masterpiece of geological fractal patterns: with layers upon layers of triangular mountain peaks, alluvial deposits, and dendric drainage patterns. (*Dendric*, from the Greek word *dendron*, meaning tree, is related to the term dendrite, a type of neuron also with a fractal branching pattern.) It is possible that especially fascinating views include such fractal patterns. Urban and built landscapes can also have fractal elements. The highly ornamented buildings of the Gothic and Victorian eras often embody fractal relationships, with progressively detailed levels of carvings. As mentioned earlier, almost any continuous perspective view, whether it be buildings, telephone poles, or mountain ranges has a fractal nature to it. A perspective view of simple row houses creates a fractal pattern, as each house farther away replicates the shapes of those closer in, mentally pulling us farther and farther out into the landscape.

Zooming In and Out

I have often wondered why humans are so good at mentally changing scale. As an architect, I was trained to understand a building from a set of plans at 1:10 scale or a city from a map where one inch = one mile. In my first experience visiting a house under construction which I had designed, I strangely felt myself to be suddenly an inch and a half tall, as if I had been miniaturized in order to walk around inside the 1/4" scale white foam-core model I had worked on so diligently. Other professions also mentally zoom in and out, with remarkable agility. Surgeons and dentists looking through microscopes see their work in expanded detail, while still correctly controlling their muscles to work in real scale. Mariners use binoculars to understand their environment in the opposite scale, navigating by distant landmarks, and maps that reduce their world to a tiny fraction of reality.

It is easy to understand that a hawk, as a predator, needs to have the mental capacity to identify prey, such as a mouse in a field far below, and be able to swoop down, descending at very high speed, all the while keeping the mouse fixed in its sights in order to grab it in its talons. So the hawk needs to perceptually understand the mouse at many scales, from a dot in the meadow to a body in its beak. Likewise, imagine a hawk deciding to perch in a distant tree. The hawk needs to understand the tree as the same object from far away, close up, and even from within, as flies inside the tree branches to find a perfect perching spot. Thus, the hawk must have a continuous understanding of the structure of the tree branches at multiple scales. This is inherently a fractal conception of the tree, as it changes in visual scale during the hawk's flight.

Humans didn't evolve with as much speed or three-dimensional agility as a hawk, and yet still we have easily accommodated to moving about on skis, bikes, and cars which enable similar degrees of speed and movement. Our mental ability to zoom in and out of scales is truly remarkable. It may be that part of our aesthetic pleasure in fractals is based in this mental capacity for zooming in and out of scales so freely. The fractal pattern you contemplate may be vast, like a sweeping vista of Death Valley's geology, or intimate, like a tiny bonsai tree on your window sill. Our brains seem to be wired to understand the world at a continuous range of scales, and it may give us pleasure to exercise that capability, even if it is only from glancing out the window now and then.

Three Layered Views

Advanced mathematics, neurology, and psychology may eventually give us tools to better understand the characteristics of a good view, and why. But in the meantime, building designers look for simple 'rules of thumb' to provide immediate guidance on what constitutes sufficiently good views for building occupants. Some voluntary building standards, such as Leadership in Energy and Environmental Design (LEED) or WELL, have adopted simple metrics to give qualifying credits for better view access, derived from the best available research at the time.

Perhaps a simpler approach is that adopted by the British Design Standard, based merely on simple logic.[27] It contends that the best views consist of three layers: a view of the sky, a view of the ground, and a middle layer in between. A view of the sky likely includes clouds, sunsets, birds, and horizon. The view of the ground can include pathways, waterways, meadows, and agricultural fields, and people and cars moving along those horizontal surfaces. The middle layer in between includes all the vertical elements that make the 'stuff' of our cities and countryside, such as buildings, trees, rocks, and walls, and any landmarks rising vertically from the ground. Thus, such a simple rule of thumb guarantees that most of the desirable elements in this chapter will be included, and that there will likely be enough distance and complexity to satisfy our yearnings for fractal patterns, ambiguity, motion, and change of scale.

Indeed, given such a simple construct, it is then possible to quantify the proportion of each layer's contribution in any given view as a way of assessing its balance.[28] Computer simulation programs promise great analytic power to predict the quality of a visual environment, whether based on illuminance patterns or view content, once we agree on the basic factors to be considered.

However, there is much more to the successful design of well-daylit spaces with satisfying views than mastering the physics, physiology and psychology. Buildings are also very much an expression of our social systems and cultural priorities. The following chapters in Part 3, Motivation, explore the social context, examining the changing priorities and passions that shape the forms of our buildings.

There is often a considerable time lag between the people who are responsible for the initial design of buildings and cities, and the people who later inhabit those places. History provides some insight to why various forms were once favored, including the cultural, economic, and technological pressures of the time, and why some forms have proven more enduring than others, by being more easily adapted to new uses and priorities. Places which can fully satisfy occupants' desire for daylight and views are likely to be the most enduring over time.

The following chapters examine a number of building types, focusing mostly on places where people spend much of their day, at work, school, or play. We start with schools for young children and end with hospices for the dying. In between, there are many stories from the trenches, about how daylight and views help people form emotional bonds with their workplaces, and what motivates building owners, managers, and occupants to successfully maintain the daylighting systems of their buildings.

Part 3: Motivation

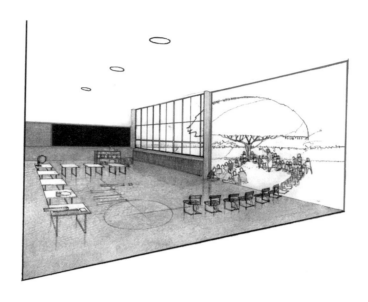

10. Daylighting Education

The design of public schools in the United States provides an especially interesting case study in the history of attitudes towards windows, daylight, and views, as those attitudes have changed radically over the years. I spent a number of years designing schools, which taught me that people are more passionate about the design of schools than almost any other building type, partly because schools are imbued with such a deep public purpose, and partly because everyone has some personal history with schools, whether as student, parent, or teacher.

Public education in the United States began in the New England colonies, based on the Protestant belief that universal literacy was essential for reading the Bible, enabling all the colonies' citizens to cultivate a direct relationship with God. Massachusetts was the first colony to set up publicly-funded schools, in the 1600s, and the first to mandate compulsory education, in 1852. Each township was required to build a schoolhouse for its local population of children. These buildings often looked like small churches or town halls but were most easily identified by their extra tall windows, providing sufficient daylight for the young scholars.

Other states soon followed Massachusetts' lead, such that by 1900 there were 34 states which had laws requiring minimum school attendance at least through elementary school. As the population grew in the mid-west and western states, one-room schoolhouses were often replaced with larger multi-grade 'union' schools, unifying the education for more children from multiple towns. Many guidebooks to schoolhouse design were available providing standardized layouts and design advice, especially an admonition that large classroom windows should ideally be on both sides of the students' desks to avoid shadowing, or if that was not possible, then to the left of the students to avoid shadowing their right hand, required for writing. A widely used guidebook[1] published in 1910 carefully specified window sizes and configurations, including advice that *"The sill should, however, not be higher than 3 ½ feet from the floor, as it is desirable that the pupils should be able to rest their eyes at times by looking out at more or less distant objects ..."* A recent history of school design noted that *"This simple way of explaining the need for views would largely disappear in the century to follow, as school classroom design became increasingly engineered and economized."*[2]

The period immediately after the First World War saw an enormous boom in public school building, as the country rededicated itself to democratic values. The American school buildings of the 1920s were typically two- to three-story brick buildings, modeled after factory construction, with high-ceilinged, high-windowed classrooms lined up along an interior hallway. Daylight was still the primary illuminant, with a minimum of three footcandles (30 lux) of incandescent electric lighting recommended to supplement the daylight. These schools ended up serving generations of students, because construction of new schools almost ceased during the next 15 years, due to the Great Depression and the Second World War.

Meanwhile, a few other design trends were taking hold. A progressive movement in nineteenth-century Germany initiated the concept that even very young children could benefit from schooling, but that they should spend most of their day learning via free play, in a garden-like setting. From this movement developed our kindergartens (from the German *kinder* = child and *garten* = garden). Thus, while schools for older children featured orderly rows of desks facing the teacher at the front of the classroom, kindergarten rooms were more free-flowing, with free-choice activity centers allowing children to select their preferred environment. The Waldorf schools set up by Rudolf Steiner in Germany were an outgrowth of this movement, as were the Montessori schools named after founder Maria Montessori in Italy.

In the United States, this progressive movement influenced a number of young American architects with European roots, such as Eliel Saarinen and Alvar Aalto, and especially Richard Neutra, who proposed a new design approach in the 1930s known as the 'open air school' movement, due to the emphasis placed on air, light, outdoor learning and easy circulation through the school buildings.[3] At the time, before vaccinations and antibiotics became common after the Second World War, fresh air and sunshine was considered the primary strategy for prevention of tuberculosis and the Spanish flu that had ravaged the country in 1919. Neutra had grown up in a family of doctors and engineers in Austria, and became one of the prime proponents that architectural design should serve public health by creating healthier indoor environments. Neutra designed a ground-breaking elementary school near Los Angeles with exterior walls comprised of continuous sliding glass doors, similar to the shoji screens of a Japanese house, that opened out to a teaching courtyard for each classroom. (See Neutra's conceptual sketch for the Corona Avenue School on page 187.)

By 1940, 50% of American adults had a high school education. When the Second World War ended in 1945, there was again renewed enthusiasm for building public schools, and ever greater urgency given the rapidly expanding population of 'baby boom' children of returning soldiers. A new generation of architectural theorists espoused ideas for what 'modern' schools should look like and how they should serve the country, certain that these modern schools would look nothing like those of previous generations.

A popular type of school plan of the 1950s was termed 'the finger plan,' largely derived from open-air school movement's ideas about the need for plenty of daylight and fresh air. These were one-story buildings, with lightweight steel construction, inexpensive and quick to construct, where the 'fingers' were long rows of classrooms with ample, operable windows on opposite sides. In colder climates, an interior corridor served the classrooms; in warmer climates, exterior circulation pathways were preferred. However, by the 1960s, forces were afoot that would challenge the primacy of windows as a determinant of school design.

Air conditioning was becoming ever more affordable and desirable, especially in hot, humid southern climates. Operable windows were considered an unnecessary complication for mechanical ventilation systems, since if teachers were able to open a window, the ventilation system became unbalanced, preventing it from distributing thermal comfort evenly. The rise of inexpensive fluorescent lighting in the 1950s also convinced many architects that windows were no longer needed as a light source. The Illuminating Engineering Society (IES) had raised its recommended light levels in classroom from three footcandles in 1920, to 30, then to 70 footcandles by 1959.[4] Although classroom illumination levels were still assumed to be a combination of daylight and electric light sources, daylighting was considered increasingly unreliable compared to the flick of a light switch.

There were also important economic pressures, forcing school districts to look for ever cheaper ways to build all the new schools that were needed to house this burgeoning baby boom generation. The popular finger plan used up a great deal of land, whereas more compact schools could be built on smaller sites. Windows were seen as *the problem*. If classrooms could be designed with fewer or no windows, school districts could save on both land and building costs.

The Michigan Study: Early 1960s

The prestigious Architectural Research Laboratory, at the University of Michigan School of Architecture, decided to address this question head on, with a major study funded by the Ford Foundation.[5] As they explained in their introduction: *"It was just about this time—September 1961—that the attention of school architects and school administrators throughout the United States was drawn to the problem of windowless classrooms. A number of underground structures designed to do double duty as fallout shelters and as elementary schools were being built in New Mexico and elsewhere. The whole concept of* fenestration *had come into question as the result of advances in air conditioning and artificial illumination. In fact, many air-conditioning engineers and lighting specialists were contending that windows are not only an unnecessary building expense but an operational nuisance as well, particularly insofar as they introduce problems of heat transmission and visual glare."*

American children in the 1950s and 60s Cold War era were all taught 'duck and cover' drills to protect them from the immediate effects of a nuclear blast, such as flying glass and blinding light. (The Cuban Missile Crisis was in 1962.) Thus, the idea of windowless classrooms also promised important civil defense benefits in addition to energy savings. However, this new trend in windowless classrooms was not without controversy, with many people protesting that they were simply not good for children.

The Michigan researchers hoped to resolve this controversy with carefully formulated and unbiased research. They assembled a stellar research team with 29 professors contributing diverse expertise from architecture, engineering, education, psychology, and public health. They added prominent advisors, including Michigan's Director of Public Education and Edward Hall, the noted anthropologist. They also acknowledged input from three teachers from their candidate school district in Wayne, Michigan, the only women on this 43-member study team.

The researchers identified two little elementary schools which they considered perfect for their study, each with only four classrooms, housing kindergarten through third grade. The Mann School would serve as a control, while during the second year of the three-year study, windows at the Hoover School would be replaced with opaque panels. (Not coincidentally, in the second year, the ventilation and fluorescent lighting were also permanently increased to compensate for the lack of operable windows.) In order to overcome early resistance to the study by parents, the researchers promised to monitor the children's mental and physical health throughout the project.

However, the parents were not particularly won over. While the report's abstract claims that "... *minor resistance to the study was encountered ...*," within the body of the report the parents' 'minor resistance' seems a bit more formidable. A handful of the parents were labeled objectors and the researchers noted that they continued to object throughout duration of the study. One of the more vocal parents was quoted numerous times: "... *she felt the parents should have been consulted first, since this concerned their children. She felt the parents were treated like they were stupid. On another occasion she said, 'God gave us the sun to enjoy, and no one has a right to take it away from us.'*"

There were also problems with retention of both teachers and students. At the Hoover School test site, the researchers reported that three of the four teachers did not return for the second year when the windows were removed. Plus, "*in the recruitment of new teachers for the Hoover School several candidates declined because they did not want to teach in windowless classrooms.*" The researchers did not consider this recruitment challenge to be problematic for their study, but rather simply par for the course of a small elementary school manned by young women teachers. Kindergarten absences at the Hoover School went up dramatically during the windowless year, but this also was not deemed cause for concern, as it was considered a likely anomaly.

While each school housed about 130 students across the four grades, given yearly graduations and general mobility, only about 90 made it through two years of the study, and only 30 students completed all three years. The researchers attempted to track student grades across the study period, but found the teachers' subjective grading too 'elastic' and the number of students too small for detecting any meaningful trends. However, they took this lack of a clear pattern as a positive, in that no obvious negative effect had been detected.

The researchers reported on interviews they held with all the children about their opinion of the windowless classrooms. During the second year at the Hoover School, 71% of the students missed the windows. Kindergarten children fared even worse, with 87% complaining they missed the windows. However, the researchers put more faith in the teachers, who reported the children really did not care much one way or the other.

The four teachers at Hoover, on the other hand, liked the lack of visual distractions, and the improved HVAC system. The report explained: *"The one positive finding that does emerge from the Hoover School experiment is the remarkable shift in attitude by the teachers. There is no question as to their preference for windowless classrooms, once they have had the experience of teaching in such an environment, and they are unanimous in their reasons for not wanting the windows: the children are no longer distracted by outside happenings when the classrooms become windowless, and besides, the extra wall space can be put to good instructional use. Several professional educators, however, have questioned whether the elimination of outside distractions is always something to be desired."*

After three years of careful study, the Michigan researchers concluded that overall windows had little effect on student learning. Based on their *"one positive finding"* that the Hoover teachers preferred windowless classrooms, they felt comfortable recommending: *"In building planning, fenestrated classrooms should be considered only when educational purposes are served by an outside view."* The opinion of those four teachers, three of whom were specifically hired conditional on their willingness to teach in a windowless classroom, was enough to support a definitive conclusion.

The Michigan report was widely disseminated. Towards the end of the 1960s windowless classrooms had been embraced by many school districts as a good solution for their new schools, including the one where I attended high school in Los Angeles. Previously, Birmingham High School had been housed in old wooden bungalows, built as a temporary army hospital in the 1940s, with tall triple-hung windows lining both sides of the classrooms.[6] In my senior year, we moved into the new campus, built of pre-cast concrete, with one narrow slit window at the back of each classroom. I took it very personally. In calculus class I found I could no longer sit still. I squirmed and fidgeted, feeling like I was being force-fed math, with no mental breaks to chew or digest the new information. In French and physics I found every possible excuse to go work outside. In history class I just fell asleep. My memories of that final year still make me feel stressed and anxious. The one highlight was my English class, which continued on the old campus, so I had one hour of windowed-relief per day. Apparently, the English teachers had refused en masse to move over to the new campus!

Ten years after the publication of the Michigan report, the controversy still continued. Belinda Collins at the National Bureau of Standards was tasked with investigating the issue. In 1975 she published a very thorough literature review which could not find sufficiently credible studies to support the argument one way or the other.[7] She quoted Robert Sommer, an environmental psychologist, to capture the then current attitudes: *"At present the pro-window forces still lack behavioral data in support of their case and argue on the basis of metaphor and supposition, but their arguments must be weighed against statistics ... from the windowless schools ... reported to have 40 percent greater efficiency in heating and cooling, constant light to prevent eye strain ... 35 decibels or more noise reduction, and reduced maintenance costs."* He continued: *"Opponents [of windowless schools] now take recourse in the need for communion with nature, contact with the outside and stimulus variation, which are more difficult to measure, and whose importance is not readily apparent."*[8]

In Collins's view, the engineers who considered windows an *"operational nuisance"* had clearly made their case, while those concerned with the well-being of students had no evidence to stand on. Collins did note, however, that the number of people who were passionate about the need for windows for psychological reasons merited *"further consideration."*

The California Studies on Daylighting in Schools: Early 2000s

Twenty years after Belinda Collins wrote her report, I encountered a unique opportunity for the *"further consideration"* of daylighting in schools. My venture into field research on the impacts of daylighting picked up in the 1990s and continued through 2010. Previously, I had been working as a school architect for a number of years, mastering the intricacies of state funding for school construction, and learning how to optimize what little funds were available to design the best schools possible.[9] For me, trained as a passive solar architect, that meant schools that used minimal energy while also providing a high level of physical comfort and a welcoming environment for learning.

At that time, the standard practice at the firm where I was working was to specify darkly tinted glass for all classroom windows, colloquially referred to as 'limousine glass' with only 14% visible light transmittance. The thought at the time was that the dark glass reduced unwanted glare, reduced cooling loads, provided greater privacy for the teacher, and reduced the need for additional blinds or curtains. Of course, it also essentially eliminated any daylight in the classroom and made the views to the outside somber and muted. I proposed classrooms with well-balanced daylight using skylights and clear windows, but was often shot down by a whole fleet of consultants and facilities managers who wanted to keep doing things the same way, and often claimed that 'district standards' prevented them from considering daylit classrooms. It was clear that resistance to daylighting was highly institutionalized, and that it would require passionate advocacy from a district superintendent or angry parents to change course. Frustrated, I quit my job as a school architect and returned to working in building energy efficiency research. Fortunately, in retrospect, this work prompted me to master a new set of data collection and analysis skills—skills which later translated directly to studying the impacts of daylight on a big scale.

A rare alignment of interests occurred in 1997 which enabled my new consulting firm to do our first set of studies on daylighting and human performance. The California Public Utilities Commission was looking for ways to accelerate market adoption of new energy efficiency measures for buildings. The goal was to reduce the need to build more electric power plants. In the late 1990s they briefly embraced a philosophy called 'market transformation,' whereby they were willing to fund efforts that could logically increase utilization of efficiency measures by helping to overcome market resistance to adoption.[10]

At the time I already had plenty of evidence that there were great energy savings to be gained from wider deployment of daylighting in non-residential buildings, by using photocontrols to turn off the electric lighting during peak daytime hours. We also knew that daylit and naturally ventilated schools were more resilient, by enabling operational continuity during power outages and natural disasters. However, even though we could show that a daylit building with photocontrols had an attractive financial payback, building owners hesitated. Given my experience with school district policies, I understood many of the institutional barriers to change. I figured if we could change the *motivation* of the decision makers, by clearly demonstrating other daylighting benefits, then the building owners would likely embrace daylighting for those benefits, and the energy savings would follow along.

I proposed to attempt two different studies of the benefits of daylight—one comparing the performance of daylit versus non-daylit schools, and another doing the same for a large manufacturer or retail chain—with the hope of completing at least one of them. I was extremely fortunate that there were already strong advocates for daylighting at the utility company, Pacific Gas and Electric (PG&E), who agreed to fund my proposal.

I called these 'epidemiological-type studies,' using the metaphor of public health research, in that we would use large pre-existing databases of building performance to ascertain if there was an association between more daylight and better building outcomes. These days they are just referred to as 'Big Data' studies.

The Power of Big Data

I had not yet read Belinda Collins' report, and knew only parts of the history recounted above about daylighting in schools. This was also before the circadian pathway between ipRGC and the SCN was identified; thus, it was before there were any recognized cognitive or metabolic mechanisms that might have explained such an association.

My rationale for proposing to study daylighting in schools was simple. Having been the architect for many school projects, I understood the building type very well. I knew that there were hundreds of similar classrooms per school district, all the same size, with teachers teaching a similar curriculum, and students being tested on standardized tests. I knew that large school districts were continually evaluating those test scores to gauge the impact of recent curriculum or policy changes, while controlling for student and teacher demographics. I had used similar types of databases to evaluate the energy performance of large populations of buildings in energy efficiency programs, and I understood the power and limitations of the statistical methods used for those evaluations.

Thus, I reasoned that this building type—schools—was perfect for the type of large-scale statistical analysis that I proposed. It had the three critical components I needed for such a study: 1) lots of nearly identical buildings, but with slight variations in daylighting conditions; 2) a highly valued quantitative outcome (standardized test scores), tracked in an existing database which could be uniquely tied to a specific building location (the classroom); and 3) lots of other explanatory data, such as student, teacher, and curriculum characteristics, that I could easily access.

I narrowed the search to just elementary schools, reasoning that these students spent the majority of their time at school with just one teacher in a single classroom over the course of a year, and thus we were more likely to be able to isolate the effect of each classroom's design. We also specifically looked for districts whose schools had a wide range of daylighting conditions, from none to a lot, including some toplit classrooms.

The desire to include toplighting was part of our early concern about trying to differentiate daylight illumination effects from view effects. The project report explains why: "*Skylights generally provide a simple illumination function, whereas windows may have a far more complex effect on people. Windows typically offer a view, which may provide relaxation, inspiration or distraction. They are often operable, which may add ventilation, air quality, and thermal comfort issues. Daylight illumination levels from windows are highly variable within a space and over time, and may include components of unacceptable contrast and glare. User control of blinds or curtains also adds another dynamic variable that is difficult to measure. Windows are also connected with personal status and may have psychological implications beyond their mere physical attributes. Skylights would not seem to be as imbued with as much cultural meaning and tend to have less variability in user control.*"[11]

My study team was able to identify and recruit three large school districts that met our criteria and were willing to participate in the study, in Seattle, Washington, Fort Collins, Colorado, and Capistrano in Southern California. These three districts allowed us to review their building plans and visit their school sites to assess their daylighting conditions, and provided us with two years of test and demographic data, for a total of over 21,000 students. No one had ever done a study of this magnitude: the Michigan study had followed 30 children in four classrooms; a few other previous studies had compared two schools, or surveyed a few hundred students about their attitudes. We had no idea what we would find.

My team spent a year obtaining permissions and collecting data. We reviewed dusty old plan sets, visited hundreds of classrooms, took photographs, and classified daylighting conditions in over 1,000 classrooms. For each classroom we created two sets of daylight variables. One set classified the type of toplighting (none, skylights, roof monitors, clerestories), and the relative amount of window area modified by its visible light transmittance. For the second set, we distilled all daylight sources into a simplified daylight code, from 'zero' for none, to 'five' for the best, i.e. a classroom that could operate successfully with no electric lighting for much of year. We created a database with information about each school, such as building vintage, total number of students, and neighborhood demographic data, and assigned each classroom an identification code. The classroom identifier linked the physical data to the (anonymized) student demographic data and test scores provided by the districts.

Having succeeded in collecting comparable input data for all three school districts, we felt triumphant just to have reached that point. We then collaborated with a master statistician, Dr. Roger Wright, to set up the analysis and test our hypotheses. Wright was experienced working with building data sets in the energy efficiency world, with considerable experience in human factors analysis. We also consulted with the educational research firms who created and administered the student tests to make sure we were handling the student data correctly and were accounting for known influences on test performance.

Finally, after verifying the validity of *twelve* sets of multi-variate linear regression models—one each for math and reading test scores for each of the three districts, times two versions of daylight variable definition—we found that, all other things being equal, more daylight in classrooms was associated with improved math *and* reading test scores, in every single model!

In simple language, those children in classrooms with the *most* daylight had test performance that improved by 7% to 26% compared to those with *no* daylight, depending on which district and whether we were looking at math or reading tests. All our analysis models showed this finding with 99+% statistical certainty in all cases.[12]

Our analysis team was frankly astonished by the magnitude and certainty of the findings. We double-checked our numbers, added many caveats to our conclusions, then submitted our report. The program managers at PG&E were also amazed by the significance of the findings, and immediately asked us to have our analysis reviewed by a team of building scientists and statisticians convened by Lawrence Berkeley National Labs. Another six months passed while we satisfied all the questions and comments from the reviewers and succeeded in earning their approval. At last PG&E released the report and we were allowed to talk about it in public.

The study's findings made waves immediately. The next day a story about the study was on the front page of the Sacramento Bee. That night the story went out on the Associated Press news wire and was picked up by newspapers around the world. Within days I was receiving requests for radio interviews from Australia, Russia, and South Africa. The response from the school architectural community was equally fervent. Architects around the country quickly embraced daylight as a 'must have' for their school designs. Within two years I noted that almost every architectural award for school design was touting the amount of 'natural light' in the school buildings. Long ago I stopped keeping track of all the press that has been written about this study, but most gratifying are the school superintendents and facility managers who now request daylight in their new schools as a matter of course.

The Reanalysis Report: Teachers Speak Out

The story might end there, but even with 99% statistical certainty after examining all the elementary schools across three school districts in different climates over 1,000 miles apart, a few prominent academics continued to question the validity of the study, especially on the basis of the 'effect size.' They reasoned that if detecting a 'daylighting effect' required such a large study population, maybe the effect wasn't big enough, or precise enough, to be important. Since most of these researchers were more familiar with controlled laboratory studies, conducted with just a few dozen test subjects (most likely other college students), rather than Big Data field studies, with all the messiness and uncertainties of field work observing thousands of real-life subjects, they were not used to evaluating findings with lower predictive power. The California Energy Commission (CEC) was eager to see if we could address these critics, and add even greater certainty to the Capistrano findings, so in 2000 they funded two additional studies of daylit schools.

The first follow-on study, called the 'Re-Analysis Report' enabled us to go back to Capistrano School District to test some additional theories about the study. For example, we were able to consider if more daylighting was associated with a reduction in absenteeism (it was not statistically significant). Our primary purpose was to determine if there was any 'teacher selection bias' in our original data analysis, whereby better teachers might have been preferentially assigned to daylit classrooms. Thus, we conducted a formal survey of all teachers remaining in the Capistrano elementary schools a few years after the initial data collection and were provided further information about their tenure and qualifications by the district. We interviewed teachers and principals about their classroom assignment procedures. The surveys asked teachers to express their preferences for classroom features. For example, 15% of the teachers preferred portables over their permanent classroom options. We learned that overall, the preferences of Capistrano teachers were for: 1) more space; 2) a convenient location; 3) more storage; 4) running water; and 5) windows, in that order. Analyzing this new data, we found that more experienced, credentialed or highly paid teachers were not more likely to be assigned to classrooms with more daylighting. Thus, we concluded that there was no systematic teacher selection bias in the original findings.

Most importantly from our point of view, adding additional information about teacher qualifications back into our original equations did not change the strength or magnitude of our findings about daylight. This second round of analysis specifically on the Capistrano dataset, with additional teacher characteristics, provided an even more refined assessment of the 'daylighting effect.' We were able to determine that, on average, the children in classrooms with the most daylight were progressing 21% faster than those in the classrooms with no daylight, or 11% faster than the district average.[13]

In the written surveys, the teachers were also invited to provide open-ended comments. We received 250 surveys back from the Capistrano teachers, of which 200 included extended comments, many with a plea for immediate attention to their classrooms. We learned that the teachers were highly opinionated about the physical environment of their classrooms on many, many topics. We reported that the teachers had a *passionate* desire for more comprehensive environmental control of their classrooms: they considered it a basic right to be able to control light levels, sun penetration, acoustic conditions, temperature, and ventilation in their classrooms. Daylighting featured in a handful of the comments, but they were always quite explicit, using emotive words like 'love' and 'excellent':

"The best schools I've seen were old ones - with banks of windows to open (on both sides of the room, for cross ventilation) and a sink with water. I know [my school] won architectural awards but it's not a good building for a school. Note: Please provide windows so we're not closed in!"

"I loved my previous room because it had a large skylight with adjustable blinds. I wish my current room had more windows instead of narrow slits."

"The light provided by the skylight makes teaching with an overhead projector excellent."

In retrospect I think that the word 'passionate' was an understatement. For a teacher to be required to spend a year in a classroom where he or she cannot control the basic conditions of environmental comfort, while being solely responsible for the well-being of 30 children, does sound like a stressful situation!

After completion of the surveys, we also interviewed a subset of teachers and asked if they had heard of our initial study findings. Most had not. But when asked if they thought the findings were reasonable—that student performance seemed to improve with more daylight and windows—they would typically give us a stunned silence, smile slightly, and then respond with disbelief that this question even merited study, as in: *"Well, duh! Of course. Windows improve my mental well-being too!"*

Fresno: Classrooms and View

The enduring desire by teachers for the physical control of their classrooms motivated another school district to sign up for our second follow up study. The California Energy Commission wanted to see if we could replicate the Capistrano findings in another California school district. Based on a careful list of selection criteria, we selected the Fresno Unified School District (FUSD) as our next study subject.[14] Now, with a bigger budget and a seasoned research team, for the Fresno study we planned to do a much better job controlling for the potential confounding effect of window views on any 'daylighting effect.'

Unfortunately, FUSD did not have any toplit classrooms to help differentiate the impacts of view from daylight illumination. However, we did our best to make up for that deficiency by recording much more detailed information about each classroom's windows, including window sizes, position, orientation, glass tints, and types of window coverings. We categorized sun penetration and reflected glare potential, along with key characteristics of views, including size, distance, and content. In the final analysis, once again, classroom window and view characteristics significantly predicted student performance, this time with up to six times more precision than the Capistrano analysis! However, the full story is far more complex and merits deeper consideration.

In 2002 FUSD was the fourth largest school district in California. It enrolled over 80,000 students and operated 61 elementary schools. And it was about as different from Capistrano as could be imagined. Whereas Capistrano benefitted from a mild coastal climate in Southern California, Fresno sits in California's Central Valley where summers are very, very hot, and winters can be cold and dreary. While Capistrano benefited from fresh ocean air, Fresno had some of the most polluted air in California, and among the highest rates of childhood asthma in the nation. While Capistrano's student population was fairly representative of California's overall demographics, Fresno's was one of the poorest in the state, with vast numbers of immigrant families and English-language learners. And while the Capistrano district had an interesting mix of school building types, from older to recent, and a wide range of daylighting strategies, Fresno had mostly older schools which the district struggled to maintain. There were no skylights, and very limited range of daylighting conditions. We faced challenges on every level.

Early on in the Fresno study we met with the FUSD research department, responsible for evaluating student performance based on standardized tests and recommending evidence-based improvements to District policies and procedures. (One of our reasons for selecting Fresno was that the district used the same careful testing protocols as Capistrano.) The Director of Research explained that she would be extremely interested to learn if, and how, classroom design and condition impacted student performance. This was because there was a long simmering war going on between the district teachers and the maintenance department. The Director of Research was hoping that we could help resolve the dispute.

We learned that maintenance staff wanted to implement centralized control for HVAC units in all classrooms. The teachers' union strenuously objected, insisting that teachers retain control of the thermostat and fan. (One teacher explained to us how her contractor husband had secretly rigged a way to defeat the central controls in her classroom!) The maintenance staff wanted to board up any operable windows with insulating panels, to improve the energy efficiency of the classrooms, and prevent the teachers from opening windows when the HVAC system was on. The teachers thought the fans were too noisy, and they desperately wanted to keep their window views. The maintenance staff thought the teachers could not be trusted to operate their classrooms efficiently. The teachers thought the maintenance staff had no regard for their need to individually manage their classroom environment. This was, indeed, a heated war that we stepped into.

In support of our efforts, the District gave us access to a treasure trove of data: two years of student fall and spring test scores, along with teacher, student, and school-level demographics. We began our study with site visits to every elementary school during the summer break, when we had free range to take photographs and measurements. However, in the process we discovered that, unlike Capistrano, FUSD had selectively assigned both students and teachers to classrooms based on daylighting characteristics. Gifted or younger children, and teachers with more tenure, were preferentially assigned the more daylit classrooms. As a result, although we controlled for these variables, our FUSD data was more confounded than Capistrano.

In the final FUSD data set, we had very discontinuous conditions: a small handful of older, well-daylit classrooms, but with poor air quality, thermal comfort, and acoustic comfort; a huge number of portable classrooms, with mediocre everything; and a fair number of more modern classrooms, generally with better air quality, acoustics, and thermal comfort, but very little daylight or views. When we plotted the net effect of all the window characteristics considered in our regression analysis against the daylight code of each classroom, there was a decided U-shaped curve, with the poorest performance in the middle of the range, and the best student performance at both the lowest and highest ends of the daylight code.[15] Thus, the older finger plan classrooms with ample daylight and views were performing well, in spite of having poor thermal and acoustic conditions, while the newer classrooms, with better control of air quality, acoustics, and thermal comfort, but poor daylight and views, were performing equally well.

Ultimately, we found that many window characteristics were highly significant in predicting student performance, especially those associated with views. As mentioned earlier, the cumulative effect of the window characteristics considered in the Fresno study had *two to six times* the predictive power as the daylight characteristics considered in the Capistrano model. Thus, we came away with a high degree of certainty that windows in classrooms were powerfully associated with student performance. A simplified summary of the study's findings was included in the final report:

- An ample and pleasant view out of a window, that includes vegetation or human activity and objects in the far distance, supports better outcomes of student learning.

- Sources of glare negatively impact student learning. This is especially true for math learning, where instruction is often visually demonstrated on the front teaching wall. Per our observations, when teachers have white marker boards, rather than black or green chalk boards, they are more likely to use them and children perform better in math.

- Direct sun penetration into classrooms, especially through unshaded east or south-facing windows, is associated with negative student performance, likely causing both glare and thermal discomfort.

- Blinds or curtains allow teachers to control the intermittent sources of glare or visual distraction through their windows. When teachers do not have control of their windows, student performance is negatively affected.

For any well-trained school architect, none of these findings should be surprising. Given that they are all consistent with commonsense expectations, one might reasonably ask what is the value of undertaking such a detailed and quantified study? The answer is that we were able to quantify the contribution of the physical conditions of a classroom to student learning, and test their significance and predictive power, in such a way that they can be compared to other factors in education. The report explains that holistic analysis of the FUSD dataset showed that *"the window characteristics were as significant and of equal or greater magnitude as teacher characteristics, number of computers, or attendance rates in predicting student performance."* It was a remarkable achievement to put the social impact of architectural design into this wider context.

Effect Sizes and Decision Making

In response to the earlier critics of the Capistrano report, our research team put special emphasis on detailing the precision and effect sizes of variables in the statistical models. And just as with the Capistrano findings, we found a very consistent pattern. In all four districts (Capistrano, Seattle, Fort Collins, and now Fresno), we were able to create a mathematical model that explained about 25% of the variation in student test scores over time. Of this 25%, about 10% of that was based on the individual student's past performance. Demographic variables, such as gender or ethnic background, predicted an individual's performance with an order-of-magnitude less precision, or about 1% per variable. The physical variables, describing classroom design and condition, dropped another order of magnitude, each predicting only about 0.1% of student performance. Considered all together, the physical classroom descriptors in our equations predicted about 1.5% to 2% of the variation in student test scores.

So, you might wonder, if all the physical conditions of a classroom are only predicting 1–2% of a student's progress over time, why would such a small effect be interesting and valuable to know? The Fresno report responds with a powerful argument to this key question:

"Perhaps the most compelling reason is that the physical conditions of the environment are completely within our human control when we make design decisions about new buildings. We typically have no control of our demographic characteristics, such as age or ethnic background. And it requires enormous and persistent political will to change social conditions, like the transience of the student population or the education level of parents. But design decisions about the physical environment are completely within our control, and once made, have very long-term effects. A school building in California is likely to have at least a fifty year life span."

"Thus, a decision about the physical environment, even though it has a relatively small amount of influence on individual performance, will continue to have an effect for fifty years and will influence hundreds or thousands of individuals over its lifetime, which greatly multiplies its importance."

"We might think of the life-cycle value of various effects. For example, buying ten more computers for a classroom is predicted to improve math student performance by 10%, with a partial R^2 of 0.2%. However, the computers may only last for 5 years. Thus, they have five-year's worth of influence at 0.2% precision. Providing a window with a pleasant view of trees and grass from a classroom is also predicted to improve math performance by 10%, with a partial R^2 of 0.1%, but will probably last for fifty years. The view may have slightly less precision in achieving the desired goal, but will have ten times as long to influence performance. With this perspective, the view has at least five times the long-term impact on student learning and so should be a more important investment decision."

When our first schools study came out, with a simple finding that more daylight was associated with better student performance, people quickly embraced the findings, not because they carefully reviewed the analysis methodology, but because they loved the concept. *"Let the Sun Shine In!"* was the (inappropriate) headline for practically every newspaper story. The Fresno study, on the other hand, though far more detailed and nuanced, received far less attention. It did not have the consistent finding that more daylight illumination was always better. Rather, sometimes thermal and acoustic comfort and air quality proved more important. However, the positive effect of bigger, more interesting views came through loud and clear. It was this Fresno study that really pushed me to ponder the many differences between daylight illumination and view. Did they have related, or distinct, mechanisms to influence student performance? This book is a continuation of the effort to better answer that question.

By 2003, when the Fresno study was published, the ipRGC had been identified, and the importance of exposure to daylight illumination was beginning to be recognized as a primary driver of circadian rhythms. Thus, there was a logical causal mechanism available to explain the Capistrano findings. Other researchers jumped in and attempted to replicate the findings. At first graduate students from various universities around the world would set up a small study which tracked student performance in one or two classrooms, rarely with a study population of more than 30 students or a time span of more than a few weeks. These first efforts at replication inevitably came up with no significant findings due to the low predictive power of their study designs, with small populations and short time frames. However, more recently some larger, more carefully designed studies have analyzed data from substantial populations, including thousands of students in hundreds of classrooms or even hundreds of schools.

For example, Peter Barrett and colleagues in the UK compared learning outcomes from 3,766 students to the physical attributes of their 153 classrooms across three school districts. They considered 30 classroom design factors, including variations in physical layout and measured comfort conditions such as acoustics and temperature, and analyzed how each factor was associated with measured annual progress on reading, writing, and math. Of all the physical factors considered, the presence of daylight and view had the largest and most significant impact on student learning.[16] One interesting detail was that a factor called 'window views to nature' proved to be most significant for progress in writing scores, suggesting a connection to creativity. In speaking about this study at a conference in 2017, Barrett explained: *"I am not a daylighting specialist. I did a study that was not obsessing about daylighting, but it found that daylight actually was the biggest factor influencing learning among children."*[17]

Lecture Halls and Sleeping Superintendents

It is admittedly easier and more convenient to study the impact of daylight and view on learning progress in elementary school children. However, there are many reasons to believe that the outcomes may be similar with other age groups, from teenagers through adults. Let's consider some more personal forms of evidence.

I have given hundreds of lectures and talks in a wide variety of settings over the years. My least favorite settings are the big conference rooms in hotels or lecture halls on campuses where there are no windows. The room is completely dark if the electric lights are turned off. The visual environment for the speaker is inevitably either very drab, with uniform overhead lighting throughout, or very glary, with spotlights directed right at the speaker's face. If the desire is to provide a video recording for people who could not attend the talk, the lighting is likely even worse, optimized for the people who are not in the room over those who are there. I find these settings stressful, creating a huge visual divide between the speaker and the audience, because, blinded by the spotlight, the speaker cannot see the audience's faces. This is a performance setting, while the audience listens passively.

My favorite lecture halls have some ambient daylight, ideally from skylights or side windows, and maybe even a modest view off to one side. In my experience, where there is some daylight and view, the audience remains more engaged in lecture venues and is more likely to initiate an animated conversation and linger after the talk. The audience is certainly less likely to settle in for a nap while I'm talking.

I have visited many, many daylit classrooms over the years to observe teacher and student behaviors, and always learn something from the experience. In general, as per the lecturing story above, I have the impression that daylit classrooms are just livelier, and more participatory, then their non-daylit brethren. I don't have any systematic observations or data to back up that observation. But I do have one very funny experience which I think sums up the difference.

One sunny spring weekend I went to a big statewide conference on funding for California public schools. I especially wanted to visit a demonstration portable classroom that had been set up outside the conference facility by a skylight manufacturer. It was there to allow school administrators to experience a well-designed skylit classroom for themselves. This demonstration module was just like most other portable classrooms, 24' deep by 40' long, with smallish windows plus one door on the narrow ends. But it also had four generous diffusing skylights overhead, each with a motorized black-out roller shade.

When I knocked at the door of the classroom, the hostess, a representative from the skylight company, greeted me and immediately put her finger to her lips, asking me to be quiet. She stepped outside and explained that while the module was generally open for public viewing, right at the moment it was being used for an important continuing education course for school superintendents, teaching them about new rules for school financing. *"Can you come back tomorrow?"* she asked. Unfortunately, I could not, so I asked if I could just peek inside to see the daylighting quality from the skylights. She explained that also wasn't possible, since right then the skylights were completely covered by their black-out shades. I was noticeably disappointed. She pondered for a moment, then brightened up. Not to worry! She realized she could use the motor to open the black-out blinds. I was concerned that this would be disruptive. *"Oh, no problem,"* she exclaimed. *"Look: they are all asleep! They won't care!"* So, we stepped quietly inside, and sure enough, there were 32 district superintendents, all sound asleep, their heads drooped, some snoring away, while an educational video played on two TV screens at the front of the classroom.

The lady in charge switched on the motors, and the black-out shades slowly, and quietly, rolled open. The room brightened. The overhead electric lights, which had been operating at half power, dimmed further in response to the daylight. The sleeping superintendents gently roused, shifting their slumped bodies, lifting their heads and opening their eyes, and resumed watching the video as if nothing had happened. Within two minutes of the skylights being opened, they were all awake. I have never seen a more powerful demonstration of how daylight helps people stay alert. I'm sure those superintendents have no memory of this experience. They had just dozed off watching a video, just like all of their students do. They were not aware of why they woke back up. Kindergarten teachers and parents have long known the trick of opening curtains to help children wake up gently from their naps. These skylights, with their quiet motorized black-out shades, obviously had exactly the same effect for this group of mature, highly professional educators.

11. Selling Daylight

Much of the early work of my consulting company was to document the energy performance of buildings. We were hired to collect data on site to answer the question: are the buildings really saving as much energy as promised by the designers? But there was always a secondary question: will the energy savings persist without sacrificing the comfort of the occupants or productivity of the organization? Sacrifice was a big part of the conversation around energy efficiency back then. There was always an assumption that building owners had to give up some degree of comfort or convenience to achieve greater efficiency.

But, I wondered, what if more efficient designs resulted in buildings that exceeded expectations, where the occupants were happier and more productive, or the organization more profitable? We undertook a series of case studies (including those about the Remo and Standard Abrasive factories recounted in the Introduction), where there was growing evidence of the many 'non-energy benefits' of daylighting. One case study featured Industrial Development International, a company which was building gigantic skylit warehouses in the Inland Empire region of Southern California. I visited the company's vice president one day and he took me on a tour of a new warehouse recently occupied by Timberland, the shoe manufacturer. He explained how the skylights were giving his leasing business a huge sales advantage: *"Our buildings just show better! When potential tenants first walk into the empty building, they are immediately impressed with how nice the space looks. When we point out that there aren't any lights on—then they are really impressed! As a result, we lease our buildings sooner, and they are out from under us before they are even completed."*[1]

High performance skylights were dotted in a repeating pattern across 3% of the warehouse roof area. They lit the warehouse's 30-foot high stacks, they lit the sorting and packaging area, and they especially lit the loading docks, where a dozen forklifts zipped back and forth. But the most remarkable area was the 'overflow storage' area. My tour guide explained that Timberland had initially leased only ¾ of the warehouse, but: *"As soon as they moved into their building, they found that orders had increased dramatically and they needed additional space immediately. They arranged to lease the remaining 100,000 square feet in the building. To save time they asked that any tenant improvements be delayed until after their rush period was over."*

As a result, at the time of my visit, the overflow storage area had been operating full-tilt for five months with only the illumination provided by the skylights, and Timberland management had no sense of urgency to spend money on an electric lighting system they didn't yet need.

Despite reliable cost savings from a well-designed skylighting system paired with automatic photocontrol of the electric lights, we still had trouble convincing architects, engineers, and building owners to take action. Architects worried about skylights leaking. Electrical engineers and lighting designers worried that the more variable lighting conditions would be too annoying. Mechanical engineers worried about skylights contributing too much heat in the summertime and loosing too much heat in the winter. And owners worried about safety and security. We provided excellent examples of how to address all those concerns, and still people hesitated. Beyond all the energy dollars saved, and the good engineering, there was still a hurdle holding people back. What was it? One answer was provided by another huge building owner: Walmart.

Walmart

Walmart, the giant discount retailer, a private company based in Arkansas, was on a massive national growth spirt when they decided to enter the California market in the early 1990s. As the story was told to me, architects working for Southern California Edison (SCE) helped persuade them to consider some new energy efficiency features for their first new store in Los Angeles. Skylights were one of those features. Shortly thereafter, the company also decided to build a demonstration 'eco-store' in Lawrence, Kansas, testing out many new purportedly environmentally-friendly building systems. At this point, folks at the Rocky Mountain Institute (RMI), a non-profit advocate for energy efficiency, got involved, and helped persuade them again to incorporate skylighting into their demonstration store.

However, as a last-minute cost-saving measure, Walmart decided to install skylights in only one half of the store. This created a most serendipitous natural experiment, as reported on the front page of the Wall Street Journal in December of 1994: *"Walmart claims energy savings from drawing natural light through the skylights. But 'something else has gotten the corporation's attention,' says the [Rocky Mountain] Institute. In every Walmart store, each cash register is connected in real time back to headquarters in Bentonville, Ark. According to Tom Seay, who was then the company's vice president for real estate, sales were 'significantly higher' in those departments in the daylit half of the store, and they were also higher there than in the same departments at other stores. Employees in the half without daylighting continue to try to have their departments move to the daylit side."*[2]

As I later heard the story from Walmart executives, the company did switch the departments around, and found the same results: notably higher sales under the skylit one-half of the building. However, neither the Wall Street Journal story, nor Walmart themselves, attached any actual sales numbers to this story. The executive management team back in Arkansas were reportedly dismayed to have their 'secret sauce' building innovations being discussed on the front page of a major national newspaper. That was the end of any public communications about environmental experiments from Walmart for a very long time. However, the company did continue to pursue skylighting aggressively, perfecting designs and specifications, and eventually adopting it as a design standard for all their new stores, resulting in millions of skylights and photocontrols being installed in their big-box retail buildings across America. All those dubious architects, engineers and building owners began to take notice, thinking *"Well, if Walmart is doing it, it must be cost effective!"* and *"Not all those skylights can leak!"* Walmart's adoption of skylighting was a game-changer, and ultimately led to my own studies examining how daylighting impacts human performance.

A Brief History of Daylighting and Retail Design

Selling products, whether groceries or crafts, has long been done in the open air. In ancient Rome, merchants displayed their wares under awnings along the street edge, while plazas and forums were set up for larger farmers' markets, and street peddlers hawked their wares wherever they could find an open corner. In the middle east, old Roman traditions were continued in Islamic market towns, with the development of the *souk*, a street devoted to shopping, covered with shade cloth. In the middle ages, European market towns began to build covered markets, so that merchants could continue to peddle their wares even if it was raining or snowing. In the late eighteenth century, the development of plate glass technology, combined with cast iron construction, lead to experimentation with covering courtyards and shopping streets with a glazed roof to keep out the rain: first in Paris with the Palais Royal in 1791, then the Passage du Caire in 1798.

These efforts were a mere run up to the grande dame of skylit retail, the Galleria Vittorio Emanuele II built in Milan in the 1860s. Five stories of shops and apartments were covered with a barrel-vaulted glass roof over 50 feet wide and 25 feet high. Four of these covered streets converged at a great glass dome in the center, rising another 50 feet above the beautifully marbled mosaic floor. It created one of the largest enclosed volumes in human history, rivaling the grandest of basilicas. Soaring high overhead, the delicate glass and iron work was awe inspiring, and the engineering ingenious.

The Galleria in Milan became the prototype for many other 'gallerias' subsequently built around the world, all hoping that their covered streets would attract the most well-heeled clientele looking to purchase luxury goods. (Galleria Umberto in Naples, circa 1880, graces page 207.) The Galleria's central skylight dome also become a much copied feature in the new nineteenth-century concept of a 'department store,' which united many types of shops all within one building and business. Luxury department stores in Paris, then worldwide, started to feature a grand central court covered with a beautiful stained-glass skylight, uniting the sensibilities of Art Nouveau and Tiffany stained glass with royal courtyards such as the Palais Royal. The Milan Galleria, with its interior pedestrian streets, also served as inspiration for much more modest suburban shopping malls developed after the Second World War. As those suburban malls grew ever larger, many experimented with various forms of skylighting for the central concourse, perhaps best exemplified by the gigantic Mall of America, in Bloomington, Minnesota.

Thus, skylighting was nothing new in retail buildings when it was re-adopted by Walmart in the 1990s. What was new was an intention to save energy, and an understanding that the presence of daylight might impact sales, the lifeblood of any retailer. The Walmart skylights were strictly utilitarian: four-foot by eight-foot diffusing acrylic domes, they sat in neatly spaced rows to provide highly uniform illumination across the vast stores, with up to 260,000 square feet of floor space below. Indeed, nothing in the Walmart store design spoke of luxury or indulgence. The design goal was to convey no-frills retailing, so that shoppers would always assume that they were getting the absolute lowest possible price with no money wasted on aesthetics or indulgences. As a result, most other retailers chose to avoid doing anything that might mimic the utilitarian Walmart look. Although they were starting to believe that skylights might not have all those other problems they feared—leaking, security, heat gain and loss—there was a new mantra I started to hear: *"We don't want skylights to make our stores look like a Walmart!"* However, they remained curious about those higher sales reported in the Wall Street Journal story. I wondered if we could get real numbers to back up those claims, since higher sales should be irresistible to any retailer. And then most fortuitously, a window of opportunity opened to test the proposition: the same opportunity that funded the first round of school and daylighting studies described in the previous chapter.

The Grocery Store

I approached many companies, offering to study the economic impact of their skylights, and was turned down many times. Finally, one company stepped up, with a most generous offer. Ralph's, a large chain of grocery stores, originally begun in 1873 in Los Angeles, had been persuaded by the local utility company to try skylighting as an energy efficiency measure. By the time I came on the scene, they had tried out a few design options, liked the cost savings, refined their design approach, and built many new stores with skylights. At that time, they had over a hundred store sites, and about 2/3 of them had skylights.

Ralph's preferred skylit store design was ingenious. Called a 'high-hat design,' it featured a 25' high central ceiling, painted white, with exposed beams and skylights, surrounded by a ring of lower bays with suspended ceilings and fluorescent fixtures. The central space was daylit by a dozen or more four-inch by eight-inch diffusing skylights, placed 16 to 20 feet apart. As a result, during the day, the center of the store glowed with bright diffuse daylight. Shadows were non-existent. The bright center pulled customers into the store, and made shoppers feel energized by the light. The outer ring, with the lower ceiling and all the ventilation equipment, was used for the more service-intensive sections, such as the fish and meat markets, deli, florist shop, and bakery.

At the time, Ralph's had a policy of aggressive expansion and renovation, with the goal that every site would be upgraded and remodeled every five years. They kept detailed data on the status of each store, monitoring the impact of new configuration ideas on sales. How did adding a bakery affect store sales? Should the florist be at the front or the back of the store? The corporate energy manager was charged with reducing energy costs in every way possible, especially by taking advantage of all the rebates and incentives available to upgrade the energy efficiency of store design and equipment. He suspected that some of his upgrades might also have an impact on sales, but he did not have the means to study that question. Then I offered to do the study for him, for free, courtesy of my funding from the market transformation program run by Pacific Gas and Electric. He agreed to give me access to 18 months of sales data, along with store characteristics, on the condition that I would not make the identity or type of store public.

We started by touring the Los Angeles stores to verify the data I had been given. I visited a sample of both skylit and non-skylit stores to look for any other systematic differences between the two types, and talked to managers and shoppers. The whole chain seemed remarkably uniform, with similar product displays, interior furnishings and layout, parking lots, marketing campaigns and signage. Convinced that we had a clean data set, we ran regression analysis on store sales versus the presence or absence of skylights 'yes/no.' A multi-variate equation allowed us to control for store age, size, hours of operation, location, and renovation history. We used zipcodes to add information about neighborhood demographics. The results of the analysis came back with a startling number: all other things being equal, those stores with skylights were outselling their sisters by 40%! This number came back with 99% statistical certainty.[3]

Once again, our analysis team was astounded by the magnitude of the findings. Once again, we double-checked our numbers, added careful caveats to our conclusions, then submitted our report. The expert reviewers convened by Lawrence Berkeley National Labs were less suspicious of this report than the schools study, since the predictive power of the model was considerably higher. The mathematical models were able to explain 58% of the variation in the retail dataset, compared to only about 25% for the schools study. Given their greater comfort with the findings, they did not request any further analysis on the retail study before it was released.

However, compared to the schools study, the reception for the retail study was lukewarm, despite the magnitude of the daylighting effect and the greater predictive power of the model. There were no front-page stories in newspapers. When I spoke about the study, my audience was much more skeptical of the findings, insisting I should identify the chain, or the type of store studied: hardware? clothing? food? Of course, I couldn't say. Many people immediately jumped to the conclusion that the study subject *must* be Walmart, which I adamantly denied.

In the report we considered five ways that the skylights might be helping to increase sales: 1) Increased customer loyalty, in that shoppers preferred the shopping at the skylit store; 2) More relaxed customers, who were happy to spend more time shopping; 3) Better visibility, making product information easier to see; 4) Better color rendering, making products more attractive; 5) Enhanced employee morale, translating into better service and thus increased customer sales. (This was before the discovery of the ipRGC and thus no direct circadian pathways were postulated.)

I did have some anecdotal evidence that some shoppers traveled out of their way to shop at the skylit stores. However, even if people were emotionally drawn to the skylit stores, it was clear they were mostly unaware of the skylights themselves, as explained in the final report: *"Informal interviews with shoppers repeatedly confirmed that the vast majority of shoppers were not aware of the skylights. The questioner, looking just like any other shopper, would approach a shopper and ask: 'May I ask you a question?' The response was universally affirmative. We then asked, 'What do you think of the skylights in this store?' The typical response was to look up, look puzzled, and then say, 'That's funny. I never noticed them before.' Out of 42 interviews in skylit stores, only three shoppers could be found who were already aware of the skylights. Two of those volunteered that they had only noticed the skylights because their small child had pointed them out on an earlier trip, while looking up at a helium balloon that had floated up to the higher skylit ceiling."*

Ralph's grocery has long since changed ownership. It is now just one of over 20 subsidiaries of Kroger's, a corporation which operates well over 3,500 grocery stores nationwide. The energy manager has long since retired. The company recognized him as a hero for saving so much energy, but I don't think he got much credit for helping improve sales. (In anticipation of a pending acquisition, he was especially hoping the study might convince any new owners to keep the skylights.) And I kept my promise: for over 20 years not even my children knew the identity of the chain I had studied.

When I presented my findings at an IES conference there was also great skepticism. One highly respected member of the society stood up and declared: *"A photon is a photon! It doesn't matter where they come from. There is no logical reason for any difference between daylight and electric light."* A well-known educator also expressed skepticism, arguing that electric light could easily replicate any daylit design, and therefore any differences that I was finding must be attributable to differences in illumination levels and light distribution patterns. Luckily, a few years later, I was able to arrange a collaborative project with this second fellow. When he came out from New York to visit our offices in Sacramento, I took him on a little field trip to observe some of our local stores that had skylights. I took him into a big office-supply store first, lit with pendant fluorescent fixtures. Then right next door, in an identical box, we went into a home-supply store, lit with the same fluorescent fixtures, but which were dimmed in response to ample skylights overhead. He stood in the second store, transfixed. *"You know, there is a difference. I can feel it."* he exclaimed. Thereupon I concluded, that regardless of how compelling the information about the benefits of skylights might be, the real transformation would happen only when people could *experience* the difference themselves, by putting their bodies directly in a well-daylit space.

A few years after our first retail study came out, Walmart overcame their reticence at discussing the energy efficiency features of their stores. I was told that the second generation of family owners decided that the company should start to proselytize for environmental stewardship. As a result, Ralph Williams, then the store development manager at Walmart, often spoke alongside me at conferences, detailing the benefits of skylighting. Hundreds of engineers and retail architects from around the world flocked to take behind-the-scenes store tours, to see how Walmart did it! I'm sure these tours had an enormous impact on the adoption of not only skylights and photocontrols, but also many other advanced energy efficiency features, like white 'cool' roofs and eventually photovoltaics, also mounted on the roofs. Members of the construction industry seem to prefer a very direct, physical learning style; they want to see things for themselves before they consider adopting a new technology or design strategy.

The Hardware Store

Also few years later, I got a second opportunity, courtesy of the California Energy Commission, to try to replicate the Ralph's skylighting study with another chain retailer. This time I hoped to control for more variables, and have the opportunity to investigate some of our hypotheses about causal mechanisms. For this second study, I was able to persuade a large Northern California hardware chain to participate. Orchard Supply Hardware was founded as a farmers' cooperative in San Jose during the Great Depression in 1931, back when the primary product of Silicon Valley was prunes rather than software. It eventually evolved into a beloved neighborhood hardware store, known by its initials OSH, with locations around northern California. It had run into hard times itself during the 1980s, and had been sold to a variety of new owners, the latest of whom, when I came along, was Sears.

The managers of the OSH subsidiary were interested in the same question as the Ralph's study: could they convince their new corporate owners that adding skylights to stores was a wise investment? I made the same promise of strict confidentiality, that in my report I would not reveal any information about the identity or type of chain. Unfortunately, the story of OSH does not result in a happy ending. After another series of corporate bankruptcies, OSH was eventually bought by Lowes in 2013, and then completely closed down in 2018. Since the company and brand name no longer exists, I now feel comfortable telling this story.

The OSH management team at the time was enormously supportive of our research approach. They provided detailed data on the characteristics of each of their stores, and allowed my team to visit every OSH site to take measurements, photographs, light readings and to interview and survey staff. The Vice President of Marketing explained the variables that they considered most important to their sales, such as traffic on feeder roads, and size of the parking lot. Ultimately, we received 34 months of sales data for 73 store sites, of which 24, or 1/3, were considered daylit.[4]

This second study was much more detailed and nuanced than the first in many ways. Although OSH had fewer daylit stores and the daylighting was less aggressive, it had a greater variety of daylighting design strategies. Some stores used unit-skylights like Ralph's, while others used clerestory windows. We were able to estimate the amount of daylight, and energy savings, from each store site using annual simulation tools. Thus, rather than a simple yes/no variable, the amount of daylight in each store was described as a continuous variable, based on the percentage of yearly hours that electric lights would not be needed.

With more detailed data, we were able to do a better job explaining variations in store sales over time. Most importantly, we found a dose-response relationship: all other things being equal, more daylight resulted in more total dollar sales value per store, and also a higher number of transactions per store. Thus, more people were shopping at the daylit stores, and they were each spending a little more money. We found that the most aggressively daylit OSH sites had dramatically increased sales (+37%), similar to the Ralph's study (+40%). However, since the OSH stores generally had lower daylight illumination levels than Ralph's, the *average* daylight effect across the chain was also less: about a 6% increase in sales.

Most interestingly, we were able to compare the dollar value of the daylight energy savings to the increased sales effect. The energy savings had been the initial corporate justification for installing the skylights and photocontrols. However, the value of the increased sales associated with more daylight provided about *45 times more revenue* to the chain than the energy savings alone. Clearly, daylighting was no sacrifice for this company!

We waited for feedback from the OSH management after what we considered to be a triumphant report. Instead they were distracted, unhappy with decisions being made up at corporate headquarters. There was great uncertainty if more stores would be closed or who might lose their job. Oddly, from my point of view, the OSH management seemed most concerned about interviews I had done with store managers. One store manager had told us that he loved his store's skylights so much that he never wanted to work anywhere else. Apparently, such loyalty was worrisome: if skylights made employees less likely to want to move, that could be a big problem, resulting in less management flexibility!

Long Life, Loose Fit

My company, and many other consultants, have since worked with numerous retailers, large and small, along with owners of offices, factories and warehouses, to help them utilize daylight in their buildings. While there have been notable success stories, I'm sorry to say that there have also been spectacular failures.

In our highly competitive and unpredictable business world, most companies are looking for quick payback on investments, often within two years or less. Given that, little time or resources are allotted for careful consideration and analysis. Furthermore, there is so much turnover in the staff that institutional knowledge is quickly lost within a few years. *"Building at the speed of retail"* was one phrase that I heard often. Thus, most building decisions are made in response to immediate company needs, with little thought to long-term benefits or impacts, let alone larger social benefits. With the accelerating pace of change in the retail industry, including online shopping and overnight deliveries, the future of brick-and-mortar retail buildings is ever more uncertain. One result is a major shift in employment from small local shops to giant regional warehouses, with buildings that are designed more to optimize automated sorting systems rather than employee welfare. In risky times, a company's focus is understandably on strengthening their core business elements, not on the nuances of better physical building design.

The buildings themselves, on the other hand, endure for decades, if not hundreds of years. Once initial design decisions are made, the resulting buildings typically pass from one owner to the next, perhaps with a bit of remodeling, upgrades, and adaptions to new uses along the way. Thus, the buildings become part of the cultural infrastructure that affects everyone living nearby. Each new building constitutes not only a solution to an immediate need, but also a resource for future use.

Some architects working on concepts of sustainable design have coined the concept of "*long life, loose fit*" as a more sustainable approach to design, whereby buildings are designed to accommodate many changes in use over time.[5] Such an approach stresses the importance of long-term societal benefits as compared to immediate utility or short-term investments. Our next chapter addresses many of these societal decisions affecting access to daylight and views in more detail.

12. Enduring Urban Forms

According to the United Nations, the world's population is growing towards 10 billion, and by 2050 over two-thirds of us will live in cities.[1] That means that for every two cities today, there will be more than three of the same size by 2050. Cities will also need to get bigger and denser to handle this population growth. Will all these new cities and their buildings be planned to preserve access to daylight and views for their residents?

We can plan for the future by learning from how various cities have handled growth pressures in the past—some gracefully offering their residents ample access to light and air, some becoming increasingly more unlivable. There are many fundamental urban planning decisions that support access to more daylight and views, and there are many smaller scale fixes that can help a city improve incrementally over time.

In considering what strategies might be employed at an urban scale to improve access to daylight and views, it is useful to consider the time scale of each decision. Cities and buildings may seem very permanent. In reality, they are constantly in flux. Little improvements are made to update the wiring or the carpet. Bigger changes are made to move a wall or add a porch. At the urban scale, empty lots are filled in and new buildings replace old. Even historic preservation districts inevitably change the use of streets and buildings as cultures and technologies evolve.

Stewart Brand, in his masterful book, *How Buildings Learn*, explains how various building systems change over time.[2] "*Site is eternal*" he quips. Largely determined by topography, and urban infrastructure, property lines last for hundreds or even thousands of years. Brand classifies building systems into the 'six S's,' each with a different time dimension. In addition to *Site*, there is *Structure*, the foundation and load-bearing elements which are likely to last for at least 50 years, and perhaps up to 300 years, in stable societies. Next in time scale comes *Skin*, the fenestration and cladding of a building wall, designed to resist the onslaught of weather. On a well-built structure, the skin might last 50 or more years before it needs serious maintenance or upgrading. The other three elements—*Services*, *Space Plan*, and *Stuff*—have much more rapid turnover schedules. "*They wear out or obsolesce every seven to 15 years*," explains Brand, and are regularly changed and upgraded to meet the needs of the new occupants and advances in technology. It is the first three categories—*Site*, *Structure*, and *Skin*—that are the primary determinants of access to daylight and views.

Property Lines and Permanence

Land use patterns, such as property lines, are some of the most persistent marks that humans make on the planet. The gridded streets and small lots of Roman cities from 2,000 years ago can often still be seen in the cities that have persisted in the same location, even after the original structures are long gone. Similarly, the original property lines carved out by the Spaniards in New Mexico, using 'long lot' development which sliced up all the land along important waterways into skinny holdings perpendicular to a river or creek, still persist in property lines today. They can be clearly seen from the air and are beautifully illustrated in the massive mapping project *Every Building in America* published by the New York Times.[3] Likewise, the layout of the original Dutch colony of New Amsterdam persists in the narrow winding streets of Manhattan's financial district, a.k.a. Wall Street, 400 years later.

Not only property lines, but also the corresponding street layouts, have enormous influence on building size and orientation, and thus ultimately the availability of daylight and views inside of buildings. Traditional settlements often have small blocks or irregularly shaped properties, while some cities follow strict grids with precise orientations. For example, all the streets of Boise, Idaho follow a grid at 45 degrees to the cardinal directions, such that every building façade in the city faces NE, SE, SW, or NW, with nothing in between. Salt Lake City, originally laid out by Mormon settlers for family-based agriculture, has the largest city block sizes in the United States, 660 feet square, and some of the widest streets, 130 feet wide. City blocks in Portland, Oregon, in comparison, are only 200 feet square. As a consequence, new daylit buildings may be easier to achieve in Portland, with its smaller block sizes, than in Salt Lake City, where a single building filling up a city block could be over ten times as large. Thus, the initial act of laying out new streets or drawing property lines may impact daylight availability for hundreds or thousands of years.

Modern real estate developers are often keen to amass adjacent properties that can be combined into a larger property, which will then support a bigger, deeper, taller building. The transformation of many downtown areas, from older ownership patterns of small lots, to consolidated ownership enabling bigger, taller buildings follows this pattern. There may be many justifications for this trend, including reduced building costs, greater design flexibility, or improved energy efficiency. But as building volume increases relative to exterior skin surface area (e.g. the surface to volume ratio), a clear consequence is correspondingly fewer opportunities for daylight, view, and natural ventilation per unit of floor area.

Code, Standards, and Resiliency

Most great cites have developed with simple rule sets and constraints that informed the shape and location of their buildings. Sometimes these constraints were physical, determined by the landform and building materials. Sometimes they were cultural, based on the social customs, religious edicts, and/or aspirations of the times. And often they were political, enforced with laws, regulations, and public investments. We can find many examples of the latter in zoning laws, building setbacks, height restrictions, and view-shed protections that have been enforced in various cities around the world.[4]

Building decision makers, on the other hand, be they developers, owners, architects, or engineers, are often resistant to such constraints on building form. Codes and standards are generally seen as annoying and overly restrictive, a blunt instrument, which can rarely account for all the subtlety required of good design. I felt this way too, as a young architect, certain that I knew how to design far better buildings without the hassle of codes constraining my design, dumbing it down to the lowest common denominator, and forcing me to spend extra hours to demonstrate compliance. However, over my career I have seen how the many building codes in my state have gradually made our building stock safer in earthquakes and fires, more energy efficient, more accessible to people with physical challenges and more resilient, saving the citizens of the state a great deal of financial and emotional trauma from major building failures.

For example, the daylit schools in California have proved their worth many times over during various earthquakes, storms, fires, and other events causing power outages: classrooms in well-daylit schools can continue to operate, while those students in schools without daylight must be sent home. Likewise, code requirements for dimmable lighting in daylit retail stores played a major role in managing California's power supplies during the electric power crises of 2001–2002. After Hurricane Sandy devastated New York City in 2012, knocking out both grid and emergency power supplies throughout the region, residents of multi-story apartment buildings wished that their stairwells simply had a little daylight to ease the trauma of living without electric lighting and functioning elevators. During the COVID-19 pandemic of 2020, people all over the world treasured their window views as a precious connection to the outside, as they stayed home to avoid exposure to the virus.

Thus, in addition to their many other benefits, windows and skylights can provide important social resiliency by enabling buildings to continue to be habitable under extreme conditions (*operable* windows and skylights even more so, by also enabling natural ventilation). Designing our cities and buildings for long-term resiliency, in the face of climate change along with the mounting pressures of rapid technological change and population growth, is likely to become a key imperative for ensuring more daylight and views in buildings.

Voids in the Urban Fabric

Perhaps equally important as the street and block pattern of a city, are the voids, the unbuildable areas, be they bodies of water, mountains, bluffs, or man-made parks. In order to have daylight, you need a direct, or indirect, view of the sky; and likewise, to have a view, you need a void to look across. Courtyards and atria create small voids; parklands and parkways create bigger voids; and major landforms that decisively limit the spread of buildings— oceans, rivers, lakes, hills, and mountains—create the biggest visual voids and the most spectacular views.

In addition to natural barriers of unbuildable land, there are many types of man-made voids in the urban fabric. In ancient times, and through the middle ages, defensive walls served to create a 'hard edge' that defined the limits of the city. Many of these massive walls, or their portals, became an important part of the city's visual identity. Citizens could both climb up the walls for a view out, and look back to see the walls from afar. As defensive walls lost their purpose in the age of modern warfare, they have often been repurposed for more benign public uses. Witold Rybczynski, in his wonderful biography of Frederick Law Olmstead, writes: "*The first leisure promenades in European cities were on top of abandoned city fortifications. These promenades came to be known as boolevarts, or boulevards, after the German bollwerk (bulwark).*"[5] Creating a public promenade on top of the wall transformed a utilitarian void into a social and scenic void (sort of an early version of New York's 'High Line' park!). Royal palaces and parade grounds, enclosed within an expanding city, are another important source of voids and parklands within many European and

Asian cities. Often the royals selected the best site for their palace and gardens, with favorable microclimates and panoramic views. Rome's many old palace sites are typically up on top of hills, benefiting from a freshening breeze and lovely vistas, as is Tokyo's Imperial Palace and garden.

With no royal heritage, the United States evolved another model for preserving a void in the center of a city. The New England town square became the prototype for many northern cities, with one or more blocks set aside for public lawns and gardens in the center of town, surrounded by the most important civic buildings. In the southern United States, the early settlers of Savannah, Georgia, pioneered an egalitarian approach to town planning, based on the Enlightenment ideas of James Oglethorpe, laying out a super grid of identical neighborhoods, each with one central block dedicated as a public park. Today, this part of Savannah is considered one of the most beautiful historic districts in the country.

In the middle of the nineteenth century, New York City undertook a radical experiment in city planning, and decided to devote a huge plot of land that could serve as the 'lungs of the city,' a lushly landscaped parkland that would provide relaxation and recreation for all its the citizens. Central Park was conceived as a democratic alternative to the royal gardens of Europe. Frederick Law Olmstead was awarded his first public commission to design the park and implement its construction, which at that time was located far out in the hinterlands of Manhattan. As development densified the city, high-rise buildings began to line up along the edge of the park, defining an ever-sharper edge between urban grid and void. Today Central Park preserves daylight and views in the dense interior of Manhattan, while the Hudson and East Rivers define hard edges on two sides of the long, skinny island (see map of Central Park on page 303).

These hard, un-buildable edges surrounding natural or intentional voids are much of what make these cities livable, and memorable. It is being able to look at the city from a distant perspective that gives it an 'image.' It is being able to get to the edge, and see *out* of the city, that gives the city a cohesive identity. Having a strong civic identity motivates people to take care of their city, and perhaps preserve more land for public use, a feedback loop that is likely to enrich any city over time.

The Danish city Copenhagen took an interesting approach to bringing more greenspace and view-shed into its urban fabric. Recognizing that with population pressures the city would need to grow substantially after the Second World War, in 1947 Copenhagen adopted a 'Finger Plan' strategy to guide future development which mimicked biological systems. Old Copenhagen along the waterfront was the 'hand' while five fingers of development would reach westward out into the countryside, with commuter rail lines and stations along the center of each finger, as diagrammed in Figure 12.1. In the opposite direction long fingers of green space would penetrate in toward the city from the countryside, lined with new housing that could benefit from the expanded linear edge. These interlacing fingers work much like the villi that line the digestive tracts of humans and animals, greatly expanding the surface area of the intestine available to absorb nutrients into the body. Similarly, the fingers

Figure 12.1: The finger plan of Copenhagen, with transit lines down the center of the digits and green space between

of greenspace greatly increased the urban edges providing access to daylight and views for the city's citizens. Paired with a complementary transit system providing the lifeblood of a city, the efficient circulation of people and goods moves both inward and outward. Today, largely because of this approach to managing growth, increasing urban densities while still maintaining access to green space, Copenhagen has been consistently rated as one of the greenest cities in the world. Not coincidentally, Copenhagen is also a city of extensively daylit buildings, looking outward into the voids, the harbor, the green fingers, and many smaller courtyards preserved throughout the city.

Roman Precedents

The Roman empire provided a model for much of later European urban and building design, first simply via cultural continuity, as each generation modified the cities and buildings they inherited from their ancestors. Then in the Renaissance, the rediscovery of Vitruvius's *Ten Books of Architecture* prompted architects to closely study his prescriptions for building plans, orientation, and construction details. In turn, architects from later centuries modeled their buildings on those from the Renaissance.

Pompeii was a prosperous Roman city of 20,000 people when it was buried in twenty feet of volcanic debris by the Vesuvius eruption in 89 CE. Preserved completely intact for centuries, Pompeii gives us one of our most detailed insights into how people lived over 2,000 years ago, at least in Italy. The city plan featured a classic Roman grid layout, densely packed with one- and two-story buildings, filled with shops, factories, simple homes, and grander mansions, all separated by stone and brick party-walls defining interior property lines.

The walls of Pompeii as we see them today are a mosaic of building vintages, embedded with lintels and arches hinting at past uses, as walls and openings were repeatedly modified. At the lowest levels, the walls start with hefty Greek or Etruscan stone foundations, narrow doorways and massive stone lintels. The Romans eventually learned that walls made with smaller pieces of stone or brick were easier to modify and repair, especially after earthquakes. In later years they also mastered the use of the brick arch, as seen in the massive Colosseum and aqueducts stretching out into the countryside. Thus, as the masonry walls of Pompeii grow upward the stones are ever smaller, and openings grow larger. Vitruvius carefully describes each type of wall construction and its potential for future modifications, even including equations for real estate valuation.

Public streets came with rules about property-owner obligations and allowable actions: street level façades were limited to an entrance door and a few tiny windows, usually with heavy iron bars to protect against thievery. Holes drilled into the street curbs and building façades attest to poles that held out awnings stretched out in front of doorways to provide shelter for small shops. Above, a second story might feature a few larger windows, also fitted with stout wooden shutters that could be locked for security.

Thus, Pompeii's urban plan, and that of most other Roman towns of that era, resulted in buildings with no opportunities for openings on the three sides defined by shared property walls and very limited opportunities facing the street. The only reliable opportunity for procuring daylight and ventilation was from above. Therefore, the primary method of providing daylight was an opening in the roof, what we would call a skylight and what the Romans called a *compluvium*, because it not only let in daylight and air, but also rain (from the Latin *com* = with, and *pluit* = rain). The *compluvium* was set at the center of a downward sloped roof, above a corresponding pool (*impluvium)* set in the floor, which collected the rainwater and channeled it to an underground cistern for household use. This whole assembly constituted the *atrium*, usually the most splendid and ceremonial space in the house (and best lit), where a family altar might be set, and guests received, before being escorted to the smaller rooms surrounding the atrium. (Figure 12.2)

Larger properties in Pompeii might also have a peristyle (*peristylium* in Latin), a courtyard or garden area surrounded by columns supporting a roof over a central walkway, and surrounded by many smaller service rooms. Compared to the atrium, the larger peristyle allowed in much more sunlight, used for drying clothes or foods, thus a location for industry within the household. It was one of the few places that upper-class women, cloistered in the home, had access to direct sunlight. The Roman peristyle later formed the prototype for many monasteries in the Middle Ages, where the monks and nuns could live securely in an inward facing cloister.

Views to the outside world from within these homes were almost non-existent. At best, one could watch the street activities from the front doorway. A few homes might have been able to

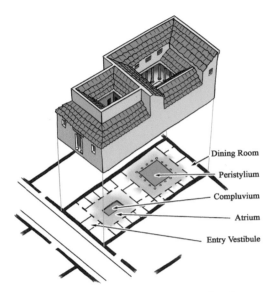

Dining Room
Peristylium
Compluvium
Atrium
Entry Vestibule

Figure 12.2: Typical Roman house plan in Pompeii, with atrium and peristyle courtyard

see Mount Vesuvius from a back courtyard. It is interesting to note, therefore, that the subject of much of the artwork found inside of Pompeii homes are frescos with elaborate scenes of the natural world: gods cavorting out in nature, hunting parties set in forests full of animals, and walled gardens full of flowers, birds and bird baths. HW Janson, in his monumental book *The History of Art* describes the progression of Roman fresco art across eras, including a growing fascination in later years, as evidenced in Pompeii, with *"make-believe windows"* and illusionistic architectural perspective, as if an increasingly urbanized people longed for their rural roots.[6]

An atrium is the quintessential toplighting strategy, bringing daylight into the center of a building from overhead. In the mild Mediterranean climate, concern about extreme heat or cold, or accumulation of snow, was no concern. The Roman atrium formed a prototype for many of the traditional courtyard buildings later found throughout the former Roman empire, from Egypt and Turkey, to Spain and Morocco.[7]

The Roman atrium also serves as a prototype for more recent buildings, such as multi-story apartment buildings centered around a central courtyard atrium. The atria of these buildings may be much taller and larger than the Roman version, but still have similar proportions of an approximately cube-shaped void open to the sky above, surrounded by walkways leading to a ring of apartments or rooms. During the nineteenth century, glass technology advanced to the point where it became economical to cover an atrium with a monumental glass skylight. Many older museums, such as the Prado in Spain and the Legion of Honor in San Francisco, utilize this classic form, with their sculpture gardens and art work lit by grand skylights in a central atrium (unfortunately, the glass skylights are now too often covered over and replaced with hidden electric light sources). Interestingly, the term *atrium*, or atrial cavity, is now also used in biology and zoology to describe the central chamber of the heart. Thus, the daylit void at the center of the Roman home also became a metaphor for the functioning of the body's circulation system.

The larger domestic peristyle formed a prototype for the Roman commercial building type known as the basilica, where lawyers and contractors conducted their daily business. The basilica was one of the largest buildings in any Roman town, sort of a downtown commerce district all housed within one building. The basilica consisted of one huge elongated central room, surrounded by a line of columns, supporting second floor balconies overhead. On both floors, a walkway ringed the columns, serving a row of many smaller functional rooms off to each side. However, unlike the domestic-scaled peristyle, the large central court of the basilica was not open to the sky, but instead covered by a long, gabled roof from end to end. The eaves of this central roof were raised up enough from the colonnade to provide a continuous ring of daylight. Originally, this framed opening was open-air, or sheltered with awnings or shutters to protect the businessmen working directly below from rain and wind. After the first or second century CE, Romans had mastered glassmaking technology sufficiently to enclose some of these buildings with windows made with flat squares of glass pieced together. Thus, the high windows surrounding the central hall of the basilica became the first glazed clerestory window.

The Roman basilica was designed to shelter large indoor crowds. Early Christians, who wanted to invite everyone to come participate in worship, found these existing commercial buildings best met their needs for large gatherings. Thus, they repurposed them to serve as churches. The term 'Basilica' eventually denoted the grandest of the medieval churches, where bishops conducted religious services in the center of important cities. Cathedrals based on this prototype included a large central gathering area, lit from clerestories high above, and surrounded by columns defining the edge of an ambulatory serving many side chapels and niches for smaller scale or more private worship.

Letter-Shaped Buildings

Washington DC is a city full of buildings following ancient prototypes, with colonnades and pediments providing suitably grand historical references.

But instead of churches or former palaces, as in Europe, these are mostly government office buildings. By the late nineteenth century, the ever-expanding size of government created pressures to consider building forms beyond the simple Roman prototypes of a square 'O' with an atrium, or 'T' of the basilica.

The building designers realized that in order to provide access to windows for all the government office workers—absolutely essential in the time before electric lighting and mechanically powered heating, cooling, and ventilation systems—they needed to increase the overall exterior surface area. The result was increasingly crenelated floor plans, with extra building wings, each just wide enough to provide sufficient daylight and natural ventilation for a row of offices on either side of a double-loaded corridor. Thus, an I-shaped building, became an L, E, or an H.

The primary challenge for designers was to optimize the view outwards. The deeper and narrower the folds on an E-shaped building, the more windows would be looking directly at each other. This was not desirable for light or view, or especially acoustic privacy, back in the day when opening windows was necessary for basic ventilation and could easily result in overhearing conversations from nearby offices. S, U, V, W, Y, and X were not far behind. These pressures produced the ubiquitous 'letter-shaped' buildings of Washington DC, such that one can practically make out words when looking down from an airplane.

The largest of all DC government buildings, the Pentagon, headquarters of the US Department of Defense, broke the mold of alphabet shapes when it was built in 1941. Instead, the massive five-sided building sports five pentagonal rings, one inside the other, each 50 feet wide and five stories high. Dozens of courtyards separate each ring of the pentagon. The Pentagon's thousands upon thousands of office windows face each other squarely across these narrow courtyards, in military precision. Apparently, visual and acoustic privacy were not a concern of the military at that time.

Stairs and Building Heights

The height limits of cities used to be constrained by building technology. Vitruvius first discussed the constraints of building height, relative to those shared stone property walls in Rome and Pompeii. They were originally built to support only one additional floor above grade. Higher walls were subject to disastrous failure, especially in earthquakes. However, economic pressures in the Roman empire eventually created reasons for property owners to add a third, or even a fourth floor to their homes and businesses. The upper floors were often built in wood, to reduce the structural load on the original stone or brick walls. However, built of wood, they were also highly flammable, and created a new fire risk for the city. Eventually, the solution was to ban all cooking and fires in the upper apartments, forcing ever more Roman citizens to rely on street food for their daily meals.

In dense urban areas, as streets became the domain of the common people, the wealthy began to withdraw their living and dining quarters to a level built above the street. Crowded medieval streets became famous for their filth, odors, and noise, such that by the early Renaissance, Italian architects were constructing mansions and public buildings with a standard plan of service rooms at grade, or partially submerged in a half-basement, with the major public floors raised up on a platform above the street by 8 to 12 feet. Another two to three floors could then be built for more private uses above that. Thus, the best floor in the building was what Americans would call the second floor (first floor in Europe), also known as the *piano nobile* (Italian for the 'noble floor'). It was located just one flight up from street level, more protected from thievery, flooding, and other street-level insults, plus it had better views. The *piano nobile* was built with the highest ceilings and the grandest windows the owner could afford. Thus, it would be the floor with the very best light, the best ventilation, and the best views.

At some point in their histories Paris and many other European cities formally adopted a five-story building height limit, or some equivalent formula, which was considered the maximum flights of stairs that a person could be reasonably expected to climb on a daily basis. As in ancient Rome, the height limits were also predicated on other concerns, such as fire safety and sanitation. Sometimes the height limit was predicated on the width of the street, to ensure adequate light and ventilation, so that the wider the street, the higher the façades. This greatly contributed to the real estate value of owning property on major avenues and boulevards. The net result of the five-story height limit was that a few important public buildings, like a cathedral spire or parliament dome, rose far above the overall height limit and remained highly visible landmarks.

Paris and Washington DC are two of the very few major world cities that have steadfastly maintained their nineteenth-century building height limits, with the added benefit that the Eiffel Tower in Paris and the Capitol Dome in Washington DC are still visible from almost every property in downtown neighborhoods. Eventually, this concept of view preservation was also adopted as a rationale for building height limits by a few other cities in the latter half of the twentieth century. Most famously Athens, Greece, maintains a maximum building height to preserve a view of the Parthenon, while Portland, Oregon has set height limits within the city to preserve views of its famous landmark, the magnificent Mount Hood volcano.

However, cities with height limits also created a trade-off for building owners and developers to squeeze more rentable floor space within a given allowed building height. The solution was often to make the topmost floors very short, as often found in Paris or Edinburgh, with minimal ceiling heights to accommodate the garrets or servants' quarters. Accordingly, there was ongoing tension between overall building height limits and floor-to-floor ceiling heights. This tension continued until the dawn of the twentieth century, when a few new technologies disrupted this equation.

Elevators and Towers

Mechanical dumb waiters were a new concept in the early eighteenth century. Thomas Jefferson built one into his innovative home Monticello. Louis the XV purportedly had one built to secretly transport his mistresses into his bed chambers. But development of mechanically powered elevators really accelerated with the industrial revolution and the need to move lots of material in and out of factories, and move lots of men down into coal mines

By the mid-nineteenth century, architects started to experiment with installing mechanical elevators in buildings. An insurance company, the Equitable Life Assurance Company in New York City, first recognized the economic potential of the elevator and included one in their new headquarters office building in Manhattan. The resulting building was only seven stories tall, but quickly proved that, with an elevator, upper floors could command higher rents! Other companies in New York City quickly followed suit.

These early 'skyscrapers,' while able to add additional floors because of the elevator, were still bogged down by the use of load-bearing masonry construction, which required ever thicker walls at their base in order to support their greater height. Meanwhile, a thousand miles away in the midwestern boom town of Chicago, architects like Daniel Burnham and Louis Sullivan were experimenting with a new approach to high-rise buildings, using steel frame construction to lighten up the structure. Steel-framed buildings seemed to promise a future freed from constraints of gravity, where windows could be ever larger. With steel beams and less weight above, grand openings could be framed at the base of the building to invite the public in. And of course, the elevator would carry patrons up to the topmost floor with no thought to the exhaustion of climbing stairs. A livery-uniformed elevator operator, or 'lift attendant,' welcomed patrons into the contraption and safely delivered them to the desired floor, much like a doorman or butler in a fancy dwelling, with a personable 'good morning' and 'good evening' added to the mix.

However, it was the use of elevators at the Eiffel Tower at the Universal Exhibition in 1889 that really captured the world's imagination. Suddenly the ride in the elevator was more than a utilitarian transport, but now an exciting event, taking tourists up to the top of the (then) tallest structure in the world! The power of view became the economic power of tourism. Going up to the top of the tallest tower in a city has become a standard tourist attraction in almost every city in the world. For example, the Tokyo Tower in Japan, built of steel lattice work like the Eiffel Tower, has been visited by over 150 million people since it opened in 1958 as the world's tallest tower. In 2012, it was superseded by the Tokyo Skytree, with an observation deck mounted at 1,476 feet above the ground, 50% higher than the Eiffel Tower's.

There seems to be no limit for people's fascination with getting ever higher up for a look around, providing the vantage point to help form a cognitive map of one's surrounds. In this sense, these grand towers serve as both landmarks from below—unique forms demarking a special place visible from all around the city—and as the center of a cognitive map created while contemplating the view from above. Just as a table and chair set on out a patio invites you to conceive of yourself inhabiting the patio, so too a tower invites you to envision yourself at the top of the tower, commanding the sweeping view.

Stairways had once been one of the grandest architectural features of a building, an opportunity to visually connect people at different levels of a building. However, with the success of elevators moving people up to the highest floors, stairs quickly became relegated to windowless concrete shafts, a bleakly uninviting environment. In high-rises they served only as the 'back-up-plan' fire escape, designed to minimum fire code standards, no longer a social event. Only recently have architects tried to lure occupants back onto using stairs, often by adding daylight and views, to create an 'irresistible stair' that once again invites people to move, to encounter each other, and to enjoy the view as they move between floors.[8]

View Sheds and Solar Envelopes

Another problem with towers is that, sooner or later, someone is likely to build a taller one, blocking some of the sweeping view from the first. And so it goes, the war of the tall urban buildings, each one taking something away from its neighbors, especially unrestricted access to daylight, sunlight, and view. A 1,000-foot-tall tower, with 70 to 80 floors, will cast a shadow that impacts a huge semicircular area, on the order of 150 acres. With a sun angle at 30 degrees above the horizon, the leading edge of the tower's shadow will sweep across the city like the hands of a giant clock at the rate of five to ten feet per minute, or one to two inches per second, and then linger for an hour or two, depending on the width of the building. Deep in the urban canyons, with shadows compounding from many tall buildings, sunlight may never reach the lowest floors or street pavement.

As cities started to grow ever denser in the nineteenth century, building owners in England increasingly evoked a common law doctrine of 'ancient lights'; 'lights' in this case meaning windows. The ancient lights doctrine says that if a window that has provided useful daylight for twenty years or more is blocked by a new neighbor, the owner of the window can sue for damages, due to a loss of easement to the sky. The ancient lights doctrine created a motivation to negotiate monetary damages paid from new developers to existing building owners, but did nothing to protect rights to sunlight, daylight and views for future generations. The history and interpretation of this law is long and complex, and has been criticized for unduly constraining development in Britain.

Around the end of the nineteenth century, American cities tried a different tactic to address the threat of ever denser cities with ever taller buildings. They adopted city planning regulations that required progressive setbacks for high-rise buildings, creating the common tiered form of early skyscrapers, such as the Empire State and Chrysler Buildings. These regulations resulted in 'wedding-cake' stacked buildings that opened up more of the street to the sky, but filled in entire blocks with the bottom floors of the building, resulting in no public space at street level.

Later, by the middle of the twentieth century, a new deal was struck with developers, allowing them to build taller blocky buildings if they dedicated more space at street level to a public plaza. The Seagram Building and its entrance plaza, designed by architect Mies van der Rohe and completed in 1958, became the prototype for this type of urban regulation. The plaza in front of the Seagram Building was later studied by the sociologist William Whyte who pointed out all the ways the designers misunderstood how real people would inhabit the plaza. Whyte used this case study to help New York City refine its planning regulations, including guidelines for where people at street level were observed to prefer to sit, relative to exposure to sun, wind, trees, water and other amenities.[9] The Project for Public Spaces, founded in 1975 to continue Whyte's work, has helped over 3,000 communities worldwide to design their public places for better utilization, following his simple method of observing resulting behaviors.[10] While the effort has resulted in better urban plazas and streetscapes where people will happily gather, a major component of the equation—the fundamental layout and structural forms of the city—is still often ignored.

Ralph Knowles, a USC professor of architecture, took on the challenge of how to maximize urban form for the benefit of the people both inside and outside of buildings. In 1976 he coined the term 'the solar envelope' as a zoning concept to ensure solar access to all buildings within a mid-rise, mid-density plan. He claims to have been inspired by the design of the ancient Acoma Pueblo in New Mexico, where terraced houses face southward, their thick masonry walls providing ideal passive heating in the winter, and cooling in the summer.[11] His studies demonstrate how the solar envelope, i.e. the largest theoretical container of space that would not cast shadows off-site for given day of the year, varies with street and block orientation, and property sizing within a block. For example, those giant N–S city blocks in Salt Lake City have a very different result than the unusual NW/SE streets in Boise, Idaho. Knowles's work suggests that there is generally a mid-rise building maximum height of six to seven stories that optimizes urban density while still preserving solar access for buildings and streets.

San Jose, the center of Silicon Valley in California, has embraced mid-rise apartments as its housing solution as it transforms from a sprawling city of ranch-style homes built in the 1950s and 1960s to the dense urban center of the digital revolution. Typically, four floors of apartment units are built on top of a concrete 'podium' that houses retail stores and parking. This approach can achieve 65 to 100 units per acre at costs considerably less per unit (and thus lower rents) than high-rise style tower construction. The top of the concrete podium becomes a livable roof deck, with gardens and pools raised above street level. At the base, walkable streets are lined with modest-sized retail outlets adjacent to the housing. The resulting urban plan also generates considerably less shadowing, and much less windy streets than a comparable city of high-rise towers.

Knowles's work is prospective, providing guidance for future city planners who want to optimize solar access while maintaining urban densities. In 2016, the New York Times took the opposite approach, publishing a massive interactive map displaying the cumulative shadows cast by every existing building in the city.[12] This map can be filtered for different seasons, allowing anyone to quickly locate the darkest urban canyons, or the plazas and parks that receive the most yearly sunlight. The oldest part of town, in the financial district near Wall Street, has some of the darkest streets, exposed to less than 10% of the sky dome and rarely seeing sunlight. The edges and center of the voids are the brightest areas, especially Central Park which preserves unimpeded access to the sky and sunlight all year round. Given the diversity of building types and vintages around the city, the map allows quick comparison of the shadowing impacts of various urban design approaches. Using similar information to create a three-dimensional model of all buildings in a city (such as already exists for cell phone coverage), it should also be possible to create city-scale maps of daylight access and view sheds.

The Future of Urban Form

We began this discussion of urban form with the observation that as cities grow ever larger and denser to accommodate population growth, basic access to daylight and views from inside of buildings, where we spend most of our lives, will become ever more threatened. Unfortunately, something becomes truly precious only when it is scarce. Simple access to daylight, sunlight and views of the outdoor world should not be a zero-sum game, where whoever gets there first gets the goods, and everyone else must live with less. Without governmental action to mandate such access, developers of new buildings will inevitably try to maximize access for their property at the expense of their neighbors. It is not hard to imagine a future dystopia of very dense cities where real daylight and views have become so scarce that the only alternative is to offer people 'virtual reality' simulations.

Urban planning is extraordinarily complex, and its consequences have an exceedingly long timeframe. We have already reviewed many factors that impact daylight and view access, such as definition of city edges and voids, orientation of streets, size of properties, building height limits, ceiling heights, top- versus side-lighting opportunities, bulky versus more folded building shapes, accessibility of vista points, towers and views to landmarks, solar envelopes, and view sheds. Ensuring widespread daylight and view access in our cities is indeed a complex three-dimensional and policy problem, but one which needs to be urgently addressed in the growth of cities around the world.

As Stewart Brand explained, basic siting decisions such as street orientation and property lines can endure for millennia. When older, smaller properties are merged into larger properties for redevelopment, buildings tend to get bigger, taller, and deeper, reducing opportunities to preserve access to daylight and views. Likewise, basic building forms and shapes are also very enduring, representing the elements of *Structure* and *Skin* which persist almost as long as *Site*. Once a new building restricts access to daylight and views to either its own interior or that of its neighbors, there is rarely much chance to improve the situation short of tearing the building down. Alternatively, it is worthwhile looking at older generations of buildings and considering which are the easiest to retrofit for our purposes today. Those which provide ample access to daylight and views are often easiest to retrofit, continuing to support human needs as they are remodeled to serve ever-evolving purposes, thereby demonstrating their 'loose fit.'

American building codes instituted in the early twentieth century took a first step in insuring that everyone had a right to a minimum level of daylight and ventilation *in their homes*. We should undertake a similar effort as a favor for future generations, and expand that mandate to include schools, streets, workplaces, and the many other places where people spend their days. To do this well, architectural and urban designers need to deeply understand all the financial incentives, social structures and technical limitations that constrain the problem, along with the range of physiologic needs, perceptions, motivations, and cultural imperatives that drive people's desire for daylight and view. Which is where we turn our attention next.

13. The Value of View

Shortly after I had moved into my current home, I toured a house for sale across the street. It was small, old, poorly built, and terribly overpriced. However, the living room had the most amazing view: large corner windows looked out through a lacework of oak trees to a lovely grassland beyond. I immediately recognized that I had 'view lust.' I didn't want to own the house, but, oh my, I wanted that view!

There is an old real estate maxim which cites the three most important factors in determining the value of a property: 'location, location, and location!' However, on further inquiry real estate agents are usually willing to admit that nice views also figure in fairly prominently into both the desirability, and thus value, of an office building or a home.

When showing a home for sale, real estate agents often give advice that you should first wash all the windows and then open all the curtains and blinds, or better yet, remove them entirely, in order to emphasize how big the windows are and how bright the space can be. Interested buyers rarely notice the lack of window coverings, remembering instead the big, bright views out the windows. As one realtor I know likes to quip: *"In my 40 years in this business, I have never had anyone ask for a dark and gloomy house!"*

A friend who has long lived on the upper west side in Manhattan recounted the story of a family that purchased a newly remodeled condo on the second floor of their ten-story building, for $1.2 million, telling everyone that they loved the location. However, just a few months later an older apartment with an *identical* layout came up for sale on the tenth floor. The new family immediately sold their second-floor apartment, purchased the tenth-floor apartment upstairs at *twice* the price of the first, and then spent another $2.5 million renovating it. Thus, the tenth-floor unit, with a sunny, southwestern corner view (plus an elevator ride), was clearly worth four times the amount of the second-floor unit to them.

The central value of view for luxury homes is also exemplified by the level of effort that a commercial real estate developer expended in order to demonstrate the quality of the future views from their new luxury high rise, tellingly named Lumina, then under construction in San Francisco.[1] Long before the building was completed, a sales room was constructed elsewhere with a full size mock-up of the apartments to show to prospective buyers. The faux apartment windows looked out onto a blank curved wall, 72 feet long by ten feet high. A cutting-edge visual technology firm, Obscura, was hired to create an immersive projection system for the sales gallery. Images from 3D digital models were merged with high resolution photographs taken from each floor level, so that dozens of projectors could create panoramic images of the cityscape outside the window, at different times of day and night from any floor or orientation. A sales agent could flip through options via her mobile phone to display the appropriate view from any apartment unit under consideration: *"Would you like to see a view of the Bay Bridge at dawn or sunset? Or how much more can you see from ten floors up?"* On their website, Obscura happily reported: *"This is one of the first times immersive simulation projection technologies have been used to support the real estate sales industry. To date, [our] technology has enabled the LUMINA showroom to become the most successful residential sales gallery in San Francisco."*

Clearly, the developer believed that for this building they were primarily selling views of San Francisco, and was willing to invest serious money in their high-tech sales gallery to help make those sales.

Assessing Value

These stories illustrate the extreme value that some people place on what they deem to be a desirable view. Most realtors have plenty of experience with what motivates buyers to pay top dollar for a property, and can easily recount similar stories where they have personally seen the selling price of a home, or rental rates in an office building, escalate far above neighboring properties due to an unusually nice view. They are inevitably asked by other prospective sellers *"So then, how much is* my *view worth?"* But the market is quixotic, and it is very difficult to generalize outside of one's own immediate experience. The financial value of view has been an interesting, but often elusive, topic for many people studying daylight and views in buildings.

A Seattle-based residential broker attempted to break the valuation of view into four key components. In her blog, she suggested four key questions to consider. First, what is the view potential of the lot, independent of any existing buildings? If a building can be put on the lot which *could* have a great view, then the value of the lot is correspondingly greater. The second question is what is the potential view quality? Is the view panoramic, or just a peek-through? Is it year-round, or available only in the winter after deciduous trees have dropped their leaves? The third question, based on the home's design, is how accessible is the view? Do all the major living areas enjoy the view, or just the attic? Is the view seen only from a deck, where enjoyment is dependent on good weather? And finally, the fourth question to answer is how well the view is protected from future obstructions, such as from the growth of neighbors' trees, or a taller building which could be constructed in the future.[2]

These are all good questions to ask, but they do not actually quantify the value of view. Ideally, a real estate appraiser would like to be able to look into a data base and add a dollar value for a view, based on objective, observable features: bigger versus smaller, near versus far, east versus west, protected versus unprotected, etc. Such a database might be a Rosetta Stone for monetizing the qualities of a view. Indeed, some promising efforts are headed in this direction, but to date, so far success in distilling large urban databases seems to be focused on the value of daylight and sunlight exposure rather than the quality and content of views.[3]

Killer Views

One study which did address the content of view, done on behalf of the website Realtor.com, reported on the value of 'killer views' in select real estate markets in 2017. A 'killer view' was defined as the iconic view for a given city that was most commonly identified in advertisements. According to an article by Sara Ventiera, "*[The Realtor.com] data team collected the prices for all the homes for sale on the site that highlight these sought-after panoramas, and then compared them to similar-size properties in adjacent ZIP codes with no view to speak of.*"[4]

This analysis found that there was a considerable price differential, from hundreds of thousands, to millions of dollars, for a these 'killer views.'

At that time, if a home in San Francisco could claim a view of the Golden Gate Bridge, an average $600,000 premium was added to a home with such a view, or an additional 33% of overall value. A local realtor is quoted in the article explaining why a view of the Golden Gate Bridge is so highly prized: "*It's what makes San Francisco special ... If you have a glorious view of the water, the bridge and Alcatraz, then you know you're in San Francisco!"* It seems questionable that someone would spend hundreds of thousands of dollars in order to be reminded of where they were living. Surely, there is more to the value of such a view than a simple reminder of your current location?

In Chicago, a view of Lake Michigan essentially doubled the price of an apartment. Likewise, in Miami, a view of South Beach doubled the value. One way to think of this situation is that in these markets renters and buyers are comparing two aspects of a potential property: the physical apartment (with its location, square footage, layout and amenities such as a modern kitchen and bath) versus the 'killer view': the two are judged to have equal monetary value!

In Las Vegas, the value of a home tripled if the famous Las Vegas Strip was visible from a window or patio. The Vegas Strip sits at the bottom of a topographical bowl, creating a natural amphitheater of residential neighborhoods, full of homes trying to position for a view of the glittering high-rise casinos and hotels at the center of the valley. An agent who works there is quoted as saying: *"People pay this premium because the Strip is to Vegas what the beach is to Malibu: That's our ocean."*

In New York City, Venteria explained: *"Manhattan is notorious for its exorbitantly priced, itty-bitty apartments, with windows that look into a grand expanse of brick wall. Or alleys. But for those New Yorkers who can afford the* privilege *of natural light, there's one view that matters above all others: Central Park"* (emphasis added by the author).

This study found that, on average, a view of Central Park added over a million dollars to the value of a condominium. Interestingly, she also reports that floor level and orientation matters. The higher the better, and views on the south side of the park, looking northward onto the sunlit trees, are by far the most desirable. The east and west side of the park are also both in demand, but the east side has slightly higher prices, because those homes also command a view of the sunset sky. She quotes a local agent who summarizes the allure of a view of Central Park: *"It's really all about status. Apartments with views of the nation's most famous park are about showing off* what you have *and* who you are" (emphasis added by the author).

Privilege and Ownership

There are some interesting concepts expressed here that figure into a lot of real estate assumptions. The first is that natural light and views are a *privilege*, that therefore they are part of the structure of the market, where wealthy people can afford to pay the extra price or rent to secure them, and less wealthy people must make do without.

The second concept is that a view is something *you have*, i.e. you can own it, it is part of your personal property, implying that you have property rights to this view that *you have,* and that this ownership of a view conveys something about *who you are*.

Erik Gunter, also writing in Realtor.com about the importance of views to luxury real estate, contends that *"When it comes to multi-multimillion-dollar listings, views are the key. You're not opening your wallet to stare at a partial view of your neighbor's fence—you need to feel like the master of all you survey."*

Of course, unless a view is of a grand private estate that extends for miles, where the owner actually is the master, people rarely own the contents of their view. In the case of Central Park, the view is of a public park, maintained by the City. In the case of a view of Las Vegas, you are looking at nothing but other people's private property. In the case of Chicago's view of Lake Michigan, it is a natural body of water, presumably owned by all of the citizens of the surrounding states. Outside of the private real estate market, people also express a sense of *privilege* at having daily access to a beautiful view from a public place.

The University of California at Santa Cruz, near where I live, sits up on a hill, overlooking the waters of Monterey Bay, which stretches out in a grand half circle, to the mountains forming the spine of the Monterey Peninsula 30 miles away. On a clear day, of which there are many in this climate, this is indeed a breathtaking view. In interviews, both faculty and students frequently used the word *privilege* to describe their daily access to that view from various spots on campus. They felt that access to that killer view was one of the treasured benefits of working on campus. Asked why it was so treasured, more than one person responded *"It makes you feel expansive."* One fellow explained: *"As I come over the rise, and suddenly see the view of the Bay, I instantly take in a deep breath and feel my body relax. My life feels that much bigger and a little bit easier."*

The term 'commanding view' is also commonly used, and while it might be interpreted most directly as an 'unobstructed view,' it also speaks of a feeling of mastery and ownership that views can convey, as if inherited from a distant royalist past, when a king or military commander overlooked his domain from the castle on high. Daniel Menaker, an editor for *The New Yorker* magazine for many years, reflected on his view of Manhattan as essentially a view of other hundreds of other windows. His sense is that: *"Each person looking out any one of those other windows is the master and commander of his view, just as I am the master and commander of mine. Every window is literally and metaphorically a point of view, and everyone who looks out a window is a sovereign of what he sees.*"[5]

Menaker also uses the term *sovereign*, which implies independence from others, and even some form of control over the territory being viewed, i.e. the scope of the view designates the sovereign's dominion. There is an inference here that the act of looking at a view is also a way to possess that view. Possessing a view might be interpreted loosely as a metaphor of emotional attachment, or for some people it is literally interpreted as a form of proprietary rights.

Tree Wars and Spite Walls

There are many stories of wealthy or eccentric people whose sense of privilege at 'owning' a view extends to taking action to preserve their view at any cost. Many arborists make a good living pruning trees to maintain views. One arborist working around upper Lake Michigan told me that he is routinely paid tens of thousands of dollars to open up a view to the lake for a new homeowner, sometimes on their own land, sometimes on a neighbor's, which might also include the purchase of a legal 'view easement' attached to property records in perpetuity. Other less scrupulous homeowners have been known to find ways to kill trees that obscure their view. When I lived near the American River in Sacramento, California, a park ranger discovered an old grove of oak trees newly girdled—a continuous ring of bark removed—and all dead or dying. Eventually a homeowner on the bluffs directly above the dead trees was convicted of felony destruction of public property for trying to secure an unobstructed view of the river.

The flip side to tree wars are stories of 'revenge walls' or 'spite fences' where one neighbor builds an excessively tall barrier to cut off a neighbor's view. Perhaps the most famous of these is a forty-foot high fence built in 1876 on Nob Hill in San Francisco by the wealthy goldrush banker Charles Crocker, blocking light and view on two sides for his neighbor who refused to sell the corner lot on the block where Crocker wanted to construct his new mansion. The towering fence surrounding the neighbor's tiny cottage become a local curiosity, persisting for decades. Charles Crocker's famous fence eventually formed the basis for laws banning 'spite fences,' which has since become an official term in American property law. Nowadays most localities have ordinances that prohibit walls or fences over six or eight feet. Many, especially in areas with highly prized ocean or mountain views, also have view ordinances restricting the height of trees. In some subdivisions, a written set of rules governing the neighborhood, such as covenants, conditions, and restrictions

(CC&Rs), may protect views, while in others, owners are left to sue each other for any perceived infringement.

Perhaps part of this intense sense of ownership of views is predicated on the fact that it is actually possible to permanently block a view, i.e. to physically restrict access to who is allowed to partake of a particular view, or alternatively, to purchase a legally enforced 'view easement.' In comparison, very few other environmental pleasures are so entwined with our system of property rights. The experience of sounds and fragrances can be intensely evocative of place, but it is difficult to prevent a sound or fragrance from migrating over property lines. Nuisance laws do exist to protect residents from obnoxious smells or noise emanating from neighbors' property, but I can think of no comparable concept of 'owning' pleasant natural sounds, like bird song, or the smell of a nearby fragrant forest, because there is simply no way to enforce its presence.

Views may also evoke a feeling of ownership since they have a sense of durability, in that you can expect to return to the same spot and re-experience essentially the same view again and again, whereas most our other sensory experiences are fleeting, not so easily repeated. Indeed, views are a stable enough experience that they are widely marketed, not only in advertisements for hotel rooms or to sell a home, but also in place names. American developers long ago learned the appeal of naming a new development after its purported view qualities, such as 'Mountain View' or 'Panorama City,' now both well-known cities in California. Expressing the idea of a beautiful view in French, Italian, or Spanish, such as *Bellevue*, *Belvedere*, or *Buena Vista*, added a touch of class and increased the naming possibilities. Likewise, we rarely have places names named after other sensory experiences, such as 'Harbor Melodies' or 'Park Aroma.' View and vision seem to be intricately embedded in our sense of place and location, with a permanence that is not provided with other sensory associations.

I think this expectation of permanence fuels a full spectrum of emotions, from the passionate possessiveness of entitled ownership, as seen in angry lawsuits, to the reassuring calm and nostalgia of returning to a much-loved view. While in reality, views are constantly changing—plants change and grow with the seasons, pedestrians and traffic come and go—but the deeper structure is very slow to change, providing reassurance about our place in the world.

A Point of View

Let's return to the quote from Daniel Menaker, that *"every window is literally and metaphorically a point of view,"* i.e. a unique perspective that comes from that particular location in time and space. Somehow this point of view fuses with the sense-of-self of the person doing the viewing. How, I wonder, does a particular view get internalized into a 'point of view,' which conveys that sense of ownership? This merging of the viewer's outward perspective and inward identity is intriguing.

Matteo Pericoli tells an illustrative story about when he first realized that his own sense of self had become entwined with his daily view. One day, just as he was getting ready to move to a new apartment, he writes: "*I remember looking once again at the view and was struck by a bewildering feeling of loss. 'I can't leave this behind!' I told myself ... 'How great it would be if I could capture the view by simply peeling off an imaginary thin film from the glass, rolling it up, and then taking it to our new place.' ... I had looked out that window for seven years, day after day, taking in that particular arrangement of buildings, and now my wife and I were about to move out of our one-bedroom apartment. Without my knowing it, that view had become my most familiar image of the city. It had become mine. And I would never see it again.*"[6]

Pericoli emphasizes "*It had become mine,*" implying a form of ownership, but in this case with a much more emotional connotation, more like 'it had become a part of me' than the sense of property rights discussed earlier. Realizing how important this view had become to him, his very sense of self, he decided to try to document it, perhaps as a way to preserve that ownership, or more likely to preserve that feeling inside of him, so that he could bring it with him to the new place.

At first, he tried to photograph it, "*... from all possible angles and perspectives with the room. But photographing the view meant photographing the window frame, too, for there is no such thing as a 'window view' without a frame ... Soon [I] realized that the photos didn't work. They were not able to convey my view, but simply what was outside the window.*"

Instead, he decided to draw it on a big sheet of brown wrapping paper, and as he did, he noticed ever more things about the view, "*things I didn't know that I had been looking at for so long. Where had they been hiding in my brain?*"

Here we have Pericoli, the illustrator, i.e. a highly visual person, telling us that he had stared out this window for seven years while working there every day, and yet he had not noticed significant details in that view. He had become so fond of it that he felt separation anxiety at the prospect of leaving it, and yet he still had not consciously absorbed all of its details. This suggests that much more was going on in his brain when he was staring out of the window other than just 'looking.'

I would argue that, while looking at a routine view, our brains are building up layers of memories of moments and emotions experienced while looking out the same window again and again. Familiarity breeds fondness, such that the more time we spend with a view, the more likely we are to find something to like about it, and eventually even love about it. It may not be a great view, but it is *our* view. I think this evolution is especially likely with the types of views where we have the luxury to pause for a few moments, just randomly staring, pondering, mind wandering. This might be standing at a kitchen window where you spend a lot of time washing dishes, or the bench where you wait every day for your commuter bus. Depending on your type of work, it might be the window at your desk or the breakroom window. The longer you spend with a view, and the more opportunities you have to pause and reflect, the more likely you are to develop a fondness for it, regardless of how 'nice' the view is to begin with. The view instead becomes a subtle reminder of all those past moments and emotions, now somehow sublimated into a feeling about the view itself.

View as Vortex

Michelle Huneven, a novelist and UCLA professor, describes how the constancy of her garden view in Los Angeles helps her get down to work. Like remembering the tail end of a dream, the reminder of this reliable view pulls her back into the imaginary worlds of her novels: "*My office is a small hut in the backyard about 50 feet from the house ... It's very private. I see only our neighbor's trees—there is not a powerline, a street, or even a roof in sight; it's like working in a park or another century ... For years now this has been what I see when I work; not surprising, it's what I visualize whenever I so much as think of getting down to it. This setting has become the base camp, the portal of my imagination; from here, day after day, I begin.*"

It is this special power of a view, as a 'portal' to other thoughts, feelings, memories, and ways of thinking, that is perhaps most fascinating. Huneven seems to be suggesting that her garden view provides a mental landscape that she inhabits when she is at work. Looking at the view helps to cue her brain that it is time to enter into this different mental landscape, return to where she left off a day or two ago, and get down to working.

Mike McCormack, an Irish science fiction writer made a similar observation. His home office view is of a very ordinary suburban street, with driveways, garages, lamp posts, and a few little trees planted in a nearby lawn. He wrote: "*I have lived in this house on the edge of Galway City for over five years now, and for a couple of hours a day I sit with my feet up on the windowsill and look out over this cul-de-sac ... The place is constant, nothing much to hold the eye or interest. Of course this is precisely the kind of stillness in which the mind's eye gets lost—vista as vortex."*

Thus, while McCormack's view is quiet, also importantly it is constant. In its very stillness, his view pulls his mind into a vortex, another dimension of thought. That is quite a contradictory image: a vortex implies a violent swirling, a whirlwind of mental activity, all set in this very quiet and ordinary street. Perhaps it is the very quietude and constancy of the suburban street that provides a stable context, safe enough for him to head off into that vortex of imagination.

Getting lost in a fantasy world is actually a very real danger for humans. We learned earlier about 'intrusive thoughts,' the category of unwanted mind wandering that is out of the control of the subject, and accounts for many forms of mental illness. Depressed or suicidal people have lost the ability to exclude negative thoughts. Obsessive thoughts can become paralyzing; paired with agoraphobia or other anxiety disorders, they prevent people from acting according to current conditions. Fiction writers also talk about 'the story' taking control of them, such that external reality temporarily ceases to exist. But as writers, they carefully manage their descent into the fantasy world, such that they can experience and document it and then reemerge whole and functional in the everyday world.

This balancing act, between internal and external worlds is a recurring theme among the narratives in Pericoli's books about writer's workplace views. They explicitly select and manage their environment to get just the right level of stimulation versus distraction, engagement versus detachment, companionship versus solitary focus. They seem be trying to maintain a delicate equilibrium between an expansive outward view and an inwardly contracting mental focus.

The Balancing Act

Rebecca Walker is explicit about this balancing act, describing her relationship to her writer's studio view in Maui, Hawaii: *"I have been looking out this window for three years. I have stared out of these rectangular panes full of hope and also despair, giddy with inspiration to connect and overtaken with a throbbing desire to disengage. I suppose this is what writing is to me: gripping the rope that swings between reaching out and pulling in."*

Rana Dasgupta, who writes from his home in new Delhi, India, describes an opposite experience from the Irish writer McCormack. A constant tumult of activity outside his writing window helps to balance his mental isolation as a writer. He writes: *"The rampant energy of Delhi, this city of almost twenty million people, presses in on my leafy street. ... I have come to realize that I do not love solitude as much as I think. It is always with happy anticipation that I arrive in my study: alone, at last, to write! But once the door is closed, I have a paradoxical sense of loss, as if I am cut off from my source. Is this why I spend such an unreasonable amount of time staring of the window?"*

Oliver Sacks, the famous neurologist quoted earlier, always wrote while viewing the activity outside his writing window in Greenwich Village— *"the constant movement of life of New York City"*—as a needed counterpoint to his inner thoughts while writing. Orhan Pamuk, a historical novelist writing in Istanbul, suggests a reason why this balance is so essential: that with such concentration on the imaginary world of their books, writers especially need reassurance that the real world happily continues on outside, regardless of the writer's internal state of mind. He explains: *"Most of my writing time is spent forming the next sentence in my imagination. When my mind is busy with words, all by itself my eye moves away from the page [to his sweeping view of Istanbul and the Bosphorus] ... To the popular question inquisitive guests and journalists ask—'Doesn't this wonderful view distract you?'—my answer is no. But I know that some part of me is always busy with some part of the landscape, following the movements of the seagulls, trees, and shadows, spotting boats and checking to see that the world is always there, always interesting, and always a challenge to write about: an assurance that the writer needs to continue to write and reader needs to continue to read."*

The issue of balance takes many forms. Not all workers have the intense inner life of writers, but most do have a need to balance multiple demands on their attention while at work, especially relative to interaction with fellow workers and focus on their own tasks and priorities. Views in the workplace is the topic of the next chapter.

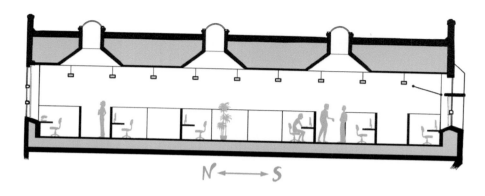

N ←——→ S

14. Working with Daylight

In any workplace, finding the right balance between engagement with the outside world and maintaining inward privacy, security, and focus is always a challenge. This is not just an issue for daylight and view, but also for the many other indoor environmental quality (IEQ) concerns, such as thermal comfort, fresh air, and acoustics. In fact, the history of modern office building design might partly be thought of as engineers and designers struggling to gradually separate all those IEQ concerns into independent systems—for example, where ventilation can be controlled separately from thermal, acoustic, and visual conditions in the space. However, if you open a window, they all come rushing back together again! Reynard Banham wrote a wonderful history of indoor environmental systems in the 1970s, *The Architecture of the Well-Tempered Environment*. It provides an essential history of building systems from the nineteenth century through the 1970s. Our story picks up where Banham left off, focusing of course on daylight and view, but also with a sub-theme of how they interact with all the other concerns that arise in various workplace environments.

As an initial thought experiment about the many ways that daylight and view might impact workers, I decided to review my own work history over 50 years, from when I was a teenager until now. I remembered 30 places that I had worked inside a building over those years, discounting the few times when I had a job working outside as a construction worker or camp counselor. I tried to remember some key visual impressions or fond memories of those workplaces and found that they were sorely lacking. As I listed the 18 times that I was working for someone else as an employee, I realized that the quality of the daylight and views in those places ranged from highly forgettable to completely non-existent. Eight of my jobs offered no views to the outside;

zero, zilch. I worked at a telephone switch board, retail sales, a library, and for various architecture firms where my workstation had no access to any windows. Ten other employee positions offered minimal views, with windows far, far away from my desk. Over those years, I looked out onto a lot of bare walls and parking lots. It may not be coincidental that I also felt constrained, controlled, and generally thwarted.

On the other hand, the 12 places where I worked for myself as a student, a self-employed freelancer, or head of my own company, all tended to have pretty nice views, and some were downright spectacular. For example, my freshman dorm room in college looked out across the San Francisco Bay to the Golden Gate Bridge. I felt so alive as I wrote those freshman essays! My future possibilities seemed similarly immense. Once I had the opportunity to choose my own workplace, as head of my own company, the views just kept getting better and better. Our final offices featured a gorgeous Japanese garden in the interior courtyard, and huge cottonwood trees ringing the outer offices, such that everyone in the office had a view out to some serious greenery. As an employer, I found that a good view was certainly not the only aspect of a successful workplace, but it definitely added an element of motivation for showing up to work at the office every morning.

The Number One Office Perk

Indeed, recent surveys of office workers have found that access to daylight and views is often the top desire of employees. An article in the Harvard Business Review titled *The #1 Office Perk? Natural Light* explained that in a research poll of 1,614 North American employees, access to natural light and views of the outdoors were found to be: "*the number one attribute of the workplace environment, outranking stalwarts like onsite cafeterias, fitness centers, and premium perks including onsite childcare.*" The author went on to explain that: "*The study also found that the absence of natural light and outdoor views hurts the employee experience. Over a third of employees feel that they don't get enough natural light in their workspace. 47% of employees admit they feel tired or very tired from the absence of natural light or a window at their office, and 43% report feeling gloomy because of the lack of light.*"[1]

But, we must ask, if daylight and views are so important to office workers, why is the marketplace not generating more workplaces that meet these desires? One comprehensive study of existing office buildings in California found that two-thirds of the *existing* office floorspace had *no* access to daylight.[2] Thus, while daylight and views might be the most highly desired office 'perk' among employees, evidence shows it is still far from the norm.

In order to encourage more daylight and views in *new* office buildings, many voluntary environmental and building performance standards, such as BREEAM, LEED, and WELL have adopted language that incentivizes building owners to include daylight and views in new buildings. However, in spite of good intentions, there is evidence that these standards are not (yet) having a very widespread effect. For example, an assessment of recent LEED applications conducted in 2018 found that only 18% of all new projects applied for daylighting credits, and only 2% used the more sophisticated annual hourly simulation daylight modeling techniques.[3] This puts the number of LEED-certified projects with daylighting credits across the United States in the hundreds, not thousands, a tiny fraction of new construction.

A Brief History of the Open Plan Office

Back in the 1980s, as a young architect, I was involved in the design of a number of high-rise office buildings in San Francisco and Oakland, California. I quickly learned that the design of the building was largely determined by the rentable-space formula. At that time, standard practice was still to ring the perimeter of a building with private offices, each of which had one or two windows: this was the high-rent district. The more private offices that a designer could pack around the exterior of the building, the higher the rents for the building owner, and thus the greater the value of the building. The central interior space was reserved for administrative support staff—the secretaries—who did all the typing and sat at desks in an open office area, where they might get a peek out a window when the door was left open to the boss's private office.

As desktop computers took over in the 1990s and more people did their own typing, personal secretaries became increasingly rare. Instead of rows of private offices, 'open office' planning became popular, where mid-level and junior professionals were assigned an L-shaped or U-shaped desk separated by five-foot high partition walls. Revealing the minimalist, one-size-fits-all nature of these workstations, they were called 'cubicles,' i.e. the cubic area of office space allotted to each worker. The interior design of office buildings devolved into a simple geometric packing problem, with only four basic workplace types—big and small private offices, and big and small cubicles. The architectural challenge was to see how many of these standard rectangular units could be packed most efficiently into a given floorplan. Vast landscapes of cubicles were often ridiculed as 'cube farms,' creating a perverse social environment, as amply captured at the time by Scott Adams in the popular Dilbert comic strip.

FL Wright's Johnson Wax Building

Actually, open plan office design has a long and storied history. One of the most influential early open plan offices was designed by Frank Lloyd Wright for the Johnson Wax Company in Racine, Wisconsin. Occupied in 1939, it featured a vast open floor for the company secretaries, with 20 foot tall mushroom-shaped columns, or as Wright preferred to call them, 'dendriform' (i.e. tree-like), that rose from a narrow base of nine inches to 18-foot wide caps at the top. Most importantly, the space between the round column caps was filled in with skylights, with the intention of flooding the space below with daylight from above. The initial reactions to the space were glorious, with occupants overjoyed with the sense of spaciousness. The 'Great Workroom' was bright enough and tall enough such that early photographs show large potted trees also filling the space, although later photos show a much more utilitarian layout.

Wright thought the legacy of the building would be his gently curvilinear forms, which he equated with democracy, while avoiding creating any 'boxes' that he equated with fascist ideology. Instead, the Johnson Wax building became the inspiration for the increasing use of open plan office design. Germans picked up the idea in the 1950s with the concept of *Bürolandschaft* (German for 'office landscape'), that allowed informal, non-linear plan layouts of desks, and portable partitions. An American manufacturer of office furniture, Herman Miller, quickly followed suit, advertising an 'Action Office' system of re-configurable curved partitions that allowed for a fluid, adaptable open plan layout. Soon office managers and real estate agents discovered the space-saving, and hence the cost-saving, advantages of open plan offices. As ever more furniture manufacturers took over the traditional architectural role of office space planning, the race was on to pack as many people as possible into the floorplates of modern high-rise office buildings.

With the advent of ubiquitous overhead fluorescent lighting and mechanical ventilation, floor-to-ceiling heights could be reduced by eliminating any concern for the distribution of natural light and natural ventilation. High-rise office buildings were designed in horizontal layers, with precise allowances of how many vertical inches could allotted to each engineering discipline: structural, mechanical, electrical, acoustic. Many big architectural offices, famous for their high-rise office buildings, prided themselves on their ability to manage how tightly each of these layers could be compressed. This compression of vertical space, however, also created problems for the overhead lighting and ventilation systems, both of which required horizontal distribution to be effective. As the ceiling was lowered, the gap between the ceiling and partition became ever smaller, resulting in more shadows and ventilation dead-spots.

Towards the end of the century, people were beginning to notice a myriad of problems with recently constructed office buildings. Legionnaires disease, a form of pneumonia first identified in 1974, was associated with the huge air conditioning systems of large buildings, and launched larger concerns with 'sick building syndrome,' where office workers complained of a general malaise. Investigations of the problem sometimes closed down entire buildings for months at a time. The public health cost of poorly operated office buildings was becoming painful.

A huge amount of floorspace was still devoted to private offices, but these pricy perimeter offices were often empty as their resident executives attended meetings elsewhere. A few companies innovated by placing private offices in the interior core of the floorplan, allowing the folks in the cubicles to have greater access to windows. (Executives were loath to give up their windows, but even more loath to give up their doors.) Meanwhile life in the 'cube farms' barely improved. In innovative projects, like the New York Times headquarters opened in 2007, the heights of the cubicle partitions were lowered, to allow more access to daylight and views deeper into the rows of cubicles, but acoustic conditions worsened. A mechanical solution was often undertaken, with 'white noise' or 'brown noise' added to mask the intelligibility of nearby voices. However, a number of studies found that noise from co-workers was still one of the primary complaints of people working in open office settings, even among some of the most high-end office buildings with a prestigious green certification.[4] The problem of contagious diseases spreading through open office ventilation systems became even more acute during the COVID-19 pandemic of 2020. The progression of office design seemed to be continuously two steps forward, three steps back, with the future increasingly uncertain.

Re-Imaging the Office Workplace

The United States General Services Administration (GSA) is a huge agency that operates the buildings for a large portion of the federal workforce. In 2017, the GSA was responsible for managing about 350 million square feet, about 50% of all US federal government office space, calling itself 'the largest landlord in the world.'[5] As such, the GSA decided to take on some responsibility for the well-being of its office workers and launched a major effort to inform and demonstrate a new type of healthier, more efficient, more productive office workplace.

Observations in their traditional office buildings showed that government employees were actually sitting at their desk for only about one-third of the workweek; they were elsewhere in the building for meetings or breaks for another one-third; and physically absent, due to travel, field visits, telecommuting, vacations, or sick leave for the remaining one-third. However, with the increasing availability of portable laptops and cell phones, employees were no longer tethered to a fixed location with a telephone line and a desk top computer. Given this, GSA decided to give up on the concept of permanently assigned offices or desks and instead favor a new policy of flexible 'hoteling,' Using a software reservation system, similar to making a hotel reservation on-line, employees could reserve a workspace for a few hours, days, or weeks at a time.

Hoteling was a radical approach to try to address many space planning problems by adding a temporal element: reduce the amount of unoccupied space by allowing multiple occupants to use the space in sequence. They could choose a gracious private office with a door one day, a collaborative team space the next, and next an isolated cubicle for focused work. GSA space planners began to focus more on designing for variety rather than mere packing efficiency. Thus, employees could choose more or less acoustic and visual privacy as needed, or more access to daylight and views when most desired.

Not coincidentally, this change resulted in GSA's ability to accommodate far more workers within a given area. A building that previously was designed to hold 2,000 employees could now accommodate 4,000. With ever more people telecommuting from home, that ratio could easily increase further. Adaptation to frequent technology upgrades and ease of furniture reconfiguration became a driving force for space planning. Likewise, mechanical and electrical systems were selected for ease of reconfiguration, so that space plans could quickly respond to changing needs.

With all these redesigns and reconfigurations, much office building design has been reduced simply to 'core and shell' architecture, where only the fundamental shape and structure of the building are considered: floor-to-floor heights, stairs and elevators, vertical plumbing runs, weather skin, and apertures. As a result, aperture size and location, i.e. determining the placement of windows, skylights, and doors, is one of the last remaining and most enduring, design decision for work space architects. Ideally, apertures will be chosen to provide the spatial variety, flexibility and loose fit needed to meet future challenges.

Observing Behaviors

A very interesting research opportunity has presented itself with the advent of 'hoteling' office spaces, where office workers have freedom of choice to select their preferred work environment. In addition to GSA, many other large corporations, such as Genentech, a pharmaceutical research company which runs a massive campus of new buildings in San Francisco, and new office-services companies such as WeWork, have adopted similar hoteling protocols for their workspaces.[6] With enough diversity of options, such situations offer the opportunity to make non-invasive, anthropological-style, observations of where, when, how, and why people prioritize various attributes of their work environment.

I decided to conduct my own small observational studies with a number of companies located near where I live in California, especially those experimenting with new office layout paradigms. These included, in addition to Genentech, a few major software companies in Silicon Valley, and a handful of smaller local companies. (And, because office buildings comprise less than 20% of workplaces in the United States,[7] I also toured a variety of other building types, such as hospitals, courthouses, industrial buildings, hair salons, and recording studios.) Many friends and colleagues graciously gave me tours of their workplaces, often arranging for me to interview co-workers and discreetly observe office behavior.

Many people I spoke with were willing to sacrifice daylight and/or view in their workplace if they believed the situation was *temporary*, or if it was for only a few hours or few days a week. When I interviewed people who frequently telecommuted, and thus only came into an office setting for a day or two a week or a few hours per day, they were much less particular about their workspace. Likewise, short-term interns and temporary employees expressed little concern about their workplace conditions.

More senior and long-term employees, on the other hand, were insistent that they have just the right balance of daylight, view, privacy, and social connection. One manager explained how he carefully positioned his desk and chair so that, with just a slight change in position, he could have either a view of fellow workers and the windows beyond, or swivel inward for privacy and no social distractions. A proposal writer explained that she needed to maintain intense focus for long periods, but also wanted to work in ambient daylight and have a view. Her interior office provided her with just the right balance: a high partition window provided some borrowed daylight while a floor-to-ceiling glass wall and door let her look out over the larger open office area. She could work all day with her electric lights off, and had enough view of other people's activities to prevent her from feeling isolated. Keeping the door in the glass-wall closed most of the time gave her sufficient social and acoustic privacy so she could maintain focus.

Those long-term employees who felt that they had achieved just the right balance—between privacy and view, stimulation and distraction, engagement and detachment—were extremely tenacious in defending their rights to keep their workplace, and very resistant to any suggestions that they move elsewhere. These folks could articulate every nuance that they liked about their windows, their lighting, their views and their control of social interaction. It seemed that they felt they had finally achieved a mastery of their work environment.

An especially interesting site for my observations was a recently renovated printing plant, transformed into a LEED gold-rated office building by its new owners, Ecology Action, an environmental non-profit, and CruzIO, a local internet provider.[8] CruzIO had decided to devote part of their first floor of the building into an office-services business, very similar to WeWork, providing a wide range of office spaces, workstations, meeting rooms, and other support facilities. At the time of my observations, they were offering about 30 private offices with monthly rentals, of which slightly fewer than half have some access to daylight. *"Those offices facing the windows are always full,"* explained the manager. They also provided another 50 or so workstations of varying flavors, with daily rental options. A huge window, 15 feet high and 25 feet wide, dominated the central two-story high workspace. Facing due north and well protected from sunlight, it sported no blinds or curtains. It was also supplemented by an array of skylights directly overhead, such that the north area of the room swam in a pool of bright diffuse daylight. The daylight gradually dissipated deeper into the space, about 50 feet back, and 20 feet on each side. Large cubicles and small study carrels filled in on one side, while glassed-in conference rooms filled in on the other. In the back, a dark blue wall loomed over the double height space, and a few private offices with floor to ceiling frosted-glass walls led into a back corridor. Thus, this hoteling space provided a wide range of daylight and view conditions for the members to choose from.

Like pigeons on a wire, the subscribers at CruzIO's shared workplace tended to distribute themselves equally around the main room, with almost uniform spacing between each worker. And once settled in, their spot became fixed. There was a row of six standing desks lined up along the front window, which typically had one or two people using them. The rest of the sitting desks lined up in rows, typically grouped in pairs facing each other, and mounted on wheels for easy reconfiguration. Thus, the occupants had at least a binary choice of orientation, with an equal number of chairs facing the front and back walls, and they could have also easily rotated a desk or chair to another orientation. But nobody did: everyone faced the window.

I interviewed a lawyer who worked there two days a week, frequently using the standing desks. She explained that, due to the confidential nature of her work, she spent most of her time sitting in a small carrel facing a blank wall, in the hope that no-one could see any private information on her laptop screen. But she also worked at the standing desk for an hour or two a day, "*bathing in full-body daylight,*" she said, whenever she could work on paper, which had fewer visual privacy concerns. I estimated an average of 1,000+ lux of daylight at this desk. "*I couldn't work here without this big window. I need a visual break at least a few times per day,*" was her summary (see also page 156).

I talked with a number of people who chose to locate far away from the window, such that it was completely out of sight, or maybe just in a narrow upper corner of their field of view. Most of these people spent much of their day on the phone, and so were especially sensitive to acoustic privacy. But they all said the presence of the window was still very important to them, that they snuck a glance outside every so often, by standing up or walking past. Along the back wall, 50 feet from the big window, was where many of the 'regulars' sat, in the same spot every day. I gave it a try myself and found the view of big mullioned window particularly satisfying, providing a reference grid for every movement outside, from cars to clouds. There were only 20 to 30 lux of daylight reaching the desk, but my eyes were flooded with light from the view. The CruzIO layout seemed to have achieved a good balance between fluidity and security, view and privacy, engagement and detachment, and offered their members enough choices that everyone seemed comfortable with their selected option.

Windows and Street Noise

Upstairs from CruzIO, the Ecology Action offices make extensive use of skylights for interior offices and conference rooms, and also provide a ring of operable windows for workers at the periphery, along with a few glass doors accessing balconies. In my interviews with these workers, they uniformly treasured their window views, but many had issues with the associated heat and noise.

In Santa Cruz's mild climate, employees loved to keep the windows and doors open for the fresh breeze, which introduced the second issue with the windows: street noise. Outside were the usual street noises, from traffic, delivery trucks, and construction, which might be annoying, but not especially disruptive. The bigger problem was with intermittent sounds that could signal danger or distress—like sirens or voices of people arguing on the street— which left the office workers worrying: perhaps they should consider running outside to help? In this way, the open windows created the biggest distraction for their offices.

Urban life is full of non-actionable alerts: car alarms are perhaps the most egregious example of noise that disturbs too many while helping too few. It may be that one of the attractions of high-rise office buildings is that with sealed windows, high above the street, you get the views without any social connection to the street below. You can see plenty of sky and weather, and a few birds flying past, but the sounds of the street all seem far away, muted by the insulated glass, reducing any sense of social obligation for what might transpire down below. Not so surprisingly, there seems to be a strong connection between how we evaluate sound and what we can see. Sounds that have a clear visual source are generally less distracting than those which have no embodied source. You can try this yourself sometime, by looking towards, or away, from a source of noise and consider which is easier for you to accommodate or ignore. As an interesting corollary, sound engineers who were attempting to create new biophilic sound environments tested people's reactions to various sources of masking noise, including those of running water, such as a babbling brook or ocean waves. They found that without some visual cue to the source of water, people generally made very negative assumptions about the source of the sound: a flooding basement! a running toilet! On the other hand, when an image was nearby that could explain the source of the water, such as a photo of a waterfall or video of ocean waves, they made positive assessments of the sounds.[9] Once again, our brains seek to integrate all sensory input into a holistic assessment of the environment.

Programmers, Troglodytes, and Dark Places

Computer programmers were one of the groups that I interviewed who were most extreme in wanting to avoid any audio or visual distractions. In various companies where I have worked, we have humorously referred to the engineers who wanted to work in the dark as the 'troglodytes,' i.e. the people who prefer to live in caves. When I have asked these folks why, they generally insisted that it was a purely personal preference. A few were suspectable to migraines and so preferred a darkened environment. Many were night-owls, and believed that their preference for black screens and dark environments came from a preference for nighttime work. Yet none of these answers really satisfied me, as programmers' preference to work in dark places seems so pervasive.

When visiting one technology company, on a floor full of computer programmers, the window shades were all closed, followed by black-out blinds for extra protection. In their dimly lit cubicles, the software engineers worked on black screens with color-coded fonts—an intensely visual task. They quickly objected to any source of light which added more reflected glare to their screens. When asked, one programmer explained that when he is working in code, he is inhabiting a region within his own brain, and wants no reminders of the outside world. There was no interest in talking about window views.

There are many other types of workplaces that traditionally do not have access to daylight or windows. It is worth considering some of these extreme cases, to understand how people cope with such a work environment. Most large urban buildings and campuses have certain jobs that are usually relegated to the basement levels. This commonly includes the janitorial, maintenance, and facility management offices, along with mail, delivery, and parking functions—basically all the support staff for the building. In hospitals and medical buildings, it also often includes laboratory workers, pharmacy workers, the business department, and specialists managing the big equipment that doesn't fit anywhere else.

I have made a habit of asking people who work in the basements of hospitals, such as pharmacies and X-ray labs, what they think about spending all their working hours in a place with no daylight or window views. *"Oh, I'm used to it,"* is the usual reply. They might add that they take their breaks outside, or get off work early, or only work a few days a week, which makes it easier to tolerate. In sum, they all seem completely resigned that their job requires work in a windowless setting. But when I ask, *"What if your office (or break room) had a window?"* the reply is usually enthusiastic: *"Oh, that would be great!"* followed with a more dubious query, such as *"But how could that be possible?"* Of course, they are not thinking like an architect. To them, the building design is a given, not a variable.

I had a revealing encounter with a basement worker years ago, a man who was attending one of my classes for the federal government electrical engineers, teaching them how to implement more efficient lighting in their buildings. After I gave a brief presentation on lighting and health, this man wanted to share his own experience. He was in his fifties, overweight, and did not look very healthy. He said that he worked his whole career for GSA, managing a number of federal buildings around the New York City area. His office was down in the basement of one of those buildings, where he spent most of his working hours. He said: *"Now I understand why when I get home in the evening, I just want to sit outside on the steps outside my house for an hour or so, just staring at the sky. I do it rain or shine, especially in the fall and winter, as the days are getting shorter and colder. My wife thinks I'm nuts, but I just can't motivate myself to do anything until I've had that time to sit outside at the end of the day."* That man's sorry demeanor and observation, searching for some way to make his life more tolerable, has haunted me now for decades.

A rapidly growing area of employment is service work in the underground transit centers that are proliferating around the world. Grand Central Station in New York City has long had a vibrant retail hub that served commuters as they rushed into and out of the city, with quickie snack shops, pharmacies, and gift stores. The array of shops has more recently expanded to include banking centers, clothing, technology, and luxury goods stores, following along a transit hub model similar to 'the airport as shopping mall.' These grand underground shopping concourses can now be found in major cities around the world, providing retail services to millions of commuters, but also employing hundreds of thousands of workers who spend their work days entirely below ground. In Montreal, Quebec, *la ville souterraine* is purportedly the largest underground network in the world, supporting over 2,000 shops and 40 cinemas, while providing a semblance of an 'outdoor' pedestrian experience during cold Canadian winters. In addition to the many miles of underground retail concourses that already exist in many cities, such as Tokyo, Osaka, Singapore, and Seoul, development of massive new underground urban complexes with multiple levels are planned for many of the fastest growing Asian cities.[10] This begs the question how essential daylight and views are for all the people who will work in those places.

Unusual Work Conditions: Submarines and Space Stations

Working on a submarine constitutes one of the most extreme cases of daylight and view deprivation I know of. Jim Sciutto, CNN's National Security Correspondent, spent a few days aboard the nuclear submarine USS Missouri, and filed a report describing the experience.[11] The Missouri spent 90% of its time on a recent six-month deployment underwater, 163 out of 181 days. *"Night and day are indistinguishable on board. It is an endless series of eight-hour shifts. To keep a sense of sanity, the mess rotates breakfast, lunch and dinner every few days so the late shift isn't stuck eating meat and potatoes for breakfast."*

Since the sailors work in eight-hour shifts, someone is always sleeping, and sleep is one of the most precious commodities on a sub. There are only beds for about 2/3 of the crew, so 1/3 is always on duty; 1/3 may be sleeping, and 1/3 engaged in personal activities. The crew spend most of their free time exercising, playing cards, watching movies, or reading books. Given that we know that both physical exercise and social interaction can provide some circadian stimulus in the absence of daylight, these are excellent substitutes. When the sub does surface, sailors often take a sunbath topside for some vitamin D, or if the conditions are right, even go swimming in the ocean, with floats marking off the swimming area.

All the sailors are volunteers, and undergo a year of rigorous training to be sure they are physically, psychologically, and mentally fit before they head out on their first mission on a sub. A humorous website offered suggestions for how you could simulate life on a submarine to see if it suited you.[12] The suggestions used ordinary household objects and situations to simulate the experience of working, living, and sleeping on a submarine, for example:

- Spend as much time as you can indoors during the daytime, stay out of direct sunlight. Go to work only before sunrise and come home after sunset.

- Fix-up a shelf in your closet that will serve as your bunk for the next six months. Take the door off of the hinges and replace them with curtains. While asleep, have family members shine a flashlight in your eyes at random intervals and say either "*Sign this!*" or "*Sorry, wrong rack!*"

- Have a fluorescent lamp installed under your coffee table and lie underneath it to read books.

- Repeat back everything spoken to you. Repeat back everything spoken to you.

Thus, as best I can tell, daylight deprivation on submarines is largely dealt with via a combination of tight military discipline and dark humor. However, it is also an increasing concern for the circadian health of the military, as evidenced by the studies quoted earlier (see page 24).

Another extreme work environment worthy of consideration is space travel. America's first space traveler, Alan Shephard, aboard Freedom 7 Mercury capsule in 1961 was provided with two six-inch circular portholes, which were considered essential for mitigating the extreme claustrophobia that might set in during the dangerous mission. The pioneering Mercury astronauts pressed for larger windows. Only a few months later, the Liberty Bell 7, flying a sub-orbital loop, included a trapezoidal window 19 inches high by 11 inches across. (By way of comparison, passenger windows on the Boeing 747 are 10 inches wide by 16 inches tall.) Astronauts continued to insist on the importance of windows, which grew slightly larger with each new model of spacecraft, but were always tightly constrained by engineering demands of space flight. Even so, returning astronauts spoke in poetic terms about how stunningly beautiful the Earth was seen through those little portals. In 1968, astronaut William

Anders took the famous *Earthrise* photograph from lunar orbit, which captured the world's attention and helped spark the environmental movement.

NASA also recognized the essential nature of windows in the space station where astronauts would spend extended periods of time, up to a year at a time. When the International Space Station (ISS) was first being assembled in the early 2000s, the largest window was 20 inches in diameter. A new era began for the ISS crewmembers with the arrival of the Cupola in 2010, a module specifically designed to allow 360-degree views, through six trapezoid-shaped windows, the largest window yet to orbit the Earth.

"Windows are a vital experience of space travel," said Karen Scott, an optical scientist and member of the design team for the commercial Dream Chaser space plane. She explained that staring out to watch the Earth pass by below was a major free time activity for ISS astronauts. *"Many astronauts have described emotional experiences seeing the Earth from space. They have taken millions of photos trying to capture the beauty that they see and they say that the photos never do the view justice."*[13] Given this, those companies vying for near-future space tourism dollars have recognized that there are just two key experiences that people seek when paying many thousands of dollars for the privilege of a near-space experience: weightlessness, and a view of earth from space. Scott explained the essential nature of the windows to the space travel experience: *"The view of our beautiful planet is the destination, on the short ride into suborbital space ... otherwise space tourists are just weightless sardines in a can."*[14]

Apple, Technology, and Visual Security

While space stations, submarines, and even hospital laboratories, have obvious physical limitations on access to daylight and view, there are other types of workplaces which have imposed their own limitations, primarily over the issue of visual security. Most companies have some sensitivity to visual security. Traditionally, employees dealing with sensitive information worked inside private offices, with lockable doors. Later, in open-pan offices, companies have commonly dealt with this concern via use of polarized films or other devices that restrict the viewing angle of a computer screen.

However, there are some companies who have taken concern about visual security to an extreme—restricting all employee access to windows. I first encountered this phenomenon years ago when I did some brief consulting for Apple. At the time, they were growing at a phenomenal rate, and were leasing practically every existing building that they could find in and around Cupertino, California. (Their giant donut-shaped headquarters was still in the planning stage.) The facilities manager told me that his job was to lease, design and furnish enough space for 50 new employees *per week*, for the next three years. That's the equivalent of occupying about one new 10,000 square foot building per week, every week, for the foreseeable future. These were mostly existing one- and two-story buildings dotted around Cupertino's suburban landscape.

The hitch was someone in upper management had decided that no one should ever be able to see *into* any building occupied by Apple, not from the street, the sidewalk, a parking garage, or even overhead from a helicopter or drone. The facility manager wanted to know if he could preserve some sense of view of the outdoors for the employees, while preventing any possibility of view into the building, day or night. I was flummoxed. Optics is generally a two-way street; what works in one direction is perfectly reversed in the other direction. I suggested that they carve out some interior courtyards and cultivate some interior gardens; but that idea was rejected as consuming too much valuable space that could house a few more employees. As best I know, the windows of every leased buildings were therefore covered over with a thick frosted film, like an impenetrable fog encasing all employees, in order to prevent any imaging equipment from ever seeing into Apple's very private enterprise.

The great irony was that Apple's new, 2.8 million square-foot headquarters building opened in 2019 featured four floors of massive floor-to-ceiling clear glass windows, curling around an iconic circular building, as a visual metaphor for the company's purported transparency and vision of the future (while ignoring every precept of thoughtful solar orientation and shading). A review of the new headquarters building in Wired Magazine interviewed Tim Cook, the new CEO of Apple who took over after Apple's founder Steven Jobs died in 2011. He explained that Jobs' aims for the great circular building "were not just aesthetic. He did his best thinking during walks and was especially inspired by ambling in nature, so he envisioned how Apple workers would do that too. Can you imagine doing your work in a national park? … When I really need to think about something I'm struggling with, I get out in nature. We can do that now! It won't feel like Silicon Valley at all."[15]

I cannot report if Jobs and his design team succeeded in their mission to recreate the blissful experience of working in the midst of nature for the 12,000 employees who would eventually inhabit the massive 'mothership,' because the public has not yet been invited in, and journalists are specifically excluded. I've never been able to mentally resolve the discrepancy between these two very different design mandates from the same company. However, I continue to be disturbed that a company with such driving vision for its future headquarters could completely ignore any present needs of the tens of thousands of employees already working in leased space.

Apple may have begun the paranoia in Silicon Valley for trade secrets being stolen through windows and skylights, but many other companies have picked up the infection. This seems especially odd to me at a time when an encyclopedia's worth of information can be stored on a tiny USB flash drive and hundreds of cell phone cameras walk in and out of a building every day. How did old fashioned glass windows come to be considered such a twenty-first-century security threat? I am reminded of the older Islamic cultures' concern with privacy and security that engendered many inward-looking buildings, with beautiful courtyards maintained behind high walls. That was back when physical and visual barriers were considered sufficient for security. Now in a digital age, when remote hacking is the critical international security threat, we have tech companies who are still so worried about visual spying that they are willing to sacrifice daylight, views, and the comfort of all their employees.

Courthouses and Jury Rooms

One traditional building type in the United States that has recently experienced a turn-around in attitude towards visual security versus transparency is the courthouse. Courthouse design, at least in the Anglophile world, traditionally followed the old British model where 'the bar' was literally a polished wooden railing that kept the public separated from the judge, who was elevated on a dais wearing his black gown and curly gray wig. American courthouses generally followed this model throughout the twentieth century, complete with lots of dark wood paneling and classical details borrowed from the Romans. The design emphasis was on tightly controlled environments, where the judge and jury were protected from outside influences while the accused was literally kept 'in the dark' about conditions in the outside world. While in the first half of the century high clerestories windows were included to provide daylight, by the 1950s the typical courtroom had no windows at all, relying entirely on electric lighting.

The adjacent spaces similarly tended to be inward-looking spaces, walled off from the outdoors, designed primarily for security and the clear separation of the prison population from the jurors and the public. The steady flow of jurors and the public were considered temporary visitors, shepherded through the halls of justice and deserving little in the way of environmental amenities. Jurors, especially, were collected in large waiting rooms awaiting processing, often approximating a bus terminal in creature comforts and aesthetics. A recent review of courthouse designs in Australia found that *"The work environment of the jury was portrayed as singularly unpleasant ... Fundamental problems included cramped, airless, windowless quarters and a broken juror chair.*" The author noted "*the paradox that jurors charged with immense responsibilities are required to work in a fairly hostile work environment, without fundamental assistance and tools.*"[16]

However, more recently courthouse designers have started to question the old design paradigms and tried to reconceive the courthouse as a more welcoming, transparent and supportive social space. New design guidelines offered by the AIA Justice Knowledge Community stress the importance of the courthouse as a public landmark in a town, but also the importance of views from the courthouse outward to other local landmarks, as a way to knit the social fabric together. It explicitly recommends that views be available from 90% of all regularly occupied spaces, following LEED v.4 definitions: "*Sunlight, daylight and views that cue time of day, weather conditions, and psychological connection to nature are provided for informal waiting/meeting areas, family law spaces, staff work areas, public waiting and circulation areas.*"[17]

The new United States Courthouse in downtown Los Angeles, was commissioned and managed by the US General Services Administration (GSA) according to their new sustainability design guidelines.[18] Designed by the architecture firm Skidmore Ownings and Merrill and opened in 2016, the design team worked to both optimize public security and safety from physical threats like earthquakes and terrorist blasts while also featuring extensive daylighting and views throughout, all despite a budget that was dramatically reduced midway through the process.[19] I was lucky to be given an inside tour of this brand new federal courthouse in order to observe how this change in design philosophy played out.

The ten-story building, including 24 courtrooms and 32 judges' chambers, sits as a giant glass cube perched on its prominent downtown site. Its perimeter is sheathed in floor-to-ceiling glass on the upper floors, which are hung from a central core structure that provides earthquake resistance. The high-performance glass façade is also faceted to provide better solar control. The central public space on each floor rings a ten-story high atrium, brightly daylit from sawtooth skylights above and from a tall window wall facing north to a carefully framed view of the San Gabriel Mountains looming a few miles away. Ultimately, the courthouse was awarded a LEED platinum certification.

Half of the courtrooms also feature a view of these mountains, out through high windows located above the judge's platform. The courtrooms were furnished with light blond wood and white surfaces throughout, to better bounce the daylight around and emphasize the airy modernist aesthetic. A courtroom with ample daylight and a beautiful view is indeed a novel experience! It was lovely, but empty, when I toured.

I was most interested in the jury deliberation rooms, where a jury may end up spending weeks or even months deliberating a difficult case. Jurors work in an extremely stressful situation, needing to cooperate with complete strangers on life and death matters. The deliberation rooms in the new Los Angeles Federal Courthouse were designed as large conference rooms, with attached kitchen and bathroom facilities. They each featured a large window across the narrow end looking out across the Los Angeles basin. These rooms did not feel claustrophobic, as if you needed to be held against your will to endure weeks of jury service. A little relief in terms of a view of distant scenery goes a long way to reducing stress and giving the jurors the mental space to consider the details of case and its consequences. I would love to see a study comparing juror outcomes between deliberation rooms with, and without, such windows!

Windows and Organizational Productivity

Can we actually pinpoint what Apple and the other security-minded companies gave up when they blocked off their employees' views to the outside? In this and previous chapters we have discussed many of the ways that a view to the outdoors might support better health, as well as emotional and cognitive function. For example, we've reviewed evidence that mind wandering is associated with self-awareness, increased working memory, incubation of problem solutions, and creative thought. We've also considered how window views provide both the motivation and opportunity for about ten times the circadian stimulus of simple daylight illumination in the same space. With more appropriate circadian stimulus in our everyday lives, we know that people who spend 90%+ of their time inside of buildings are likely to maintain a more robust circadian rhythm, resulting in better sleep, better metabolic health, better memory formation, and better emotional resilience.

This type of evidence provides a logical, but admittedly somewhat indirect, pathway from the provision of window views to employer benefits. The logic is that with healthier, happier employees, the company will also benefit as a whole; but worker health, comfort, and satisfaction may not add up to organizational productivity and ultimately be noticeable in the company bottom line. There is, however, a growing body of laboratory and field studies that do provide evidence of a more direct connection between worker access to windows and measures of organizational-level performance.

At the same time as the second round of school and retail studies were undertaken, my company was also given funds to study how daylighting and/

or view impacted office worker performance. The study undertaken with those funds, conducted at the Sacramento Municipal Utility District (SMUD) offices, was an early effort to conduct a rigorous field study under real office conditions. It ultimately provided a number of paths of evidence that window views do indeed improve employee performance, and that these effects can be traced down to the financial bottom line for a company.

The Sacramento Municipal Utility District offices offered an excellent study site to differentiate between how ambient daylight illumination, versus window views, might each impact worker productivity. Three very different buildings on the same campus provided a wide variety of daylighting and view conditions, while employees all sat at similar cubicles, operated similar computers, under identical climatic and social conditions—an excellent physical set up for our study. (The chapter title page shows a cross section of the top floor of one SMUD building with its windows and skylights.) SMUD agreed to allow us free access to their facilities over a two-year period, and provided us with detailed demographic data about their employees (while maintaining strict confidentiality). Ultimately, we conducted two completely separate studies, with different populations and performance outcome metrics, but with similar data collection and analysis methodologies. The first is called the Call Center Study; the second, the Desk Top Study.

The Call Center Study

The first SMUD study is called 'The Call Center Study', because it specifically focused on the 100 workers who handled incoming calls about SMUD programs and services. Similar to call centers around the world, these workers did nothing but handle coming in calls, working in three shifts, spanning 7am to 7pm. They all worked in the same open-office wing of the Customer Service Center, with big view windows facing both north and south. Those workers near the north windows also received plenty of daylight, while the south-facing windows were more commonly obscured by perforated vertical blinds. We collected continuous environmental data, such as air temperature, humidity, and illumination levels, and assessed each workstation for physical conditions, such as ventilation settings, presence of personal fans and task lights, and the size, direction and quality of window views. The study differentiated between 'Primary View,' i.e. the amount and quality of window views that could be seen while looking directly at the computer, versus 'Break View,' the amount and quality of view that could be seen when rotating the worker's chair in other directions.

Call center employment is a rapidly growing service sector around the world, employing many millions of people.[20] As in most call centers, the calls at the SMUD center were highly automated and continuously tracked. This data is intensely analyzed to understand how to improve call center efficiency. We worked with the SMUD statisticians to understand the most meaningful performance metrics for our purposes, such as 'average handling time' reported per person per hour, and how to control for other pressures and anomalies in the workflow. For example, we learned that the first and 15th of the month were especially stressful as bills came due, plus the day after any holiday or weekend. Thus, we excluded those days, and analyzed data collected only from Tuesday through Friday on non-holiday weeks.

In the Call Center analysis, increased illumination, whether daylight or electric, as measured in horizontal lux, was not found to have much effect on worker performance. However, distance from the north windows did importantly predict better performance, such that workers sitting within ten feet of a north-facing window answered calls 3% faster than those located in the core of the facility. In addition, those workers who had access to the largest 'break view,' i.e. the ability to look out a large window area from their office chair, were answering calls 7% faster than those workers with no access to view. These effects are additive, such that the workers with both conditions were working 10% faster than those with no access to a window view.

This is a remarkable finding, and highly valuable to the organization's bottom line. In the case of the Call Center Study we were able to make a direct connection between employee productivity and organizational productivity, as valued and measured by that organization. Working with SMUD's financial department, we determined the yearly operating cost of the call center per employee, and per square foot. It turned out that, at that time, a 7% improvement in call center efficiency would save $195 per square foot per year in net operation costs. To put this into context, $195 per square foot was also about the cost of an average new office building in Sacramento. The exemplary SMUD Customer Services Building had been constructed for about three times that average cost. Thus, the savings achieved by providing ample view windows to all Call Center employees would have been the equivalent of a two-year payback not just for the windows, but for *all* the high-performance features of the building!

The Desk Top Study

The Desk Top Study tested the performance of 200 professional employees sitting at their regular desk on a suite of visual and cognitive tasks via their desk top computer. We recruited a balanced population of volunteers who were evenly distributed around the three buildings and across 12 administrative units, including engineering, finance, and human resources. We assessed and monitored the environmental conditions at each volunteer's desk location. Once a week for six weeks, between 10am and noon on each Thursday, the volunteers were invited to take a five-minute series of standardized computer-based tests, which examined their visual and cognitive performance. At the end of the study period, the participants were also asked to fill out a comprehensive survey, assessing the physical comfort conditions in their workspace and reporting on any health symptoms experienced within the past week.

On the key test of working memory capacity, called 'Digit Span Backwards,' it was found that, all other things being equal, that those employees with access to the most daylight performed significantly better. The amount of daylight exposure had the greatest explanatory power in predicting performance on this test of any of the physical or demographic variables that we tested, even more than years of education or seniority with the company. All other things being equal, those employees who received the most horizontal *daylight* illumination at their desks, as measured in lux by a nearby light monitor, basically had 20% better working memory performance than those with no access to daylight.

A test of long-term memory also came back positive for access to window views. The study found that: *"When a participant had the best possible Primary View, they could remember 16% more objects correctly than those participants with no Primary View ... Likewise, those employees with the best Break View also increased their performance by 9% over those with no Break View. These two results are additive, so any employees with both the highest Primary View and Break View would be performing 25% better than those with none."*

This long-term memory finding was also modified by a negative effect of any probable glare from the window. The visual acuity tasks followed the expected pattern, with more glare probability reducing tested visual acuity. Thus, the results of the computerized tests were very consistent: cognitive performance was improved with more daylight and access to window views, while visual task performance was reduced by likelihood of glare.

Window Views and Worker Fatigue

The concluding survey of these 200 office workers also told a very interesting story. First of all, we were very happy to see that participants' subjective assessment of their comfort conditions closely tracked the data collected by our research staff. Even more interesting were the correlations we found between environmental conditions at the desks and self-reports of health symptoms. Overall, the fewer complaints the employees had about the *physical* environment at their desk, the fewer negative *health* complaints they also reported. Although the causal relationship could easily go either way, the consistency of this relationship was striking. Furthermore, the size and quality of their view was the single strongest predictor of overall environmental satisfaction and comfort. When workers had a view that they liked, they were less critical of *every* other aspect of their office environment!

Digging into the health reports a bit deeper, it became clear that the quality of the window view—whether assessed by the worker or measured by the researchers—was highly correlated with reports of fatigue. Increased fatigue was positively correlated with the frequency of eight common health symptoms experienced within the past week, in the following order: difficulty concentrating, eye strain, headache, high stress level, stomach upset, back or joints ache, neck or shoulder ache, and flu. The next most strongly associated variable, almost as strong as flu symptoms, was "*My view is boring.*" Next in line came "*There is not enough daylight.*" Thus, claiming to have a boring view, or not enough access to daylight, predicted fatigue at work almost as much as having been sick with flu symptoms in the last week. On the flip side, "*My view is relaxing*" was by far the strongest environmental predictor that a worker did not report experiencing fatigue in the past week.

It is the consistency of the findings about the importance of views that is most striking in all these studies. The final report on the two SMUD studies noted: "*Having a better view out of a window, gauged primarily by the size of the view and secondarily by greater vegetation content, was most consistently associated with better worker performance in six out of eight outcomes considered.*"[21] As with the Capistrano and Fresno schools study, it is also useful to consider the *predictive power* of the statistical models (see pages 202–204). In the Call Center models, we were able to predict about 20% of the total variation in *daily* worker performance, and 7% of the variation in their *hourly* performance. Of this, only 1% to 3% was predicted by all of the physical conditions considered, such as air temperature, partition height, and illumination. The quality of views predicted on the order of 0.5% of the variation in worker performance. On the other hand, 'access to views' had more explanatory power than many things workers themselves thought was important, such as membership in different workgroups or shift schedules for the Call Center Study, or years of education and tenure with the company for the Desk Top Study. These small effect sizes explain why large study populations are needed to detect these relationships. And again, they are importantly countered by the long-term stability of environmental effects. Just like interest rates compounding in a bank, a small but very consistent influence on human behavior can have a powerful cumulative impact.

15. Healing Daylight

The architectural community involved in healthcare design embraced the concept of data-driven design decisions, often referred to as 'evidence-based design,' long before other areas of the profession. Likely, it was via their close association with the medical profession, which had already adopted a highly coordinated research agenda that resulted in 'evidence-based' medical treatment.[1]

Roger Ulrich helped launch this shift in healthcare design with his seminal 1984 study showing that patients in a hospital recovering from abdominal surgery had better postoperative outcomes if they were assigned to a recovery room looking out on a view of trees, rather than a brick wall.[2] This is probably the most cited and well-known study on the association of better views with health outcomes. With the attention he received for his initial study, Ulrich helped to start a journal, Health Environments Research and Design (HERD) and a non-profit organization, the Center for Health Design, dedicated to publishing and archiving research on healthcare environments. Subsequently, the research field studying the health impacts of environmental design has blossomed into a major practice area, featuring professional certifications, conferences, and university-based research institutes worldwide.[3]

In 2008, Ulrich and his colleagues wrote an extensive literature review, citing almost 500 peer-reviewed papers on evidence-based healthcare design: evidence of a maturing field 25 years later! The scope of inquiry had expanded widely, to include such topics as patient room design, improved acoustics, and electric lighting controls. Here we concentrate only on their key findings relative to daylight and view. The report summarized that fully one-half, or eight out of 16, of all types of health outcomes considered were significantly improved by access to daylight, whereas views of nature influenced seven out of 16. The evidence for these associations is carefully detailed in their report, worthy of serious considerations by anyone involved in healthcare design.[4]

One of the most unambiguous findings is the relationship between daylight exposure and sleep quality. The study explains (citations removed): "*Hospitalized patients have an increased need for sleep because of their illnesses. However, in reality, they often suffer from diminished circadian rhythms and poor sleep while hospitalized, which may lead to increased stress, impaired immune function, ventilatory compromise, disrupted thermoregulation, and delirium. These effects may hinder the healing process and contribute to increased morbidity and mortality.... The research team identified more than 70 articles about sleep in healthcare settings, including descriptive, correlational, and intervention studies. The literature confirmed that sleep disruption and deprivation were very common problems in healthcare settings, especially for high-acuity patients who are more susceptible to unfavorable environmental conditions ... Findings suggest that patient rooms should be carefully oriented and designed to receive natural daylight and maintain the normal light-dark cycle of 24-hour periods to help patients retain normal circadian rhythms and improve sleep.*"

Thus, the reports recommended that deploying daylight and view to reinforce the circadian health of hospital patients should be standard practice. What is surprising is that this basic concept was ignored in hospital design for over 50 years.

A Brief History of Hospital Design

An early healthcare practitioner who advocated for the importance of daylight and views in a healthcare environment was the famous British nurse, Florence Nightingale. In 1863 in her *Notes on Hospitals* she wrote: "*Second only to fresh air, however, I should be inclined to rank light in importance for the sick ... Among the kindred effects of light I may mention, from experience, as quite perceptible in promoting recovery, the being able to see out of window, instead of looking against a dead wall: the bright colours of flowers; the being able to read in bed by the light of a window close to bed-head. It is generally said that the effect is upon the mind. Perhaps so; but it is no less so upon the body on that account.*"

Back in Nightingale's day, hospital beds were lined up next to big windows. The windows provided both ample daylight for the patients and so their doctors could examine them. Patients were often moved out onto sunporches to increase their exposure to daylight and sunlight, facing out to views of the extensive gardens cultivated around the old Victorian hospitals.

Just as in our brief history of schools, daylight continued to have a very prominent role in hospital design in the late nineteenth and early twentieth century, especially in the design of sanitoriums for the treatment of tuberculosis. In 1903 Neils Finse, a Danish/Icelandic physician, was awarded the Nobel Prize in Medicine for his work in 'heliotherapy' (from the Greek word for sun, *helios*), demonstrating that sunlight could cure tuberculosis. However, by the Second World War, with the advent of antibiotic treatments for many diseases and cheap fluorescent lighting to supplant daylight illumination, daylight waned in significance in healthcare design.

Hospitals grew ever larger, and ever more dependent on mechanical ventilation and electric lighting. The concept of hospital design as therapeutic for patients lost favor. The primary concerns in hospital design were for ever greater sanitation and ever greater efficiency. When Ulrich's early studies showed that patients in rooms with daylight and views recovered faster and so had a shorter stay in the hospital, it immediately got the attention of hospital administrators. By reducing 'average length of stay,' hospitals could treat more people for less cost. Looking at a future where hundreds of *billions* of dollars were planned for new hospital construction within the coming decade, hospital administrators became acutely interested in other ways architectural design might improve their bottom line. They realized that the potential was not only to reduce medical costs and risks, but also improve the quality of care that they delivered, with better patient outcomes, better staff performance, satisfaction and retention, and increased satisfaction of the families who paid the bills. All of these pathways have helped to raise the prominence of research supporting evidence-based healthcare design.

One organization that has embraced evidence-based design with great passion is the Kaiser Permanente Group, the largest managed care provider in the United States, with over 12 million members in 2018.[5] In the late 1980s, Kaiser Permanente set up its own research unit to probe the relationship between facility design and patient outcomes and to test out prototype designs. Based on these investigations, Kaiser developed very precise design guidelines for their new facilities, and now maintains a network of pre-qualified architectural design, engineering, and general contracting firms who *"understand our vision,"* according to a 2007 interview with their national head of facilities, Christine Malcolm.[6]

This same article explains that this new paradigm of research-driven design can create conflict within the design professions: *"There is a certain level of mutual frustration ... Architects complain that Kaiser Permanente restricts their creativity with too many predefined elements and components. Kaiser Permanente complains that some architects fiddle with the small stuff at the expense of bigger, more important issues."*

John Kouletsis, then head of planning and design at Kaiser Permanente explained: *"It's like higher education. We've done the undergraduate course work ... We look for firms that can take that knowledge and build on it."* The real source of the conflict, as Kouletsis sees it, is a paradigm shift for architects to pay less attention to what the building looks like as an object, and more attention to how the building functionally impacts people: *"It's not about being published in Architectural Record ... It's about creating better health outcomes."*

A friend of mine grew up within the Kaiser Permanente healthcare system, as her father was a Kaiser doctor in Los Angeles. Decades later she found herself spending hours and hours in various Kaiser hospitals around town as she helped her elderly mother navigate cancer treatments. *"You can't believe the difference between the old and the new hospitals! You have to come see it!"* she exclaimed on the phone to me one day. *"The old hospitals are dark and dingey, with endless corridors. The cafeteria is always in the basement. They are so depressing! The new hospitals are all light and view. The cafeteria is upstairs, with beautiful views, full of sunlight! Even the cancer treatment rooms have windows looking out to a garden."*

So, here was my friend, upbeat on the phone, *happily* describing a day spent in a new Kaiser Permanente hospital with her dying mother. I will call that quite a design accomplishment!

Depression and Pain

One of the major areas of discussion in the Ulrich literature review is the reduction of depressive symptoms. Writing in 2008, the authors noted that although knowledge about the interaction between light and depression was still limited, exposure to light was already being acknowledged as equally efficacious as pharmaceutical treatments: *"A meta-analysis of 20 randomized controlled studies ... reached the powerful conclusion that light treatment for nonseasonal and seasonal depression is 'efficacious, with effect sizes equivalent to those in most antidepressant pharmacotherapy trials.' Additionally, light exposure offers the important advantage of being faster acting than antidepressant drugs. In this regard ... light can produce significant reduction of depression after less than 2 weeks of treatment, while antidepressant drugs require at least 4–6 weeks before effective onset."*[7]

It is not only the design of hospital buildings, but also their siting and location that can have an important impact on patient outcomes, especially relative to depression and other psychiatric diagnoses. In California, many older Veterans Administration hospitals were located in the most fabulously beautiful locations available, often up on a hill, looking over lovely valleys or lakes. Patient rooms are situated to enjoy these views, which were certainly intended to help lift the vets' spirits. Those early hospital designers certainly knew what they were doing!

The Ulrich literature review also addressed pain, explaining that: *"Pain is a pervasive and serious problem in hospitals."* Reducing pain can also reduce the need for pain medications and the complications that they cause. It turns out that exposure to both daylight and views of nature have been shown to reduce pain across many types of illnesses and injuries. The Ulrich report continues: *"... it is encouraging that mounting scientific evidence, including that from prospective randomized controlled studies, has shown that exposing patients to nature can produce substantial and clinically important alleviation of pain. Limited research also suggests that patients experience less pain when exposed to higher levels of daylight in contrast to lower levels of daylight in their hospital rooms. The state of knowledge on the environment-pain relationship has grown to the point where a leading international pain research journal recently published an article that emphasizes the importance of designing healthcare facilities to harness nature, light, and other environmental factors to enhance pain."*

The report explains that the causal mechanisms for daylight and nature views are distinct pathways, and details one study which quantified the reduction in pain for surgical patients. This reduction in pain was not only a benefit to the patient, but also to the hospital, which saw lower costs as a result: *"The presumed pain reduction mechanism for daylight is different than for nature. Sunlight exposure increases levels of serotonin, a neurotransmitter known to inhibit pain pathways ... A well-controlled prospective study of the effects of daylight on pain [was conducted] in patients undergoing spinal surgeries, who were admitted postoperatively to rooms either on the bright [sunlit] or shaded side of a surgical ward ... Findings indicated that patients in rooms with more sunlight reported less pain and stress, and took 22% less analgesic medications, resulting in a 21% reduction in medication costs."*

The report also emphasizes that site planning issues also must be considered in order to achieve the benefits of daylight and view, linking the very intimate outcome of a patient's pain levels to the consequences of large-scale urban planning: *"Finally, the evidence implies that careful attention should be given to building orientation and site planning in healthcare projects, and that plans where some buildings block pain-relieving nature views and daylight from others should be avoided."*

In this one example we can find all the levels of daylighting knowledge discussed so far, from planetary rhythms, to impacts on vision, cognitive and hormonal processes, to real estate valuation, and the deeply personal emotional sensations of pain and recovery, all linked to proper architectural design!

Of course, patients are not the only people who are affected by hospital design. Doctors, nurses, administrative, and maintenance staff also spend their careers working in hospitals. Family members spend very stressful hours or days visiting their loved ones in hospitals. And there are also healthcare settings other than hospitals which should be considered when thinking about daylight and views

Views for Nurses

I interviewed a nurse, Barbara Cordes, who spent over 40 years of working in various hospital and healthcare settings. She had spent the majority of her career as an emergency room nurse, but also worked in maternity wards, operating and recovery rooms, and ambulatory surgery centers; about a dozen hospital settings in total. Just like with my own workplace reflections mentioned earlier, she realized that those memories involving windows tended to be her most positive memories of all the places she had worked. She also reflected on how the design of the windows and access to the outdoors in those spaces impacted her work as a nurse, and her ability to help her patients.

Of three emergency room (ER) settings that she worked in, one had no windows or any openings to the outdoors, the second had glass doors through which she could see the parking lot in one direction and reception room in the other, and the third had narrow strip windows, mounted high up near the ceiling, with only a view of the sky outside. *"Those windows meant a lot to me!"* She told me: *"They brought me peace. They reminded me there was another world out there, besides just the stressful world of the ER."*

In one of her most vivid memories of those windows the ER team was just getting ready to start a procedure when she noticed some thick smoke off in the distance. One of the doctors immediately excused himself, realizing that the fire must be near his home. He got home just in time to save his pets and a few household treasures from a wildfire, reinforcing how critical the contextual awareness of 'alerting events' provided by windows can be in an emergency.

The ER setting with the glass doors also provided some visual benefits: "*At least we could see what was coming in the door and have a moment to prepare mentally*." She explained that when ER patients were brought in by ambulance, the ER team received warning about the patient's condition ahead of time from the ambulance radio communications (this was before cellphones), but that half of their patients just arrived by private car or walked in. "*The situation in an ER can go from calm to intense in just a matter of seconds, so it helps to have those few extra seconds to prepare yourself*," she explained.

She found that the best relief from the strain of the job was to take a walk outside, to "*get some air*." Sometimes, if there was a break in the action, one nurse might ask another to cover her patient for a few minutes, declaring "*I need to go outside!*" That request was understood as an *urgent* mental health moment, and the nurses did the best they could to cover for each other. Going for a walk in the sunshine was the best possible therapy. The nurses also took their lunches and breaks outside whenever possible; but, she explained, if there was no daylight also available inside the building, it was even harder to go back to work.

She also described the intense environment of a surgery nurse, working in a dangerous, high-anxiety environment, where patients' lives are at stake, but at the same time that you also must quickly handle sharp objects, chemicals, and potentially explosive gasses. She said that surgery rooms can become particularly claustrophobic, especially once you have 'scrubbed in' with sanitary coverings head to foot, and you know that you will be in the surgery room for the duration of the procedure. "*Things can get very tense in surgery. Often interpersonal relationships are very hard, because everyone in the room is under pressure ... A little bit of a view out goes a long way in helping relieve that stress.*"

The stress of working in a healthcare setting is something that many people speak of. But there are some people who may experience the stress, and especially fear of the unknown, and yet cannot speak up for themselves. These include young children, patients who have lost the ability to communicate, especially the elderly suffering from dementia, and even our beloved pets. In many ways, animals are a good proxy for pre-verbal children, or patients without the ability to communicate, as we try to think through how patients relate to their physical environment. We tend to empathize deeply with our own pets, with whom we share our homes during their short lives. We observe them closely and get to know their quirks and unique behaviors, but also appreciate their many commonalities with us.

Views for Animals

I have had many pets, large and small, over my life. It is very clear to me, and I think most pet owners, that animals have clear preferences for views, and given the opportunity, will locate themselves to enjoy their favorite lookout. And while a place to live and play outdoors would be preferred by almost any animal, our increasingly urban lives mean that many pets have to spend most of their days indoors while their owners are at work or school. (Given how much people love their pets, it may be more motivating to ensure that the animals have proper views, than to provide the same for their fellow humans!)

As any cat owner has noticed, indoor cats love to sleep in a spot of sunlight, and will occasionally relocate their nap as the sun moves across the floor, a favorite subject of cartoonists. They also love to perch somewhere up high, up on the windowsill or on top of the refrigerator, where they can keep an eye on what everyone else in the room is doing. The ideal cat haven, then, is a high sunny windowsill, offering both a view in and a view out.

Dogs like to feel in charge of whatever is going on, and so want to be where they can get a clear view of activities around them. Visually supervising the neighborhood gives a dog a sense of purpose and something to think about during the long day waiting for their master to come home from work; and as many pet owners have learned, a bored dog often becomes a neurotic dog. Left inside all day, other dogs will try their best to figure out some way to see out a window onto the street, whether it means jumping up on the forbidden kitchen table or lying up on top of the sofa back.

Thus, a view is important to our pets, both to provide them with appropriate mental and emotional stimulation and to reduce anxieties. A group of veterinarians and architects recognized this and put together a list of recommended best design practices for veterinarian hospitals, called *Fear-Free Hospital Design Guidelines* which includes many very specific recommendations about access to daylight and views for their animal patients.[8] *Fear Free* is an intriguing objective for any hospital or healthcare setting. It implies an effort to prevent unnecessary anxiety and uncertainty, and provide patients with something positive to occupy their minds instead of worries. This veterinarian hospital design guide recommends the use of skylights throughout the facility to provide ample daylight and help the animal patients maintain their appropriate sleep-wake cycles. It recommends doggie or kitty eye-level views to the outdoors from all holding cages, exercise pens, and even exam rooms whenever possible, to provide a positive distraction. Ideally, cats can watch birds flit about outside, dogs can watch activity of humans or other dogs.

(However, since dogs and cats often perceive other members of their own species as a threat, the guide recommends preventing a view of other animals within the facility, especially avoiding double-loaded corridors with holding cages facing each other down an aisle.)

Zoos also have to give careful thought about how to provide adequate access to sunlight, daylight, appropriate views, and likewise darkness at night, for their animal wards. Zoos have a special responsibility to try to understand the native environment for all their animals, and to provide an approximation in the enclosure design for each type of creature. Polar bears and penguins need ice cold water to swim in. Lions and leopards need a sunny spot where they can doze, while keeping a lazy eye on the surroundings. It is well understood that if zoo designers cannot provide an appropriate environment tailored to the needs of each species, some animals will eventually sicken and die. It is not so different for humans.

Pediatric and Elder Care

Pediatric healthcare is a well-defined medical specialty, as is pediatric hospital design. However, while hospital design for adults has seen a recent renaissance in evidence-based design, studies of how children relate to healthcare settings has lagged behind. Perhaps this is because it is much more difficult to get institutional permission to study children. It is also much more difficult to generalize about children, given their range of ages and sizes: a newborn has very different needs from a toddler or a teenager.

Healthcare settings designed specifically for children often emphasize bright colors, and cartoon figures, as if that is all that the adults designing the space can remember about childhood. But children have much the same physiological and emotional needs as adults, only they may be even more sensitive to subtle changes in the environment. Newborn babies are just learning about their world, trying to make sense of strange sounds and new patterns of light. The closer the visual and acoustic environment can approximate a healthy home life, the sooner they are likely to adapt to life outside the womb. Small children are especially emotionally dependent upon their family members, and so making places where families can stay together throughout all healthcare treatments can significantly reduce anxiety and fear. This implies a need for family social spaces enriched by daylight and views. A recent study of pediatric hospitals in Britain, which conducted in-depth interviews with child patients, recommended that 'positive distractions,' especially views of nature, daylit playrooms, and access to outdoor gardens, were key features for keeping children happy and comfortable, and reducing anxiety in hospital settings.[9] For children in long-term care facilities, any inducement to go outdoors can help improve circadian rhythms and sleep quality. For children in rehab, regaining their physical capabilities is key, and thus any motivation to increase physical activity will be positive.[10]

Physical activity has been recognized as one the greatest contributors to all aspects of health, and thus has recently become a major focus of public health initiatives. Anything that increases physical activity is likely to also improve overall health.

A study of residents of long-term care facilities in the United States found that only 22%, or one out of five, residents were observed to go outside routinely. Sadly, 16% went outside less than once a day, 30% less than once a week, and the remaining 32% went outside less than once a month.[11] When the same researchers interviewed the staff, they found that less than 5% of the facilities had organized programs that included daily time outdoors and almost one half, or 48%, *never* had any organized activities outside. This strongly argues for ample access to brightly daylit areas and window views that can provide regular circadian stimulus and visual engagement. Facilities can be designed such that daily activities, such as meals, games, or socializing, take place in normally sunlit areas. In many climates and seasons, indoor sunrooms and atria may provide more routine access to daylight and nature than outdoor gardens and activity areas. I recall visiting many plazas in Spain and Italy where their elderly citizens sat closed packed on the benches, sharing gossip and commenting on all the crazy tourists passing by, but most importantly having a welcome place in the sun.

Circadian disruption is a significant concern for people living with Alzheimer's disease and related dementias (ADRD). Kyle Konis, a research architect at the University of Southern California, has been studying the effect of daylight on such people in institutional care settings. He writes: *"Clinically significant depression occurs in about 20–30% of people with ADRD. Treatment of depression in people living with ADRD can improve well-being, quality of life and individual function, even in the presence of ongoing declines in memory and cognition. Exposure to sufficient daylight is a potentially effective non-drug treatment option for depression and other neuropsychiatric symptoms of dementia."*

His early pilot studies have suggested that architectural design can indeed have an impact on depression rates among the institutionalized. He points out that simple approaches to architectural design which increase residents' exposure to daylight and views *"has the potential for fewer side effects [than pharmacological treatments] and has less practical limitations than specialized electric lighting devices."*

Eunice Noell-Wagner has been one of the most tireless campaigners for improvements to the architectural and lighting design of care facilities. In 2017 she was given an IES award recognizing her lifetime of work, especially for launching the publication *Lighting and the Visual Environment for Seniors and the Low Vision Population*.[12] This document details the range of visual challenges faced by older people and others losing their vision for various reasons, and how that impacts their relationship with the architectural spaces they inhabit. It goes on to make specific visual design recommendations by space type. It makes a strong case for the greater use of daylight and views in senior care facilities, both for improved visual quality and circadian health, noting: *"Providing easy access and strong visual connection to the outdoors encourages seniors to go outside,"* where they will receive more circadian stimulus and vitamin D synthesis from direct sunlight. It also notes that daylight and settings with ample access to nature provide vitally important social spaces, not only for the residents but also for their visiting families and medical personal, affording *"a relaxed space for difficult conversations."*

Hospice

The transition from skilled nursing to hospice care makes an even more poignant case for the importance of access to daylight and window views. Everyone at a hospice, the patients, their visitors, the doctors, and staff, all need that access, to nurture their bonds with each other under that most extreme condition, facing the end of life. Rachel Clarke, a hospice doctor, wrote an editorial for the New York Times, titled *In Life's Last Moments, Open a Window*[13] and subtitled: *My hospice patients were dying, but they still longed for fresh air and birdsong.* She tells the story of a terminally ill patient who was thrashing uncontrollably, and unable to speak clearly due to cancer of the tongue. Finally, a young doctor leaned in and listened very carefully to understand what he was trying to accomplish: to have his chair turned so he could see out the window. She observed, once his request was met, *"Now he sat calmly, transfixed by the trees and the sky. All he had wanted was that view."*

My brother also died, far too early, of lung cancer. He spent his final weeks resting at home, his favorite spot sitting out on his front porch, nodding to neighbors as they walked by, and especially keeping an eye out for the local wild bunnies. When I asked him what else he would like to do during his final days, he answered *"spend more time dreaming."* At first, I thought that was an odd activity, not something 'you do,' but then I realized that as a professional artist, he had a very rich visual imagination, and just loved watching the images his own mind would create. My brother spent his very last days in the intensive care unit of a local hospital. I lived there too, sleeping in the chair by his side, next to a window, that looked out onto a tree and a patch of lawn. I bless the designers of that hospital for that window and tree every time I think of the experience, because they provided solace when there was none available elsewhere.

Dr. Clarke writes: *"Shortly before his death from pancreatic cancer at 59 ... British playwright Dennis Potter described the exaltation of looking out at a blossom that had become the 'whitest, frothiest, blossom-est blossom that there ever could be' from his window. 'Things are both more trivial than they ever were, and more important than they ever were, and the difference between the trivial and the important doesn't seem to matter. But the nowness of everything is absolutely wondrous,' he told an interviewer."*

Dr. Clarke continues: *"People often imagine hospices to be dark and dismal places where there is nothing left to experience but dying. But what dominates my work is not proximity to death but the best bits of living. Nowness is everywhere. Nature provides it."*

The emphasis on the word *nowness* is mine, because it captures the essence of the difference between a real view, and a simulated view, whether from a painting, a photograph, or a video display. There is no way to deny the *nowness* of real life, lived in the current moment.

Another one of Dr. Clarke's patients was told that she had terminal breast cancer at age 51. Her patient described her thought process as she adjusted to the dire prognosis: *" 'My first thought, my urge, was to get up and find an open space,' she told me on that first meeting. 'I needed to breathe fresh air, to hear natural noises, away from the hospital and its treatment rooms.' At first, she fought to preserve herself digitally, documenting every thought and feeling on her computer before they, and she, were lost forever. But one day, as she was typing frantically, she heard a bird singing through her open window. 'When you come to the end of your life, you get the sense that you don't want to lose yourself, you want to pass something on,' she told me later ... 'Somehow, when I listened to the song of a blackbird in the garden, I found it incredibly calming. It seemed to allay the fear that everything was going to disappear, to be lost forever, because I thought 'Well, there will be other blackbirds. Their songs will be pretty similar and it will all be fine. And in the same way, there were other people before me with my diagnosis. Other people will have died in the same way I will die. And it's natural. It's a natural progression. Cancer is part of nature too, and that is something I have to accept, to learn to live and die with.' "*

Dr. Clarke's observations suggest that maybe biophilia is especially strong at the end of life. Why would we not want to treasure every bit of life we can experience in our last precious moments? Connection to the rhythms of the planet, whether it is a bird singing brightly in the morning, as birds have always done, or experiencing the changing colors of sunrise or sunset, connect us more strongly with the life we all share. Enabling those experiences is what good design is all about.

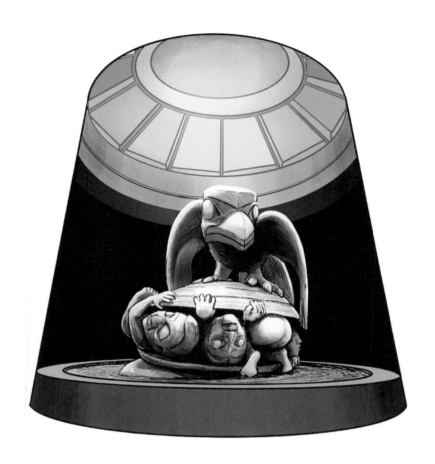

Part 4: Meaning

16. Iconic Daylight and Views

The way that we incorporate views and daylight into our built environment can become an important expression of cultural attitudes. Daylit spaces, carefully designed, can create such iconic visual experiences that they intensely reinforce the cultural meaning of a place, whether by conveying religious, historic, or philosophical concepts. Likewise, iconic views can become such treasured components of landscape that they help form emotional bonds among the citizens of a neighborhood, a town, or a country. Whether bringing the focus inward, as with an intimate daylit chapel, or outward, as with a panoramic view, when these constructions also embody cherished cultural attitudes, they transcend the practicalities of mere building or urban design, and instead become a form of social communication which endures across time, and spans generations.

At certain times, daylight can have a strange power to transform an ordinary experience into an ineffable moment. How is that possible? Likewise, some views are so beloved that they themselves become iconic images of a place, or a whole culture. How and why does that happen? Let's begin by considering some examples of places that consistently have that transcendent quality, and then consider how views of seemingly ordinary places might become transformed into icons of their culture.

Our brains are wired to make certain default assumptions about the visual environment, as we discussed earlier regarding visual illusions (see page 82). One of these is a presumption that light will come from above, such as from the sky, and that there will be only one primary source of light, such as the sun or the moon. This makes evolutionary sense, given that it is one of the most common natural experiences that human beings are likely to have on our planet.

However, there are moments, and places, where these default assumptions are shifted, creating distinctly different flows of ambient light. Sunrise and sunset are the most familiar examples of such a moment, when the balance of colors and the direction of direct light shifts. Rather than coming from somewhere overhead, the direct beams of sunlight cross the plane of the earth in a nearly horizontal direction; vertical surfaces facing the sun are then intensely illuminated. Sky colors also shift: oranges and reds radiate around the sun while the sky overhead transitions into deeper blues. These dramatic shifts in daylight character might last for a few minutes or an hour, but it is enough to mark the moment as special. Likewise, clouds and mists can reflect and refract daylight in strange ways, transforming the view from obvious to ambiguous, from dependable to fleeting. Understanding these atmospheric effects offers a designer an additional set of tools to emphasize certain kinds of experience and emotional response.

Otherworldly Light

Natural landscapes and architectural form can also alter the flow of daylight, and create an ambient daylight condition that seems extraordinary. Yosemite Valley is one of those places that always has a magical light to it. The very first American visitors to the valley in the 1850s were transfixed. They wrote odes to its beauty, which were published widely around the country. Huge oil paintings were toured to dazzle audiences with Yosemite's splendor. In the middle of the American Civil War, Frederick Law Olmsted felt compelled to make the grueling overland trip to visit the valley in 1863, and inspired by its magnificence, became the chair of the commission appointed by President Abraham Lincoln to oversee its eternal protection and transfer as a public park to the state of California. In 1906 the naturalist John Muir convinced President Theodore Roosevelt to take national control of the park, making it the third national park ever created. Just a few years later, the renowned photographer Ansel Adams made his first visit to Yosemite as a young teenager with his family and took his first photos with a simple Brownie box camera. In his autobiography, Adams explained how that visit set the course for his life as a photographer: *"the splendor of Yosemite burst upon us and it was glorious ... One wonder after another descended upon us ... There was light everywhere ... A new era began for me."*[1]

Adams struggled for years to find just the right techniques to capture the sensibility of the light in the valley in his black and white photographs. In the process, those images made him one of the most famous photographers in the world and defined the iconic images of Yosemite Valley that continue to draw millions of tourists per year.

What is responsible for this magical light in Yosemite that has inspired so many? I think that it is created by the sheer granite walls, rising 3,000 to 4,000 feet above the valley floor, which bounce daylight back and forth, until there is a much stronger horizontal component to the light than experienced elsewhere. Shadows are softened, glowing with an unusual luminosity, and highlights appear in unexpected locations. The sunlit façades of these granite massifs silhouette trees and people in new directions, while the cliffs' walls in deep shadow create a stunning backdrop for sunlit images.

A similar rearrangement of normal daylighting expectations occurs in Venice, Italy, where the omnipresent waters of the lagoon reflect sunlight into the nooks and crannies of the Venetian canals. The vertical walls of the buildings in Venice lining the canals inter-reflect daylight, just like the granite walls of Yosemite, creating a horizontal flow of light that creates unexpected highlights and illuminated shadows. Daylight inside of buildings has an unusual upward bounce, off of the water below. Due to the sun's movement, these geometrical relationships among sun, water, and wall are constantly shifting throughout the day and the year, riveting the attention of every artist who arrives in Venice, eager to capture one special moment in time.

Another constructed setting which transforms normal daylight into a transcendent experience is the Fushimi Inari Taisha in Kyoto, Japan, where thousands of vermillion torii gates line pathways up and down the sacred mountain, dedicated to the Shinto god of rice, Inari. A torii is the traditional Shinto gateway that marks the boundary between the sacred and profane. For hundreds of years people and companies have erected torii at Fushimi Inari to give thanks for good fortune, resulting in pathways that are lined with literally thousands of these structures, each consisting of two hefty legs supporting two horizontal members overhead, all cloaked in shiny red paint.

The experience of walking the pathways is remarkable, as sunlight streams first through the leaves of the forest and then between the dense rows of columns, reflected back and forth within the lines of torii, intensifying red wavelengths in every direction. Crowds of religious pilgrims and secular tourists make their way through the passages up and down the mountain, continuously bathed in this amazing light, and enraptured by how exceptional everything looks, especially each other's faces. It is a memorable experience, as much for the unusual quality of light as for the cultural and historical implications of the shrine. (See illustration on page 287.)

Mimicking the effects of clouds and mists, many religions have used smoke to send offerings up to the gods above. Smoke, whether it comes from fires, candles, or incense censers, can make patterns of light far more apparent as beams of sunlight, and their contrasting shadows, are newly seen as three-dimensional shapes. The first time I experienced the use of a censer in a church was as a teenager when I was visiting an Armenian Orthodox church with a friend. The priests in gold-embroidered robes walked slowly down the center aisle swinging their shiny brass censers on long chains while they chanted some form of blessing. The aromatic smoke slowly spread throughout the church. Unfamiliar with the meaning of all the rituals, I was fascinated instead by how the quality of light in the church was transformed, from mundane to magical. The daylight, streaming down from the stained-glass windows high above became tangible in the soft smoke of the censer. The saints' portraits, set in golden mosaics, continued to sparkle through the smoky mist, implying an enduring presence even through that veil of smoke. Melodic chanting, fragrant incense, gently colored shafts of light—it was an intense multi-sensory experience.

The Pantheon

The directionality and color of daylight have long been used to convey religious experience. The Pantheon in Rome was built towards the end of the Roman Empire, sometime around 120 CE, replacing previous temples on the site which had burned multiple times. The origin of the name is usually interpreted to mean 'temple for all the gods,' from the Greek (*pan* = all, *theon* = of the gods). However, a contemporary historian, Cassius Dio, in his *History of Rome,* seemed to imply Pantheon was just a nickname, "*my own opinion of the name is that, because of its vaulted roof, it resembles the heavens.*"

Indeed, the Pantheon took a unique form, unlike any previous Roman temple, a monumental dome shaped of poured, un-reinforced, concrete. It is still the largest such dome in the world. Special construction techniques helped to stabilize the giant structure, with volcanic pumice stone used in the concrete in the upper portion of the dome to lighten the load, and the top of the dome, the most fragile portion, left out entirely. Instead, at the top of the dome is a 27-foot diameter hole, open to the sky, called the 'oculus,' from the Latin word for 'eye.' At slightly less than 4% of the domed roof area, the oculus is more than sufficient to be the sole source of illumination for the floor below. Sunlight and rain both fall freely into the space, unfiltered, just as a few birds also fly within the vast rotunda, welcome as visitors from the natural world outside.

The Pantheon survived the sacking of Rome and was later converted into a Catholic church during the middle ages. Chapels were fitted into the niches formed by the cylinder of columns marching around its perimeter. Later it also became the burial site of Italian kings. The technical mastery of the Pantheon was clearly in the construction of the concrete dome, which still looks flawless 2,000 years later. However, the Pantheon's enduring power is the symbolism of the rotunda mimicking the vault of the heavens, lit by a single shaft of sunlight, revealing the passage of time within its consecrated volume.

As the beam of sunlight moves throughout the day, it highlights different areas of the mosaic floor, the sculpted walls and the coffered dome. It fills the enormous volume with reflected daylight and softly sculpted shadows. The sun itself is not visible, only its result. It is perhaps best to think of the Pantheon not as a daylit building, but rather as an elaborate vessel for capturing and displaying one ray of sunlight, so that we can experience the essence of it, and its power to illuminate.

Cathedrals and Chapels

In the great Gothic and Renaissance cathedrals of Europe, daylight was architecturally manipulated to create a numinous environment where ordinary people were invited to experience the sacred realm. As discussed earlier (see page 227), Gothic churches favored the form of the basilica from Roman times, with rows of clerestory windows high above the columns supporting the main roof. Light filtered down in shafts from above, a metaphor for heavenly blessings, perhaps emphasized by the ceremonial use of smoke from candles and censers to make the shafts even more apparent. Wealthy sponsors added stained glass windows to tell biblical stories, which further intensified the colors within the sanctuaries. Medieval architects quickly learned how to reinforce the outward thrust of the roof with flying buttresses, which allowed ever larger and taller openings in the exterior walls of Gothic churches for more windows. The interior of these cathedrals become a daylit landscape themselves, with the Gothic structure and ornament providing almost as much fractal detail as a real forest.

Sainte-Chapelle in Paris has survived as one of the greatest achievements of Gothic architecture, dissolving structure into light. Built in the mid-1200s as the private chapel of King Louis IX, who was later canonized as Saint Louis, huge stained-glass windows surround the chapel on all sides, rising 50 feet overhead, and filled with the largest intact collection of medieval stained glass. Like Yosemite, vertical surfaces dominate and light flows horizontally from the windows, with an animation and variety that is ever changing.

Renaissance architects continued with the theme of sacred daylight, ushered in by Brunelleschi's masterful dome over the Florence Cathedral, inspired by the Pantheon in Rome. He replaced the Pantheon's open oculus with a glazed cupola at the very top of the dome, allowing daylight to enter at the highest point of the church, and highlighting the church altar, located directly below at the crossing of the nave and transept. With daylight available from the highest points of the roof, the ceilings of Renaissance churches became a well-lit canvas for elaborate frescos and mosaics, further lifting the attention of the churchgoer upward, towards the heavens. Some Renaissance architects added sundials, plotted on the floor of the church, to explicitly mark the movement of the sun. They also often added small hidden skylights over the niches which lined the walls of a church. Each daylit niche then created a more contained version of the heavenly illumination which metaphorically blessed the statues of saints housed in the niches' contemplative chapels.

In the modern era, American architect Eero Saarinen took the idea of a skylight over the altar to an extreme, in a small contemplative chapel he designed for the Massachusetts Institute of Technology, opened in 1955. The chapel sits inside of a perfectly round brick drum, with one round skylight set directly over the altar. The light from the skylight is caught and reflected by a cascade of metallic rectangles hung from its rim. They shine brightly against the dark brick walls and emphasize the descent of light from above. That one skylight provides almost all of the light of the chapel. There are no views, other than the inward view to the sculpture dancing in the daylight.

However, Saarinen added another unusual design element, supporting his brick drum on little arches, and setting the feet of those arches in a pool of water that rings the chapel. A narrow line of glass follows the interior walls, allowing daylight to be reflected upward onto the heavily textured brick walls. Thus, by day, the brick walls of the chapel are illuminated by gently undulating light reflected upwards from the pool outside, with subtle shifts of light produced by the caustic patterns of the wind-rippled water below, while visual focus is kept on the dramatic cascade of metallic squares seeming to float upward. One recent visitor wrote: *"While the exterior only gives a slight hint of the possibilities of the inside, nothing prepares one for the eccentricities of this room ... Its dark, undulating walls pulsate ... The darkness is comforting and intimate, penetrated by only two otherworldly sources of light ... The effect is sublime."*[2]

Saarinen's chapel is a very urban solution. The double brick walls insulate the visitor from traffic noise from busy Massachusetts Avenue, and the extremes of New England's winter and summer weather. Inwardly focused and visually divorced from its surroundings, the chapel's very simple visual environment provides a soothing contrast to the intense academic world outside.

The Wayfarer's Chapel, in Palos Verdes, California, also known as the Glass Chapel, is the architectural antithesis of Saarinen's Chapel, especially in terms of daylight and view. Designed by Lloyd Wright, son of Frank Lloyd Wright, in 1950, the Wayfarer's Chapel sits at the very edge of a peninsula overlooking the Pacific Ocean. The walls are entirely glass, as is most of the roof, allowing congregants to look beyond the sanctuary to the land and sky outside. A grove of redwoods and cedar trees was planted to shelter the glass structure, and ivy was encouraged to grow over some of the glass. Plants also grow inside of the church, to further blur the distinction between indoors and out. Wright, with his love of complex geometric forms, employed a naturalistic structural theme, based on 60 degree angles to mimic the fractal branching of trees outside. The chapel is now listed on the American National Register of Historic Places, and is a favorite setting for weddings and films. (See illustration on page 315.)

When I was a child, I lived nearby. My family officially belonged to a church down the hill, but come Sundays I would beg my mother to take me to the Glass Chapel instead, because I thought it was the most wonderful place I had ever been. I could sit quietly for an hour happily if I could watch the clouds and the birds outside. I thought that the naturalistic setting was the perfect idea for a church. Much later I learned that the Wright was asked to design Wayfarer's Chapel to epitomize the philosophy of Emanuel Swedenborg, eighteenth-century founder of the Swedenborgian Church. Swedenborg was a well-known philosopher in nineteenth-century America, quoted by Thomas Jefferson and Ralph Wadsworth Emerson, among others. Swedenborg believed that 'nature' was the ultimate expression of a loving God. John Chapman, better known as Johnny Appleseed, who traveled the country by foot in the early nineteenth century planting apple trees to feed the settlers who were sure to come later, is perhaps the most well-known member of the Swedenborgian church in America. Lloyd Wright translated that philosophy into a church design, embracing a maximum amount of daylight and view, which even a five-year-old child could understand.

The Raven and the First Men

There is a special use of daylight in the British Columbia Museum of Anthropology, designed by Canadian architect Arthur Erickson, to evoke the origin story of the Haida people, a First Nations tribe in the Pacific Northwest.

There are many parallels to the story of the Pantheon, with the sky dome symbolizing the origins of humanity.

Bill Reid, a master carver of the tribe, was commissioned to create a singular sculpture for the museum, *The Raven and the First Men*, carved out of multiple blocks of yellow cedar, kiln-dried and bonded together into a massive wooden cube, seven feet on each side. The sculpture took seven years for Reid and his assistants to complete, finishing the work only after it was moved into place at the museum. Upon its unveiling in 1980, the sculpture was celebrated by the Haida community with a ceremony of song, dance, and feasting. It has since become a favorite of museum visitors, and an icon of Canadian First Peoples' culture.

As visitors enter the museum, they first experience a forest of giant totem poles, set in a glassy atrium space overlooking the nearby coastline, as if the totem poles were still out in the raw wet weather of the shore, standing sentinel in front of the cedar-bark lodges that housed the Haida. There are more totem poles to visit, set deeper inside the museum, surrounding an exhibit where visitors can go inside one of the cedar log homes and feel the darkness and earthiness of the interior. Beyond this darkness is the special room set aside for the sculpture.

The piece is set under a circular skylight, that captures the experience of the first light, as proto-men emerge out of a clam shell (see the illustration on page 285). The skylight provides the light of the larger world that they are just beginning to experience, as explained by Reid himself: "… *It wasn't long before one, then another of the little shell brothers, timidly emerged. Some of them immediately scurried back when they saw the immensity of the sea and the sky and the overwhelming blackness of the Raven. But eventually curiosity overcame caution and all of them crept or scrambled out. Very strange creatures they were, two-legged like the Raven. There the resemblance ended. They had no glossy feathers, no thrusting beak, their skin was pale and they were naked except for their long, black hair on their round, flat-featured heads. Instead of strong wings they had stick-like appendages that waved and fluttered constantly. They were the original Haidas, the first humans.*"[3]

Thus, this sculpture celebrates the moment of first vision, as the humans look out into daylight for the first time. The eye of the Raven is immense, and intent. The eyes of the humans are also wide open, expressing their curiosity and wonder at their bright new world. The polished yellow cedar wood glows golden in the soft daylight falling from above, while the shadows within the clamshell emphasize the darkness of the humans' previous existence. Without the daylight from above, this creation story could not be told.

Memorial Landscapes

It is not only in origin stories, but also memorials for the dead, that daylight and views can epitomize cultural and philosophical concepts. Egyptians buried their mummified dead shrouded inside of coffins within more coffins, and then entombed in stone, as if trying to ensure the dead would stay within the depths of the earth. For the Egyptians, the great pyramids served as the primary cultural landmark noting the ceremonial passage of life for their rulers, while hundreds of state bureaucrats were entombed in vast mortuary cities surrounding the pyramids. The Romans continued with giant monuments honoring their rulers, while ordinary Romans were buried in family vaults in cemeteries ringing the outskirts of their cities. The scale of the cemeteries with their elaborately carved stone vaults, crypts, and statues bespeaks of the level of investment made to ensure the living remembered the glories of the past.

In sharp contrast, the Parsis in Persia and India, along with some Native American tribes, placed their dead on raised platforms, where the carrion birds could carry their flesh off into the sky. Once decayed and consumed, the body had seemingly disappeared into the sky. The Mongols in Central Asia took this disappearing act even further. When their great ruler Genghis Khan died, Mongol legend has it that the Great Khan was buried in an unmarked grave far out in the empty steppe, and then thousands of horses were run back and forth to obliterate any sign of the location. In these societies the dead disappeared into the atmosphere. The sky itself became the memorial to their existence. This is not unlike the more modern practice of scattering ashes in a place the person loved, whether it be the ocean, a grassy hill, or a red-rock canyon, in which case the dead literally merge with the landscape. For these cultures, there is no landmark, but only the native landscape to speak for the dead.

Early in the nineteenth century, Europeans and Americans began to turn away from the older concept of the 'graveyard' on consecrated ground adjacent to a church or temple, to a more secular 'cemetery' (from the Greek for 'sleeping place'), often built on the outskirts of cities where there was more room to inter the rapidly growing population. The first American garden cemetery, Mount Auburn Cemetery, was opened near Boston in 1831. Sponsored by the Boston Horticultural Society, Mount Auburn also became an arboretum, featuring hundreds of specimen trees planted along the rolling landscape overlooking the Charles River. By the middle of the nineteenth century, tourists were flocking to Mount Auburn and taking home the concept that a cemetery should be a romantically designed landscape. As such, a sense of melancholy was key, with perhaps a few weeping willows and swans gracing the site, creating an idealized image of new heavenly home for the dearly departed. Later American cemeteries took this notion a step further, selecting sites with great vistas and grand boscs of trees. Forest Lawn in Los Angeles is one of the most famous modern examples, the burial site for many of Hollywood's celebrities, which has become a tourist attraction itself.

In a much more humble vein, my town has begun a new tradition whereby families can fund a public bench as a memorial to their loved one, strategically located for a nice view of a park, hillside, or harbor, along with a short inscription. Thus, each bench along an evening's walk offers communion with someone who also loved that view in the past. It is another way of sharing a special view across time.

Japanese and Chinese Gardens

The gardens of Zen Buddhist temples in Japan, designed to aid Zen monks in meditation, are unequaled in their use of symbolic elements to represent philosophic concepts. A covered porch surrounding the temple offers a sheltered location to sit quietly and contemplate the garden maintained within the temple walls. Some contemplative Zen gardens have small ponds or streams, surrounded by carefully selected plantings that change colors with the seasons. Trees are meticulously pruned, and even miniaturized via bonsai techniques, sustained within miniaturized meadows of immaculately maintained moss, in order to represent a highly idealized form of nature. But the most iconic Zen gardens are those made largely of rocks and gravel, such as the fifteenth-century Ryōan-ji in Kyoto. Specially chosen rocks are arranged to represent islands in the ocean, such that at least one rock is always hidden from any given vantage point. Fine white gravel or sand is raked to resemble the waves rippling endlessly around the islands. The white gravel also can be thought to represent purity, or the mental distance, detachment and tranquility that the monks seek to reach with their meditations. In the case of the Zen Temple garden, the garden is a highly evolved art form and the view contains the message.

Other Asian landscapes have also been carefully curated and became cultural icons. Xi Hu—also known as West Lake—in Hangzhou, China, provides an example of a set of curated views that have not only endured over a millennium, but also established a cultural prototype that has been copied throughout Asia. Located at the southern end of the great canal connecting northward to Beijing, a large swampy area was dammed early in its history and turned into a freshwater lake. In 1129 CE, Hangzhou became the imperial capital of the Southern Song dynasty. The Song Dynasty was a time of great cultural and technical innovation, including the first use of paper money, the compass, gunpowder, and a standing navy. It is believed that Hangzhou may have been the largest city in the world from 1180 to 1315, with a population of one to two million.

The shallow lake was gradually improved by successive emperors. Continuous dredging to maintain some depth and flow in the lake resulted in a meandering shoreline and numerous islands, which were then connected with picturesque bridges and canals. Xi Hu became the playground of the palace courtiers, who then painted images and wrote poetic odes to its beauty, capturing all the romantic moments that they experienced in its thrall. It was nature within easy reach of the imperial elite, and so inspired literally thousands of poems and paintings. With its thriving culture and beautiful lake, Hangzhou attracted thousands of foreign visitors, including Marco Polo sometime in the 1200s and the great Moroccan explorer Ibn Battuta in 1345.

Two hundred years ago Emperor Qianlong codified the most perfect viewing locations on the lake, each marked with a four-character inscription carved in a stone stele, identifying ten quintessential experiences, by season, time of day, and weather. There is *Leifeng Pagoda in the Sunset* and *Three Ponds Mirroring the Moon*. One of the best-known scenes in Hangzhou is *Spring Dawn at Su Causeway* where six bridges connecting multiple islands are overhung with blossoms and new willow leaves. The causeway is named for Su Shi, also known as Su Tungpo, the governor of Hangzhou responsible for building it. Su was also a Renaissance man, 300 years *before* the Italian Renaissance, a grand master of technology, painting, poetry, and calligraphy. Today a museum at the lake is dedicated to his artwork and writings, reinforcing the lake's enduring cultural connections.

These ten scenes of West Lake may be one of the earliest examples of officially-designated tourist vista spots. West Lake continues to inspire; now listed as a UNESCO World Heritage Site, it is one of the top tourism draws for China. According to Eric Weiner, who visited the lake in his research for his book, the Geography of Genius, "*The lake does not disappoint. Surrounded on three sides by lush green mountains and specked with countless pagodas and temples, it exudes quiet beauty ...*" Weiner went to Hangzhou to interview Jack Ma, the billionaire founder of China's biggest software company, Alibaba. Ma explained: "*When Alibaba was in its infancy and had no office space to speak of, the employees used the lake as their conference room, finding a grassy spot along the shores and holding their meetings there.*"[4] In his search for places that uniquely nurture genius, Weiner summarized his interest in visiting West Lake based on his belief that "*Great cities are never fully divorced from the natural world. They always retain visitation rights. New York's Central Park*

... Tokyo's Imperial Gardens. A city completely detached from nature is a dead place, and not a very creative one."

Edinburgh and Urban Intimacy

Weiner visited seven cities that he felt had sparked a period of remarkable cultural innovation at some point in history, trying to identify unifying themes that might also support future genius. Weiner is an unusual mix of science journalist and travel writer who claims his key interest is in the intersection of places and ideas. *"Cities are the places where ideas go to have sex,"* he quips. Edinburgh in Scotland was another of his city-subjects, which hosted a scientific and philosophical constellation of geniuses in the late eighteenth century, including inventor James Watt, philosopher David Hume, geologist James Hutton, economist Adam Smith, and the world's leading medical school of the time. Weiner contends that the physical layout of Edinburgh captures one aspect of genius: surprise mixed with historical continuity. In his first visit, he spent a good amount of time traversing the town on foot. *"Edinburgh is a compact city, designed for shoes, not cars,"* he writes. *"The first time I catch a glimpse of Edinburgh Castle, sprouting from the basalt like some giant stone apparition, I am caught off guard. I'd seen pictures of it, read about it, and so I had, modulated by expectations, discounted my reaction ... [but] when I turn a corner and it suddenly materializes, towering over Edinburgh from one of the city's many extinct volcanoes, I am stunned ... All of Edinburgh is like that. It surprises, and surprise, along with the attendant phenomena of wonder and awe, lies at the heart of all creative genius."*

Weiner visited the old Surgeons Hall Museum, which tells the story of Edinburgh's revolutionary medical school, when he was struck looking out a hallway window: *"It's a wonderful view. I can see the hills off in the distance, including Arthur's Seat, the old volcano that sits at the edge of town. I look for a long time, marveling at how the scene before me is virtually unchanged from what a young medical student would have seen nearly three hundred years ago."*

Edinburgh has many opportunities for sweeping views, but generally you have to hike up a windy mountain or hill to get there. In the old sections of town, views out are highly constrained—down a street, over a wall, between two buildings—and contrast intensely with the old soot-blackened buildings. An Edinburgh native, Robert Louis Stevenson, wrote of the contrast and surprise of Edinburgh's views in the nineteenth century: *"You peep under an arch, you descend stairs that look as if they would land you in a cellar, you turn to the back window of a grimy tenement in a lane—and behold! You are face to face with distant and bright prospects."*

Unable to quite resolve Edinburgh's challenging northern climate with the deep love so many locals feel for the city, Weiner asked a famous Scottish historian, Donald Campbell, why he chose to live there. *"Intimacy"* the man replies. *"It was not a word I was expecting, but when I heard it, something clicked,"* explains Weiner. *"Places of genius are not only densely populated, but they are also intimate, and intimacy always includes a degree of trust ... Today, the cities and companies that excel creatively are those where trust and intimacy are high."*

I find this a very interesting concept, the idea of *urban intimacy*, as a quality of a city. Certainly, social behaviors and customs must be key to creating such an atmosphere, but beloved cultural landmarks may also play a role in helping to forge an urban intimacy, creating a bond between locals, and even with tourists: a shared love. This is not hard to recognize in the myriads of people, locals and tourists alike, making the pilgrimage to walk across the Golden Gate Bridge in San Francisco, or the folks who come to picnic at the foot of the Eiffel Tower in Paris. There is an emotional bond in knowing that everyone loves the same thing. Viewing the landmark, while seemingly passive, is an active reminder of shared experience and may help foster the sense of community that Weiner was seeking in his book. It may also help explain the extreme real estate valuation that is placed on views of such landmarks, as discussed in Chapter 13, as a way of purchasing a greater sense of intimacy with the city of your choice.

The *trust* part of the equation posited above comes from a faith that the urban landscape will be relatively stable over time ... that someone like Eric Weiner can walk the streets of Edinburgh and feel that he is reliving the experience of a medical student from 300 years ago, or perhaps, that you will be able take your grandchildren back to an important vantage point from your childhood, to merge cognitive maps across generations. Thus, landscapes and views that reinforce a sense of history can also provide an emotional stability and context that reinforces trust, an assurance that memories can be conveyed to future generations.

Emerging Landmarks

Where I lived once, in Fair Oaks, California, there is a special oak tree that is the revered symbol of the town, but known only to local residents. The old oak tree grows on the very edge of a bluff about a hundred feet up above the American River. In times past, before the dam was built farther up the river, the river used to flood every few years, ferociously washing away banks and structures in its way. Once the dam was built, the river no longer flooded, and its banks and bluffs stopped eroding. This one oak tree had been in danger of being the next to go. It still clings precariously at the edge of the bluff, with half of its root structure dangling in the open air over the cliff's edge. Locals know how to follow a little path up the bluff to this unique tree and are rewarded with a view of the river flowing in broad bends below. There aren't many other vantage-points nearby to help you get a fix on where you are in the world, so this spot is especially valuable.

The oak's sheer tenacity to keep growing, despite its dangerous position, also engenders affection. The improbable tree became a favorite subject of local artists and photographers. I have a lovely photograph of it framed in my living room to remind me of where I once lived, and I have given paintings to my children, who now live far away, to remind them of happy times where they grew up. Eventually the town purchased a bit of land around the oak to help preserve it. Perhaps, now that you know this story, you will look for the tree when you visit Fair Oaks sometime in the future, and take your own photograph or selfie to commemorate the occasion. If and when you do, the dangling oak tree will be a little further on its way to icon status before its inevitable demise.

Humble urban structures can also become beloved landmarks. Novelist Nathan Englander described how he came to love rooftop views of New York City's water towers. Initially they were not inherently interesting to him, but a friend passed on the contagion: *"My favorite New York feature, one of the things I'm most attached to, is the wooden water tower. There's one on every roof ... When I first moved to the city, a friend pointed them out as things of great majesty. He was obsessed with them. I'm not sure I would have noticed the water towers without his help, or that I'd have decided they were some kind of wonder. But I've long since come to agree. Now I wouldn't trade them for mountains in the distance. They are very much this city to me."*[5]

Nathan Englander is not alone in his love of New York city water towers. Water towers have become so emblematic of the New York City skyline that artists have taken to recreating them as sculptures. For example, artist Tom Fruin transformed the skeleton of an old water tower with a new patchwork skin of translucent colors, radiating bright colors in the sunlight like a jeweled cylinder high up on the rooftops. Likewise, British artist Rachel Whiteread created a public sculpture called *Water Tower*, now mounted on the rooftop above the Museum of Modern Art's sculpture garden. Cast in translucent resin from the inside of an old wooden water tower, in order to replicate its inner textures, it represents the unseen contents of all the city's ubiquitous water towers.

These oak tree and water tower stories illustrate a vernacular process whereby a local landmark acquires more elevated status (pun intended) over time. First, it marks a special spot that is meaningful to local inhabitants. The landmark endures and is remembered by more than one generation, creating ties to history. Locals start to create images of the landmark, write poetry, make movies that feature it as a local landmark, sharing their enthusiasm. At first this artwork or literature is just for the local *cognoscenti*, but if and when a larger audience becomes engaged, then the landmark also expands in importance. The more repetitions, the greater the reinforcement; just as in any marketing or branding campaign. References in artwork and literature tend to create an echo-chamber, making more people aware of the landmark, and thus making it more well-known, enjoyed and valued, and thus more likely to be further referenced by others. Eventually it is recognized as iconic to that place and culture.

These stories also make it clear that affection for views is not determined so much by the inherent beauty of natural scenes, as by cultural associations and layers of meanings that build up over time. Especially in cities, iconic views often include constructed landmarks, such as the Eiffel Tower or Golden Gate Bridge. Yet, when asked, people will often say that they prefer their window view to include 'nature.' Given that very common response, we should inquire more deeply: "*Exactly what do you mean by 'nature'?*"

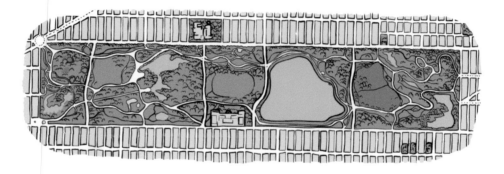

17. Visions of Nature

Many of the research studies discussed in this book, those which tried to better understand human response to views or physical immersion in 'nature,' employed a methodology based on showing study subjects photographs or videos representing 'views of nature' versus a 'built or urban' environment. This dualist construct implies that it should be obvious to all what constitutes a view of nature. The nature images I have seen used in these research studies are typically photographs of an urban park-like setting, with leafy trees and a lawn. A wider view might include some sky above and/or a bit of mountainous landscape beyond. The key element in these photographs seems to be that 'nature' equals greenery i.e. plant material, growing in happy isolation outdoors, while 'urban or built environment' typically consists of streets, cars, and rectilinear buildings, with rarely a hint of topography, people, plants, birds, or weather. Before we buy into the findings from these studies, it behooves us to explore a bit further into the many possible meanings of 'nature.'

The English word nature is derived from the Latin word *natura*, meaning 'of birth, an essential quality or innate disposition.' But the word nature has many more meanings in the English language. It can also mean the essential character of something; native; all that is not man-made, i.e. not manufactured. Various dictionaries provide five, ten, even 17 different meanings of the word, the broadest of which is *"the sum total of the forces at work throughout the universe."* If so, then not only trees and grass, but also weather, atmospherics, gravity, and geology should provide an image of 'nature.'

An urban park is far from the original native landscape of most cities, especially if most of the park's trees are imported or hybridized specimens. Rolling expanses of lawn in a park do not occur naturally, given that they must be graded, seeded, fertilized, weeded, irrigated, and mowed in order to survive.

The Japanese epitome of natural beauty, a Zen temple garden, is certainly beautiful to contemplate, and yet there is hardly anything natural, i.e. not man-made, about it. The ponds are constructed, the craggy rocks are brought in from afar, the old pine trees have been meticulously pruned into their expressive shapes, and the moss is swept clean every morning. In a more modern vein, should an interior 'green-wall' of succulents featured in an office lobby be assumed to constitute 'nature'? There is nothing very natural, let alone self-propagating, about a constructed vertical wall of succulents hung on an interior wall, maintained by drip irrigation and artificial illumination.

Therefore, the question can rightly be asked: what are the essential components of a view of 'nature' that are beneficial? Our concepts of nature have certainly evolved over time, and are still rapidly evolving. If 'nature' is thought of as the opposite of 'man-made,' then perhaps wilderness expresses the very essence of nature? Yet the concept of wilderness, too, is fraught with cultural baggage. In the Bible, the origin story for three major world religions, there is a tightly guarded paradise which forms the basis for many Western concepts of virginal nature, before it was 'contaminated' by humans. Adam and Eve were cast out of this paradise after gaining carnal knowledge from the serpent. In his book *Second Nature*, exploring the relationship of people to nature via their gardens, Michael Pollan comments that *"once a landscape is no longer 'virgin' it is typically written off as fallen, lost to nature, irredeemable."*

European explorers tended to think of the western hemisphere as a vast untouched wilderness to explore, with so much land which was obviously new to them. Yet the landscape that they first encountered had already been heavily cultivated and formed by the indigenous populations. The Europeans generally were not aware that they were entering a recently depopulated landscape, since most of the native peoples had died from waves of disease which advanced far ahead of the European colonists. Thus, European, and subsequently American, concepts of a wilderness that exists free from human intervention, are very much at odds with the historical reality.[1]

In contrast, a concept of wilderness is not common in aboriginal cultures. There is no wilderness in Africa: there are just the lands inhabited by the neighboring tribes. Among the Australian aborigines, their mutual homeland occupies a seamless landscape during the 'everywhen,' of past, present, and future. American native peoples have a wide range of origin stories that explain how they came to their homelands, but I know of none that include a distinct district that is forbidden or inaccessible, a wilderness kept separate from human endeavors.

Topophilia

Yi-Fu Tuan is a geographer who studied various cultures' concepts of nature and helped found the discipline called humanistic geography. He coined the concept of 'topophilia,' or love of place, for the title of his masterful 1974 book on environmental perception and values, in which he explores how cultural perspectives influence our relationship to the land around us. Born in 1930 in China to an upper-class family, Tuan received an international education, which took him to Australia, the Philippines, and England before receiving a doctorate from UC Berkeley, which may help to explain his fluency with cross-cultural concepts. Tuan's perspectives were an interesting mix of geography and cultural anthropology, seeking to understand how culture acts upon a natural landscape to produce a 'cultural landscape' that is an amalgam of both natural conditions and cultural attitudes.

Early in his career, Tuan lived in New Mexico, and studied the different interpretations of the landscape there by five local cultures: the indigenous Navaho and Zuni, plus the Spanish, Anglo, and Mormon settlers. He found that perceptions of the New Mexico landscape were clearly formed in relationship to previous experience. He draws a striking contrast between the comments in the journals of the early Spanish explorers looking for mineral resources, moving north from the Sonoran Desert of Mexico, and those of the Anglos, arriving from the plains of Texas. "*Spaniards and Mexicans, when they moved north into New Mexico, did not find the country barren. On the contrary, they remarked frequently on the presence of streams. Barreiro went so far as to say that 'the greater part of the country consists of immense plains and delightful valleys, clothed with very abundant pasturage.' In contrast, the Anglo explorers arrived in New Mexico from the more humid east. They complained of the barrenness and aridness of the country. They called the landscape 'naked' and 'sickening' 'barren and uninteresting in the extreme.'"*[2]

Tuan compares ideas of 'pretty' and 'ugly' among these groups, and how it applies to landscape elements. For example, he explains that: "*'Ugly' to the Zuni means the difficulties inherent in livelihood and the maliciousness of human nature. The Navaho, on the other hand, tend to see 'ugly' as the disruption of the natural order; it stirs memories of hardship, parched land, illness, accident, and aliens.*" Thus, interpretations of views and landscapes are inherently driven by cultural perspective.

Taoist and Hindu Cosmologies

Mai-Mai Sze, a twentieth-century Chinese–American painter and writer, explored how Taoist philosophy interacted with concepts of nature, in her book, *The Way of Chinese Painting*, published in 1956. She returned to the ancient texts to gain insight into how Chinese philosophies interacted with landscape painting styles. Indeed, the very term for landscape painting, Shan-shui, literally means 'mountain water,' and is symbolic of the *Yang* and the *Yin*. She explains: *"From the evidence of the earliest beliefs, it is known that mountains were associates with Heaven and the Yang principle ... symbolizing the element of fire, and thus also the sun, heat, red, power, spirit and literally the fires of life ... similarly shui (water) represents the Yin principle is the nourishing element, both the depths and the source, and in its apparent stillness possesses both motion and strength."*[3]

And although Chinese landscape painting may be termed 'mountain-water,' it is very much the presence of sky—as in mists, air, void, spirit, or transformation—which is the key element. Even though Taoist philosophy had a strongly dualistic component, it also was based on an underlying principle of unity, derived from the concept that both *Yin* and *Yang* are constantly in the process of being transformed into their opposite, as represented by the well-known *Yin-Yang* symbol ☯. Thus, a Taoist painter's goal was not merely to capture a pretty picture of nature, but to express the philosophy that everything within view—the rocks, water, trees, and atmosphere, and by extension, the artist and the viewer too—are all participating in a unified and ever transforming existence. According to Sze, *"The usual proportions of sky and earth in a Chinese landscape painting allow a conspicuous amount of space for sky, mist and voids in relationship to that given to mountain, trees, and other terrestrial features: an overall statement of the dominance of sky (Heaven, Yang, spirit) over earth (Earth, Yin, matter)."*

While the Chinese were mastering the delicate art of ink painting on the finest silk scrolls, not too far away to the south, landscape aesthetics in India followed a very different path. Hindu monarchs in India were commissioning stone carvings to capture their cosmology of gods and goddesses, saints and spirits who inhabit an enduring landscape, as permanently represented in granite. Whereas for the ancient Chinese, the abstract forces of nature themselves were divine, for the Hindus, the tangible landscape was teaming with divine spirits, some embodied by everyday animals, others floating about, just outside of view, just before our time.

A monumental rock sculpture at Mahabalipuram, near Chennai, in India captures this blend of naturalism and animism. Elephant families, carved 800 years ago, are rendered in stone so naturalistically that they look as if they were photographed just yesterday. A waterfall is populated with fat monkeys who comically imitate gaunt monks meditating at the side of a stream, while deer look on curiously from the rocks above, and gods and bodhisattva fly about overhead. The implication seems to be that there is always far more going on in every landscape than you can actually perceive at any given moment. The moment in time may seem fleeting, but the illusion is permanent.

In Hindu teachings, high mountain peaks provide access to highest levels of consciousness. Mount Meru, a mythical mountain, is the center of all creation, and as the home of gods, also the inspiration for the form of many Hindu temples in India, Cambodia, and Indonesia. The massive towers which rise high above the inner sanctuary and the *gopurum* (gateways) into the temple compounds invoke the holy mountains, while also serving as a landmark to guide pilgrims to the temples. Intricate carvings on the towers represent all aspects of Hindu cosmology, from mythical stories to mathematical principles. The ancient stones pulsate with their representation of life, simultaneously both highly individualistic and uniformly elaborate.

Sacred mountains are found around the world, from Uluru (Ayers Rock) in the Australian outback, and Mount Fuji in Japan, to Mount Olympus in Greece, the home of the gods in Greek mythology. In today's world where a majority of people live in cities, and given our increasingly dense settlements, a mountain often provides one of the best urban views, an enduring, and often sacred, landmark that can be easily seen over the tops of nearby roofs, and so can be equitably shared by everyone in the city. Yi-Fu Tuan described how, in both Asian and Western traditions, there have been similar cultural progression in attitudes towards mountains: *"Chinese attitudes towards mountains changed over time. The detailed shifts did not parallel those of the Occident, but in broad outline a common sequence can be discerned: in both civilizations the change was from a religious attitude in which awe was combined with aversion, to an aesthetic attitude that shifted from a sense of the sublime to a feeling for the picturesque; to the modern evolution of mountains as a recreational resource."*[4]

European Landscape Aesthetics

Following Tuan's thesis, European landscape aesthetics have had many radical changes over the course of history, as evidenced in art and design. Since Roman times, the geometrical garden was long favored by Italian architects and painters, whose walled gardens demonstrated a desired dominance of human endeavor over rampant botany. This somewhat defensive, or even hostile, view of the natural world changed to a more benign interpretation during the Italian Renaissance, with painters who started to use flowers and fruit as evidence of purity and earthly rewards, and elaborate cloud formations as a visual metaphor for God's omnipresence.

Of all the great Italian renaissance painters, Leonardo Da Vinci most loved a naturalistic landscape, having spent his boyhood climbing the mountains around his Tuscan home. He was a close observer of geology and also fancied himself a hydraulic engineer; his technical fascination is clearly reflected in his paintings. However, there is also a compelling vision of a deeper human relationship to landforms evidenced in many of his religious paintings, which represent a landscape that is both tumultuous and serene. His life's work includes many versions of the Madonna and Child set in in front of complex landscapes, with a hazy blue sky filtering through distant mountains, then resolving in blue water pouring forward towards the viewer as a river and waterfall. The Madonna of the Yarnwinder perhaps best epitomizes this image of the Virgin as fully integrated into a landscape: the blue of the sky and water are then repeated in the fluid blue robes of the Virgin, which continue to flow down the painting towards the viewer. Just as the Madonna is portrayed as part of the ethereal fluid landscape, her naked baby Jesus leans into the flesh-colored rocks, very much a part of the earth.

The European fascination with a mountainous aesthetic was renewed centuries later, with the birth of the picturesque movement in landscape art, continuing through the romantic period of poetry and music in the nineteenth century. In 1757, the budding young Irish-Anglo philosopher and statesman Edmund Burke published his treatise on aesthetics, *A Philosophical Enquiry into the Origin of Our Ideas of the Sublime and Beautiful*, wherein he defined 'the sublime' as a type of natural beauty driven by inconceivable vastness, and even a touch of terror, in order to properly heighten the emotions.

The European Alps provided one of the most definitive examples of a sublime experience, sometimes dark and stormy, sometimes bathed in light, but always vast. Following Burke's lead, young noblemen began to travel to the Alps to experience the passion of this aesthetic experience. These wealthy young men sometimes hired an artist to travel with them, to document their experience, not unlike taking a selfie today with a grand landmark in the background.

In 1782 the English cleric, William Gilpin, published a highly influential book which refined the concept of touristic travel specifically to savor the picturesque beauty of England's landscape.[5] 'Picturesque' means literally 'like a picture.' The book instructed English travelers how to judge the beauty of the natural world, much along the lines of Burke's philosophic thesis. Because Gilpin's book focused on domestic examples, his picturesque tours were more modest, and within the economic reach of upper-class Britons, helping to establish a tradition of landscape tourism. The tourists were encouraged to bring their watercolor canvases with them, to capture the perfect image of sylvan beauty, or better yet, to purchase a painting to remember their trip.

As these paintings became increasingly fashionable, the English countryside, in a clear case of life imitating art, began to resemble the most iconic of the paintings. The English gentry commissioned gardeners and architects to transform their estates into picturesque landscapes. A hidden wall set into a sunken ditch, called a 'ha-ha,' was built to protect the gardens from grazing animals while preserving uninterrupted views into the agricultural lands far beyond—the very antithesis of the walled Italian gardens of old. Architectural 'follies,' such as a diminutive faux temple or castle ruins, were dotted about the landscape to provide a visual exclamation points, often copied straight from the revered landscape paintings.

Olmsted's Vision of the Future

Such was the condition of English landscape design when the young American, Frederick Law Olmsted, visited the great parks of Europe in 1850. He had read Gilpin and other English authors and wanted to see the landscape for himself. Olmsted, his brother and a friend took themselves on a six-month walking tour of the English and French countryside, including farms, parks and estates. He was enchanted by the sheer greenery of the land. Within in a few days of arriving, he wrote in his diary *"green, dripping, glistening, gorgeous!"* As Olmsted's biographer Rybczynski writes: *"For any American the first experience of the English countryside is a revelation. It is greener. The light, thanks to the 'watery atmosphere'—a beautiful phrase—is different. The temperate climate lacks the scorching summers and freezing winters that annually batter the [New England] landscape. The land is not only gentler, it appears more tended ... In England the wilderness disappeared a long time ago—much of the country is a garden."*

Rybczynski continues: *"England became the touchstone of Olmsted's ideas about rural scenery. He swallowed the English countryside whole, but he did more than merely succumb to its visual delights ... [He had] a desire to understand exactly how natural elements could be manipulated to create an effect of picturesqueness or sublimity."*[6]

A few years before his trip to Europe, Olmsted served as the corresponding secretary for the Staten Island Agricultural Society, and wrote an impassioned plea for support of the Society's efforts: *"We believe [the society] will increase the profit of our labor—enhance the value of our lands—throw a garment of beauty around our homes, and above all, and before all, materially promote Moral and Intellectual Improvement—instructing us in the language of nature, from whose preaching, while we pursue our grateful labors, we shall learn to receive her Fruits as the bounty, and her Beauty as the manifestation of her Creator."*

Clearly, Olmsted thought that there was much more to landscape design than proper plant selection and fertilization. Rybczynski notes that this plea, beyond the usual florid Victorian language, presents the vast range of ideas that Olmsted was incorporating into his approach to landscape, long before he even realized that he had a future as a professional landscape designer: *"Ostensibly about farming, the statement is representative of the broad, encompassing vision that Olmsted is beginning to develop [early in his career]. It reflects his reading of Carlyle, Emerson, Ruskin, and Downing. He is trying to combine economics, aesthetics, landscaping, nature, moral and intellectual improvement, and salvation. It is a bewildering mix of ideas, but he is persevering. He is making his own way."*

Once his career was flourishing, and a full decade after crafting Central Park in Manhattan, Olmsted had another opportunity to shape the landscape of New York City. In 1871, his design for Prospect Park opened in Brooklyn, which has been described as *"a meditation on post-Civil War America."* Rybczynski explains how, after the national and personal trauma of the Civil War, Olmsted sought to use park design as a tonic to a shattered nation. Prospect Park provided *"a transcendental vision of a unified, peaceful country, in which the meadows represent agriculture, the wooded terrain is the American wilderness, and the lakeside terrace and its more refined architecture, civilization."* To those readers who are not steeped in landscape design, it may seem odd to think of the layout of an urban park as a vision of the future, or as symbolizing a larger social construct. And yet, Olmsted and his partner Vaux definitely conceived of their park designs as an art form. While they used natural elements, their designs were clearly artificial, an artform representing a highly idealized form of 'nature.'

In part of their proposal for Prospect Park, they spelled out their vision of landscape design as art, at the same time that they formally gave a name to their new profession (the emphasis is mine): *"A scene in nature is made up of various parts ... It is unlikely that accident should bring together the best possible ideals of each separate part ... and it is still more unlikely that accident should group a number of these possible ideals in such a way that not only one or two but that all should be harmoniously related one to the other. It is evident, however, that an attempt to accomplish this artificially is not impossible ... The* result would be a work of art, *and the combination of the art thus defined, with the art of architecture in the production of landscape compositions, is what we denominate landscape architecture."*[7]

Olmsted and his firm left a long legacy. He went on to design hundreds of parks, campuses, and estates all over the United States, and essentially invented the modern profession of landscape architecture. His sons continued the firm's work through the twentieth century, while also teaching at Harvard, thus greatly expanding the reach of the Olmsted philosophy across the country. Olmsted's work is remarkable in how it spans across centuries, starting with the influences of Burke and Gilpin from the eighteenth century; through the many philosophers and naturalists he encountered during the nineteenth century, such as Thomas Jefferson, John Ruskin, Andrew Jackson Downing, and John Muir; and the influence of his own work continuing through the twentieth and twenty-first centuries, as people continuously rediscover the nature of his art by simply walking through a park.

Rybczynki describes in the forward to his book how he came to learn about Olmstead and his influence in Canada and America. As a college student in Montréal he had loved to hike in *Mont Royal*, a local park encompassing a broad hill in the middle of its namesake city, surrounded by the Saint Lawrence River. (The park is commonly just called 'the Mountain' by locals.) *"I remember as a college student being told that the Mountain was the work of someone called Frederick Law Olmsted, the same man who designed Central Park (in New York City). Like most people, I took the landscape of the Mountain for granted; I thought that it was simply a nature preserve. Here was the most significant man-made object in Montreal—arguably the city's most important cultural artifact—and I thought of it as 'natural.' How wrong I was."*

New Urban Landscapes

If Olmstead's parks are a highly curated cultural artifact, where is the line between nature and man-made? Perhaps, per Yi-Fu Tuan, understanding the cultural landscape may be the more important task. Given that most people now live in cities, the urban landscape is increasingly becoming our cultural landscape. Ever fewer children grow up with nearby agricultural fields to roam or a creek to play in. Instead, their urban playgrounds are brightly-colored pre-fabricated play structures anchored to a carpet of chopped-up recycled tires, or else just the forgotten corners of cities, the weeds and cracked asphalt of an empty corner lot. Such early childhood experiences create a very different cultural context and expectation of what may constitute 'nature' and a beautiful view.

One of the earliest examples of the emergence of a new urban aesthetic is the quirky Gas Works Park in Seattle, that occupies the site of an old coal gasification plant. The gasification plant occupied a prime peninsula with views across the water to downtown Seattle. A considerable source of local pollution, the plant loomed menacingly over the community and fenced people off from the waterfront. When it finally closed down in 1956, a local landscape architect, Richard Haag, was hired to transform the contaminated site, covered with machinery and old tanks, gigantic pipes and smokestacks, into a public park.

Contrary to the wishes of the city councilwoman who had worked for decades to raise funds for remediation, Haag instead recommended preserving most of the structures on the site, as a form of historical urban sculpture. In his design, toxic industrial waste was encased in clay and covered with soil and grass to make mounds for picnic views and flying kites. Rusting pipes were painted and turned into climbing structures for children. Old tanks and towers were fenced off to remain as sentinels of the past. Richard Haag describes the motivation for his unusual design: "*I haunted the buildings and let the spirit of the place enjoin me. I began seeing what I liked, then I liked what I saw ... industrial middens were drumlins, the towers were ferro-forests and their brooding presence became the most sacred of symbols. I accepted these gifts, and decided to absolve the community's vindictive feel towards the gas plant.*"[8]

It took almost 20 years to open the park to the public. The public is still not allowed to enter the water or mud flats adjacent to the park, as the pollution levels are still too high. Ultimately the city councilwoman who led the charge to acquire the land for a public park disavowed the project, refusing to let her name be associated with the park since it did not restore the peninsula to a 'natural state.' Instead the park has become a home to many quirky Seattle celebrations, and has won Richard Haag great acclaim as the harbinger of a new style of urban landscape, the 'industrial preservation park.'

A similar 'industrial preservation park' was created in Duisberg, Germany, on the site of the old Thyssen iron smelters. A river that had been used as an open sewer was transformed into a variety of publicly accessible water pathways and reservoirs, cisterns were repurposed as garden areas. Many of the old industrial structures were left as historical landmarks, and some became climbing structures. Completed in 2002, the Landscape Park at Duisberg Nord was one of about 100 projects implemented to establish new ecological, economic, social and cultural resources in the old industrial Ruhr area.[9] These restoration projects were very much in line with Olmstead's efforts a century and a half earlier, per Rybcznski: *"trying to combine economics, aesthetics, landscaping, nature, moral and intellectual improvement, and salvation"* all in one landscaping project.

The industrial preservation park that has received the most attention in the United States is the High Line Park in New York City, a pedestrian parkway installed on an abandoned raised railway threading its way through a mile and a half of dense urban blocks in Manhattan. The High Line was modeled after a similar re-use of a railway line in Paris, the *Coulée vert René-Dumont*, otherwise known as the *Promenade plantée*, opened in 1993. The first leg of the High Line was opened in 2009, and the last was completed ten years later in 2019. However, that timeline betrays decades of painful history that led to its creation: first, beginning in 1847, 80 years of dangerous street-level railway line that resulted in hundreds of pedestrian deaths, then a brief 30 years of active use for the new elevated rail line serving a number of manufacturing buildings, followed by another 50 years of disuse and decay. The dilapidated railway became a strange anomaly in the city fabric, supporting a fringe of tough urban trees, bushes and grasses growing wild along the tracks high up above the streets: an eyesore to some and an intriguing refuge to others.

Now the carefully curated meadow grasses and diminutive trees that grow along the High Line speak to the reclamation of old structures by natural forces. A huge success with both locals and tourists, as of 2019, 10,000–20,000 people visited the parkway every day. In response to the opening of the High Line, local property values soared, and retail properties scrambled to capitalize on the increased pedestrian traffic.

The High Line park certainly provides an inspiring model for how an active parkway can be opened up through seemingly random voids found between existing buildings, transforming urban brownfields into a place more worthy of a view. In 2017, Seoul in South Korea transformed an inner-city highway into a 1 kilometer long 'Skygarden,' very similar to the High Line in concept. This raised pedestrian garden, open 24 hours a day, is located high above the Cheonggyecheon river, which also newly runs through the center of the city, restored to daylight after being covered over with concrete for decades. Singapore has announced plans to add parks and parkways such that 85% of its residents live within 400 meters of a green space. Interweaving more of the natural world back into cities seems to be the emerging project of the twenty-first century.

Given such wide-ranging attitudes towards nature and landscapes, we should ask, how do we distinguish mere fashion from foundational philosophy, art from artifice, biological imperatives from placebos? The next chapter considers the question further: how can we distinguish those qualities of a window view which might seem adequate and attractive, but without enduring benefits, versus those which are most inherently beneficial, and therefore worth preserving at considerable cost?

18. Biophilia and Technophilia

Edward O Wilson, a professor of biology at Yale University, first proposed a Biophilia Hypothesis in 1984. Wilson defined biophilia as *"the innate affiliation people seek with other organisms and especially with the natural world."*[1] He borrowed the term from American psychoanalyst Eric Fromm who earlier had used it in 1973 to describe *"the passionate love of life and of all that is alive."* From his work as an evolutionary biologist, Wilson strongly believes that there is a genetic basis to many aspects of human nature. He uses the term 'epigenetic' to describe processes that are encoded in our genes, but only activated under certain environmental conditions.

Wilson writes: *"Human nature is the collectivity of epigenetic rules, the inherited regularities of mental development. These rules are the genetic biases in the way our senses perceive the world, the symbolic coding by which we represent the world, the options we open to ourselves, and the responses we find easiest and most rewarding to make."* Thus, Wilson proposes that careful observations of what humans naturally do, that which comes most easily to us and gives us joy, are likely to provide insight into our inherited behavioral patterns, and into preferences and biases that are hardwired into our genes.

Wilson proposed biophilia as a scientific hypothesis that should be tested; however little formal testing has yet been done to prove or disprove the theory. Perhaps the most compelling evidence for biophilia to date comes from its polar opposite, bio-phobia, or fear of nature. For example, intrinsic fears of heights, spiders, and snakes have been documented with measurable physiological responses.[2] Logically, where fear and repulsion are naturally exhibited, attraction, and enjoyment may also be innate responses at the other end of the spectrum.

Yet, in spite of its lack of formal proof, the concept of biophilia has greatly captured the imagination of many people in the design community and of environmental psychologists. Biophilia is frequently mentioned as a rationale for provisions in green building criteria. A book published in 2008, *Biophilic Design*, provided dozens of essays by leading thinkers in the field. In the introductory chapter, editor Steven Kellert, also from Yale, describes over 70 potential elements and attributes of biophilic design.[3] Likewise Alex Wilson, executive editor of Environmental Building News, proposes another list of *29 Biophilic Design Strategies and Priorities.*[4] Over two thirds of the items on of this list directly address creating better view sheds and access to views. Thus, daylight and views to the outdoors tend to be high on designers' lists of how to enhance the biophilic component of their designs.

Steven and Rachel Kaplan, a married team of environmental psychologists, made a career of studying the human relationship with the environment, and taught generations of students at the University of Michigan. They formulated the Attention Restoration Theory, which postulated that exposure to nature helped to restore depleted attentional resources. The Kaplans conducted numerous studies trying to ferret out how exposure to 'nature' influenced behavior, attitudes, and attention. The Kaplans also extended the work of other researchers interested in landscape interactions, such as Jay Appleton who first proposed a theory of 'prospect and refuge' in 1975. Appleton's proposal was that humans naturally seek out environments where they both feel protected (refuge) and able to monitor their surrounds (prospect). This concept of 'prospect and refuge' has since become one of the most commonly cited theories informing environmental design.

The Kaplans expanded the concept of prospect and refuge to include an informational model whereby humans are considered to be naturally motivated to explore and understand their physical environment. They proposed four dimensions for the key qualities of views: *coherence, complexity, legibility,* and *mystery*. These theories and models have strongly influenced many generations of environmental psychologists. However, a recent meta-analysis of research studies based on these theories did not find consistent results over 30 years of studies.[5] It may be that the variables were imprecisely defined, or that the methodologies were inconsistent. However, the outcome of such a meta-analysis does provide a cautionary tale that the rigorous criteria applied to other scientific literature is often still lacking in the study of environmental design.

'Nature Contact' and Public Health

In 2017, Dr. Howard Frumkin, then Dean of the University of Washington School of Public Health in Seattle, along with ten other colleagues, undertook a review of recent research on nature contact and human health.[6] Citing the biophilia hypothesis as an open question, they provided a wide-ranging summary and critique of the range of existing studies and their limitations. Key in this discussion are ambiguities about *"what constitutes nature contact?"* and indeed, *"what constitutes nature?"* And while they found the breadth of available evidence compelling, they concluded that *"large gaps remain in our understanding."* They proceeded to propose a coordinated research agenda that could help identify causal relationships and introduce more rigor to evidence-based design interventions.

While Frumkin and his team undertook a broad, cross-disciplinary approach, which included window views as a form of nature contact, it is disconcerting to note that their literature review leaves out any mention of daylight exposure or circadian stimulus as a possible mechanism for 'nature contact' benefits. Such an omission only emphasizes how little awareness various research disciplines have of each other's work. In searching for precise measures of nature exposure, Frumkin's team noted that: *"much contemporary research focuses on* greenspace *as the exposure of interest, perhaps because of ease of measurement ..."* Let's take a closer look at one of the most compelling of these recent 'greenspace' studies.

The Chan School of Public Health at Harvard University has recently started applying classic epidemiological methods to the study of health and the built environment. Using large datasets available to medical researchers, they have added information about the nearby outdoor environment via GPS (global positioning system) databases and LiDAR (Light + RADAR) imagery and monitoring. In a landmark paper published in 2016, the group reported on a study of the health and mortality of over 100,000 American women from the national Nurses' Health Study over the course of eight years.[7] The greenness surrounding their home address was quantified using LiDAR satellite imagery, within both a one block and a five block area. The greenery data was updated four times per year to account for seasonal effects, and the addresses were updated if the women moved. Over the study time span, 8% of the women died.

The study found that, after accounting for other risk factors such as age, ethnicity, smoking, local pollution, and economic status, those women who had the most access to greenery near their homes had a 12% lower rate of non-accidental mortality compared to women with the least. Their death certificates were examined for cause of death. Accidental deaths, such as from car accidents, were not correlated to the surrounding level of greenness, which is logically consistent and thus a reassuring negative finding. Causes of death that were most significantly reduced in association with increased greenness included cancers, and respiratory and kidney diseases. This methodology has been replicated at a smaller scale in various European and American cities, with very similar findings.

The public health implications of this study are difficult to overstate: daily access to more greenery significantly lowers mortality rates from many diseases! While the findings are dramatic, demographic studies like these do not help to elucidate the physiological, psychological, or behavioral mechanisms that are responsible for these important effects. More detailed studies are needed to try to isolate specific pathways that enable these observed outcomes, and certainly a better understanding of which aspects of 'greenery' and 'nature contact' are involved.

Actual Versus Simulated Nature

As mentioned earlier, many researchers trying to understand the human response to nature, whether via window views or a walk outdoors, have resorted to the convenience of substituting images of nature for the real thing. The assumption is that if looking at nature is purely a visual phenomenon, then any kind of image should be a sufficient substitute. Early on, studies used photographs, printed on cards or posters, and sometimes projected images, which were thus luminous. With the dawn of the digital age, such tests transferred to computer screens or TVs, including videos with soundtracks. The latest technologies to grab researchers' fancy are forms of virtual reality where participants, wearing a headset, can visually navigate around a 3D image of a space using their own head and body movements.

The question logically arises then: how valid are such substitutions? This is a challenging question, since clearly, the technologies are a moving target. If posters are a reasonable substitute, as some people believe, then surely videos or virtual reality are even better! A handful of researchers have tried to answer this question.

Coralie Cauwerts at the Catholic University of Louvain, in Belgium, wanted to learn which types of visual experiences could be considered valid research surrogates for the real world. She conducted a study where participants were asked to assess the visual and emotional parameters of a given spatial experience, while viewing images or within the actual space. She tested two-dimensional sketched and photographic images, three-dimensional computer-rendered images, plus an early version of virtual reality, called Quick Time Virtual Reality. She found that, across the board, the virtual reality experience had much more in common with the photographic or rendered images than with the real experience.[8]

A research group in Hong Kong took another approach: they compared a simulated window view to no view, with or without real potted plants. This group was particularly interested in how to improve the experience of underground workspaces (which are becoming increasingly prevalent in large Asian cities). They set up an underground laboratory with four conditions: a control condition, with just furniture and bare walls; the same setup but with six living plants; the same furniture set up with curtains drawn to reveal a projected image of a city park set inside a window frame; and then a combination of the live plants and projected image. They recruited the usual college student participants and collected their subjective evaluations of the quality of the space, their electrodermal activity, and their response time to simple computer tasks. They reported that the live house plants improved the subjective evaluations of the space and improved task response time, whereas the artificial window had the opposite effect. (The electrodermal measurements, which are thought to measure arousal, did not show any significant variations among the four conditions.) The researchers concluded that, while living plants could be used to improve windowless underground spaces, further work was needed to make artificial windows more realistic.[9] This is indeed a logical conclusion when the assumption is that working in windowless underground spaces is inevitable, and the primary challenge is to improve them. It is unfortunate and ironic, however, that they had no experience of a real view for comparison.

Shinrin-Yoku

Masahiro Hirouchi and his colleagues at the Mount Fuji Research Institute in Japan conducted the opposite experiment: they removed a real view. They are part of the research team in Japan trying to document tangible and intangible benefits of 'forest bathing,' whereby people are advised to spend a few hours per month immersed in a natural forest. Forest bathing is somewhat similar in concept to sunbathing—full body immersion in a healthful environment. The Japanese are very serious about their forest bathing, *shinrin-yoku*, first introduced as a medical concept in the 1990s. The first rigorous experimental studies began in 2004, and have since continued to accelerate in number, scope, and detail, focused on trying to understand the specific inputs, outcomes, and causal mechanisms of what they believe to be a profound and reliable benefit from spending time outside, specifically in a forest. It may be that the Japanese researchers will assemble the most concrete evidence of changes in physiology attributable to biophilic experiences. Based on the findings to date, the Japanese government has since created dozens of certified forest-therapy bases, where doctors can prescribe therapeutic time in the forest to treat a variety of conditions, especially those related to stress.

Hirouchi and his team took 15 volunteers into the forest and had them each sit in a large, loosely constructed tent. For 15 minutes of the experiment the fabric tent wall looking out into the forest was open, and for another 15 minutes it was closed. Thus, the participants experienced essentially the same environment—the same sounds, the same smells, the same air quality, breeze, and air temperature. The primary difference between the two conditions was an unobstructed view or a blank curtain. Overall, they found that when the subjects were looking out into the forest, their cognitive and psychological indicators improved, but their cardiovascular profiles did not change.

Dr. Qing Li, who leads the forest-therapy research at Nippon Medical School in Tokyo has written a book in English, explaining his findings to a lay audience. He attributes the benefits of time in the forest to a number of factors including multisensory stimulation, such as rich visual patterns and sounds, plus chemical interactions with soil microbes and particles in the air released by trees (phytocides). Not coincidentally, Li finds many parallels between the concept of biophilia and Japanese traditions of nature worship in both the Shinto and Buddhist religions. There is *yūgen*, "*the profound sense of the beauty and mystery of the universe*," and *shizen*, one of the seven principles of Zen aesthetics. He writes: "*The idea behind shizen is that we are all connected to nature, emotionally, spiritually and physically; and the more closely something relates to nature, the more pleasing it is, whether it's a spoon, or a piece of furniture, or the way a house is decorated.*"[10]

Technological Nature

Peter Kahn and his team in the Department of Psychology at the University of Washington in Seattle are concerned that the theory of biophilia is cast so broadly that it can never be confirmed, or disproved. They have been trying to take a disciplined approach to testing sub-hypotheses derived from Wilson's theory of biophilia, asking researchable questions such as: "*Does biophilia also include love of non-living nature, such as canyons, caves and geysers?*" Or "*Do the benefits of nature break down somewhere along the continuum from full nature immersion to analog viewing?"* As such, they have been investigating 'technological nature,' i.e. various forms of technologies that simulate nature, such as robotic animals, videos and live webcams of nature, and immersive virtual environments.[11]

More fundamentally, Kahn asks the question: *"Two world trends are powerfully reshaping human existence: the degradation, if not destruction, of large parts of the natural world, and unprecedented technological development. At the nexus of these two trends lies technological nature—technologies that in various ways mediate, augment, or simulate the natural world ... Does it matter for the physical and psychological well-being of the human species that actual nature is being replaced with technological nature?"*

Kahn has conducted a number of clever experiments to explore this question. To consider the question most relevant to this book: *"Can simulated views usefully replace real window views?"* he conducted a series of experiments with large high-definition plasma televisions. In a pilot experiment he installed these TVs in seven faculty and staff offices that had previously only had blank walls. The TVs continuously displayed real-time images of local nature outside of the building. After 16 weeks of exposure, the participants reported that they enjoyed their plasma-display windows and seemed to benefit both psychologically and cognitively. All of the participants reported they would prefer a plasma-TV-pseudo-window over a windowless office.

Kahn then conducted a laboratory-based experiment, where subjects were recruited to experience one of three conditions: 1) the laboratory room with a real window view of the outdoors; 2) the same room with a curtain covering the window; or 3) the same room with a plasma-TV-pseudo-window displaying essentially the same image as the real window. The research team tracked participants' heart rate and where they were looking throughout the experiment. In this case, with measured physiological indicators, the researchers found no difference between outcomes in the blank wall room versus the pseudo-window room. However, in the real-window room participants' heart rate recovered faster, and the more time they spent looking out of the real window, the more rapidly it recovered.

Kahn concludes that, when considering both the pilot and laboratory studies together, *"the plasma nature window appears better than no nature, but not as good as actual nature."* He found a similar pattern with his other studies of simulated nature, such as robotic pets, where the simulated nature has some positive effect, but not nearly as much as the real thing. Given this, Kahn has a deeper worry, based on the 'shifting baseline syndrome,' where people tend to lower their expectations about what is *normal* as environmental conditions slowly degrade over time. He terms this problem 'environmental generational amnesia.'

Kahn describes a rather bleak view of the process: "*Let us imagine that, as more research emerges on the topic of technological nature, the general trend we have found so far holds up: namely, that interacting with technological nature provides some but not all of the enjoyments and benefits of interacting with actual nature. At first glance, such a finding would speak to how we can improve human life: When actual nature is not available, substitute technological nature. But such substitutions contribute to an insidious problem. Let us explain ...*"

"*... members of each generation construct their conception of what is environmentally normal based on the natural world they encountered in childhood. The crux is that, with each ensuing generation, the amount of environmental degradation can increase, but each generation tends to take that degraded condition as the ... normal experience.*"

"*We will be drawn to increasingly sophisticated and pervasive forms of technological nature, which will provide some but not all of the benefits of actual nature. In turn, there will be a downward shift (as there has been already) in the baseline across generations for what counts as a full measure of the human experience and of human flourishing.*"

Nan Zhoa of the MIT Media Lab is one of the researchers developing new ideas for how 'technological nature' can be integrated into our workplaces and personalized for each worker. She is working on a concept she calls 'Mediated Atmosphere,' intended to create a virtual environment for office workers, whereby they can always be surrounded by an optimal environmental condition created via multi-sensory simulation. Her website explains: "*Using modular, real-time control infrastructure with bio-signal sensors, controllable lighting, projection, and sound, Mediated Atmosphere creates immersive environments designed to help users focus, de-stress, and work comfortably.*"

The idea is that with non-invasive 'bio-signal sensors' which can detect a person's body temperature, activity level, facial expression, heart rate variability, or perhaps even visual focus, a computer could select an appropriate ambient environment for an individual worker, to either calm or stimulate them, as needed for an appropriate counterbalance. Alternatively, a worker might designate preferred parameters on a sliding scale, such as natural versus urban, quiet versus noisy, or social versus private. Based on these inputs, the computer could then offer up a selection of ambient space types, such as 'coffee house,' 'library,' 'babbling brook,' or 'deep forest,' adjusting the video image surrounding the workstation, plus ambient lighting, air movement, sounds, and maybe even fragrance to match. Explains Zhao: "*We want to create an 'environment player' that can recommend or automate your space similar to how Spotify or Pandora gives you access to a world of music. We want to help people to manage their day by giving them the right place at the right time.*"

Nan Zhao's research sponsors include national and international manufacturers of lighting systems, acoustic environments, and furniture systems. Logically, if these companies can incorporate the benefits of windows and views into their products, then they have added an important feature to their product which increases its value. It makes sense that if the quality of a view is a key financial asset of a building, worth millions of dollars on the real estate market, then it could also be worth investing in simulated views to help sell a product such as a furniture or an audio-visual system. Furthermore, this value would then be under their marketing control and pricing, while subtracting that value from building design and urban infrastructure. Location becomes less important. Building design becomes less important. If so, then people can be optimally productive anywhere, in the depths of a warehouse or working underground. It is clear that Zhao is working on developing that 'better artificial window' that the Hong Kong researchers envisioned.

There are many commercial companies already at work perfecting their version of simulated windows or skylights, to deliver a facsimile of daylight or window views wherever desired. For example, the Sky Factory, founded in 2002 in Fairfield, Iowa is moving onto third and fourth generation video-simulated skylights, priding themselves on high-quality 'biophilic illusions,' where even a basement room can have a bright blue sky on a dark and stormy day.[12] Many of their clients are hospitals, seeking to make their massive medical buildings more humane. At what point, we should ask, does such an effort become a mere placebo, substituting simulated experience for authentic experience? Or, more perniciously, when do such technologies further enable the very problem they were hoping to correct?

Biophilic Billboards

The lobby of the new Salesforce Tower in San Francisco, which sits atop that city's transit hub and is currently the city's tallest office tower, provides another tale of an immersive video environment, that may, or may not, provide insight into the future direction of biophilic design. The lobby features a monumental high-definition video display, ten feet tall and spanning the full 108 foot width of the building's lobby. Mike Mazza, Salesforce's Brand Manager in charge of the company's image, realized that this screen in the tower's lobby offered an important opportunity to express the company's new presence in San Francisco. In a video interview, he describes the opportunity: *"Imagine the lobby before the screen—a lot of granite, a lot of glass and a few elevators—a very sterile place ... We had a 100 foot lobby screen, this amazing blank canvas. What do we do with it?"*[13]

Mazza envisioned that the giant video wall could become a dynamic canvas to celebrate California's natural beauty, and so hired Obscura, the same media company that produced the Lumina high-rise apartments simulated-views sales room (see page 238), to create another video masterpiece. He thought the huge video wall could *"function like a window, or a giant painting"* for the thousands of office workers who pass in and out of the building lobby on a daily basis, offering them awe and wonder at the natural environment, rather than just more urban granite and glass.

The image designers at Obscura were given artistic license to use their cinematic and computer graphic wizardry to *"bring life to the lobby."* They set out to capture the essence of the redwood forest experience. Packing a camera crew up into the virgin redwood forests between California and Oregon, they used multiple large format cameras to develop a composite stereo image that could be projected onto the LED screen in full size and real time. Web images of the lobby screen show the resulting evergreen forest waving gently in the breeze, extending into the infinite distance, while in the foreground giant redwood tree trunks tower above the people in the lobby. The Obscura digital artists then sprinkled digital pixy-dust about the image: improbable little visual jokes that are hidden *"like Easter Eggs"* within the visual complexity of the forest. A tiny man, antlike, walks directly up the side of a tree. A strange white object lurks behind a tree trunk, floating slowly into view.

The redwood forest video was just the beginning. The digital artists at Obscura created other videos via computer wizardry, some to resemble real environments, others complete visual fantasy. They called their design goal 'hyper reality.' The video loops change frequently: at one point the people in the lobby are surrounded by giant fish, swimming though a clear mountain stream. Then, courtesy of computer-generated imagery (CGI), the wall transforms into a massive waterfall, with water splashing wildly over each elevator lobby entrance.

On a recent trip to San Francisco, I wanted to experience the immersive lobby myself. Walking downtown with a few friends late one winter afternoon, we first discovered that there was not just one giant lobby screen, but four, since the company now occupied all four buildings at the corner of Mission and Fremont streets. Each building had its own massive video wall, each playing a different 'channel,' so to speak, rotating through various animated images like a giant screen saver. As we watched through the lobby windows, the huge videos lit up the street with their colors and flashes, not unlike the massive animated advertisements that line the façades of buildings in New York's Times Square. (The City of San Francisco soberly required Salesforce to keep all their video displays inside the buildings.)

My friends and I finally made our way to the original and biggest screen in the Salesforce Tower lobby. I was hoping to experience the full force of the redwood forest, or to have CGI water poured over my head. Instead, the lobby had been turned into an immersive environment for the company's latest human resources campaign, code name 'Trailblazers.' Trailblazers featured cute cartoon animals and a cartoon Albert Einstein finding their way through a cartoon national park. The video animation was crude—crude enough to embarrass a Saturday-morning children's TV program. The lobby was also full of giant stuffed animals, kiosks and booths packed with promotional literature, all left over from the big sales convention held earlier that month. Thus, through the infinite flexibility of digital programming, the lobby of the city's new transit hub was no longer a testament to the natural beauty of California, or even the digital artistry of the Obscura team, but rather merely a very high-tech billboard for the company's branding campaigns.

Technophilia

In all of these stories I think there is a recurring theme of 'technophilia.' Technophilia can make for a strange bedfellow with biophilia. Although a term usually applied to a love of all things digital in the twenty-first century, technophilia can also be defined as an innate human love of technology. The technophile sees a utopian future in the application of new technology, while the technophobe sees potential danger, dependency, or addiction. Humans have been inventing things for a long time, and we tend to be very impressed with how clever we can be. An interesting analogy might be with the development of music.

Steven Paolini, founder of the digital lighting company Telelumen, speaks of wanting to create 'daylight replicators' which can both record and play back the subtle changes of natural daylight, via elaborately controlled LED light sources. His concept is that multi-colored LED light sources can be programmed to provide the same gradual transitions in lighting quality that we would normally experience in a beautifully daylit space. Paolini often uses the metaphor that his daylight replicators may be similar to recording music, so that the dynamics of daylight can be captured and played back with high fidelity like a symphony, enjoyed whenever desired.

Daniel Levitin, the neurologist quoted earlier who studies music and brains, makes an important point that music is not 'natural.' It does not exist in nature. Yes, there are certainly lovely natural sounds—waterfalls, bird song, leaves in a breeze—that we love to listen to; but music per se is constructed by humans. From Neolithic drums and flutes, to today's digital play-lists and Dolby Surround Sound, we humans continue to be enthralled with the music that we make.

Levitin writes about the art of composing music: "*Composers imbue music with emotion by knowing what our expectations are and then very deliberately controlling when those expectations will be met, and when they won't. The thrills, chills and tears we experience from music are the result of having our expectations artfully manipulated by a skilled composer and the musicians who interpret that music.*"[14] This description reads very much like the goals of the Obscura digital artists in composing the videos for the Salesforce lobby screens, manipulating our expectations of a natural image, and then providing subtle changes from those expectations.

Levitin explicitly compares modern electronic music to other modern visual forms such as videos, and explains the intrinsic fascination that can result: "*Recording engineers and musicians have learned to create special effects that tickle our brains by exploiting neural circuits that evolved to discern important features of our auditory environment. These special effects are similar in principle to 3-D art, motion picture, or visual illusions, none of which have been around long enough for our brains to have evolved special mechanisms to perceive them [accurately]; rather, they leverage perceptual systems that are in place to accomplish other things. Because they use these neural circuits in novel ways, we find them especially interesting.*"

This line of thinking would argue that all visual illusions, whether from a Renaissance fresco or a giant digital screen, are an art form that can be appreciated as such. But, as Levitin points out, they are "*leveraging perceptual systems*" which evolved to perceive the real world, and then subtly manipulating expectations to maintain the illusion and "*tickle our brains.*" The more we understand about how the brain makes sense of visual sensations, the more sophisticated we can be in creating those illusions and artfully manipulating them to tickle our brains.

And here, I think, is the critical question to consider: should we? Should we have as a social goal the creation of technologically advanced visual illusions that can enthrall their audience, or create a perfect placebo so that the true natural world is not missed? As Peter Kahn worries, does the acceptance of various automated 'technological nature' devices lower our expectations for authentic experience?

On the one hand, daylighting replicators and simulated windows providing biophilic illusions offer the possibility of a new art form, focused on beauty and ambiguity, or provocative and controversial, either of which might continue to delight and intrigue us. Architectural-scale video images might just be considered high-tech super graphics, updated from 1970s fashion, or modern versions of the monumental frescos of the Renaissance. On the other hand, isn't it reasonable to wonder what happens after the audience becomes inured to the incessant video loops, walking under the CGI waterfall over and over again? The sheer amazement at the technological virtuosity quickly fades as we become desensitized and then expect ever more spectacular achievements. Entertainment technology tends to traffic in surprise and awe, with a need to continuously intensify the experience.

The deeper lesson from the Salesforce Tower story may be that wherever there is an infinitely programable surface, like an LED screen, it will tend to become irresistible to marketers. When any organization controls the 'simulated window,' the allure of using programable digital media for public communication and advertising is just too tempting for the company to resist, such that even with the best intentions, simulated windows will also always be latent billboards.

Figure 18.1: Artificial windows may become obsolete, incompatible, or simply fail

As an alternative perspective, in one of my many interviews with office workers, I was especially struck by a computer manager who had specifically chosen to work in the only private office in the building that had absolutely no access to any daylight or views. I asked him why he chose this dark interior office. He explained that he was tired of getting moved around, and he knew that nobody would try to take this windowless office away from him! Thus, he felt that with this office he had permanency and complete control of his personal environment. Because it was so private, he explained, he could even keep his dog with him in his office during the day. Then I noticed the screen savers on his two big computer monitors, plus an additional digital picture frame on his desk, each slowly rotating through an array of photos of his family and their recent camping trips. Mountain sides and seascapes surrounded him, while nature slept at his feet in the form of his dog. He was personally in control of his simulated window views, which happily reminded him of his loved ones and their time together on vacation. Furthermore, he said whenever he felt the need for some more daylight, he just took his dog outside for a walk. He felt happily in control of his own environmental choices.

19. Synthesis and Next Steps

Whenever I give a lecture about the importance of daylight and views in our buildings, I can always count on at least one person, usually standing in the back of the room, asking the question: *"But can't we just simulate that? What if there was a webcam that continuously took a video from the roof of the building which was displayed on screens around the building? Wouldn't that be good enough?"*

Peter Kahn attempted to answer that question with his experiments. He found that people preferred an office with a webcam simulated window when the only alternative was an interior windowless office. But he also found that none of the measurable physiological and cognitive benefits of real windows transferred to the webcam version. Thus, my answer is generally: *"Something is probably better than nothing, but why should we have to settle for technological substitutions for real life?"*

Solutions that will endure for generations are surely more valuable than those that may last only until the next technology upgrade. And direct information about the world in real time is far superior to a simulation that attempts to be *"good enough,"* determined by someone else's priorities. Certainly, I tend to give primacy to architectural solutions because I am an architect, and my profession is about making physical places that are supportive of human life and activities. I acknowledge that there are many solutions possible for every problem, and that 'technological nature' and 'biophilic illusions' may sometimes serve a useful function. However, I also think there is an important societal choice to be made, of where to invest our creative energy in developing solutions that will benefit generations to come.

Thus, I want to advocate for a pervasive effort to design cities and buildings, and retrofit all existing places, to include daylight and view as an essential ingredient of people's daily lives. Who can make this happen? How can we, as a society, make this a priority and sustain the effort long enough to have a permanent impact? And, ultimately, can we fully grasp all the intersecting ways that daylight and views contribute to the well-being and delight of occupants? This chapter takes on those questions.

Professional Roles and Opportunities

A cultural commitment to daylight and views will involve thoughtful contributions from everyone who touches our buildings: city planners, landscape designers, architects, engineers, interior designers, lighting designers, building owners, managers, and occupants. It will flow from policies, products, and procedures all predicated on the fundamental value of a healthy human habitat.

It should be built into the most permanent aspects of our cities—urban density and voids, property lines and orientation, building form and façade. We learned from Stewart Brand's book *How Buildings Learn* that *Site*, *Structure* and *Surface* are very persistent, often over centuries and sometimes even millennia. In other words, the form of our cities and the form of our buildings are some of the most permanent interventions that we make in shaping our physical environment. Working to create cities that have a good balance of density and voids, of built space and green space, enables more access to daylight and views in the interior of buildings. The shaping of cities is always a work in progress. While some cities may change very slowly, *all* cities will eventually change over time. If everyone making decisions about changes to the physical shape of a city—such as new roadways, new buildings, new parks, what to preserve and what to tear down—gives primacy to the importance of view and daylight, then access can be gradually improved even in the densest or oldest cities.

Rehabilitating older buildings, especially those built before the Second World War, before the dominance of modern mechanical ventilation systems and electric lighting reduced the imperative for windows and daylight, is one of the easier paths to enhancing access to daylight and views. However, given the will, any existing building can be improved. Existing windows can be upgraded. New windows can be added. Often, an even more attractive option for retrofits is to add skylights and atria, bringing in daylight from above.

Within existing buildings, prioritizing the location of spaces where occupants spend the majority of their day to be within the daylit zones is another logical step. For example, why not locate the cafeteria or break lounge at the top of the building instead of in the basement? Interior designers can have a huge impact on daylight and view accessibility, by selecting window treatments and controls that make it easier for occupants to manage their relationship with windows, allowing workers to fluidly transition from outward to inward focus, or from social engagement to privacy. Likewise, building managers can acknowledge the primacy of daylight and view by allowing occupants to choose the visual conditions that they find the most comfortable, and to personally modify them as appropriate. If both building managers and occupants have a wider variety of space conditions and window management options available, instead of a 'one-size-fits-all' approach, it is more likely that everyone will be able to find their happy balance.

Ultimately, in order to make the primacy of daylight and view a permanent feature of our cities and buildings, we need to reach across generations to convey the importance of this as a societal priority. First of all, everyone should understand that the design of cities and buildings is a social choice, not a given. Helping students to learn the history of the built environment is key, and especially *first-hand* experience of how daylight and views have been optimized in cities and buildings over the centuries. As I learned during my retail studies, the direct experience of beautifully daylit spaces is the most compelling way for people to grasp the difference between artificially and naturally illuminated spaces.

To further realize this vision, academic programs can help by documenting and analyzing the greatest achievements, and evaluating the successes or failures of new design approaches. Case studies of real buildings help students directly observe details and consequences of design choices. We also can convey the importance of successful buildings by giving them awards, honoring their designers, preserving them for posterity, or by declaring them sacred in some form. Owners love to display a special star of recognition on their building. A visitor to such honored buildings is thereby advised to take notice, to look a little deeper, to pause for a moment in order to better remember what happens there.

We can also convey the social importance of daylight and views by mandating access to them in building codes and design standards. Of course, in order to do so, there need to be tools, metrics, and guidelines that accurately predict success. Thus, research is needed to develop those tools and metrics, and case studies to analyze success or understand failure. Finally, market demand is a very powerful force. Tenants who insist upon good daylight raise its market value. Workers who insist that they have a right to daylight and views in their workplaces change the financial equation for landlords and building owners. Each voice, asking for more, has an impact. There is a lot to do, by all of us, in order to secure a long-term future with healthier buildings.

Neutra's Concepts of Bio-Realism and Perilous Nonsense

I had an interesting experience with cross-generational communication one day when I was invited to give a lecture at the Parson's School of Design in New York City. Richard Neutra, the famous Los Angeles architect, and I were apparently soul mates, but I only discovered this more than 40 years after he died. In the 1960s, when I was a teenager and he was an old man, we were both living in Los Angeles, distressed by the environmental degradation all around us, and wishing that someone would take up the cause to improve it.

I grew up in the ether that Neutra helped create in mid-century Los Angeles. I went to school in buildings influenced by his ideas. I visited my father working in modern buildings that mimicked Neutra's designs. As an adolescent interested in architecture, I even knew his name and saw plenty of glossy photographs of his homes and buildings around town. But I did not know then that our paths would cross.

In 1969, a year before he died, he wrote an impassioned plea to the architectural profession, called *Cross Section of a Credo*,[1] written as a design manifesto much in the style of other charismatic twentieth-century architects, such as Le Corbusier and Frank Lloyd Wright. Neutra's plea was for the profession to step outside of its normal boundaries and to embrace a much broader sense of responsibility for how humans could and should relate to their environment:

"As an architect, my life has been governed by the goal of building environmental harmony, functional efficiency, and human enhancement into the experience of everyday living. These things go together, constituting the cause of architecture ... Shaping man's surroundings entails a lot more than spatial, structural, mechanical and other technical considerations, certainly a lot more than pontificating about matters of style ... Our organic wellbeing is dependent on a wholesome salubrious environment, therefore exacting attention has to be paid to our intricate sensory world."

"This is primary if our surroundings are to stimulate our abundant perceptual, intellectual and spiritual capacities, while at the same time accommodating our physiological nature, and functional needs in a durable fashion ... Architecture is charged with influential memories and tenacious emotions, expectant hopes and stark practicalities, with moral obligations and written contracts. It never lets up. It is a full blast occupation ..."

"I have framed these miscellaneous essays for those who can kindle this kind of resolve. The coming couple of generations, their moral imagination is most needed now ... My musings are for an interdisciplinary spectrum of students of whatever age; people who have not stopped thinking because they have convinced themselves that they have all the answers ..."

In 1969, as Neutra was writing this final essay, I had just graduated from high school and was heading off to study architecture at UC Berkeley. Somehow, I hoped I could help create better cities than the version I had grown up with in Los Angeles. I had been told that in order to become a city planner first you had to be trained as an architect. But when I arrived at Berkeley, I was dismayed by the core curriculum in the architecture program. I would have to take three years of dry required courses—more calculus and physics, plus drafting methods and concrete structures—before I was ever allowed to take an elective. How, I wondered, could the architecture department be so very sure about what exactly I needed to learn that they could offer me no choices? I was in far too much of an adolescent's hurry to save the environment.

Instead, I quickly opted into a new experimental major called Conservation of Natural Resources that would allow me to take courses ranging across every department in the University. I took biology, physiology, ecology, statistics, economics, anthropology, law, and journalism classes. This was during the great 1970's wave of enthusiasm for interdisciplinary studies. (This experimental major proved so successful it was made permanent, then became its own department, and then a college!) The intellectual freedom I found across disciplines was heady. Eventually I was also able to enroll in some upper-level architecture and urban planning classes, which inspired me to recommit to my original dream.

My first job out of college was working for Christopher Alexander, then a UC Berkeley professor highly regarded as an architectural theoretician. He had a consulting job to help plan a new town in the Canary Islands with a famous Spanish architect, César Manrique. It was an amazing opportunity to rub shoulders with some visionary thinkers. But while I admired Alexander's writings, I quickly concluded that working for him directly was not my cup of tea. Fortunately, however, the brief experience helped get me into graduate school, where I could finally learn how to become a real architect. While there, far across the country in Boston, I became more interested in California's architectural history. Whenever I traveled back home, I visited buildings by famous architects. I recognized that Neutra's designs provided an important precedent for all that I knew about modern Los Angeles; but still I did not read his writings.

Learning about Neutra's deeper motivations had to wait for an evening on the Parson's stage in 2011 when we were brought together by Jonsara Ruth, Professor of Interior Design, who had organized a symposium called *Immaterial Environments*.[2] I was there to speak about *Thermal Delight*, and how such an intangible sensory experience as thermal comfort could inform architectural design. The event was opened with a dramatic reading of Richard Neutra's essay by Karen Ludwig, a Professor of Theater Arts. At first, I thought it was an odd choice, to open a symposium with a reading of a rather strident manifesto from an architect who had been dead for decades. But as the actress read Neutra's words, I realized that he was speaking directly to me, especially to the high school student I had once been. He clearly loved words as much as he loved buildings, and was trying his best to reach out across time. Finally, we connected.

Although Neutra was highly technical, he always saw all aspects of life as interconnected. He wrote about the need for an architectural profession that respected the environment, that was multi-disciplinary, and especially that recognized the intimate relationship between humans and their environment. In this final essay he wrote: *"The processes of life are dynamic and interwoven ... as imperceptible or subtle as this impact often is, our very health is tethered to nature's principal cycles and rhythmic fields of force ... Lawyers are not independent of the courtrooms in which they plead their cases ... teachers and students are not independent of the classroom in which education unfolds ... The environment ties us together, it determines who we are, how we feel ... it colors our behavior and in even more subtle ways shapes our beliefs, our values, vitality and productivity."*

Neutra called his design philosophy 'bio-realism,' based on a foundation of understanding the biological forces that shaped human evolution. He pleaded with his readers to continue forward with further evolution of this understanding: *"I have built up my philosophy of bio-realism ... over half a century. But this does not mean that it has any complacent or pedantic finality. It bristles with unanswered questions. Hopefully what I have to say will impel you to appraise the environment from your own angle of perception, experience and expertise. And to widen this angle as you think about what insights and skills you can bring to its enhancement."*

What a call to action! "*It* bristles *with unanswered questions,*" he said. The year 1969 saw the amazing achievement of the first human walking on the moon. Neutra called for a similar level of collaboration across disciplines to help create a healthier built environment for humans: "*This is a collaborative mission, as expansive and significant as any we might undertake to the moon or Mars. People of many different callings, lines of work and educational backgrounds must participate, especially in our era of super-specialization. We must never be lulled into believing that any one academic discipline or professional field can grapple with such a comprehensive, complex challenge ... The old dualistic notion that the interior and exterior forces of the world are segregated is perilous nonsense. The common denominator of our evolutionary nature must, therefore, be held sacrosanct and nurtured ... a synthesis of our physiological, our sensory, our psychological and spiritual qualities ...*"

I stood on the stage at Parson's, stunned to hear these words spoken to me 40 years after they were written. My book *Thermal Delight* was specifically written to promote "*a synthesis of our physiological, our sensory, our psychological and spiritual qualities*" with its four chapters, titled *Necessity, Delight, Affection,* and *Sacredness.* I discovered that Neutra and I had organized our discussion of design using the exactly the same four-layered structure, a structure I have found useful many times for the way it allows a deep dive into a topic, and which I have repeated in this book. I realized that I had been spending my entire career trying to realize Neutra's vision of a more interdisciplinary profession "*governed by the goal of building environmental harmony, functional efficiency, and human enhancement into the* experience of everyday living." Of course, I hope you will choose to do the same.

Research Challenges and Emergent Properties

Since Neutra's time, architectural research, environmental psychology, and related research on human interactions with the physical environment has started to blossom, as we have seen in the many examples cited in this book. There are now a wide range of professional associations and journals devoted to research on cross disciplinary and overarching topics, and just as many specialized journals, for lighting, thermal comfort, indoor air quality, low-energy, high-performance, green and sustainable buildings. Choose a new buzz-word and a journal will spring up. Yet this very proliferation of journals threatens to reinforce the isolation of disciplines rather than knitting them together. Each group of specialists has its preferred conferences and list of publishing venues. Given this proliferation, it is increasingly challenging to follow research done outside of one's own field, and difficult to gauge its value.

Interdisciplinary research is often still the kiss of death for many an academic, as their colleagues are clueless about how to evaluate its quality or impact.

Furthermore, in pursuing such research, there is a continuing conflict between the convenience of reductionist, laboratory-based research, and more holistic methods that attempt to understand phenomena in context. Reductionist science suits an engineering mindset, where each factor influencing a system can be identified, isolated and assigned a mathematical relationship to the outcome of interest. However, such research also assumes that the broader system is understood, and we are just working to fill in the details. Holistic research, on the other hand, is better suited to the life sciences—the biologist, the ecologist, and the medical professions—where it is understood that the whole is greater than the sum of the parts. Another way to phrase this is that complex systems often exhibit 'emergent properties' that cannot be observed independently of the operation of the whole system.

Given all the complexities that have been addressed in this book—ranging, for example, across circadian physiology, vision and cognitive science, business management and urban design—we would be well advised to try first to understand the challenge of daylight and view in buildings holistically, before we try to reduce it to its component parts. And needless to say, holistic studies require knowledge from an extremely wide range of perspectives, guided by someone who can intelligently converse with every expert involved. Vitruvius, the Roman architect, admirably described this problem back in the first century CE, and cited in the introduction to this book. Neutra pleaded for it in his essays. Likewise, throughout this book I have drawn from a wide array of resources, from quantitative research to personal experience, to detail the broad reach of daylight and views on the occupants of buildings. To make further progress, we will need both compelling hypotheses and coordinated research. In this effort, I'd recommend that future research efforts be balanced like a three-legged stool, using three very different methodological approaches to triangulate towards a common understanding of the problem and its solution.

The Three-Legged Stool

One of the three legs, as I see them, is clinical work. In medical research this is clinical practice, with doctors diagnosing and treating individual patients. In anthropology, this translates into careful observational studies of one tight-knit community. In the world of building science, clinical studies equate to post-occupancy case studies of completed, fully-occupied buildings. Such clinical studies facilitate insight into one level of a complex system, because they enable holistic observations of a single entity in its natural operation. Thus, clinical studies are fertile ground for generating hypotheses to be tested via other research methods. (While to the non-architectural reader this may sound like an obvious research approach, you would be surprised to learn how extremely rare disciplined post-occupancy studies of building performance really are.)

A second leg of the stool is epidemiological studies that look at very large populations. Like the public health studies that linked cancer to smoking, these types of studies can identify outcomes that only occur over very long time periods and/or subtle effects across huge populations. We need these large demographic studies because normal human intuition is exceptionally bad at probabilities and statistical analysis. Our brains did not evolve to detect patterns larger than our personal daily experience of the world. Modern statistical methods, in contrast, can easily identify patterns in huge data sets and suggest relationships that are not apparent to the casual observer. The Harvard nurses' study quoted earlier (see page 317), which found significantly lower mortality rates for American women who had more green spaces near their homes, is an excellent example of this type of big epidemiological study. These types of studies can be very expensive and time consuming if they must generate the original data for analysis across a large population. However, they can also be comparatively inexpensive and quick if they can repurpose existing data available from other sources, such as my team did with the schools, daylighting, and windows studies in Capistrano and Fresno.

The third leg of the stool is the type of classic laboratory study which focuses on one narrowly defined outcome and attempts to isolate its relationship to a singular input. These are the studies that can clearly demonstrate a causal relationship between two phenomena. However, when an overarching theory of the larger complex system is lacking, individual laboratory studies can be very difficult to knit together into a larger coherent understanding of the world. Laboratory studies are commonly the favored approach of academics because they can be segmented into small steps, each of which can be completed within one academic year or one graduate fellowship. New graduate students look for advice from their faculty advisors about how to construct a focused experiment that has the greatest probability of success and which will build on previous findings, thereby giving it guaranteed relevance and context. Thus, this process favors very cautious research, rather than big ideas and bold theories.

Exploring Time and Reality

One of those emergent properties of the complex system of daylighting and view in buildings that I find the most interesting is how they impact our sense of time and of reality. At first glance, this may seem an overly sweeping and grandiose statement. Yet while writing this book I found I came back to these two issues over and over again. Many of the topics we have covered have an element of understanding time. There are perceptual distortions of time that show up relative to views and the visual environment again and again. The use of any type of technological nature or virtual reality techniques to study our relationship to daylight and view in buildings has the danger of excluding key unknown elements from the highly complex system, and thus missing important emergent properties.

We learned earlier from David Eagleman, the neuroscientist at Stanford University who studies temporal illusions, how very easy it is to artificially distort time perception, and how fragile our grasp of reality is when our perception of time is distorted. It follows, then, that preserving our sense of time and reality inside of buildings may be one of the more consequential functions that windows and views can provide.

Virtual reality, on the other hand, has a reality problem. If you think about it, 'virtual reality' is a misnomer, actually more of an oxymoron, since the term is inherently self-contradictory. Virtual reality also implies that someone else is creating a substitute reality for you, i.e. that your agency has been removed and you are inhabiting a space and time artificially created by others. This may be an excellent form of immersive entertainment, or an efficient way to teach people about new environments, but it also has a potentially sinister tinge to it. Horror films often traffic in distorting reality, inducing the fear that we may no longer be able tell the difference between illusion and reality, and that some nefarious person may be intentionally manipulating our perceptions. Many of the neurological diseases that people fear the most, like Alzheimer's and schizophrenia, also involve a breakdown in a perception of reality.

We know that our brains are using multiple sources of simultaneous sensory information to organize experience into identifiable objects, places, actions, and intentions. In the perception of reality, timing is everything. Understanding how visual information connects to a larger perceptual reality is a critical task for our brains. The eye assembles focal information from multiple saccades per second, all tightly coordinated with a foundational four Hertz cognitive rhythm of inward and outward awareness sampling. Synchronizing our internal sense of time with that of the outside world may be one of the greatest benefits that a good window view gives us.

Cognitive Maps and Mental Exploration

One environmental psychologist who has added a holistic component to his research methods is Russell Epstein. A professor of Psychology at the University of Pennsylvania, Epstein studies neural mechanisms underlying visual scene perception and spatial navigation in humans. He and his colleagues used what by now should sound like a very familiar methodology: they recruited college students and showed them photographs while they laid in an fMRI machine, in order to observe which parts of their brains were activated when looking at different images. The researchers were interested in understanding how the brain works to navigate via the landmarks and space types, as postulated by Kevin Lynch.

Epstein's team recruited students from two different universities and showed them a variety of images of both the inside and outside of a number of campus buildings. Some of students had actually been to the places in the photographs, and others had not. Thus, the variable of interest was not visual processing, but rather how visual processing related to previous physical experience.

The difference in the parts of the brain that were activated by the photos was striking, depending upon whether the student had actually been to the building or not. If a student had physically been to the building in the photograph their brain showed similar patterns of firing when looking at *any* photo of the building, whether inside or out. If the student had *not* physically experienced the building, then the interior and exterior photos of the same building did not exhibit similar patterns.[3] Thus, if the student had been to a building, it was recognized in their brains as an identifiable object, i.e. 'a place' in architectural lingo.

By connecting the study of photographic images to the experience of actual campus buildings, Epstein used a more holistic approach compared to other fMRI studies we've reviewed, and so was able to isolate the effect of real experience over mere visual perception. The study suggests that the previous experience of physically being in and around a building helped knit the purely visual information in the photographs into a more coherent cognitive map.

Epstein's study helps to point out some of the reasons why merely simulated window views, such as from video screens or webcams, lack emotional impact, because they are devoid of a larger experiential context. Cognitive maps are formulated from many sources of information, such as narrative experience, kinesthetic motion, and all the other sensory inputs that occur when visiting and navigating a real space. Having a coherent cognitive map helps to expand our sense of personal space and enables us to imagine taking action within that expanded space. Thus, I suggest that more comprehensive cognitive maps enabled by window views may also help to expand our mental opportunities.

Compression and Expansion

A Brazilian novelist, Tatania Salem Levy, describes how her view helps her start her day's work: "*Although I have an office in my apartment, every day I wake up and take my laptop to the dining room table. The view from my dining room has an amplitude that takes me away, and when I write I need the feeling that space and time have no end.*"[4] I find the use of the word *amplitude* most intriguing from this quote. It implies that in order to begin her work in the morning, she first needs a sense of mental expansion, "*the feeling that space and time have no end.*" Her morning view invites her mind out for limitless exploration.

We learned earlier how many of the writers quoted in Pericoli's books strive to maintain a balance between inward mental focus and connection to the outer world. In my own interviews, I found recurring themes of compression and expansion from many of the people I asked about their relationship to windows and views. People describing their most beloved views commonly spoke of the feeling of expansion, an unfolding or release. "*It feels like this:*" they would say, demonstrating the expansive feeling by spreading their arms wide: "*Aaaah!*" In contrast, people who worked in offices without views routinely spoke of feeling confined, imprisoned, constrained. They pantomimed the feeling of windowless spaces with hunched, compressed bodies and a downward gaze.

Architecturally, it is easy to create small confined spaces. Small, confined spaces are almost a default condition for buildings, part of our earliest dwellings and including the closets, cubicles, bathrooms, and basements of today. We now have increasingly competent mechanical systems to make little (or large) confined spaces more habitable with sufficient air, light, and temperature control. Thus, there is no art to creating compression. And expansion is easily provided by stepping outside under the wide-open sky. The art is in creating an interior space that can provide a balance between the two, that offers both shelter from the elements and connection to the greater world beyond the confines of a building. Perhaps this is another variation of the idea of including both 'prospect and refuge' in all aspects of environmental design.

The Zen Master's Garden

One of my favorite stories about the power of a view is a classic tale of the Japanese master gardener, told to me early in my architectural education.

He was revered in early Tokyo as the most artful designer of contemplative gardens, and was sought after by Zen monks and all the wealthy Samurai to design and construct their gardens for the tea ceremony. For his efforts, he was rewarded with a prized plot of land that had the most perfect view of Mount Fuji. After many years, he finally had enough resources to construct his own private garden. He worked on the garden for months in secret, wanting to surprise his friends. At last the first group of guests were invited into the finished garden, expecting to be dazzled by the view and his mastery of design. Instead, they were puzzled to find the garden enclosed in tall fences and trees that completely blocked the view of Mount Fuji. They followed a narrow path of irregular stepping-stones meandering towards the tea house situated at the far end of the garden. As was the custom, each visitor stopped at the *tsukubai,* the stone water basin, to cleanse their hands and mouths before entering the tea house. As they knelt down to reach for the bamboo dipper there was an opening low down in the fence from which they could now see the full view of Mount Fuji in all its glory. Thus, the iconic view of the Japanese mountain was only available from this humble position, as they knelt one by one to cleanse themselves for the sacred tea ceremony.

This Japanese garden master saved the grandest view from his garden for a specially choreographed moment, orchestrating an experience first of compression then expansion. First the guests entered the garden and were drawn inward, forced to focus on their internal balance while navigating the stepping-stones. Then, positioned exactly, with the cleansing water in their hands, they were finally allowed the expansive view of the sacred mountain. The moment may have been brief, but intensely memorable, reinforced by a progression of other sensory experiences: body position, the sound, touch and taste of the water, and then a release with a clarified mind to join the highly ritualized tea ceremony.

Inward and Outward: Inspirited Buildings

There is an old English aphorism which claims that the 'Eyes are a window into the soul.' From much of the neuroscience cited earlier in this book, it is also now clear that our eyes are indeed actively tied to cognitive processing. There is a corresponding saying that 'Windows are the eyes of the building.' Architects have long known that windows are one of the most expressive elements of a building's façade, reveling the life of the inhabitants inside, and even serving as a proxy for their presence. A building without windows is most likely merely a holding box for machinery, or a tomb for the dead.

The journalist Michael Pollan, in his book about the design and construction of his personal writing hut, had an even more poetic take on what the presence of windows contributed to his building. He had been laboring on the rough carpentry for months, and finally the custom-made windows were ready to install—a task that took only a few hours. He reports: *"From the outside, the building was suddenly much more interesting to look at—because now the building looked back. It had a face. Roused by glass from its long material slumber, the structure now seemed something more than the sum of its wooden parts, as though Oz-like, it had been inspired. Especially after we'd installed the two windows in the peak, from which they peered out with a supervisory air, the building looked, if not alive, then at least like a pretty good metaphor for consciousness, with its big awning windows reflecting back the landscape in what seemed almost a form of acknowledgment."*[5]

Pollan thought that windows *"inspirited"* his writing hut, just like a young child's drawing of her house might include two window-eyes, symmetrically placed around a door-mouth. Thus, as the 'eyes of the building,' windows provide an anthropomorphic element, allowing us to see something very human in this inanimate object we have built. Self-recognition is really what is at work here. We can easily recognize windows as providing much the same function as our own eyes: processing visual information, and offering information about the rhythms of the planet. Just as with our own eyes, we can look out from the window at the broader world, and others can peer in, perhaps trying to determine something of the inhabitant's soul.

Fractals: Self-Recognition

It is not just the windows themselves, but also the dynamic quality of daylight and the complexity of the window views that may also contribute an anthropomorphic element to our buildings. For example, fractal patterns in views and daylight variability may contribute a form of self-recognition, as described below.

Fractals, the repeating, self-similar patterns discussed earlier (see page 180), can exist in both space and time. The ability to detect fractal patterns within very complex data sets has been revolutionizing medicine. Dr. Ary Goldberger, a professor of cardiology at Harvard Medical School and a specialist in heart-rate variability, has been one of the leaders in the field, applying fractal analysis to many areas of medicine. Importantly, Goldberger has found that rhythmic complexity, and the ability to function efficiently at many scales, is an essential characteristic of healthy human processes such as cardiac function, and that conversely, the loss of rhythmic complexity is a sign of aging and disease.

Fascinated with the ubiquitous presence of fractal structures in nature and in the human body, Goldberger began to recognize them in human creations too, such as architectural structures. In a sense, he had an epiphany about apophany. 'Apophany' is defined as the human tendency to detect patterns in random information. Our brains are actively trying to discern patterns and meaning from all sensory input. It is how infants make sense of the world, gradually recognizing more and more repetitive sensory patterns as meaningful. It is how we all form cognitive maps, recognizing repetitive patterns that indicate a unique object or place. Because our brains are selectively attuned to certain evolutionarily useful patterns, like human faces, we are able to recognize those most quickly, and we also have a tendency to overpredict those patterns we naturally favor. Thus, it is easy for us to see imaginary faces in random patterns, just as the Greeks and Romans saw their gods outlined by the stars overhead. In other words, we have a natural predilection for humanoid interpretations of random data.

In 1996, Goldberger wrote a paper published in Molecular Psychiatry, comparing the fractal structures he found in medicine to those of a Gothic cathedral. He felt that the designer of the cathedral, thought to be the medieval Frenchman Abbot Suger, had somehow recognized and expressed the structure of his own mind. Goldberger's theory, somewhat similar to Alan Wilson's concept of Biophilia, is that the beauty we find in a Gothic cathedral in France, or perhaps an equally complex Hindu temple in India, may be a function of self-recognition of our own mental structures. He writes: "*The process of creation realized in the minds of geniuses like Suger may be akin to re-creation in which the artwork externalizes and maps the internal brain-work of the architect. Conversely, the interaction of the viewer with the artform may be taken as an act of self-recognition. Standing inside a Gothic cathedral in the light of multi-paneled stained-glass windows, we are able to look not only outward, but also inward. The scale-free forms and complex patterns encountered are ultimately singular loci of self-discovery.*"[6]

Goldberger' observation about "*looking inward*" brings us back to the concept of 'insight' discussed in Chapter 3, about mind wandering and daydreams. Perhaps the most appreciated views are those that best support our internal mental wanderings, and which exhibit a compatible structure of rhythms, in both space and time, allowing us to zoom in and out of fractal patterns. Goldberger is suggesting that forms of self-recognition are at play in aesthetic judgments. Based on his observations of recurring physiological patterns that exhibit fractal complexity, he thinks that humans are naturally attuned to similar visual patterns. If he is correct—that fractal complexity is an essential characteristic of healthy human physiology, and that conversely, that loss of complexity is a sign of aging and disease—then it stands to follow that humans would have a natural affinity towards complex visual environments, as indicative of life, vibrancy, and health.

Earth Gazing

The emotional power of a living view is really brought home by a story about the Apollo astronauts. A photograph of the crescent Earth rising above the moon's surface was taken from lunar orbit by astronaut Bill Anders in 1968, during the Apollo 8 lunar mission. It has been called one of the most influential photographs ever taken.[7] The first astronauts to orbit the earth, and then the moon, found themselves deeply fascinated with the view back to the earth. While many photos have been taken, the astronauts consistently claim that the photos or videos never do the view justice.[8]

Christopher Potter, a science writer, wrote a history of the American space program, called *The Earth Gazers*. He interviewed many of the test pilots and astronauts from the early space programs, from the 1920s through the Apollo missions of the 1960s, and found that the experience of looking back at the Earth had been a transformational experience, starting with Charles Lindberg and continuing through current residents of the International Space Station. Buzz Aldrin gave the book its name. Aldrin was the second man to step on the surface of the moon, right after Neil Armstrong. Potter writes: "*When he was asked if he had any regrets, Aldrin said that he wished he had looked out of the window more, Earthgazing.*"

One of the starkest realizations for the astronauts who walked on the moon's surface was how utterly still and lifeless it was. In contrast, when they looked back towards the Earth, they could see that its swirling, glowing atmosphere—that which from the Earth's surface we perceive as 'sky'—is very much a part of the dynamic, living dimension of our planet. The contrast with the moon and its lack of any atmosphere made this abundantly clear. Potter writes: "*The silence was startling. Without an atmosphere, outer space begins at the moon's surface. Even meteorites crash there silently ... How different being there than on the Earth's surface, cocooned by the Earth's atmosphere.*"[9]

Mike Collins was the third Apollo 11 astronaut who manned the orbiting capsule while Armstrong and Aldrin walked the moon's surface. In a radio interview with Potter, Collins summarized how inadequate he felt to describe the experience: "*We were a crew of three experimental test pilots. The crew should have included a poet, a priest and a philosopher.*"[10]

Potter agreed, based on his interviews with other astronauts: "*We don't really have the language to describe the view. Numinous is the best I could come up with.*" Collins continued on, trying to explain his experience: "*The*

Earth seemed quite fragile from the moon. It never seemed fragile from on the Earth. I sensed that it was inhabited. I was conscious of some presence ... not a human presence."

Ed Mitchell, an Apollo 14 astronaut who also spent two days on the moon's surface, was perhaps the most psychologically transformed by the experience. Potter writes: *"It would take him several years to assimilate what had happened to him. Out there, ten times as many stars are visible than from the most propitious vantage point on Earth, and are ten times brighter. 'There is a sense of being swaddled by the universe' Mitchell said. In space the universe seems more intelligent than inanimate."*

Two years later, in 1973, Mitchell quit NASA and founded the Institute of Noetic Studies, an organization devoted to the study of consciousness. The institute continues on today, almost 50 years later, funding research and hosting workshops. Mitchell explains his motivation in changing careers from astronaut to a sponsor of research on consciousness: *"On the return trip home, gazing through 240,000 miles of space toward the stars and the planet from which I had come, I suddenly experienced the universe as intelligent, loving, harmonious. My view of our planet was a glimpse of divinity. We went to the Moon as technicians; we returned as humanitarians."*[11]

Isn't it remarkable that the view out of the space capsule window, from the very dead moon to the very living Earth, could have such a transformational effect? Certainly, the Apollo astronauts had undergone a very unique and grueling experience, in their travel to the moon and back. And yet it was the view of the Earth that they wanted to talk about the most.

We should not underestimate the importance of views out to the larger world, some small portion of the Earth, for every other human on the planet.

Conclusion: The Case for Visual Delight

This book has set out a wide range of theories, and evidence, that daylight and views are essential to a healthy human habitat. The types of evidence include water-tight scientific research that is establishing a new understanding of human biological functions, and more suggestive epidemiological research that shows strong statistical relationships between daylight, views, and many important societal outcomes. The range of evidence also includes plenty of careful observations, case studies, and interviews, along with cultural norms, revered icons, and even ancient philosophies and myths. It all adds up to a compelling body of knowledge.

Allow me to review the evidence and summarize the case, as succinctly as possible.

We have known since ancient times that human life is intricately tied to planetary rhythms, from our efforts to make calendars and time keepers that correctly synchronize with planetary movements. We also know that these rhythms are critically determined by our place on the planet, and influenced by the global atmospheric patterns and localized weather that swirl around our homes. Recent research has only reinforced the fundamental importance that exposure to the continuously varying patterns of bright daylight illumination and darkness at night play in maintaining our biological rhythms.

These rhythms operate at many time scales. Circadian rhythms operating in daily cycles are becoming better understood. They clearly influence the quality of our sleep, which directly impacts growth, learning, and memory formation, as well as immune response, bodily repair, and overall metabolic health. During the daytime, circadian rhythms influence physical activity, alertness, attention, hunger, along with a cascade of hormonal interactions. In addition, at a longer time scale, there are annual and lunar rhythms, and at a shorter time scale, pulsating rhythms of heart, stomach, muscles, ears, and eyes. These rhythms are also coordinated with internal brain rhythms, which, like a metronome, keep a steady micro-beat that manages both our inward and outward perceptions, letting us establish reality and successfully predict the immediate future. This is true not only for humans, but also for our entire ecological system, including other animals, plants, and even the microbiome that lives on our skin, inside our bodies, and all around our buildings.

Because our bodily and cognitive rhythms are so essential to our well-being, as daytime active animals we have evolved an appetite for light and a natural aversion to darkness. We humans naturally love light as much as we love, and often develop cravings for, water, sugar, and salt. With our mastery of new technologies, we have found artificial means to satisfy these hungers and cravings. Electric lighting, since its invention just over a century ago, has quickly become the default mechanism for providing light both in the day and the night. In our rush to invent convenient technological solutions to all human needs and desires, we have neglected many simpler and more natural ways to meet our needs. Just as a well-balanced diet of organic whole foods is recognized as a healthier alternative to industrially processed foods and supplements, so too should a built environment that supports daily exposure to natural daylight and views be recognized as a healthier alternative to manufactured synthetic light and views.

Humans evolved over millennia while spending most of their lives outdoors. Now, however, the opposite is true, where the majority of modern humans live in cities, and spend over 90% of their lives inside of buildings. Thus, the interior of buildings is now the 'natural habitat' of humans. As such, the interior of buildings should be designed to support basic human needs, such as access to the natural rhythms and the intrinsic interest provided by daylight and views.

It turns out that looking at views of the outdoor environment is far more than just a pleasant pastime or an optional amenity. First of all, looking out of a window is likely to provide about ten times more circadian stimulus than the equivalent indoor daylight illumination. This is because a view of the outdoors is both that much brighter, and more interesting to look at, naturally drawing our attention. Refocusing our eyes to distant views also helps maintain eye health, via exercising the many little muscles around the eye and increasing blood flow. Regularly glancing around a window view and routine exposure to daylight may also promote normal eye growth and development in children and adolescents, improving eye tracking and saccades, and reducing their lifetime risk of myopia. The complexities of daylit environments and outdoor views provide more nuanced colors, shades and shadows, sparkle and motion, that help inform and maintain visual perception from childhood through old age. The fractal nature of many outdoor views, whether natural or man-made, beckons our deeper attention, inviting mental explorations of scale and movement.

Our brains are hungry to make predictions about the future, and the complexity, ambiguity, and continual change inherent in outdoor vistas feed those cognitive processes. Views to the outdoors may also be the preferred visual focus for the vast amount of time that we spend in micro-bursts of mind wandering, up to 50% of our waking hours. This largely unconscious process helps maintain a delicate cognitive balance between interior and exterior awareness. Mind wandering gives us the mental space to incubate solutions, formulate our personal priorities, and plan future activities. Views out to the surrounding area also help us to construct cognitive maps, by orienting to local landmarks and understanding our position relative to the outside world. A robust cognitive map can ward off disorientation in both space and time, and provide a mental armature that enhances memory formation and retrieval, along with explorations into future possibilities.

Views also enhance lasting emotional attachment to place, working at many levels of engagement. Views often provide a connection to the history of a place, and the promise of continuity with the future, resulting in an expansive sense of time. They may provide a mental portal, that efficiently transports the viewer to other imaginary worlds, or a balance that brings them back to reality. They may offer privacy and solace, or companionship and social connection. Whether partaking in a daily ritual, or a once-in-a-lifetime moment, people develop deeply personal relationships with their views that importantly contribute to their sense of self.

Buildings with ample daylight and abundant access to views are associated with a wide range of highly desirable outcomes, from improved performance on academic and cognitive tests, increased retail sales, employee engagement and loyalty, and many positive health outcomes. Occupants of such buildings have been found to have less fatigue, less stress, less pain, and faster recovery from illness and surgery. Similarly, animals kept in veterinary buildings with daylight and views exhibit less fear and anxiety. Observations and interviews of building occupants testify to increased satisfaction with their workplace, a happier balance of privacy versus social interaction, control of mental focus, and sustained productivity.

The amount of money commanded by real estate with a good view speaks to the economic value of view, sometimes far exceeding the basic value of the land area and its physical improvements. The literature and art inspired by views, especially the highly evolved arts of landscape painting and landscape design, embody the cultural value of views even more. Carefully curated views, such as Zen gardens or renowned tourist attractions, have become iconic images that exemplify the very identity of a people and their philosophies. Likewise, the daylight design of a space or place can also create an otherworldly ambience that elevates the experience to something transcendent.

The success of spaces designed to use daylight as their primary illumination is well established knowledge, and thus easily observed in many existing buildings and older cities. Daylight can also be usefully studied using physical models because it scales perfectly. Newer computer modeling techniques have been rapidly evolving, but still have lingering questions about quantitative and perceptual accuracy. Even newer virtual reality techniques offer promise, especially for accelerating learning and analysis, but also threaten to undermine the most basic value of daylight and views: their inherent reality. While we have established many metrics to assess the adequacy of daylight illumination, our understanding of view is much less mature. Descriptions of the essential qualities of window views and related management strategies are rudimentary, and untested. Glare, in these situations, is a form of visual noise: just as noise is determined by what we are trying to listen to, glare is a function of what we choose to view. This book has attempted to offer a number of hypotheses that might form the basis for more comprehensive research into essential qualities of the visual environment.

A deep embrace of daylight and views as essential for human habitat will inevitably result in a renaissance of design and research exploring new ways to optimize all of our buildings for their current and future occupants. From this perspective, daylight should become the primary illuminant for any space where people spend a substantial part of their day, and access to an outdoor view must be readily available to everyone—whether rich or poor; very young or very old; active, infirm, or bedridden; working, learning, or relaxing.

Glossary

This glossary provides definitions for 63 specialized words used in this book, or which may be unfamiliar to a reader new to architecture, lighting, or circadian biology. These glossary words appear in blue font for their first use in a chapter.

Acronym or unit	Word	Description
	adaptation (visual)	In vision science, the process of the eye and brain adjusting perception to new ambient illumination levels. Compare to saturation.
	aperture	In architecture, any type of hole in a building envelope that lets in daylight. Windows, skylights, and glass doors are collectively all apertures. From Latin: *apertura* = opening, hole. Compare to fenestration.
CFL	compact fluorescent lamp	A small fluorescent lamp, typically designed to replace a screw-in incandescent light bulb. Compare to incandescent and LED.
	chronobiology	The study of biological rhythms. From Latin: *chrono* = time.
	circadian	A biological process that is influenced by day length. From Latin: *circa* = approximately; *dies* = day.
	clerestory	In architecture, a high section of wall that contains windows above eye level. The purpose is to admit light, fresh air, or both. Compare to cupola and skylight.
	cognitive map	An internal representation or mental model of the physical space within which we operate.
	color constancy	The ability of the brain to perceive the color of objects as invariable in spite of continuously changing lighting conditions.
°K	color temperature	A numerical description of the perception of a white light source as 'warm' (<4,000°K) or 'cool' (>6,000°K), expressed in degrees Kelvin. See incandescent and Figure 3.4.
	cupola	In architecture, a small enclosure located on top of a roof or dome that provides daylight and/or ventilation to the area below. Compare to clerestory and skylight.
	daylight	Illumination from the sky, or indirectly from sunlight reflected off other surfaces. Compare to sunlight.
	daylighting	In architecture, the practice of designing a space to take advantage of daylight.
	daylit	An adjective describing a space that has been successfully designed to utilize daylight as its primary source of illumination.

Acronym or unit	Word	Description
DMN	default mode network	A recurring pattern of brain activation that shows up on fMRI scans when the brain is not engaged in an outwardly directed task. It has been associated with daydreaming, autobiographical narratives, and self-care mental states.
	diurnal	Adjective describing an animal which is most active in the daytime, as opposed to nocturnal (active at night), or crepuscular (most active in the twilight hours).
	dopamine	A neurotransmitter and hormone produced during the daytime, associated with daytime behaviors and motivational rewards.
EEG	electroencephalography	Electrical potential recordings of brain signals, presented as visual graphs. From Greek: *encephalo* = brain. Compare to fMRI.
	electrochromic glass	A type of glass that changes tint and transmission of visible light upon the application of an electric charge. There are a number of types.
	equinox	The two days per year that have a day and night that are both 12 hours long. Spring equinox is around March 20th and fall equinox is around September 21st. From the Latin for equal nights. Compare to solstice.
	façade	In architecture, the outer wall (or 'face') of a building, especially the principal wall facing a street or public place.
	fenestration	In architecture, the arrangement of windows, doors, and other transparent or operable elements in a building's skin. From Latin: *fenestra* = window. Compare to aperture.
FC	footcandle	A measure of illumination equivalent to one lumen per square foot (the light produced by a standard candle one foot away from a surface one-foot square), normalized for the photopic sensitivity of the human eye, expressed in imperial units. Compare to the metric unit, lux. See Figure 3.1 for typical illuminance levels.
	fovea	A small depression in the center of the human retina with the highest visual acuity and concentration of cones for color vision. From Latin for 'small pit.'
fMRI	functional magnetic resonance imaging	A non-invasive brain imaging system which uses magnetic fields to image the activity of living tissue via changes in blood flow. Compare to EEG.
HVAC	heating ventilation and air conditioning	A branch of mechanical engineering providing thermal comfort and ventilation systems to buildings.
HDR	high dynamic range	A photographic technique that captures greater detail in the highlights and shadows of an image, in order to better represent human perception.
IES	Illuminating Engineering Society	A society of professionals and others involved in the art and science of lighting, publishing guides and recommended standards, primarily in North America.

Acronym or unit	Word	Description
	incandescent	A type of light source that glows due to its high temperature. Incandescent light bulbs, first perfected by Thomas Edison, include a small tungsten wire that glows first a dim red or amber, then ever brighter, from yellowish-white to bluish-white, as the flow of electricity through it is increased. See color temperature and Figure 3.4. Compare to LED and CFL.
IR	infrared	Electromagnetic radiation with a frequency lower than visible red light, with wavelengths from 0.7 micrometer to 1 millimeter, primarily perceived by humans as heat. Compare to ultraviolet.
	interoception	The sensing of one's own bodily states (such as hunger, cold, fatigue). From English: interior + reception. Compare to proprioception.
ipRGC	intrinsically photosensitive Retinal Ganglion Cells	These ganglion nerve cells in the front of the retina respond to blue light and communicate directly with the suprachiasmatic nuclei.
LED	light emitting diode	A digital, semiconductor light source that emits light when current flows through it. They are smaller, more efficient, and more easily controlled than previous electric light sources. They can be formulated to produce almost any color of light. See Figure 3.4 and compare to incandescent and CFL.
LEED	Leadership in Energy and Environmental Design	A voluntary program for building owners to certify their buildings as meeting a list of performance criteria, originally developed by the non-profit United States Green Building Council (USGBC).
	luminaire	A complete electrical lighting unit, that includes the light source, optical control, power control, and structural housing.
	lux	A measure of illumination received on a surface, normalized for the photopic sensitivity of the human eye, expressed in SI units. Equivalent to one lumen per square meter. Compare to footcandle. See Figure 3.1 for typical illuminance levels.
	melanopsin	One of many opsins, a class of photo-responsive molecules. Melanopsin has been identified as the primary photo-switch within the ipRGC, most responsive to radiation around 480 nm (blue light). Melanopic refers to the light sensitivity profile of this molecule.
	melatonin	A hormone primarily released at night by the pineal gland that helps regulate circadian rhythms, such as the sleep–wake cycle. From Greek: *mela* = black, plus tonin, from serotonin. See also SCN.
	mesopic	In lighting design, the range of twilight ambient illumination levels when both rods and cones are active. From Greek: *meso* = middle. Compare to photopic and scotopic.
	myopia	The medical term for near-sightedness, which typically develops during childhood. People with myopia see near objects more clearly, while distant objects are blurred.

Acronym or unit	Word	Description
	photopic	In lighting design, the range of bright or daytime ambient illumination levels where cones, and color vision, dominate. Both lux and footcandle measurements are normalized relative to the photopic sensitivity function for the human eye. From Greek: *phos* = light. Compare to mesopic and scotopic.
	photoreceptor	A cell or other organic structure that responds to light, such as the rods, cones and ipRGC in the human eye.
	proprioception	The sensing of one's own bodily position and movements. From Latin: *proprius* = own, plus reception. Compare to interoception.
REM	rapid eye movements	Involuntary movements of the eye observed during the dream phase of sleep.
RPE	retinal pigmented epithelial cells	The outermost layer of cells surrounding the retina, responsible for nourishing the rods and codes. The dark (pigmented) color absorbs light which makes it past the layer of rods and cones.
	saturation	In medicine, the point at which a biological system no longer responds to additional input. In vision, it is the point at which rods or cones can no longer register additional changes in light levels. Compare to adaptation.
SCN	suprachiasmatic nucleus	A cluster of cells (a nucleus) which sits above (superior to) the chiasma (the X-shaped crossing of the two optic nerves in the brain, named for the Greek letter *chi* = X). It is the site of the body's master circadian clock, connecting the input directly from ipRGC in the retina to the pineal gland, which outputs melatonin.
	scotopic	In lighting design, the range of dim or nighttime ambient illumination levels where rods, and black and white vision, dominate. From Greek: *skotos* = darkness. Compare to mesopic and photopic.
	sidelighting	The design practice of providing daylight from the vertical walls around a space. Compare to toplighting.
	sidelit	The adjective describing a space that has been successfully provided with daylight from windows. Compare to toplit.
	skylight	In architecture, a transparent structure mounted in a roof designed to admit light from overhead. Also occasionally called 'roof windows,' skylights include site-built assemblies, self-contained manufactured units, and tubular skylights.
	skylighting	In architecture, the practice of providing illumination via the use of skylights. It is a specialized form of toplighting.
	skylit	An adjective describing a space that has adequate illumination provided via skylights.
	solar altitude angle	The vertical angle of the sun relative to the Earth's horizon, measured in degrees, such that the horizon is zero degrees and the zenith is 90 degrees.

Acronym or unit	Word	Description
	solar azimuth angle	The horizontal angle of the sun in the sky relative to a line running north to south. The IES defines the solar azimuth as an angle measured clockwise from true north, such that east is 90 degrees, south is 180, and west is 270 degrees.
	solstice	The two days per year when the noontime sun has travelled farthest north or south in the sky. In the northern hemisphere, Summer solstice is around June 21st, the longest day of the year. Winter solstice is around December 21st, the longest night of the year. From Latin: *sol* = sun, *stice* = stationary.
SPD	spectral power distribution	The power per wavelength (spectrum) of an illumination source, as measured by a spectrometer, typically expressed as a graph showing the relative intensity of a given light source per wavelength.
	spectrometer	A device that can measure the intensity of various wavelengths (spectrum) emitted from a light source.
	sunlight	Light from the sun, typically referring to direct beam sunlight, before it has been scattered, diffused, or bounced off of other surfaces. Compare to daylight.
	sunlit	An adjective describing a space or object where sunlight is its primary source of illumination. Compare to daylit.
	toplighting	The design practice of providing daylight from overhead surfaces, such as skylights, roof monitors, or clerestory windows. Compare to sidelighting.
	toplit	The adjective describing a space that has been successfully provided with daylight illumination from skylights, roof monitors, clerestory windows, or other overhead apertures. Compare to sidelit.
UV	ultraviolet	Electromagnetic radiation which is longer than x-rays, but shorter than visible violet light, typically between 10nm to 400nm. Ultraviolet is further divided into three categories: UV-A, the shortest; UV-B, a mid-range; and UV-C, the longest wavelengths which are mostly filtered out by the Earth's atmosphere. Compare to infrared.
	window management	The activity of selectively controlling the flow of light, heat, air, or sound through windows, via the deployment of curtains, blinds, shades, shutters, louvers, awnings, screens, grills, panels, and/or films. Devices such as these that can be added to existing windows are variously referred to as 'window treatments,' 'window fashions,' or 'window attachments.'

List of Illustrations, with Notes

All Illustrations by Garth von Ahnen, unless otherwise noted.

Notes and References

Author's Preface

1 White, D, "Collison Vision, an interview with Chuck Davis", UC Santa Cruz Magazine, October 2017, Collision vision – UC Santa Cruz Magazine (ucsc.edu) and author's personal conversation with Chuck Davis, November 2020.

2 Author's personal conversations with Alec Webster, Joop Rubens, and Elizabeth Cowell, university librarian, December 2020.

Introduction

1 https://energydesignresources.com/media/2371/EDR_CaseStudies_remo.pdf

Part 1 Prediction

1 Planetary Rhythms

1 Beale, A, et al., "Life in a dark biosphere: a review of circadian physiology in 'arrhythmic' environments." *J Comp Physiol B*, 2016, 186: 947–968. doi:10.1007/s00360-016-1000-6. Note: Scientists have not yet been able to study all creatures living in non-rhythmic environments, such as deep-sea thermal vents.

2 Numata, H, and Helm, B, *Annual, Lunar, and Tidal Clocks, Patterns and Mechanisms of Nature's Enigmatic Rhythms*, Springer, 2014.

3 Moore, M, et al., "Artificial Light at Night in Freshwater Habitats and its Potential Effects" in *The Ecological Consequences of Artificial Night Lighting*, eds. C Rich and T Longcore, Island Press, 2006.

4 http://photobiology.info/Haddock.html (7/16/15)

5 For example, see: http://andrewmarsh.com/apps/releases/soft-shadows.html

2 Chronobiology and Human Health

1 Ludovic, S Mure, et al., "Diurnal transcriptome atlas of a primate across major neural and peripheral tissues." *Science*, March 16, 2018. doi:10.1126/science.aao0318

2 Berson, DM, "Strange vision: ganglion cells as circadian photoreceptors." *Trends in Neurosciences*, 2003. doi:10.1016/S0166-2236(03)00130-9

3 Lockley, SW, Brainard, GC, and Czeisler, CA, "High sensitivity of the human circadian melatonin rhythm to resetting by short wavelength light." *Journal of Clinical Endocrinology and Metabolism*, 2003. https://doi.org/10.1210/jc.2003-030570

4 Graham, DM and Wong, KY, "Melanopsin-expressing, Intrinsically Photosensitive Retinal Ganglion Cells" in *Webvision: The Organization of the Retina and Visual System*, Kolb H, et al. www.ncbi.nlm.nih.gov/books/NBK27326/ (updated 10/1/2016)

5 www.cdc.gov/healthyschools/sleep.htm (5/13/2019)

6 www.military.com/dodbuzz/2018/03/23/ship-collisions-prompt-navy-research-sleep-deprivation.html (4/14/2020)

7 Panagiotis, M, et al., "The Role of Sleep in Human Performance and Well-being," in *Human Performance Optimization: The Science and Ethics of Enhancing Human Capabilities*, eds. Matthews M et al.. Oxford University Press, 2019. doi:10.1080/15402002.2019.1578771

8 https://blog.ted.com/the-neuroscience-of-sleep-russell-foster-at-tedglobal-2013/

9 Barron, AB, et al., "The roles of dopamine and related compounds in reward-seeking behavior across animal phyla." *Frontiers in Behavioral Neuroscience*, 2010. doi:10.3389/fnbeh.2010.00163

10 Smolensky, M, et al., "Nocturnal light pollution and underexposure to daytime sunlight: complementary mechanisms for circadian disruption and related diseases." *Chronobiology International*, 2015. doi:10.3109/07420528.2015.1072002

11 Smolensky, M, et al., "Diurnal and twenty-four hour patterning of human diseases: acute and chronic common and uncommon medical conditions." *Sleep Medicine Reviews*, 2015. doi:org/10.1016/j.smrv.2014.06.005

12 Van der Rhees, et al., "Regular sun exposure benefits health." *Medical Hypotheses*, 2016. https://doi.org/10.1016/j.mehy.2016.10.011

13 Beyer, K, et al., "Time spent outdoors, activity levels, and chronic disease among American adults." *Journal of Behavioral Medicine*, 2018. doi:10.1007/s10865-018-9911-1

14 James, P, et al., "Exposure to greenness and mortality in a nationwide prospective cohort study of women." *Environmental Health Perspectives*, 2016. doi:10.1289/eph.1510363

15 "Health consequences of electric lighting practices in the modern world: A report on the National Toxicology Program's workshop on shift work at night, artificial light at night, and circadian disruption," 2017. Science of the Total Environment, National Institutes of Health.

16 Fahimipour, A, et al., "Daylight exposure modulates bacterial communities associated with household dust." *Microbiome*, 2018. doi.org/10.1186/s40168-018-0559-4

17 Giuntella, O and Mazzonna, F, "Sunset Time and the Economic Effects of Social Jetlag Evidence from US Time Zone Borders." U Pittsburgh, Working Paper 17/009 8/2017.

18 Gu, F, et al., "Longitude position in a time zone and cancer risk in the United States." *Cancer Epidemiology Biomarkers Prevention*, 2017. doi:10.1158/1055-9965.EPI-16-1029

19 Borisenkov, M, "Latitude of residence and position in time zone are predictors of cancer incidence, cancer mortality, and life expectancy at birth." *Chronobiology International*, 2011. doi:10.3109/07420528.2010.541312

20 Ronneberg, T, et al., "Daylight saving time and artificial time zones – a battle between biological and social times." *Frontiers in Physiology*, 2019. doi.org/10.3389/fphys.2019.00944

21 Ott, WR, "Human activity patterns: a review of the literature." *Proceedings of the Research Planning Conference on Human Activity Patterns*, EPA National Exposure Research Laboratory, EPA/600/4-89/004: 1989.

22 Klepeis, N, et al., "The National Human Activity Pattern Survey: A Resource for Assessing Exposure to Environmental Pollutants." Lawrence Berkeley National Labs, 2001. doi:10.1038/sj.jea.750016

23 Diffey, BL, "An overview analysis of the time people spend outdoors." *Br J Dermatol*, 2011. doi:10.1111/j.1365-2133.2010.10165.x.

24 https://natureofamericans.org/findings/topic-summary/children (2/1/2020)

25 Smolders, K, *Daytime Light Exposure: Effects and Preferences*. Eindhoven: Technische Universiteit Eindhoven, 2013. doi:10.6100/IR762825

26 Munch, M, et al., "The role of daylight for humans: gaps in current knowledge." *Clocks and Sleep*. doi:10.3390/clockssleep2010008 (2/28/2020)

27 International Commission on Illumination, "CIE Position Statement on the Non-Visual Effects of Light" (6/28/2015).

28 American Medical Association, "Human and environmental effects of light emitting diode (LED) community lighting." *Council on Science and Public Health*, #2-A-16, 2016.

3 The Evolving and Aging Eye

1 Darwin, C, "Chapter VI. Difficulties of the Theory" in *The Origin of the Species*, 1859.

2 Moore, M, et al., "Artificial light at Night in Freshwater Habitats and its Potential Effects" in *Ecological Consequences of Artificial Night Lighting*, eds. C Rich and T Longcore, Island Press, 2006.

3 Okawa, H, et al., "ATP consumption by mammalian rod photoreceptors in darkness and in light." *Current Biology*, 2008. doi:10.1016/j.cur.2008.10.029

4 Gouras, P, "Color Vision" (7/2009), in *Webvision: The Organization of the Retina and Visual System*, eds. Kolb H et al. University of Utah. www.ncbi.nlm.nih.gov/books/NBK11537/

5 Verrelli, BC, Tishkoff, SA (9/2004). "Signatures of selection and gene conversion associated with human color vision variation." *Am. J. Hum. Genet.* doi:10.1086/423287

6 Berman, S, Clear, R, "Simplifying Melanopsin Metrology." *IES FIRES*. www.IES.org (7/1/2019).

7 For example, see www.ies.org/product/ies-method-for-evaluating-light-source-color-rendition

8 Tatler, B, et al., "Yarbus, eye movement and vision." *iPerception*, 2010. doi:10.1068/i0382

9 Tikidji-Hamburyan, A, et al., "Rods progressively escape saturation to drive visual responses in daylight conditions." *Nat Commun*, 2017. https://doi.org/10.1038/s41467-017-01816-6

10 Kawasaki, A, et al., "Impact of long-term daylight deprivation on retinal light sensitivity, circadian rhythms and sleep during the Antarctic winter." *Nature*, 2018. doi:10.1038/s41598-018-33450-7

11 Holden, BA, et al., "Global prevalence of myopia and high myopia and temporal trends from 2000 through 2050." *Ophthalmology*, 2016. doi:https://doi.org/10.1016/j.ophtha.2016.01.006

12 Lageze, W and Schaeffel, F, "Preventing myopia." *Deutsches Arzteblatt International*, 2017, 114: 575–580.

13 Carr, B and Stell, W, "The Science behind Myopia" in *Webvision: The Organization of the Retina and Visual System*, eds. Kolb H, et al. University of Utah. doi:www.ncbi.nlm.nih.gov/books/NBK470669/

14 Chakraborty, R, "Circadian rhythms, refractive development, and myopia." *Ophthalmic and Physiological Optics*, 2018. doi:10.1111.opo.12453

4 The Predictive Brain

1 Levitin, D, *This is Your Brain on Music*, Penguin, 2006.

2 Hawkins, J, *On Intelligence*, Times Books, 2004.

3 Levitin, D, op cit.

4 Carey, B, *How we Learn,* Random House, 2015.

5 Hawkins, J, op cit.

6 Brierly, S, *A Long Way Home: A Memoir*, Berkley 2013, basis of the 2017 movie *Lion*.

7 Woollett, K and Maguire, E, "Acquiring 'the knowledge' of London's layout drives structural brain changes." *Current Biology*, 2011. doi:10.1016/j.cub.2011.11.018

8 https://en.wikipedia.org/wiki/Samer_Hattar (11/1/2019)

9 Soler, J, et al., "Light modulates hippocampal function and spatial learning in a diurnal rodent species: a study using male Nile grass rat." *Hippocampus*, 2017. doi:10.1002/hipo.22822

10 Smith, S, et al., "Environmental context-dependent memory: a review and meta analysis." *Psychonomic Bulletin and Review*, 2001.

11 Isarida, T, "Environmental-context dependent memory" www.researchgate.net/publication/292937149_Environmental_context-dependent_memory

12 Smith, S, op cit, 213.

5 Attention and Insight

1 Miller, E, et al., "Working memory 2.0." *Neuron* 100, 2018. https://doi:org/10.1016/j.neuron.2018.09.023

2 Hancock, P, "On the nature of vigilance." *Human Factors and Ergonomic Society*, 2017. doi:10.1177/0018720816655240

3 Eastwood, J and Fenske, MJ, "The unengaged mind: defining boredom in terms of attention." *Perspectives on Psychological Science,* 2012. doi:10.1177/1745691612456044

4 Chin, A, et al., "Bored in the USA: experience sampling and boredom in everyday life." *Emotion*, 2016. http://dx.doi.org/10.1037/emo0000232

5 Ryan, R and Deci E, "From ego depletion to vitality: theory and findings concerning the facilitation of energy available to the self." *Social and Personality Psychology*, 2008. doi.org/10.1111/j.1751-9004.2008.00098.x

6 Smolders, K, et al., "Daytime light exposure and feelings of vitality: results of a field study during regular weekdays." *J Environ Psych*, 2013. https://doi.org/10.1016/j.jenvp.2013.09.004

7 Smolders, K, et al., "Investigation of dose-response relationships for effects of white light exposure on correlates of alertness and executive control during regular daytime work hours." *Journal of Biological Rhythms*, 2018. doi:10.1177/0748730418796438

8 Ko, WH, et al., "The impact of a view from a window on thermal comfort, emotion, and cognitive performance." *Bldg and Environ*, 2020. https://doi.org/10.1016/j.buildenv.2020.106779

9 McMillan, R, et al., "Ode to positive constructive daydreaming." *Frontiers in Psychology*, 2013. doi:10.3389/fpsyg.2013.00626

10 Nakano, T, et al., "Blink-related momentary activation of the default mode network while viewing video." *Proceedings of the National Academy of Sciences*, 1/18/2013. doi.org/10.1073/pnas.1214804110

11 Killingsworth, M and Gilbert, D, "A wandering mind is an unhappy mind." *Science*, 2010. doi:10.1126/scienc.1192439

12 Baird, B, et al., "Inspired by distraction: mind wandering facilitates creative incubation." *Psych. Sci*, 2012. doi:10.1177/0956797612446024

13 Schooler, J, et al., "The middle way: finding the balance between mindfulness and mind-wandering." *Psychology of Learning and Motivation*, 2014. ISSN 0079-7421. doi.org/10.1016.B978-0-12-800090-8.8.00001-9

14 Fox, KCR, et al., "The wandering brain: meta-analysis of functional neuroimaging studies of mind-wandering and related spontaneous thought processes." *NeuroImage*, 2015. https://doi.org/10.1016/j.neuroimage.2015.02.039

15 Faber, M, et al., "Driven to distraction: a lack of change gives rise to mind-wandering." *Cognition*, 2018. doi:/10.1016/j.cognition.2018.01.007

16 Micheal, G, et al., "Thoughts and sensations, twin galaxies of the inner space: the propensity to mind-wander relates to spontaneous sensations arising on the hands." *Consciousness and Cognition*, 2017. doi:10.1016/j.concog.2017.08.007

17 Fox, KCR, op cit.

18 Helfrich, R, et al., "Neural mechanisms of sustained attention are rhythmic." *Neuron*, August, 2018. doi:10.1016/j.neuron.2018.07.032

19 Fiebelkorn, I, et al., "A rhythmic theory of attention." *Trends in Cognitive Science*, 2019. doi:10.1016/j.tics.2018.11.009

20 Miller, E, et al., "Working memory 2.0." *Neruon perspective, Neuron 100*, 2018. doi:10.1016/j.neuron.2018.09.023

21 Schooler, J, op cit.

22 Pollan, M, *A Place of My Own: The Architecture of Daydreams*, The Penguin Press, 1997.

23 Sacks, O, cited in Pericoli, M, *The City Out My Window*, Simon & Schuster, 2009.

24 Da Vinci in *Codex Ashburnham*, cited in Issacson, W, *Leonardo Da Vinci*, Simon and Schuster, 2017.

Part 2 Perception

6 Learning to See

1 https://neurosciencenews.com/computer-vision-15862/ (4/5/2020)

2 Godfrey-Smith, P, *Other Minds: The Octopus, the Sea, and the Deep Origins of Consciousness*, Farrar, Straus and Giroux, 2016.

3 For example, see www.ritsumei.ac.jp/~akitaoka/index-e.html (6/30/2020)

4 https://en.wikipedia.org/wiki/Grid_illusion (6/1/2020)

5 Turnbull, C, *The Forest People*, 1961, cited in Yi-Fu Tuan, *Topophilia: A Study of Environmental Perception, Attitudes and Values*, Prentice Hall, 1974.

6 See, for example, the YouTube video by National Gallery of Art, 5/30/2014, "Empire of the Eye: The Magic of Illusion-Palazzo Spada's Corridor, Part 5."

7 https://en.wikipedia.org/wiki/Optical_illusion (11/1/2019)

8 Glennester, Andrew, interview, *Popular Science*, Fall 2018.

9 Bower, B, "Adults fooled by visual illusions, but not kids." *Science News*, 11/23/2009, and Dima, D, et al., "Understanding why patients with schizophrenia do not perceive the hollow-mask illusion during dynamic causal modelling." *NeuroImage*, 2009.

10 Eagleman, D, "Brain Time." *What's Next? Dispatches on the Future of Science*. Ed. M. Brockman. New York: Vintage, 2009. https://eagleman.com/blog/brain-time

11 Gavazzi, G, et al., "Time perception of visual motion is tuned by the motor representation of human actions." *Nature, Scientific Reports*, 2013. doi.org/10.1038/srep01168

12 Sanders, L, "Rat brains have a speedometer." *Science News*, August 8, 2015.

13 Gladwell, V, et al. "The great outdoors: how a green exercise environment can benefit all." *Extrem Physiol Med*, 2013. doi:10.1186/2046-7648-2-3

14 www.aao.org/eye-health/tips-prevention/ (2/1/2019)

15 www.allaboutvision.com (industry-sponsored website, accessed 2/1/2019)

16 https://psychcentral.com/news/2016/12/03/cataracts-linked-to-depression-in-older-adults/113384.html

17 Boylan, JF, "Seeing really is believing: how cataract surgery changed by my life." *NY Times*, March 20, 2019.

18 "Lighting and the visual environment for seniors and the low vision population," *ASNI/IES RP-28-16*, Illuminating Engineering Society, 2016.

19 Wueger, S, "Colour constancy across the life span: evidence for compensatory mechanisms." *PLOS One*, 2013. https://doi.org/10.1371/journal.pone.0063921

20 Turner, PL, Mainster, MA, "Circadian photoreception: ageing and the eye's important role in systemic health." *British Journal of Ophthalmology*, 2008.

7 Patterns of Daylight Illumination

1 Data collected by Steve Paolini, CEO of Telelumen, Inc. Used with permission.

2 For more about the history and properties of windows and glass, see Carmody, J, et al., *Residential Windows: A guide to new technologies and energy performance*, WW Norton, 2007.

3 For example, see the work of Jamie Carpenter and Davidson Norris. http://carpenternorris.com/

4 Isaacson, W, *Leonardo Da Vinci*, Simon and Schuster, 2017.

5 Abumrad, J and Krulwich, R, Radio Lab, "Colors," New York Public Radio, WNYC Studio, 5/13/2013.

6 Verrelli BC, Tishkoff SA, "Signatures of selection and gene conversion associated with human color vision variation." *Am. J. Hum. Genet*, 2004. doi:10.1086/423287

7 Abumrad, op cit.

8 www.nbcnews.com/science/science-news/london-skyscraper-can-melt-cars-set-buildings-fire-f8C11069092

9 https://theconversation.com/the-next-step-in-sustainable-design-bringing-the-weather-indoors-80126, see also http://vitalarchitecture.org/

10 Hirning, MB, et al., "Discomfort glare in open plan green buildings." *Energy and Buildings*, 2014. doi.org/10.1016/j.enbuild.2013.11.053

11 Van Den Wymelenberg, K, *Evaluating Human Visual Preference and Performance in an Office Environment Using Luminance-based Metrics*, PhD Dissertation, College of Built Environments, University of Washington, 2012.

12 Tuaycharoen, N and Tragenza, P, "View and discomfort glare from windows." *Lighting Research and Technology*, 2007. doi:10.1177/1365782807077193

13 Karlson, L, et al., "Occupant satisfaction with two blind control strategies: slats closed and slats in cut-off position." *Solar Energy*, 2015. https://doi.org/10.1016/j.solener.2015.02.031

14 Clear, RD, "Discomfort glare: what do we actually know?" *Lighting Research and Technology*, 2012. Doe:10.1177/1477153512444527

15 www.science20.com/mark_changizi/why_does_light_make_headaches_worse

16 Narber, M and Nakayama, K, "Pupil responses to high-level image content." *Journal of Vision*, 2013. doi:10.1167/13.6.7

17 Khanie, MS, et al., "Gaze and discomfort glare, Part 1: Development of a gaze-driven photometry." *Lighting Res. Technol*, 2016. https://journals.sagepub.com/ doi/abs/10.1177/1477153516649016 and correspondence with author.

18 Suurenbrock F, and Spanjarb G, "Exploring Eye-tracking Technology: Assessing How the Design of Densified Built Environments Can Promote Inhabitants Well-Being" in *Urban Experience and Design*, ed. Hollander J and Sussman A, Routledge, 2021.

8 Designing with Daylight

1 Heschong, L, "An Interview with William Lam." *Solar Age Magazine*, Vol 5, No 8, August 1980.

2 Lam, WC, *Sunlighting as a Formgiver for Architecture*, Van Nostrand Reinhold, 1986.

3 For example, http://andrewmarsh.com/apps/staging/sunpath3d.html

4 Thanks to Bruce Haglund and all the SBSE folks.

5 Norris, D, "The unique light of place." *Perspective*, Vol 49, 05 2017.

6 Meek, C and Van den Wymelenberg, K, *Daylighting Design in the Pacific Northwest*, University of Washington Press, Seattle, Washington, 2012.

7 Heschong Mahone Group, *The Skylighting Guidelines,* Energy Design Resources, 1997–2008 (included an Excel-based calculator, SkyCalc©, that analyzed the impact of skylighting on whole-building energy use, including heating, cooling and lighting). https://energydesignresources.com/media/19173822/skylighting-design-guidelines_final_2014-02-19.pdf

8 Heschong, L, "Daylight metrics." *PIER Daylighting Plus Research Program*, California Energy Commission, CEC-500-2012-053 Feb 2012. doi:10.13140/RG.2.2.33003.59689

9 Alexander, C, *A Pattern Language: Towns, Buildings, Construction*, Oxford University Press, 1977.

10 "LM-83-13: Approved Method: IES Spatial Daylight Autonomy (sDA) and Annual Sunlight Exposure (ASE)" IES, 2013. www.IES.org

11 Mardaljevic, J, et al., "Daylight metrics and energy savings." *Lighting Research and Technology*, 2009. https://buildings.lbl.gov/sites/all/files/lbnl-4585e.pdf

12 Saxena, M and Berkland, S, "Advanced Daylighting Blinds and Shades Assessment," Pacific Gas and Electric Emerging Technologies Program, #ET11PGE1042, 2014. www.etcc-ca.com/sites/default/files/reports/et11pge1042_adv_blinds_shades.pdf

13 Day, JK, *Occupant Training in High Performance Buildings: An Assessment of Environmental Satisfaction, Learning, and Behaviors in Buildings*. Pullman, Washington: Thesis (Ph. D.), Washington State University, 2014.

14 Day, J, et al., "Blinded by the light: occupant perceptions and visual comfort assessments of three dynamic daylight control systems and shading strategies." *Building and Environment*, 2019. https://doi.org/10.1016/j.buildenv.2019.02.037

15 Meerbeek, B, "Building automation and control." *Building and Environment*, 2014. doi:10.1016/j.buildenv.2014.04.023

16 Day, J and Heschong, L, "Understanding Behavior Potential: the Role of Building Interfaces," ACEEE Summer Study 2016. https://aceee.org/files/proceedings/2016/data/index.htm

17 Pollan, M, *A Place of My Own: The Architecture of Daydreams*, The Penguin Press, 1997.

18 Bloomer, K, "The Picture Window: The Problem of Viewing Nature through Glass" in *Biophilic Design*, eds. Kellert, et al. Wiley and Sons, 2008.

9 Elements of View

1 See Mirza, Leila PhD dissertation, "Windowscapes: A Study of Landscape Preferences in an Urban Situation" for the University of Auckland 2015, for an extensive review of literature of view research.

2 Wilson, EO, "The Nature of Human Nature" in *Biophilic Design*, eds. Kellert, et al. Wiley and Sons, 2008.

3 Keniger, L, et al., "What are the benefits of interacting with nature?" *International Journal of Environmental Research and Public Health*, 2013. doi:10.3390/ijerph10030913

4 Pericoli, M, *The City Out My Window*, Simon and Schuster, 2009.

5 Pericoli, M, *Windows on the World,* Penguin Press, 2014.

6 Pericoli, M (2014), op cit.

7 Akerman, D, *A Natural History of the Senses*, Random House, 1990.

8 Pericoli, M (2014), op cit.

9 Pericoli, M (2014), op cit.

10 Pericoli, M (2014), op cit.

11 Blakemore, Sarah-Jayne "From the perception of action to the understanding of intention." *Nature Reviews Neuroscience*. 2001.

12 Whyte, WH, *The Social Life of Small Urban Spaces*, Project for Public Spaces, 1980.

13 Lynch, K, *The Image of the City*, MIT Press, 1960.

14 Mizra, L, op cit.

15 Pericoli, M (2009), op cit.

16 Pericoli, M (2009), op cit.

17 Pericoli, M (2009), op cit.

18 Sokol, J, "The end of night: global illumination has increased worldwide." *Scientific American*, January 2018.

19 Heschong, L, et al., "Windows and Classrooms" California Energy Commission, PIER program, report P500-03-082-A-7, October 2003.

20 www.ngv.vic.gov.au/exhibition/jeppe-hein/

21 Konis, K, "Evaluating daylighting effectiveness and occupant visual comfort in a side-lit open-plan office building." *Building and Environment*, 2013. https://doi.org/10.1016/j.buildenv.2012.09.017

22 Valtchanov, D and Ellard, C, "Cognitive and affective responses to natural scenes: effects of low level visual properties on preference, cognitive load and eye-movements." *J EnvironPsych.* https://dx.doi.org/10.1016/j.envp.2105.07.001

23 For example, see http://webvision.med.utah.edu/temporal.html or https://en.wikipedia.org/wiki/Wagon-wheel_effect

24 Wilkins, A, et al., "A physiological basis for visual discomfort—application in lighting design." *Lighting Research and Technology*, 2015. https://doi.org/10.1177/1477153515612526

25 www.fractal-explorer.com or https://fractalfoundation.org/videos/

26 Ping, L, et al., "Reduced tolerance to night shift in chronic shift workers: insight from fractal regulation." *Sleep*, 2017. doi:10.1093/sleep/zsx092

27 British Standards Institute, BS 8206-2:2008, *Lighting for Buildings – code of practice for daylighting*. London BSI, 2008.

28 Madaljevic, J, "Aperture-Based Daylight Modeling: Introducing the 'View Lumen,'" IBPSA Conf 2019. www.ibpsa.org/proceedings/BS2019/BS2019_210810.pdf

Part 3 Motivation

10 Daylighting Education

1 Hamlin, A, (Ed) *Modern School Houses; Being a Series of Authoritative Articles on Planning, Sanitation, Heating and Ventilation* (Vol 1), The Swetland Publishing Co., NY, 1910.

2 Baker, L, "A History of School Design and its Indoor Environmental Standards, 1900 to Today," National Clearinghouse for Educational Facilities, 2012. https://files.eric.ed.gov/fulltext/ED539480.pdf

3 Baker, L, op cit.

4 IES illumination standards were reduced sometime in the 1980s. IES now recommends a more nuanced range, generally between 30 to 50 footcandles (300–500 lux) for various classroom types. IES handbook, 10th edition, *Illuminating Engineering Society*, NY, 2011.

5 Larson, TC, et al., "The Effect of Windowless Classrooms on Elementary School Children," U Michigan, 1965. https://files.eric.ed.gov/fulltext/ED014847.pdf

6 A few of these old buildings, then part of Birmingham High School in Van Nuys, California, are still being used over 70 years after originally built as temporary structures. Logically, they are an excellent example of 'loose fit' design, as described by Stewart Brand in his book *How Buildings Learn*.

7 Collin, B, "Windows and People: a Literature Survey, Psychological Reaction to Environments With and Without Windows," National Bureau of Standards, 1975.

8 Sommer, R, *Personal Space: The Behavioral Basis of Design*, Spectrum Books, 1969.

9 As a side note, at that time, the state was allocating more money, and three to four times more per square foot, for prisons than for schools.

10 Nadel, S, et al., *Market Transformation: Substantial Progress from a Decade of Work*, American Council for an Energy-Efficient Economy, 2003.

11 Heschong, L, "Daylighting impacts on human performance in school." *JIES*, 2002. doi.org/10.1080/00994480.2002.10748396

12 Heschong, L, et al., "Daylighting in schools," *Pacific Gas and Electric*, 1999. www.pge.com/includes/docs/pdfs/shared/edusafety/training/pec/daylight/SchoolDetailed820App.pdf

13 Heschong, L, et al., "Daylighting in Schools: Re-Analysis Report," California Energy Commission, *PIER program*, report 500-03-082-A-3, October 2003.

14 Heschong, L, et al., "Windows and Classrooms," California Energy Commission, *PIER program*, report P500-03-082-A-7, October 2003.

15 See figures 31 and 32, in Heschong, L, et al., "Windows and Classrooms," op cit.

16 Barrett, P, et al., "The impact of classroom design on pupil's learning: final results of a holistic, multi-level analysis." *Building and Environment*, 2015. doi:10.1016/j.buildenv.2015.02.013

17 http://thedaylightsite.com/symposium/2019-2/. Peter Barrett in Symposium highlights video, 30 seconds in.

11 Selling Daylight

1 https://energydesignresources.com/media/2398/EDR_CaseStudies_timber.pdf

2 "Letting the Sun Shine is Good for Business," John Pierson, *Wall Street Journal*, November 20, 1994.

3 Heschong Mahone Group, *Skylights and Retail Sales PG&E 1999*. www.pge.com/includes/docs/pdfs/shared/edusafety/training/pec/daylight/RetailCondensed820.pdf

4 Heschong, L, "Daylight and Retail Sales," CEC PIER report P500-03-082-A-5. http://newbuildings.org/sites/default/files/A-5_Daylgt_Retail_2.3.7.pdf

5 Langston, C, "Measuring good architecture: long life, loose fit, low energy." *European Journal of Sustainability*, 2014. doi:10.14207/ejsd.2014.v3n4p163

12 Enduring Urban Forms

1 www.un.org/development/desa/en/news/population/2018-revision-of-world-urbanization-prospects.html. Whereas less than one tenth of the world's population lived in cities in 1840, by 2007 it was well over one half.

2 Brand, S, *How Buildings Learn*, Penguin Books, 1994.

3 www.nytimes.com/interactive/2018/10/12/us/map-of-every-building-in-the-united-states.

4 Bridgen, T, *Value in the View*, RIBA Publishing, 2018.

5 Rybczynski, W, *A Clearing in the Distance*, Touchstone, 1999.

6 Janson, HW, *The History of Art*, 2nd ed. Harry Abrams, 1979.

7 Reynolds, JS, *Courtyards: Aesthetic, Social and Thermal Delight*, Wiley, 2002.

8 https://bullittcenter.org/building/building-features/active-design/

9 Whyte, W, *The Social Life of Small Urban Spaces,* Project for Public Spaces, NY, 1980.

10 www.pps.org/about

11 Knowles, R, "The solar envelope: its meaning for energy and buildings." *Energy and Buildings*, 2003. www.sciencedirect.com/science/article/pii/S0378778802000762

12 www.nytimes.com/interactive/2016/12/21/upshot/Mapping-the-Shadows-of-New-York-City.html

13 The Value of View

1 Lumina, 289 Main Street, San Francisco, is a 656 unit luxury high rise developed by Tishman Speyer. http://obscuradigital.com/work/lumina/ (10/12/2018)

2 http://raincityguide.com/2006/05/21/what-is-a-view-worth/ (10/15/2018)

3 For example, see Turan, I, "The value of daylight in office buildings." *Bldg and Environ*, 2020. https://doi.org/10.1016/j.buildenv.2019.106503 or www.youtube.com/watch?v=nzkFfyPQFKg

4 Ventiera, S, "Rooms With a View: From Central Park to Golden Gate, Price Premiums on Iconic Vistas." www.realtor.com/news/trends/what-buyers-shell-out-for-killer-views/ (5/1/2017)

5 Pericoli, M (2009), op cit.

6 This and all subsequent quotes in this chapter are from Pericoli, M (2014), op cit.

14 Working with Daylight

1 Meister, J, "The #1 office perk? Natural light." *Harvard Business Review*, Sept, 2018.

2 Saxena, M, et al., "Office Daylighting Potential" California Energy Commission, PIER Report # CEC-500-2013-002 2013.

3 Personal communication from Larissa Oaks, USGBC, 2019.

4 Turner, C and Frankel, M, "Energy Performance of LEED® for New Construction Building," New Buildings Institute, White Salmon, WA, Final Report for the USGBC, 2008.

5 "FY 2017 open data set," from www.gsa.gov/policy-regulations/policy/real-property-policy/data-collection-and-reports/frpp-summary-report-library

6 Konrad, A, "Inside The Phenomenal Rise Of WeWork." *Forbes*, February 2015.

7 Per the US Energy Information Agency, Commercial Building Energy Survey (CBEC) 2012, offices constitute 18% of both US commercial floor space and buildings.

8 Cruzioworks is one of over 2,000 independently operated co-working places around the world listed on https://coworkingmap.org

9 Galbrun, L, "Audio-visual interaction and perceptual assessment of water features used over road traffic noise." *Journal of the Acoustical Society of America*, 2014. https://doi.org/10.1121/1.4897313

10 https://en.wikipedia.org/wiki/Underground_city lists 27 countries worldwide with extensive underground shopping and transit next works (6/21/2019).

11 www.cnn.com/2016/05/06/politics/life-on-uss-missouri-nuclear-submarine/index.html (9/24/2018)

12 https://fas.org/man/dod-101/sys/ship/docs/simlife.htm (9/24/2018)

13 David, L, "Window Wars in Space" Quest for the 'Big View' High Above Earth." *Space Insider*, Space.com www.space.com/39691-window-sizes-spacecraft-blue-origin-virgin-galactic.html, (6/21/2019)

14 www.blueorigin.com/new-shepard/become-an-astronaut/ (6/21/2019)

15 Levy, S, "One More Thing, Inside Apple's Insanely Great (or Just Insane) New Mothership." *Wired Magazine*. www.wired.com/2017/05/apple-park-new-silicon-valley-campus/ (5/16/17)

16 Knox, M, "The secrets of the jury room." *Australian Forensic Science*, 2007.

17 AIA Academy of Architecture for Justice, Sustainable Justice Guidelines, 2015.

18 See www.gsa.gov/p100 and https://wbdg.org/

19 www.gsa.gov/about-us/regions/welcome-to-the-pacific-rim-region-9/buildings-and-facilities/california/new-los-angeles-us-courthouse (6/25/2019)

20 https://info.siteselectiongroup.com/blog/how-big-is-the-us-call-center-industry-compared-to-india-and-philippines (6/2019) Estimated 2.2 million call center workers in the USA alone; 350,000 in India; 400,000 in the Philippines. This does not include UK, Europe, Latin America, or non-English language services.

21 Heschong, L., et al., "Windows and Offices: A Study of Office Worker Performance and the Indoor Environment," California Energy Commission, 2003, PIER Report # CEC P500-03-082-A-9.

15 Healing Daylight

1 For a history of how the medical profession transitioned from charisma-based to evidence-based research, see Mukherjee, S, *Cancer: the Emperor of All Maladies*, Scribner, 2010.

2 Ulrich, RS, "View through a window may influence recovery from surgery." *Science*, 1984. doi:10.1126/science.6143402

3 For more context, see Sternberg, E, *Healing Spaces: the Science of Place and Well-Being*, Harvard University Press, 2009.

4 Ulrich, RS, et al., "A review of the research literature on evidence-based healthcare design." *HERD*, 2008. https://doi.org/10.1177/193758670800100306

5 https://en.wikipedia.org/wiki/Kaiser_Permanente (6/30/2019)

6 Kellog, C, "Kaiser permanente." *arcCA*, 07.1. https://aiacalifornia.org/kaiser-permanente/ (9/18/2020)

7 Ulrich, RS, 2008, op cit.

8 https://fearfreepets.com/fear-free-research/ and https://equimanagement.com/articles/fear-free-design-for-equine-veterinary-practices

9 Coyne, I, "Children's experience of hospitalization." *Journal of Child Health Care*, 2006. doi:10.1177/1367493506067884

10 Cooper, A, et al., "Patterns of GPS measured time outdoors after school and objective physical activity in English children: the PEACH project." *International Journal of Behavioral Nutrition and Physical Activity*, 2010. https://doi.org/10.1186/1479-5868-7-31

11 Cutle, L, School of Public Health, University of Minnesota presentation to GSA 2008, from cutle001@umn.edu.

12 ANSI/IES RP-28-16 "Lighting and the visual environment for seniors and the low vision population," *Illuminating Engineering Society*, 2016.

13 Clarke, R, "In Life's Last Moments, Open a Window." *New York Times*, September 8, 2018.

Part 4 Meaning

16 Iconic Daylight and Views

1 Adams, A and Alinder, MS, *Ansel Adams: an Autobiography*, Little Brown, Boston, 1985.

2 www.galinsky.com/buildings/mitchapel/index.htm

3 Cross, A, "The Raven and the First Men: From Conception to Completion," University of British Columbia, Museum of Anthropology, 2011.

4 Weiner, E, *The Geography of Genius*, Simon and Schuster, 2016.

5 Pericoli, M (2009), op cit.

17 Visions of Nature

1   For a deeper discussion of wilderness see, Cronon, W, "The Trouble with Wilderness; or, Getting Back to the Wrong Nature" in *Uncommon Ground: Rethinking the Human Place in Nature*, ed. William Cronon. WW Norton 1995.

2   Tuan, Yi-Fu, *Topophilia: A Study of Environmental Perception, Attitudes and Values*, Prentice-Hall, 1974.

3   Sze, M, *The Way of Chinese Painting: its Ideas and Technique*, Vintage Books, 1956.

4   Tuan, YF, *Topophilia*, op cit.

5   Gilpin, W, *Observations on the River Wye*, London, 1820.

6   Rybczynski, W, *A Clearing in the Distance*, Simon and Schuster, 1999.

7   Olmstead, FL, quoted in Rybczynski, W, op cit.

8   https://uwpressblog.com/2015/04/15/gas-works-park-a-brief-history-of-a-seattle-landmark/ (7/1/2019)

9   www.urbangreenbluegrids.com/projects/landscape-park-duisburg-nord/ (7/1/2019).

18 Biophilia and Technophilia

1   Wilson, EO, "The Nature of Human Nature," in *Biophilic Design*, ed. Kellert, et al. Wiley and Sons, 2008.

2   www.britannica.com/science/biophilia-hypothesis

3   Kellert, S, Chapter 1 in *Biophilic Design*, op cit.

4   Wilson, A, Chapter 21 in *Biophilic Design*, op cit.

5   Stamps, A, "Mystery, complexity, legibility and coherence: a meta-analysis." *Journal of Environmental Psychology*, 2004. doi:10.106/S0272-4944(03)00023-9

6   Frumkin, H, et al., "Nature contact and human health: a research agenda." *Environmental Health Perspectives*, 7/31/2017. doi.org/10.1289/EHP1663

7   James, P, et al., "Exposure to greenness and mortality in a nationwide prospective cohort study of women." *Environmental Health Perspectives*, 2016. doi:10.1289/ehp.1510363

8   Cauwerts, C, "Influence of presentation modes on visual perceptions of daylit spaces." PhD Dissertation submitted to UCL Department of Architecture, Louvain-la-Neuve. http://hdl.handle.net/2078.1/135934 (11/1/2013)

9   Kim, J, "The effects of indoor plants and artificial windows in an underground environment," *Building and Environment*, 2018. doi.org/10.1016/j.buildenv.2018.04.029

10 Li, Quin, "The Japanese Art and Science of Skinrin-Yoku, Forest Bathing," Penguin Random House, 2018.

11 Kahn, P, et al., "The human relation with nature and technological nature." *Current Directions in Psychological Science*, 2009. https://doi.org/10.1111/j.1467-8721.2009.01602.x

12 www.skyfactory.com/about/ (9/1/2020)

13 Interviews with Mike Mazza and Obscura design team. https://vimeo.com/175865167 or www.codaworx.com/project/salesforce-lobby-video-wall-salesforce (10/11/2018)

14 Levitin, D, *This is Your Brain on Music*, Penquin, 2006.

19 Synthesis and Next Steps

1 Neutra, R, *Cross Section of a Credo*, Capra Press, Santa Barbara, Calif. 1969.

2 Ruth, J, *Immaterial Environments*; for a description and videos of the event: http://sce.parsons.edu/blog/aftertaste_event/immaterial-environments/

3 Marchette, S, et al., "Outside looking in: landmark generalization in the human navigational system." *The Journal of Neuroscience*, 2015. doi:10.1523/jneruosci.2270-15.2015

4 Levy, TS, quoted in Pericoli, M (2014), op cit.

5 Pollan, M, *A Place of My Own: The Architecture of Daydreams*, Penguin Books, 1997.

6 Goldberger, AL, "Fractals and the birth of Gothic: reflections on the biological basis of creativity." *Molecular Psychiatry*, 1996.

7 https://en.wikipedia.org/wiki/Earthrise (8/26/2019)

8 David, L, "Window Wars in Space Quest for the 'Big View' High Above Earth." *Space Insider*, Space.com. www.space.com/39691-window-sizes-spacecraft-blue-origin-virgin-galactic.html (6/21/2019)

9 Potter, C, *The Earth Gazers*, Pegasus Books, 2018.

10 NPR interview, February 4, 2018. www.npr.org/2018/02/04/582534895/the-first-men-to-have-the-whole-world-in-their-sights

11 Quote from Dr. Edgar Mitchell, astronaut. https://noetic.org/

Acknowledgments

This book was in gestation for many years, and thus there are many people who contributed to its development, both directly and indirectly. I hugely appreciate the team who helped bring the book to fruition, Editors Fran Ford and Trudy Varcianna at Routledge, who remained buoyant in the most trying of times; Illustrator Garth von Ahnen, who was an absolute joy to work with, as was Clyde Compton, who helped me wrestle the book down to size. I also appreciate the early enthusiasm of Roger Conover and Thomas Weaver at MIT Press.

In addition to the work of all the authors listed in the references section (and many who are not), I am indebted to my brain trust of professional friends and colleagues who provided helpful perspective along the way, in big and little ways, whether knowingly or unknowingly: Edward B. Allen, Donlyn Lyndon, Margo Jones, Roger Goldstein, John Crowley, Davidson Norris, Ed Arens, Gail Brager, Barbara Erwine, Kyle Konis, Andy McNeal, Lindsey Baker, Jan Stensland, Greg Ward, Steven Selkowitz, Francis Rubinstein, Eleanor Lee, Charles Eley, Michael Holtz, Micheal Jouaneh, Joel Loveland, Kevin Houser, Kevin Van Den Wymelenberg, Richard Mistrick, Neall Digert, Pekka Hakkarainen, Naomi Miller, Hayden McKay, Jennifer Veitch, Eunice Noelle-Wagner, Amy Keller, Peter Ngai, Nancy Clanton, Joan Roberts, Bud Brainard, Mudit Saxena, Jon McHugh, Owen Howlett, Michael Mutmansky, Sophia Hartkopf, Abhijeet Pande, Raghu Padiyath, Veronica Soebarto, Chris Buntine, Julia Day, Michael S. Brown, Laura Malakoff, Dr. Betty Patterson, Steve Paolini, Jonsara Ruth, Marilyn Anderson, Mandana Serie Khanie, Christoph Reinhart, Dr. Richard J Jackson, Dr. Raymond Neutra, Til Roennenberg, Anna Wirz-Justice, Per Arnold Anderson, Jens Christiansen, Nickolas Roy, John Mardaljevic, Peter Tregenza, and Ellen Katherine Hansen.

I am also deeply grateful for the friends and clients who, over the years, supported my research and/or enabled my direct observations, such as Jerry Bloomberg, Peter Turnbull, George Loisos, Alan Sulieman, Jan Johnson, Randall Higa, William Vicent, David Cohan, Jeff Harris, Marsha Walton, Bruce Baccei, Connie Samla, Rabbi Emily Feigenson, Judge Dennis Purless, Judge Suzanne Segal, Shauna Casey, Chrissy Thomure, Barbara Cordes, Tara Murphy, Kyle Doerksen, David Pais, Jim Murphy, Chuck Tremper, a few who wished to remain anonymous, plus all the folks at Ecology Action, Cruz IO, and many more dedicated folks working behind the scenes at the California Energy Commission, PG&E, SCE, SMUD, NEEA, NYSERDA, AAMA, and IES.

There are many friends who provided invaluable feedback and encouragement, especially by reading early versions of the manuscript, including Annie Durbin, Rob Samish, Micheal and Lorna Herf, Margo Jones, Philip Elmer, Naomi Miller, Fred Oberkircher, Elizabeth Dauterman, Barbara Lawrence, Anina Van Alstine, Sandra Fox, Diane Pacholski, Dr. Clifford Rhodes, and most steadfast of all, my husband, Douglas Mahone.

Finally, I draw constant inspiration from my amazing family, who continue to do great things to make the world a better place: Douglas, Tyler, and Amber Mahone, Alyson McKay, Abraham Schneider, Gregg Heschong, Danny, Ruth, and David Franks.

Thank you!

Index

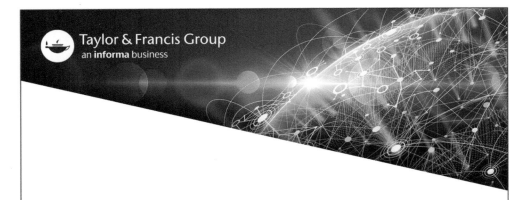